Strategic Practice Management

A Patient-Centric Approach

Strategic Practice Management

A Patient-Centric Approach

Robert G. Glaser, Ph.D.
Robert M. Traynor, Ed.D., M.B.A.

with chapter contributions from

Debra Abel, Au.D.
Glenn L. Bower, J.D.
Gail M. Whitelaw, Ph.D., M.H.A.

PLURAL
PUBLISHING
INC.
SAN DIEGO
OXFORD
BRISBANE

PLURAL PUBLISHING
INC.

5521 Ruffin Road
San Diego, CA 92123

e-mail: info@pluralpublishing.com
Web site: http://www.pluralpublishing.com

49 Bath Street
Abingdon, Oxfordshire OX14 1EA
United Kingdom

Library of Congress Cataloging-in-Publication Data
Glaser, Robert (Robert G.)
  Strategic practice management / by Robert Glaser and Robert Traynor.
      p. ; cm.
  Includes bibliographical references.
  ISBN-13: 978-1-59756-105-1 (hardcover)
  ISBN-10: 1-59756-105-3 (hardcover)
  1. Audiology–Practice. 2. Strategic planning. I. Traynor, Robert M. II. Title.
  [DNLM: 1. Practice Management, Medical–organization & administration. 2. Audiology–
organization & administration. W 80 G548s 2007]
  RF291.G53 2007
  617.80068–dc22

                                                                                    2007036505

Contents

Introduction

In 1975 Raymond Carhart, Ph.D., the father of Audiology set forth the importance of audiologists as clinicians and the importance of audiologists providing services to those in need of our specialized training. There is no better way to introduce this text than to remember these important words written in his introduction to the first edition of Pollack's *Amplification for the Hearing Impaired*:

> *The researcher can gather fact after fact at his leisure until he has a sufficient edifice of evidence to answer his question with surety. How different is the clinician's task. He, too, is an investigator but the question before him is, "What can I do now about the needs of the person who is seeking my help at this moment?" The clinician proceeds to gather as much data as possible about his client as he can in a clinically reasonable period of time. He does not have the luxury to wait several months or years for other facts to appear. The decisions of the clinician are more daring than the decisions of the researcher because human needs that require attention today impel clinical decisions to be made more rapidly and on a basis of less evidence than do research decisions. The dedicated and conscientious clinician should bear this fact in mind proudly. His is the greater courage.*

The torch now passes to a new generation of audiologists armed with Au.D. degrees and ready to practice Audiology as the clinician/providers Dr. Carhart envisioned. We trust this book will provide fuel and opportunity to keep the torch burning brightly for many years to come.

Robert G. Glaser, Ph.D. and
Robert M. Traynor, Ed.D., M.B.A.

Acknowledgments

As we reflect on our professional careers, each of us sees clearly the mentors and guides who moved us toward professional excellence. They developed the passion, the fire-in-the-belly that makes our profession come alive every day we see patients, teach classes, conduct research, or manage a department. I thank my mentors and professional role models, Drs. Kenneth W. Berger, Joseph P. Millin, and John R. Alway for providing the light and direction I needed for my professional journey. A special thanks to A. Lee Fisher, who instilled the concept of professionalism that I admire to this day. Sincere thanks and appreciation go to my longtime friend, respected colleague, and coauthor Dr. Robert Traynor. The contributions of Dr. Debbie Abel, Attorney Glenn Bower, and Dr. Gail Whitelaw raised the quality of this book significantly and I thank them for their insight and diligence. I appreciate the patience and positive attitude of Dr. Sadanand Singh and the entire team at Plural Publishing. They facilitated our efforts and fostered a strong and powerful experience for all contributors. Special thanks to my colleagues at Audiology and Speech Associates of Dayton—they tolerated my inattention well and covered the practice in their usual, excellent fashion. Last, but certainly not least, thanks to my family, Graham, Matt, Erin, and Mark, Mary Jane, Milo, and Oscar. The most special thanks is reserved for Annie, my wonderful wife who has supported my efforts through this project under difficult circumstances—always showing the world her style and grace while caring for and nurturing those around her. She is my truest inspiration, my best friend, and a fantastic editor.

Robert G. Glaser, Ph.D.

Acknowledgments

I am deeply indebted to my wife, Krista Buckles Traynor, whose support was unwavering; her encouragement was continuous during the frustrations, exhilarations, and lonely days and nights spent obtaining an MBA, and then, cocreating a textbook. Thanks to my friend and coauthor, Dr. Bob Glaser; who from the initial outline to the end of the project provided motivation, thought-provoking interaction, and held responsibility for the hardest part of the project: the tedious, but necessary, editing that has facilitated a great volume. Our collective and personal thanks to a superior group of expert contributors; Dr. Debbie Abel, Attorney Glenn Bower, and Dr. Gail Whitelaw whose expertise and superb writing skills allow this text to be the unique and complete volume on practice management. Also, thanks to my "patient-centric" office staff at Audiology Associates of Greeley, Inc., in Greeley, Colorado; Jacki Buffington-Reider, Barbara Jones, Glenda Reed, and Karen Swope who have all taken on extra projects, extra patient loads, modified schedules, and worked just a bit harder during the preparation of this manuscript. Thanks to my colleagues and students at the University of Florida who encouraged flexibility and creativity in course development that fostered insight as to the necessity for this text. And last, thanks to Drs. Keith and James Peterson lifelong otolaryngology professional colleagues and friends who said back in the 1970s . . . "Why don't you just start your own Audiology practice?"

Robert M. Traynor, Ed.D., M.B.A.

Contributors

Debra Abel, Au.D.
Hearing Resource Center
Poway, California
Chapter 5

Glenn L. Bower, J.D.
Coolidge Wall Co., LPA
Dayton, Ohio
Chapter 2

Robert G. Glaser, Ph.D.
President and CEO
Audiology Associates of Dayton, Inc.
(dba) Audiology and Speech Associates
Dayton, Ohio
Chapters 5–9, 11, & 14

Robert M. Traynor, Ed.D., M.B.A.
President and CEO
Audiology Associates of Greeley
Greeley, Colorado
Chapters 1, 3, 4, 10, & 12

Gail M. Whitelaw, Ph.D., M.H.A.
Department of Speech and Hearing
 Sciences
Ohio State University
Columbus, Ohio
Chapters 13 & 15

1

Strategic Business Planning

ROBERT M. TRAYNOR, Ed.D., M.B.A.

Introduction

Audiology is an expanding profession offering clinicians a variety of practice opportunities across a number of venues. Each audiology practice, regardless of the venue, began with a conceptual framework of the services to be provided, the populations to be served, an assessment of the competition in the market area, and projected costs to provide the services. Once the concept, the need, and other infrastructural components began to solidify, a business plan was developed to describe the operational and economic realities of the con-

cept. The business plan helped establish a clear and complete picture of what would be required to turn the concept into reality over a specific time period. It included all the important business and clinical parameters to be considered to begin the venture, and nourish it through its 3-year start-up phase and beyond. For the plan to serve as an effective roadmap it had to be exhaustive in its accuracy and depiction of anticipated costs as well as anticipated revenue.

Business plans may be labeled with other titles specific to the practice venue. In educational settings, it may be a new program proposal; in a health care facility or hospital it may be an opportunity for additional clinical services. Regardless of the title of the document, business plans must establish the need, and set forth operational and fiscal requirements to establish and maintain the new segment of care to be provided.

Independent Practice

Independent private practice is a growing sector of audiology. Practitioners are choosing not to practice in hospitals, clinics, and ENT practices which are increasingly viewed as restrictive to professional autonomy and/or financial opportunity. Armed with a doctorate, and fueled by an availability of funds for new businesses from many sources, practicing audiology as an independent, stand alone enterprise is poised to match the anticipated growth of the hearing-impaired population. Private practice has now become a "new frontier" for entrepreneurial audiologists. With the advent of the Au.D. and the successful transitioning of audiology to a doctoring profession, the dream of many audiologists who worked diligently to develop the Au.D. as a bona fide degree granted from an accredited university, younger colleagues are hanging their shingles and prospering as valued members of health care communities across the country.

The health care consumer is beginning to recognize what an audiology practice offers and they are likely to choose or be referred to an audiologist for diagnostic services and rehabilitative treatment. As the Boomer generation begins to self-manage their health care, those with hearing impairment will seek care from audiologists directly.

Although the profession of audiology is recognized by more individuals seeking resolution of their hearing difficulties than ever before, the profession remains less well known to bankers and other lenders. These professionals loan money to unfamiliar businesses every day but there are rules by which they evaluate these investment opportunities. As audiology practices are an unfamiliar type of business to most funding sources, audiologists must develop a business plan that establishes a clear strategy and realistic plans for the practice to generate revenue. The prevailing attitude among lenders is skepticism; and, therefore, to raise new capital, an emerging audiology practice must present a convincing business plan (Tracy, 2001). Without a straightforward, concise business plan lenders will not consider "partnering" with you no matter how great the opportunity.

The purpose of this chapter is to present the rationale for business preplanning and planning for both the start-up and existing audiology practices considering a facelift, expansion, or other significant modification requiring funding. Additionally, this chapter offers the mechanics of how to go about planning for an audiology practice, tips for success, and checklists to ensure that all the planning has been accomplished.

Berry's Business Plan Fable

Berry (2004), relates a fable that captures the very essence of business planning. It has been modified slightly to emphasize the importance of strategic and practical business planning in audiology.

Once upon a time there were three audiologists who had just finished their Au.D. degrees. They were out to seek their fortunes in private practice. They had carefully trained in the field at prestigious academic institutions and obtained all the licenses necessary to be audiology clinicians. Each of these new Au.D.s developed a business plan that they felt would be accepted by lending institutions so that they could obtain the necessary funding to start their new audiology practices. The first audiologist's business plan was built of straw. It was easy to complete this business plan but it was mostly puffery. For example, it had objectives like "being the best audiologists" and "to offer the best in patient satisfaction" without any methods for the measurement of these objectives. It had a lot of talk and verbal content, but few specifics. The straw business plan was written like a bad term paper or a bad public relations piece, without the really hard facts.

The second audiologist's business plan was built of sticks. It was built on what venture capitalists call, "hockey stick" forecasts. These "hockey stick" forecasts are a very common mistake in business plans in that sales have grown slowly in the past, but the forecast shoots up boldly with huge growth rates, just as soon as "something" happens. Usually the "something" that is supposed to happen is the investment of cash, often other people's money, and as soon as this plan gets the money, wonderful things happen.

The third audiologist had attended an institution where a business background was part of their audiology training program and, thus, with a sound knowledge of the necessity and process of business planning, built a business plan of bricks. Building with bricks involves the use of specific, realistic numbers and a progression of events that provide support for the business plan, not simply a plan made of "smoke and mirrors." A business plan of bricks also includes milestone

dates, deadlines, budgets, and concrete, measurable objectives.

Then came the real world to these three audiologists. The real world included phone calls, seeing patients, paying suppliers and taxes, and the host of other duties that are the recurring routines of private practice. There were real business problems and changes in the economic environment, patients and insurance companies paying slowly or not at all, costs going up on products, equipment costs higher than normal, and an increase in competition. There were additional employee concerns, such as fixed and variable pay and other personnel difficulties. In business school this is called the real world or "RW."

"RW" blew the first audiologists business plan of straw away in an instant. It was worthless, forgotten, lost somewhere in a drawer, never to be referred to again. Nobody remembered what it said; it was totally useless.

"RW" also blew the second audiologist's "hockey stick" business plan apart in an instant. No one paid much attention to the business plan of sticks because the forecasts were so wildly optimistic. Nobody had been given responsibility for objectives, and nobody would have taken responsibility for these wild optimistic concepts of the market. The plan of sticks was simply ignored. It was also useless.

The third audiologist with the plan of bricks, however, stood up to "RW." As each month closed, the plan of bricks absorbed the predicted versus actual results. Bankers and investors saw the performance and helped the young audiologist make adjustments in practice management techniques. Each kept track of the results and changes that were made in the business plan to accommodate "RW." These changes were organized, realistic, and rational modifications to "RW" that reflected actual conditions, not wild speculation. The bankers were proud of their performance, their expertise, and of the assistance that they were able to provide for the young audiologist to create a practice based on a solid foundation. The audiologist with the business plan of bricks lived happily ever after, in his patient-centric audiology practice. And, after 35 years of practice, revising the business plan of bricks many times, he sold the practice to another young Au.D. also with a business plan of bricks.

The moral of the fable is that there is no substitute for a well-developed, comprehensive business plan, whether the practice is in the early start-up phase seeking financial support or in the first quarter of the third year of the practice reviewing the plan to assess the progress and direction of the practice, and the need to reconsider aspects of the plan that, for a variety of reasons, may not be coming to fruition as initially envisioned.

Neither lending institutions nor other sources of potential funding will consider a venture without a solid, well-executed business plan.

Strategic Concept Planning for an Audiology Practice

Before the business plan is generated an audiology practice requires a strategic preplanning planning exercise. This preliminary planning allows the practitioner to consider their resources and the general economic climate to design the type of audiology practice that will be viable within the community. An organizational concept that greatly assists in preliminary planning is offered by Harrison and St. John (2004). They pose a model, presented in Figure 1–1, describing a simple preliminary planning exercise.

In their model, the practitioner must begin the planning process by reviewing the internal and external influences on

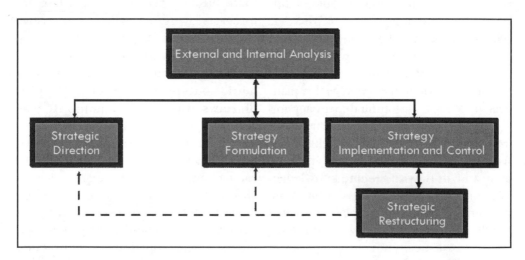

Figure 1–1. Preplanning model. (Adapted from *Foundations in Strategic Management* [3rd ed.], by J. Harrison and C. St. John, 2004, Mason, OH: Thomson Southwestern Publishing. Copyright 2004. Adapted with permission.)

the business environment. In internal preliminary planning, the audiologist must consider the internal resources that are available, such as personnel, office policies, equipment, physical location, space, and capital. Reviewing the internal resources available to the practitioner as the practice concept develops allows for the development of a realistic conceptual plan that transfers easily to the business plan. Similarly, there are external limitations for the practice that must be evaluated including the economic climate, competition, suppliers, referral sources, insurance companies, and other factors that are out of the control of the practitioner. Although there is no control over these factors, it is essential to the overall business plan that solid strategies to face these issues are developed.

Another component of the preliminary planning exercise is to strategize direction. In this exercise, the practitioner decides the direction to take the practice or what type of a practice they will choose to offer to the market place. In the formulation of a strategy to take on the market, the questions really are: what type of an audiology practice do I want? Should the practice be general audiology? Specialize in pediatric patients, or adults? Should we offer balance services, ABR, hearing instruments, cochlear implant follow-up, and fine tuning? Strategy formulation is just that, how do I take on the market and what brand of audiology do I offer?

Once the overall direction of the practice is planned, it is necessary to consider the method that will be used to interface with the market. Preplanning decisions necessary at this point concern heavy or light marketing techniques, referrals only, or some combination of both. The practice will also need to

develop a pricing strategy to appropriately price products and services within the practice as well as position their brand of audiology in the market place. Decisions as to patient centrism, risk management, and other conceptual factors must be decided to further refine the type of practice that will be introduced in the market.

As the market and practice patterns change, it may be necessary to revisit the preliminary practice planning process to restructure the proposed practice as necessary, before development of the business plan or modification of an existing business plan. Even before the business plan is considered, a preliminary strategic plan must be formulated and sometimes reformulated. This gives the business plan some direction and allows the plan to offer well-developed and unique arguments for the proposed success of the practice.

Preliminary Considerations in Developing the Business Plan

A business plan is a complete and detailed description of exactly how you intend to operate your proposed practice, as well as a communications tool for investors and others interested in understanding the operations and goals. It is a succinct document that addresses how you are going to build and maintain your practice by specifying the components of a longitudinal business strategy. Specifically, a business plan describes how the practice will function within the marketplace to stakeholders—those concerned with the long-term success of the venture.

The plan presents what is being sold, by whom, the background and qualifications of those involved in the company, prospective customers, where they can be found, what is needed to build the business, and how the practice plans to promote and determine the viability of the venture in a designated market. Not only is the plan a clarification of the practitioner's goals but it establishes a plan of action toward reaching those goals with general concepts and specific ideas.

A good business plan is also an operational tool that spells out the specific goals to optimize the success of the practice. It determines how much money will be needed for start-up costs and includes financial projections over a 3 to 5-year period. It must reassure lenders and other financial stakeholders that the analysis of the current market and the projections for the market in the future are based in sound logic, published projections about the needs of the hearing- and balance-impaired populations, and a well-described response strategy to competitive encroachment, expansion into new markets, and the opportunities that will come available by advancing technologies. Business plans should establish the specific goals of the practice for the projected 3 to 5-year period with objectives and anticipated milestones stated for each year. For example, hearing instrument sales should be *realistically, even conservatively,* projected on a monthly basis for at least the first 3 years of the projected period. Milestones to consider include hiring additional audiologists to assist in the practice, as specific milestones are met. Each decision to add personnel, or expand to a second or third office must be tied to definitive and measurable evidence before the action is put into motion in the practice.

As the business plan for the practice is so important, there are components of bad business plans that must be avoided. Berry (2004) offers some general do's and don'ts in business planning. They are adapted here for an audiology practice:

Business Plan Do's

- A Mission Statement must be crafted to reflect the purpose and long-term vision and goals of the practice.
- Use a set of concrete goals, responsibilities, and deadlines to guide the practice from start-up through 3 to 5 years.
- Milestones must be established; once achieved, other actions can develop, such as hiring another audiologist contingent on attaining specific revenue milestones.
- The competition must be exhaustively researched and accurately characterized.
- Assign action to achieve goals and milestones to a specific individual in the practice for implementation and monitoring progress.
- As part of the implementation of a business plan, schedule times for evaluation and assessment of the plan—at least quarterly in the first 3 years; semiannually thereafter.
- Good business plans provide a practical roadmap with clear metrics for achieving goals and objectives relative to the mission of the practice.

Business Plan Don't's

- Don't use a business plan to show how much you know about your business.

Nobody reads a long-winded business plan: not bankers nor other sources of capital, keep it under 25 pages.

- Don't overhype the opportunities; keep your enthusiasm visible in the document but avoid the temptation of overselling the product.
- Don't set forth unattainable goals; be realistic relative to the demographics and patients and referral sources to be served.
- Don't underevaluate the need for the services to be provided.
- Don't underestimate nor lose sight of the competition.
- Don't develop unrealistic or unattainable financial projections; be conservative in your estimates and projections.
- Don't underestimate the effects of reducing margins on hearing instruments and the necessary strategy to counteract the trend.
- Don't make the assumption that hearing instrument manufacturers would rather deal with you directly than with the consumer of their products.

Business Planning—The Advantages and Utility of a Business Plan

There were audiologists, though few in numbers in the 1970s, 1980s, and 1990s, who had both entrepreneurial spirit and the capacity to develop an appropriate business plan. They knew that the bankers and lenders of the day would not consider funding a venture that was not well conceived and carefully delineated in the context of a business plan. They understood that the business plan was (and remains) a highly stylized document involving a logical progression of information in a commonly accepted format. The content requirements may have changed over the years, largely as a function of changing technologies and advancing clinical protocols; however, the changes have resulted in additional opportunities to generate revenue. Additionally, there is improved accessibility to information important to defining the patient base, potential sources of patient referral, insurance information, and general demographic data including information about services provided by competitive practices.

One thing has not changed: the lenders of today expect exhaustive market analyses, how the patients will get to your office, and what the marketing and promotional plans will be at start-up and over at least a 3-year period. They want to understand the metrics for the practice over that period, and if they are providing serialized financial support, those metrics must be validated before each note is reissued and payment to the practice is granted. The plan must contain a complete forensic on the competition, how your venture exceeds the competition, and how your practice will provide that information to referral sources and potential patients so that they have the opportunity to choose your practice for a segment of their patient's care.

Staffing projections and equipment costs including clinical and business equipment, office furnishings, informational technologies to be instituted at start up, Web site development, and planning for a consistent Internet presence will need to be addressed in the plan. Anything less will constitute a lack of due diligence in the eyes of potential lenders. In short, the comprehensive business plan develops all the components of a successful practice based on the vision of the person seeking financial support. The audiologist seeking funding must be able to answer a single question about the business plan. If the business plan contains the appropriate balance of information, realistic projections, well-developed demographics, and information about services available within the market, the answer to the question will be simple. The question: "If you were a venture capitalist with money to invest, would you invest in this practice?" To put it another way, did your business plan develop an opportunity for a lender to become a partner in your venture with limited risk relative to the due diligence set forth in your business plan?

Brassil (2007) calls the Business Plan a management and financial blueprint of the practice that clearly identifies and defines the goals of the practice while precisely outlining the methods of achieving them. The Business Plan is a document that may be critical to the start-up of the practice. It is also critical to the ongoing good health of the practice. Some believe the Business Plan should be placed in the circular file after start-up funding has been obtained. Instead, it should be considered a vital document to be renewed from time to time as the practice grows and flourishes. The Business Plan should be close to current form at all times so that when the need for expansion capital comes about, the plan will be ready to submit with minimal intervention and revisions. Keep it handy and review it occasionally if for no other reason that to remind yourself where the venture began, how it is evolving, and whether or not the practice is on schedule as planned (Sidebar 1–1).

Continuous Business Planning

Planning is an essential, fundamental step in beginning a new practice. It is an equally important operational matter to revise and update the business plan on a regular basis. The business plan is a vital document that should change just as the practice, the patients, and the health care environment changes. There are a number of reasons to revise and update a business plan. The following are adapted from Berry (2006) who offers reasons to regularly revise and update a business plan:

- Developing a new practice.
- Orientation and direction for a start-up practice.
- Growing an existing practice.
- Seek investment for a start-up or expanding an existing practice.
- To value a practice for formal transactions related to divorce, inheritance estate planning, or tax issues.
- Preparing to sell the practice.
- Dealing with professionals, such as attorneys, accountants, and bankers.
- Share and explain business objectives with your management team, employees, or new hires.
- To provide time line and decision metrics to trigger personnel additions, to purchase new equipment, or to expand clinical offerings with the purchase of new equipment.
- Deciding if it is time to rent additional space or to purchase a building or office condominium.
- To allow the practitioner to share changes in business strategy, priorities, and specific action points with key advisors including the accountant and attorney for the practice.

Sidebar 1–1
COMPUTER-GENERATED BUSINESS PLANS

Business Plan Computer Programs

In this new century there is a computer program for nearly everything. Business planning is no exception and, as a first step, practitioners should consider the use of a software program, such as Business Plan Pro (http://www.paloalto.com), Plan Magic 9 (http://www.planmagic.com), PlanWrite (http://www.brs-inc.com), or any one of a number other programs. There are many of these programs available and most can be downloaded from the Internet for an investment of $50 to $200. Although the differences in costs among these programs are for extra features and assistance in planning, they all make the final business plan solid, accurate, and meaningful by presenting realistic milestones for assessment that are expected by lenders and other stakeholders. A good business planning computer program should be easy to learn and expedite the business planning process. If the learning curve is too time-consuming, the software can simply add to the frustration of creating the business plan, so choose the program wisely. If possible, software for business planning should integrate with the accounting software and provide templates for charts and graphs that can be customized for the presentation of the financial specifics of the practice. These programs can organize the whole planning process from start to finish, turning the business plan of straw into one of bricks in a relatively short time.

■ To allow those working in the practice to understand the Mission, goals, and direction of the practice as segments of the Business Plan are shared with practice associates.

Business Plans Change with Market Changes

The start-up business plan represents concept and vision couched in operational actions coupled with financial forecasting. It is the early roadmap for the practice. The business plan at 3 years poststart-up will likely be considerably different from the original. As roadmaps change with the addition of new highways, so too does a business plan change as the venture flourishes, hits bumps in the road, or as market changes dictate the need to redirect promotional efforts, consider relocation, or consider a second or third office location. Time changes everything and that is particularly true in health care. What was a good direction and a meaningful path for the practice at start-up may not be the best direction

3 or 5 years down the road. In a matter of a few years an office location once considered the best spot in the target demographic can change abruptly for a number of reasons: A hospital can internalize a large family practice group immediately dictating their referral patterns to providers participating in the hospital's network or provider panel; older patients move to assisted-living facilities or move in with their children outside a reasonable drive time to the practice; competitive practices move into the area and begin to impact what was once an exclusive referring relationship with several primary care practices. Other market changes are driven by factors well outside the realm of health care. If the practice was dependent on a large, single employer and the plant closes or moves to another state, the impact on the entire community and the health care market in particular will be felt across the board and perhaps especially so in the practice. In the case of an impending plant closing, the business plan should be revisited to consider adjustments such as marketing to those workers and retirees who will remain in the area following the closing or issuing information about the need to take advantage of their hearing care benefits while they remain in full force. Adapting to changing market parameters is vital to the long-term survival of many practices today —not just audiology but in primary care and other medical specialties as well.

Business Plan Format for an Audiology Practice

Business Plans, as mentioned, are stylized reports describing elemental information about start-up needs and projections, milestones, objectives, and actions needed to meet the goals established throughout the course of the practice. Business Plans conform to generally accepted guidelines of form and content. The format may vary depending on the nature of the business. Health care business plans require specificity of the patient population to be served, the referral sources as pathways to the market, equipment and personnel necessary to provide the services, and in-depth analyses across each market segment of care to be provided by the practice. A Business Plan specifically adapted for audiology practices is proposed below:

- Executive Summary
- Mission Statement
- Practice Overview
- Market Assessment
- Competition Analysis
- Personnel/Human Resources
- Operational Plan
- Financial Components

Executive Summary

The Executive Summary is the single most important segment of any business plan. It is the section that is read first and creates a first impression. If it is well crafted, it may become the basis for the decision to fund or not to fund a venture. The Executive Summary must not exceed two pages; preferably it should be completed on one page. It must be precisely written and generate a wide enough snapshot of the practice to provide the reader with the most important facts and concepts that are or will become the practice. Christiansen (2002) suggests that the best format for constructing the executive summary is to put the Issue

(Problem) and Purpose in the first paragraph to formulate interest in the reader. The Scope and Limitations as well as the Alternatives (Procedures) will go in the next paragraphs, whereas the Significant Considerations, Analysis, and Decisions will comprise the final paragraphs. Care must be taken to include only significant Considerations, Analysis, and Decisions as extra information in these sections is not appropriate. As each segment of the Executive Summary should contain key facts and information gleaned from the other sections of the Business Plan, experts agree that the Executive Summary should be written last. Each paragraph should mirror the sections of the business plan (Sidebar 1–2). Abrams (2005) suggests that when completed, the Executive Summary should answer the following questions for your readers:

- Does your basic concept make sense?
- Has your business been thoroughly planned?
- Is the management team capable?
- Is there a clear-cut market need for your product/service?
- What advantages do you have over your competition?
- Are your financial projections realistic?
- Is the business likely to succeed?
- Will investors be able to make money?
- Will lenders be able to get their money back?

Mission Statement

The Mission Statement should be considered the starting point of the business plan. It must be a concise statement that depicts both the purpose and the long-term vision of the practice. It should cover these topics: what the practice does, for whom they do it, and how (well) they do it (Klasko & Toub, 2002). The Mission Statement is a proclamation of the general nature and direction of the practice—it is an assertion of what the practice will do and what it (potentially) can be. Its value is twofold; to serve as an internal guidance statement for all working together in the practice and to inform those who come to the practice about the practice philosophy and commitment to excellence in all aspects of the services to be provided. Sample Mission Statement: *Audiology Associates will work honestly and diligently everyday to exceed the expectations of our patients and referral sources by providing the best hearing and balance care in our community.*

Practice Overview

Following an opening section describing the profession of audiology and its important contributions to contemporary hearing and balance care, the Practice Overview should delineate basic information about the practice including office locations, Web site location, legal form (sole proprietorship, LLC, etc.), a list of Principals participating in the practice, and what they will bring to the business. It should contain the history and developmental stage of the practice to date. An expansive narrative describing diagnostic and treatment procedures, hearing instrument assessment, and assistive device selection, fitting, and follow-up care must be set forth so that the reader readily understands the operational core of the practice and clinical opportunities available to patients and referring practitioners.

Sidebar 1–2
SAMPLE EXECUTIVE SUMMARY

New Practice

Mission Statement

The mission of Southwest Hearing Care, Inc. is *to always make decisions in favor of the patient or referral source at every opportunity knowing that we cannot be wrong if we are trying to be right by those whom we serve.* Southwest Hearing Care, Inc. is dedicated to working honestly and diligently everyday to exceed the expectations of our patients by providing the highest quality possible hearing and balance care.

Practice Overview

Southwest Hearing Care, Inc. is a private Audiology Practice located in Gulch, Texas that will provide hearing care products and services to the estimated 400,000 individuals in Gulch and the surrounding three county region. The practice will concentrate on providing diagnostic and rehabilitative hearing care to patients of all ages. Patients will be accepted as self-referrals and from primary health care providers as well as nonphysician health care practitioners. Hearing instruments will be dispensed as part of a rehabilitation effort and will include full range digital technologies, assistive listening devices, and a full range of support items to maintain the instruments.

Market Assessment

The estimate of patients in need of our clinical and rehabilitative services ranges from 40,000 to 65,000 within the defined demographic area. At this time, those seeking hearing care in this market area travel 75 miles to El Paso for services. That produces a hardship on these patients especially for important follow-up care necessary after hearing instrument fitting. There are no other professionals offering these services in the area described beyond commercial hearing aid dealers providing occasional visits to patient's residences for hearing aid sales and service. Recent data from the Better Hearing Institute suggest that only about 16% of the hearing impaired that could benefit from amplification devices actually own them, leaving a market of about 84% to be considered eligible for services provided and instruments dispensed in our practice. The funding requested will include marketing to primary care physicians, nonphysician health care providers, and directly to prospective patients.

Competition Analysis

In Gulch and the three county area there are three itinerant, commercial hearing aid salesmen selling hearing aids in patient's homes. None have an established office. They do not pose a significant competitive threat. Commercial hearing aid dealers have no formal degree and are licensed to assess hearing solely for the purposes of fitting a hearing aid according to Texas laws governing their practice.

Their focus in the area has been high-pressured hearing aid sales only. They may not engage in diagnostic testing and, therefore, pose no threat to that particular emphasis of the practice.

In contrast, Southwest Hearing Care, Inc. will offer full-range diagnostic hearing services and management of nonsurgical hearing impairments for all ages in a rehabilitation-centered program of hearing care. All services will be provided by doctoral level audiologists who are Board Certified by the American Board of Audiology.

Personnel/Human Resources

Southwest Hearing Care, Inc. will begin with a staff of two full-time administrative employees and Jason Jones, Au.D. Dr. Jones received his Doctor of Audiology Degree from the University of Florida and has worked as a technically competent audiologist for 12 years in various professional capacities. He was most recently employed for the past 5 years as the Director of Audiology at Adams General Hospital, El Paso, Texas. The proposed staff has worked in the other medical practices and audiology clinics for periods ranging from 4 to 10 years and offer substantial business and patient management experience.

Operational Plan

Immediate objectives for the practice are:

1. To obtain adequate funding for the project including salaries for an 18-month start-up period.
2. To obtain business and clinical equipment for start-up.
3. To lease space in a demographically sensitive area of the defined market.

4. To decorate the space with appropriate business, clinical, and patient-related furnishings.
5. To develop a marketing plan including visits to primary care physicians and nonphysician health care providers in the demographic area.
6. To establish and fund an appropriate marketing campaign in the local newspapers.
7. To secure and/or retain legal counsel to draw appropriate documents for the startup venture.
8. To secure the services of a Certified Public Accountant to establish a chart of accounts for the proposed practice and to establish the accountant's role in the fiscal management of the practice.
9. To break even at the 12- to 16-month mark from start-up date with consistent profitability occurring after the 18th month of operation.
10. To secure equipment and instrument vendors with at least a 45-day payment schedule and an understanding that they must stand behind their equipment or instruments and repairs on behalf of the patients to be served in the practice.

Financial Components

Based on the preliminary referral commitments, anticipated numbers of instruments to be dispensed, numbers of procedures to be completed and billed to third party payors, and business and clinical overhead costs coupled with the analysis of competition within the defined market area, Southwest Hearing Care, Inc. is projected to achieve an annual revenue of in excess of $1,000,000 within 36 months of operation with projected net profit after tax of $450,000.00 The company will turn profitable within the first year with after-tax earnings of $40,000 and $100,000 in year two (2008) (Figure 1–2).

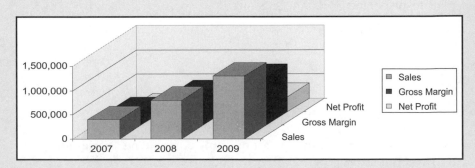

Figure 1–2. Net sales, gross profit, net profit, Southwest Hearing Care, Inc.

Existing Practice for Expansion

Mission Statement

To demonstrate to the professional community and the communities at large that we are the best source of hearing and balance assessments, hearing instrument fitting and follow-up care, and patient-centric practice operations in the Phillips County area.

Market Assessment

After 30 years of operation, Audiology Associates has stabilized profitability without growth in our current market. This has been due to population and referral sources moving to nearby markets, specifically the Horseshoe and Pinto Platte, Colorado areas. Whereas markets in Horseshoe and Pinto Platte have been steadily increasing by 15 to 25% per year over the last 3 years, our immediate demographic area has had a 10% decline in the same period.

Competition Analysis

Although there are three competitive hearing aid dealers in the area, R/R Hearing Aid Center, HearMeNow, and Bert's Hearing Barn, these competitors pose little competition in that they focus on high-pressure sales rather than professional services, rehabilitation management, and follow-up care. The referral sources that have moved into these markets recognize our practice name and understand the need for comprehensive hearing and balance services provided by audiologists in a professional setting. Re-establishing referral relationships will require personal marketing efforts and we have a plan in place and personnel resources to complete that important task. Importantly, several of our former referral sources have agreed to re-establish a referring relationship as soon as we open our office in their area.

Personnel/Human Resources

Audiology Associates has been successful in Horseshoe, Colorado for over 30 years under the direction of John Fedders, Ph.D. It is the addition of an Audiology colleague that is the key to continued success in the immediate market and in the new market area for the proposed office space. Jenny

Keller, Au.D. has joined our professional staff and will be managing the proposed new office. She will be merging her practice into ours and will bring approximately 4,000 active patients within a 30-minute drive time to the proposed office in Horseshoe.

Operational Plan

Over the past 12 months Audiology Associates has been in a preliminary planning process to open a new location in the Crossroads Center professional office complex in Horseshoe, just east of Wray, Colorado. This will permit self-referred patients and those referred by practitioners access to comprehensive hearing and balance diagnostic and rehabilitative services in close proximity to the new Scotch Pines Medical Center (SCPMC) in Wray. With the expansion of a 3,000 sq. ft. office, now under construction in the McKinley Station area just adjacent to Crossroads Center, Audiology Associates is well positioned for a new opportunity. The presence of our brand of Audiology in this area will be dramatic and profitable by offering state of the art clinical services in both hearing and balance diagnostics, high technology hearing instrument fitting and follow-up care, as well as operative monitoring services at SCPMC.

Financial Component

As requested herein, we are in need of capital infusion funding, in the amount of $100,000, with a return in a renewable 12-month period. Audiology Associates also requests interest-only monthly payments with a balloon payment at the end of this term and an option for a portion of the balance to be renewable for another 12 months. Based on our market research, our conservative estimate of increased revenues will be an income ratio increase to 45%. The funding requested will enable Audiology Associates to establish a professional presence and thereby capture significant market share in areas populated with affluent people who are more likely to spend money on health-related matters affecting the quality of their lives.

The note will be secured and personally guaranteed by Dr. Fedders.

The path a patient takes from referral source to the office and through a comprehensive hearing examination, interpretation, and counseling should be portrayed to illustrate the many interactions between the patient, clerical and clinical staff members, specialized environments, and equipment used in the clinical process. Pathways can be developed for each clinical presentation; those patients referred for hearing assessment and management, evaluation of equilibrium, and for specialized protocols such as tinnitus management and central auditory processing assessment and treatment recommendations. No matter the clinical pathways to be described, this section must be written with the nonaudiologist reader in mind.

The Practice Overview should characterize contemporary service and treatment trends in audiology and relate them to the needs of the market area. It should describe what business and clinical parameters will make the practice profitable and an effective, competitive force in the existing market. It must establish the practice's competitive edge whether based on personnel with advanced degrees and licenses, specific assessment, or therapeutic protocols not offered by others in the market (e.g., tinnitus assessment and rehabilitation), or a unique marketing approach to primary care physicians that has not been considered in the market. The reader of this section of the Business Plan should develop a clear picture of the services (to be) provided, understand what the practice will bring to the existing provider mix in the area, and an appreciation of what differentiates the practice competitively.

Market Assessment

The market is defined by individuals who will seek your services directly and by other health care providers with whom your practice will interact. Patients, physician and nonphysician referral sources in the area, hospitals, outpatient clinics, psychologists, optometrists, dentists, public and parochial schools, industrial nurses, extended care facilities, and nonprofit speech and hearing centers represent many of the people and referral sources which will interconnect with

your practice by virtue of proximity in the market. The market is also defined by a variety of demographic means including mailing codes or a 20 to 30-minute drive time to each office. Specific demographic information is readily available from a variety of sources. The U.S. Census Bureau has extensive information about population characteristics, age, income, and a variety of other information that might be of importance in better characterizing the market for your practice (http://www.census.gov). Local newspapers and telephone books as well as media outlets have specific demographic information about their readers, viewers, and listeners. The information is often available as a media information kit for potential advertisers. Examining general demographic information is a good first step in obtaining meaningful information to assess and describe a specific market area. General demographics should be periodically re-evaluated over the course of the practice to ensure that the target population remains large enough to continue to sustain the practice.

Strong target market definitions are based on observable characteristics, backed by data and research. This section of the business plan should develop a clear picture of your patients and referral sources—who they are, what they need from your practice, where they are located in relation to your practice, how they perceive the value of your services, and why they will come to or refer patients to your practice.

Competition Analysis

Potential investors reading a business plan expect to see a comprehensive assessment of the competition in the defined market area. Wherever there is a market for health care services, there is competition either directly from another audiologist practice providing diagnostic and rehabilitative services or indirectly from commercial hearing aid dealers selling hearing instruments.

To best typify the competition in the market, you must list specific competitors, estimate their market share, and consider their advertising in various media including their Web site. The competitors should be characterized by their clinical offerings, the qualifications of the care providers in the practice, and an assessment of their strengths and weaknesses. The sources of your information will vary. They will include former patients or current vendors who have had interactions with them. Qualifications and other information can be gleaned from licensing boards and other agencies that require licensing or registration information that is readily available to the public.

Understanding the offerings and competencies of direct or indirect competitors will better position you to distinguish your practice, identify factors that will make patients and referral sources choose your practice, respond to needs that are not being provided by competitors, and figure out what the practice has to overcome to advance and improve the practice's own market share (Abrams, 2005).

Distinguishing your practice from the crowd of competitors is not merely important; it is the key to both the short- and long-term success of your practice. For example, offering an assessment and treatment protocol for tinnitus can give a new practice an important edge in a market where other providers do not offer the service or fail to advise the health care community about its availability and efficacy. Patients with tinnitus

and disequilibrium are vexing problems for primary care practitioners. If they have an audiologist in the community who has made known to them that his or her practice welcomes patients with the complaints of tinnitus or dizziness, the referrals will begin and continue as long as the services and treatment exhaust the patient's need for clinical attention and valid diagnostic and therapeutic intervention or referral for further treatment. Primary care physicians appreciate the fact that their patients undergo extensive testing, competent counseling, and explanations of their particular difficulty and that their patients have some chance of remediation. Even if the outcome produces only a modicum of resolution, most patients appreciate the improvement and the fact that his or her physician has listened to their complaint and has made the referral to an interested health care practitioner who has been asked to become involved in this particular segment of their care.

Personnel/Human Resources

This section of the Business Plan must clarify both administrative and clinical positions in the practice, their respective qualifications, specific duties, and expected contributions to the overall success of the practice. Although job descriptions should not be included in their entirety in this section, they should be used as the basis of the information provided. The reader of this section must understand the need for each position, the qualifications required, and the work product expectations of each position. Regardless of the number of positions filled at the outset of the practice, every position filled or anticipated should be described. Metrics should be established in concert with time lines to hire additional personnel. For example, the addition of an audiologist may be considered when specific patient bookings exceed a 2-week waiting list on a consistent basis or when fiscal reserves reach a specified point with monthly or quarterly revenues reaching specific levels. Or it could be as simple as, when the workload at the front desk exceeds the limits of the patience of the clerical staff, it is time to add another person to the mix. First and foremost, the perceived need should be weighed against financial facts. Does the practice generate enough opportunity for billable time to support another audiologist? Is there a need to hire another front office position to meet increasing billing and reception loads? Will the addition of another audiologist improve the time a patient can be seen for assessment and follow-up? Will the new audiologist increase the numbers of procedures completed and instruments dispensed? Will the addition of another administrative staff member improve cash flow and billing turnaround time? These questions, if answered in the affirmative, represent positive indicators of growth and financial expansion of the practice.

Operational Plan

This section will be the most difficult to write due to the tendency to want to provide expansive information and support about how the practice will perform in the market, what services it will provide, immediate and long-term equipment needs, whether clinical or office equipment will be leased or purchased, and the office environment in which the

specified services and treatment regimen will be issued. Brevity must be the watchword of this section: It must include relevant information about suppliers and vendors with an indication of what performance characteristics the practice will demand from each. For example, each hearing instrument manufacturer will supply instruments under condition that the percentage of repairs by years of use will not exceed a specified amount; repair turnaround time limits should be established as should the incidence of rerepairs. The consequences of exceeding established limits should be set forth clearly (see Chapter 11 on Hearing Instrument Manufacturers and Suppliers). Both office and clinical equipment replacement schedules should be set forth in a timeline accompanied by projected costs.

A brief description of the diagnostic utility and clinical necessity of each service by CPT code should be included to orient the reader to the breadth and importance of the care to be provided. Special procedures linked to specific equipment should be described relative to anticipated use. Hearing instrument fitting and follow-up care should be explained with projected numbers of instruments to be fit over the course of the first 3 to 5 years. If you are beginning the practice with limited services, indicate the services to be added and discuss the time line or decision metric that will permit service expansion.

Business operations to be considered in this section and should include both hardware and software necessary for billing and tracking patient accounts, business equipment necessary to facilitate cash flow and patient satisfaction, office furnishings, and patient-comfort and staff-comfort items. Items necessary for informational security and compliance with

HIPAA regulations must be included. The reader of this section should develop a picture of the equipment necessary to provide all clinical services, now and in the future. The reader should understand the business operations from equipment, software, and patient-interface aspects. The office space, furnishings, and business-related supplies and services should be clarified in this section—a complete view of what it will take to support the clinical side of the venture by providing state-of-the-art equipment, billing software, and methods of information and financial management of the practice. It is best to involve all those involved in the practice, including the practice attorney and accountant, to read and comment on what ultimately defines how the business and clinical sides come together for the patients and referral sources being served in the practice.

Financial Components

This section requires rigorously realistic and objective projections with the inclusion of as much factual information as possible. Do not overstate or inflate revenue projections or numbers of services to be provided nor numbers of instruments to be dispensed. Revenue projections should be based on anticipated referrals and self-referred patients over a specified time. Incremental numbers of patients should be seen as a function of proposed marketing efforts. Break-even points should be defined based on numbers of referrals, procedures completed, and instruments dispensed over a specific time line. Projected revenues should be tied to the amount to be borrowed or the credit line draw dates to be established. Include realistic estimates of known overhead, expenses, and salary projections to the break-even point—what it will take to fund all operations until the practice is at least paying for itself including all personnel wages. Common sense should prevail: If it is unlikely you will have the referrals to support an auditory evoked potential system in the beginning of your practice, there is no need to allocate funding for its purchase until such time that anticipated referrals can support its use.

Summary

Lenders reviewing the Business Plan of start-up practices want to be convinced that the proposed venture will reach the financial projections detailed in the plan. In short, they want to be convinced that their participation as a financial partner will result in a successful practice. If the Business Plan is done well, it will provide them with a measure of confidence and an incentive to lend all monies needed to fund the venture. The document should be straightforward, as short as possible, and offer realistic financial data supported by comprehensive due diligence about the opportunities for success in the market.

As a vital and changing document, the Business Plan should be revisited periodically and updated accordingly. If the plans for the practice change, the Business Plan should reflect that change. Consider sending a copy of the revised Business Plan to your lenders, attorney, and accountant. It keeps them informed and confident that you are managing your practice as a business as diligently and with the same level of completeness as you manage your patients.

A guide for a Business Plan developed for an audiology practice is adapted from

Keller (2007) in Sidebar 1–3. It provides an extensive reminder of items of importance to lenders and investors to be applied to your Business Plan prior to its submission or during the course of your successful practice.

Sidebar 1–3
AUDIOLOGY BUSINESS PLAN GUIDE
(modified from Keller, 2007)

Executive Summary

- Audiology Business Plan in brief

Practice concepts
Marketing strategy
Products/ services,
Business management
Financing requirements
Role of investors

Practice Overview

- Historical background

Founder(s) of the practice
When founded
Development of the practice
Achievements

- Situation today

Legal structure
Key financial figures

- Additional background information

Financing for start-up depending
   on financing situation
Financing for expansion
Financing for acquisitions

Products/Services

- Products/services

Detailed description of
   products/services
Benefits for patients
Patient needs
Advantages/disadvantages
   compared with competitors'
   Audiology practices

■ Research and development

Developments/refinements in the practice
Innovations in products and services

Markets

■ Market overview

Market analysis
Patient analysis
Service and product purchase motivation

■ Practice market position

Market segments addressed
Target patient groups
Referral channels

■ Market assessment/
Market trends

Market research
Market entry barriers
Estimated patient market growth

Competitors

■ Competitor companies

Name
Location
Patient structure
Patient motivation

■ Competing products

Range of services
Products available
Differing features of services and products
Supplementary services/products

Marketing

■ Market segmentation

Target markets
Target patient groups

■ Marketing

Product and service sales
PR/advertising/promotion

■ Packaging of products/
services

Range of products/services
Pricing bundled/unbundled

■ Sales targets   Budgeted sales volumes for each
                                    market segment in the next
                                    5 years
                                    Targets for market share in each
                                    market segment

Location/Production/Administration

■ Location   Practice domicile and offices
                                    Benefits and limitations of chosen
                                        location

■ Production   Internal and external production
                                    Procurement of goods and materials
                                        (if products are manufactured in
                                        the practice)

■ Administration   Structure of administration
                                    Organization of accounting function
                                    Information technology capabilities

Organization/Management

■ Management team   Individual members
                                    Responsibilities
                                    Compensation
                                    Special qualifications

■ Clinical team   Individual members
                                    Responsibilities
                                    Compensation
                                    Special qualifications

■ Biography of each member   Training and education
                                    Professional experience
                                    Previous positions

Risk Analysis

■ Internal risks   Management
                                    Responsibilities
                                    Compensation
                                    Special qualifications

■ External Risks	Economic Environmental Legal Social

Financial Planning

■ Short-term and long-term planning	Determining financing requirements based on forecasts for the balance sheet, profit and loss (or Income) statement, and cash flow statement Cash budget

Financing

■ Financing concept	Meeting financing requirements through injection of new capital

References

Abrams, R. (2005). *Business plan in a day.* Palo Alto, CA: The Planning Shop.

Berry, T. (2004). Hurdle: *The book on business planning.* Eugene, OR: Palo Alto Software.

Berry, T. (2006). *15 reasons you need a business plan.* Retrieved February 15, 2007, from http://www.entrepreneur.com/startingabusiness/businessplancoachtimberry/article83818.html

Brassil, M. (2007). *Six important functions of a business plan.* Retrieved February 16, 2007, from http://www.websitemarketingplan.com/bplan/functions.htm

Christiansen, J. (2002). *Executive summaries complete the report.* CSUN Business writing course. Retrieved June 10, 2007, from http://www.csun.edu/~vcecn006/

Harrison, J., & St. John, C. (2004). *Foundations in strategic management* (3rd ed.), Mason, OH: Thompson Southwestern.

Keller, B. (2007). *Business plan checklist.* Presentation to the International Distributor Forum, March 20, 2007, Lucerne, Switzerland: Bernafon A/G.

Kiasko, S., & Toub, D. (2002). It's not a plan without a business plan. In J. Safalippo, T. Nolan, & Whiteside B. (Eds.), *MBA handbook for health professionals.* Valley Stream, NY: Parthenon.

Tracy, J. (2001). *Accounting for dummies* (p. 210). Hoboken, NJ: John Wiley & Co.

2

Legal Considerations in Practice Management

GLENN L. BOWER, J.D.

Usual Caveat

The statements and suggestions in this chapter should not be construed as legal advice or opinions. As noted below, readers should not act on information contained in this chapter without professional guidance based on the reader's specific relevant facts and circumstances, and then-current, applicable law.

Securing Legal Counsel and Other Professional Advisors

Establishing an audiology practice involves an array of business considerations that can be addressed by any reasonable entrepreneur aware of them. Not all such issues are intuitive. Therefore, it is helpful to engage legal counsel and other appropriate professional advisors. These professionals not only identify issues, but also provide validation of usual and reasonable alternatives as well as preferred solutions.

When selecting legal counsel, the easiest path is usually to go to someone familiar, or someone known to friends or family. This approach may yield a qualified attorney, but a more systematic approach, casting a wider net, enhances the probability of finding the most appropriate attorney. Referral services offered by the local bar association and others such as accountants, bankers, and insurance agents are also good resources for identifying qualified candidates to be considered as attorney for the practice.

Chemistry and Value

Desired qualities for legal counsel include chemistry and value. The "chemistry" element of the relationship can be very important and requires positive answers to critically important questions:

- Does the attorney really understand my legal, business, and professional requirements?
- Does the attorney really understand my approach to problem-solving and my preferences regarding how to address relevant issues that have been identified?
- Does the attorney relate to me well enough to anticipate questions I have not asked, and to provide access and advice if needed outside of normal business hours?

The "value" element consists of quality and cost. Quality legal services derive from a variety of critical factors:

- Relevant experience

- Industry insight
- Analytical ability
- Diligence in providing timely advice and appropriate work product.

Significant years of practice dealing with health care practices and associated business issues would constitute relevant experience. A meaningful degree of interaction with other health care providers, would serve as a basis for industry insight. This can include interaction with other practitioners and institutions, and involvement in relevant professional organizations, such as the American Health Lawyers Association, and health care law committees of local and state bar associations as well as the American Bar Association. Analytical ability and diligence are not characteristics easily ascertained during an introductory meeting or even necessarily by looking at biographical information in an attorney's promotional materials or on the attorney's website. Such characteristics are best determined by speaking with the attorney's current (and past if you can identify them) clients, so references are quite helpful in this regard. Obviously, a footnote to the "don't just use someone known by family and friends" warning is that if family and friends have actually used an attorney for legal services, their advice may be quite valuable in assessing the analytical ability of such attorney and the diligence with which such attorney handles projects and provides timely and useful advice or tangible work product.

Cost of legal services can certainly be very significant to a new practice. Attorneys usually charge fees based on hourly rates, with expenses passed through to varying degrees. Some attorneys pass along phone costs, mileage, and other expenses whereas others absorb these expenses into their hourly rates. Clients may be able to negotiate fixed prices for specific tasks, so it is worth discussing an alternative fee arrangement. Hourly rates are often a function of geographic area, normally mirroring to some degree cost of living in such areas, as well as size of the law firm. On the coasts or in major cities hourly rates are usually greater than in the Midwest, smaller towns, and rural areas. Although large firms normally set higher hourly rates than smaller firms, they are more likely to have attorneys with greater expertise and experience in more focused specialties and greater technical resources within the firm. The value or quality/cost function can be found in any size firm, including solo attorneys and/or multiattorney megafirms and should not be presumed according to the size of the firm.

Securing Other Professional Advisors

In addition to legal counsel, a variety of other professional advisors can be useful in establishing and maintaining an audiology practice. Selection of an accountant, a banker, and an insurance representative should follow similar systematic search process similar to securing legal counsel. An accountant normally helps with cash flow projections and budgeting, as well as with tax and other financial planning, and payroll. Potential accountants should be evaluated generally on the same basis as attorneys, with a view toward chemistry and value, quality and cost. A banker can establish a line of credit to fund initial operations, as well as set up checking and other relevant accounts. A meaningful line of credit or other type of loan will normally require

a carefully prepared business plan and some type of collateral. If the tangible assets to be owned by the practice do not suffice, a personal guaranty and/or home mortgage may be necessary. Insurance agents make recommendations regarding professional malpractice insurance; liability, property, and casualty insurance for the business; and health and life insurance for the owner and any employees. An investment advisor may be helpful to deal with personal investments of the audiologist, as well as investments associated with pension and profit sharing plans for the owner(s) and other employees.

Establishment and Operation of an Audiology Practice

For purposes of this discussion, the assumption is that the audiologist will not simply be an employee of an established practice, but intends to establish a new practice or practice group. In the process, the audiologist must consider and determine the nature of formal organization of the practice. No matter if the practice will be owned by an individual or multiple parties, important decisions are necessary including the following basic issues:

- How best to provide compensation and benefits to professionals and other employees;
- How to deal with anticipated contractual issues;
- How to comply with laws and regulations applicable to the practice of audiology.

Choice of Legal Entity

Forming a legal entity, such as a corporation, can insulate the personal assets of the owners of an audiology practice from at least the nonprofessional liabilities associated with the practice. Examples of nonprofessional liabilities that would not put personal assets of the owners at risk, if the practice were properly conducted within an entity with limited liability, include real estate and equipment leases, bank loans, and other contractual obligations not otherwise personally guaranteed by the practice owner. Landlords, lenders, hearing instrument and equipment suppliers, and others often require a personal guaranty that the owner of a start-up practice will maintain responsibility for all debts incurred until such time that firm credit is established.

"Tort" claims resulting from business operations, such as someone slipping and falling at the facility, would also fall within this category. Claims relating to professional services would normally be pursued against the professional personally, as well as against the practice, so a limited liability form of entity will likely not provide a barrier for such claims putting personal assets at risk. Note that merely organizing an entity with limited liability to own a practice does not per se insulate owners from personal liability. This protection is a presumption, which can be overcome by a showing that the business was really being operated as an alter ego of the owner(s), without its separate existence being respected by the owner(s). This "piercing the veil" concept of holding the owner(s) liable for liabilities of a corporation or limited liability company ("LLC") most frequently arises when money is not properly tracked, documented, or properly accounted for and when contracts are signed in the name of the owners rather than the business name.

Failure to formally form an entity to own the practice results in a sole proprietorship (if a single owner) or a general partnership (if more than one owner). In either of such cases, all assets of the owner(s) are available to creditors of the practice, subject to applicable bankruptcy laws that vary from state to state, but may permit certain categories or amounts of assets to be protected from bankruptcy creditors.

Corporations and Limited Liability Corporations (LLC) are currently the preferred forms of entity to accomplish insulation of personal assets from creditors of the practice. General partnerships generally do not achieve such limited liability, although states now provide for a form of general partnership commonly referred to as a Limited Liability Partnership (LLP) that limits personal liability, at least to some degree that may vary depending on statutory law in the state of organization. Limited partnerships provide such limited liability to limited partners, but not to general partners or to those limited partners participating in the management of the business.

Accountants and tax attorneys often have preferences regarding the selection of the form of an entity, a threshold question being whether a "flow-through" of tax attributes is desired. "Flow-through" entities include LLCs (unless they elect otherwise), as well as any corporation electing to file with the Internal Revenue Service as an "S Corporation." The flow-through entity is not separately taxed for federal income tax purposes and all revenues and expenses of the entity are attributed to the owners in proportion to their respective ownership interests.

Accountants for the entity prepare a Schedule K-1 annually for each owner, which provides the information needed for such owner's personal income tax return. Conversely, a corporation not properly electing "S Corporation" status (known for these purposes as a "C Corporation") would be separately taxed for federal income tax purposes. Income of a C Corporation is not attributed to owners unless they actually receive funds as compensation (which would be deductible to the entity but only to the extent the amounts are "reasonable") or dividends (which would not be deductible to the entity), and expenses would not "flow through" to the owners and be deductible on their personal federal income tax returns.

Other factors considered in determining the appropriate form of entity for an audiology practice include projected earnings, specifically in the context of federal and applicable state income tax rates and brackets; employment taxes; other state taxes; and the comfort, experience, and familiarity of the professional advisors with the various specific forms of entity.

The corporate form is historically more conventional, but LLCs have been around for a number of years now, and provide more flexibility in structure than S Corporations. An LLC operating agreement may provide that allocations and distributions are to be made other than pro-rata with equity/capital ownership. Additionally, there is no limit on the number of or nature of owners in an LLC, whereas an S Corporation may be owned by no more than 100 owners including individuals or qualified trusts. Table 2–1 summarizes certain identifying characteristics of various forms of entity.

Table 2–1. Identifying Forms of Corporate and Business Entities

	Limited Liability of Owners	Tax Pass Through	Federal or State Filing(s) Required to Organize
C Corporation	Yes	No	State
S Corporation	Yes	Yes	Federal and state
L.L.C.	Yes	Yes, unless otherwise requested	State
General Partnership	No	Yes	No (but state may require fictitious name filing)
P.L.L.	Yes, to some degree as defined by state law	Yes	No (but state may require fictitious name filing)
Limited Partnership	Yes, except for general partner	Yes	State
Sole Proprietorship	No	Yes	No

Please note this chart is not an exhaustive list of entity types, and that other potential but lesser used forms of entities, such as unincorporated associations, may exist from state to state.

The state of organization for the entity is usually, but not necessarily, the state in which the practice is located. Certain states, such as Delaware, have historically catered to companies relying on the public equities markets by business-friendly laws regarding organization, flexibility in operations, and standards of care for directors and officers of corporations. Delaware in particular has significantly more developed, and therefore more established, judicial case law relating to business issues than other states. As so many major companies have organized there, many cases with claims associated with business operations, and activities have been tried there. Many companies view the increased certainty associated with such established case law as beneficial. However, many other states have in recent years developed a more business-friendly legal environment. Closely held professional business entities do not necessarily have the same degree of concern about scrutiny of directors actions by public shareholders. Thus, Delaware is really not of preference for most closely held businesses such as audiology practices that do not commonly rely on investors to raise capital.

State taxes on business net income or revenues vary from state to state, but generally apply to operations within the state and these taxes cannot be avoided by organizing the practice in another state. In view of the foregoing, and the fact that the state in which the practice is located will also be the state with which retained legal counsel will be most familiar, normally that same state will be the logical state of organization.

Multiple Owners

Establishing a solo practice clearly avoids a number of issues associated with having one or more "partners," but there is also a perception of safety in numbers for the viability of a practice. Selection of an incompatible professional partner can adversely impact retention of other personnel, profitability, and value of the practice, as well as create various degrees of stress. These relationships are often created to increase capital or to bring greater talent to the professional or management mix of the practice.

If co-owners are needed, it is very important to establish relative expectations and ground rules for operations and decision-making as early as possible. Issues such as respective ownership percentages, associated amounts and form of capital contributions, and allocation of authority for making prospective decisions of varying degrees of materiality should be clearly identified in the organizational documents (bylaws or shareholder or "close corporation" agreements for corporations; operating agreements for LLCs). If one party is not obviously bringing more to the table than another party, in terms of initial capital, inherited practice (from a retiring parent or other acquaintance) or portable practice (bringing an existing practice from a pre-existing solo or group situation), it will be difficult to structure for other than equal rights among the owners. In the event this produces an even number of equal owners, the organizational documents should also provide for a "deadlock" mechanism to establish procedures in the event that the parties cannot agree on how to deal with one or more material issues.

In a multiple owner situation, it may be appropriate to establish one of the owners or a subset of the owners as the LLC's manager or management committee, or as the corporation's Chief Executive Officer or board of directors. Whether management is so centralized or not, there may be certain identified issues that the owners agree are so important that they should only occur on agreement of some defined supermajority vote of owners, such as 66%, 75%, 80%, or unanimous. Such supermajority issues could include amending the organizational documents, modifying compensation of owners, incurring bank debt, bringing in new owners, terminating an owner, combining with another entity, or selling the business. A supermajority vote by definition makes it more difficult to obtain the required authorization than a simple majority vote. An occasionally overlooked corollary is that minority owners have greater power (that being the potential veto power) in such circumstances. In fact, if there is an out-of-step owner, a supermajority voting requirement facilitates "tyranny of the minority," and may require the majority owners to make certain related or unrelated concessions to a minority owner in order to proceed with the matter that required the supermajority vote. I am aware of a professional firm that has grown to more than 20 owners and still requires a unanimous vote to amend its shareholders agreement (which, not surprisingly, has not been amended in any material way since it was adopted more than 20 years ago). Supermajority voting requirements can provide certain com-fort to minority owners, but may also ultimately be an unhealthy impediment to appropriate actions and organizational evolution.

Compensation and Benefits

As owners in a multiple owner scenario are usually concerned about the productivity of the other owners, compensation structures often involve a base salary or draw, with a supplemental compensation formula to reflect the relative productivity of each owner. Some health care practices allocate compensation on a pro-rata basis year after year which works when each owner takes his or her responsibilities to the others seriously. Unstated peer pressure keeps the owners at comparable and positive rates of productivity. Unless the chemistry among owners makes such an approach possible, agreeing to some productivity and measurement standards will be needed to serve as the basis to make at least annual compensation adjustments.

There are a variety of employee benefit plans, many using pretax dollars, which can enhance the compensation arrangements and financial security for owners as well as nonowner employees. Defined contribution retirement plans, such as 401(k) and profit sharing plans, are common for employers of all sizes whereas Simplified Employee Pension Plans (or "SEPs") and SIMPLE-IRA plans may be particularly attractive to employers with few employees. SIMPLE-IRAs and 401(k) plans permit employees to contribute up to a certain amount of pretax dollars to their account in the plan. Subject to legal restrictions, these plans as well as profit-sharing plans and SEPs permit employers to match or otherwise contribute to their employees' retirement accounts. Noncontributory defined benefit plans are less common for closely held companies than defined contribution plans, but that is a potential benefit plan as well. Health insurance is a typical benefit, with some portion contributory by all employees—the magnitude of employer subsidy to be determined by the owner(s). Flexible benefit plans (sometimes known as "cafeteria" or "Section 125" plans) permit pretax contributions by employees to pay group insurance premiums and otherwise noncovered health costs, including deductibles and co-pays, and child-care expenses. Other employee benefits to be considered include dental insurance, disability insurance, and life insurance. Benefit plans must be carefully designed to avoid violating government-imposed nondiscrimination tests that are intended to protect lower paid employees.

Whether subsidized by the employer as an employee benefit or not, estate planning is important for all the usual reasons of making sure desired allocations are provided for and taxes are minimized. It is important to periodically revisit the estate planning process as financial resources, survivor needs, and intended beneficiaries evolve and/or change. A qualified estate planning attorney (optimally affiliated with the attorney retained for organizational purposes so planning for business succession can be coordinated with estate planning) can make sure wills and associated documents meet desired goals in consideration of applicable federal and state estate taxes, trusts for life insurance, dependents, or others, and living will and other health care planning documents, which are generally governed by state law.

Contractual Relationships

Facilities

For a start-up practice, the location of the facility for the practice will be high on the list of things to do. Although purchasing an existing facility or constructing a facility on purchased property are alternatives, a conventional start-up practice will simply lease space. Legal counsel with real estate experience will be useful for identifying usual terms and conditions for the lease within the specific geographic area. Material terms to be considered include rent (and provisions for, and any limitations on, increases and expense pass-throughs); respective maintenance obligations of the landlord and tenant, including exterior and common areas; rights of each party to terminate or modify the lease; any limitations on subleasing or assigning the lease; any limitations on use of the facility (even if the practice is permitted, currently inapplicable prohibitions may be a problem for potential future assignees or subtenants); and allocation of risk associated with the facility, as may be reflected by indemnification and/or insurance provisions.

Events such as a fire, a major water leak or flood, or a power outage or surge can interfere with a tenant's ability to use the leased space and operate the facility. Leases characterized by a landlord as "standard form" often give only the landlord (i) a right to terminate a lease in the event of a casualty, (ii) a period of time to decide whether or not to restore damaged premises, and (iii) a further period of time to effect the restoration (6 to 9 months is common). In addition, the landlord's lender, usually the payee of landlord's insurance proceeds in the event of a casualty, may decline to make such proceeds available for restoration. A tenant with some degree of bargaining power may be able to procure a commitment from the landlord's lender, by means of subordination, nondisturbance and attornment agreement described below, that insurance proceeds will be made available for restoration if certain conditions confirming the lender's security are met. In any event, a tenant should consider what (if any) portions of the leased space are essential to operation of the practice, and options for alternative temporary space if the need arises.

The subordination, nondisturbance and attornment agreement mentioned above provides that even if the landlord defaults on its financing arrangements with the lender, including a mortgage on the leased premises, the tenant may continue to occupy the premises as long as the tenant continues to comply with its obligations, including payment of rent, under the lease. Without such an agreement, such a lender may evict a tenant of a defaulting landlord in certain circumstances. Most tenants do not ask for such an agreement, but in cases where substantial improvements are being made to the premises, or other suitable space is difficult to find, it is worth requesting.

If a need for additional space is reasonably anticipated in the foreseeable future to accommodate expected growth in the practice, it is not unusual to ask for an option or at least a right of first refusal in the lease, on identified space adjacent to the currently leased space. Additionally, the lease can be written to include the right of first refusal regarding the sale of the building.

If improvements to the leased space are required before occupancy, the landlord and tenant must agree upon what improvements will be made, who will secure the contractors to make the improvements, and who will finance the improvements. The landlord may agree to give the tenant an allowance or to finance the cost over the lease term with the tenant making periodic payments to the landlord. If the tenant is responsible for construction of the improvements, the tenant will need to obtain all necessary governmental approvals (e.g., building permit), and confirm that the improvements will comply with applicable legal requirements (e.g., zoning, Americans with Disabilities Act). These issues can be dealt with in the lease itself, or in an incorporated and mutually signed side letter.

Depending on the local real estate market, there may be opportunities to successfully negotiate more favorable terms and conditions to some degree. At least with input from an experienced real estate attorney there will be a baseline for validating that requested revisions to the landlord's proposed terms and conditions are reasonable. If this process is not satisfactory and there are otherwise desirable alternative locations available, more favorable terms might be negotiated with a more reasonable, or at least more flexible, landlord, with either a more even-handed standard form, or a willingness to negotiate more bilateral terms and conditions. Note that even if a lease does not contain obviously problematic restrictions on use of the premises, local zoning laws may have such restrictions, so a look at the local zoning map and related definitions and regulations may be prudent but usually reserved in cases where the property is being purchased.

Employees

Relationships with employees constitute another significant category of legal issues, governed by federal, state, and local laws, as well as contractual arrangements. An employee handbook is always a good idea, even if there are few employees, to establish a basis for many otherwise unstated, ambiguous, and/or misunderstood aspects of the employment relationship. When permitted by state law, confirmation on the employment application or in an employee handbook that an employee is an "at will" employee can be key to the right of the employer to terminate employment for any or no reason (unless termination is for an illegal reason such as age, race, or sex) and without prior notice. Such language can be invaluable if an employee alleges that an otherwise verbal employment arrangement was for an initial term of 1 year, and 1-year increments thereafter, where the employer during the hiring process referred to salary in an annual amount. Furthermore, an arrangement not reflected by an employee manual or other written document permits an employee to assert that the parties understood there would be no termination by the employer without "cause." Obviously such default or alleged parameters of an employment relationship may be inconvenient and costly to an employer that may have to spend time and energy to prove a valid "for cause" reason for termination, rather than simply using the "at will" concept to rid the practice of an otherwise incompatible or unproductive employee. Although formal employment agreements for key employees may be an unnecessary cost, an operational practice with more than one professional may be well served by written agreements with the professionals and perhaps other key employees to specifically cover duties, base salary, bonuses, benefits, and termination transition issues, among other things.

Other topics covered by employer-employee documentation normally include confirmation and acknowledgment of the ownership of patient records, as well as financial, personnel, and other proprietary business information of the employer. The terms usually confirm the employee's agreement that such information is confidential and proprietary and not to be used other than in the normal course of the employer's business, and are not to be removed from the employer's premises. Required compliance by the employee with identified standards of care is often set forth in such documentation as well.

Payors

An important aspect of any health care practice these days is relationships with insurance companies and other payors. The major national health insurance companies will provide their standard provider agreements. The goal of reviewing such agreements is usually not negotiation as respective bargaining power of the parties is usually far from equal. The review is to simply understand the agreement to determine if a specific relationship with a particular provider is desirable and beneficial to the practice.

Patients

The patient relationship is contractual, as well as professional. Providing new patients with contractual terms on initiation of the relationship, usually as part of the application/information forms, can be important. This is particularly true in the context of establishing primary payment responsibility. Applicability of insurance coverage is often not clearly discernable until after services are provided and claims are submitted, because of employment status and satisfaction of premium payment obligations. Within certain parameters, insurance companies may deny coverage to patients when employment of the primary covered person with the subscribing employer has terminated, or when that employer has failed to pay premiums. At the time of service the audiologist may not know these facts which can substantially impact payment for services rendered or instruments dispensed.

Regulatory Compliance

The practice of audiology is subject to state licensure or registration. As criteria vary from state to state, it is very important to become familiar with the requirements of the state(s) in which a license is likely to be desired, to ensure that such requirements are met before application for a license is made. A careful review of the state law and administrative rules should provide the information needed. If not, contact the executive director at the licensing board for specific clarifications.

In addition to state licensure, the practice of audiology is subject to a various federal, state, and local laws and associated rules, some unique to the health care industry, and some applicable to businesses generally.

Federal laws that specifically apply to the practice of health care, and therefore impact the practice of audiology directly or indirectly, include:

- The Health Insurance Portability and Accountability Act (known to its friends and others as "HIPAA"), which sets certain standards, including those relating to confidentiality;
- The "Stark" laws, prohibiting referrals to entities in which the referring

party has a direct or indirect interest, for certain "designated health services" covered by Medicare or Medicaid;

- The federal antikickback law that prohibits and makes criminal any offer, payment, solicitation, or receipt of value for influencing referrals to health care providers for services or items covered by Medicare or Medicaid;
- The False Claims Act, which dates back to the Civil War and creates a private right of action—any citizen can bring a claim—for fraudulent billing of the federal government.

The various states have laws that contain a variety of similar and parallel restrictions. Chapter 5 provides a more thorough discussion of these federal and state regulatory concerns.

Other federal laws that could impact an audiology practice but may not seem obvious include federal antitrust laws. Laws relating to price fixing and group boycott are most likely to become relevant if audiologists confer with one another in an effort to maximize revenue or minimize costs in the context of establishing fee minimums for services, or refusing to deal with (or threatening to deal with) particular vendors or other third parties.

Risk Management and Dispute Resolution

Risk management for an audiology practice, like most businesses, is addressed primarily by complying with applicable professional standards of care, and by procuring appropriate insurance. Malpractice is an obvious risk, but insurance to cover nonprofessional liabilities of the practice, as well as property or casualty losses, life, health, and disability of owners and/or employees must also be considered.

Sometimes events lead to disputes with third parties that cannot be resolved informally by an insurer or otherwise, in which case selection of the method of, and venue for, dispute resolution can be very important. Contractual arrangements described above can be structured to require mediation and/or arbitration as alternatives to litigation in a judicial setting. Even in situations where the dispute is not governed by mandatory alternative dispute resolution, the parties can agree at the time of the dispute to utilize such alternative methods.

Mediation is nonbinding, but mediators are quite often former judges who can help the parties see the weaknesses of their respective arguments, as well as likely results of a prolonged and costly formal litigation process. This, in turn, often yields a compromise that is mutually advantageous (compared to proceeding with litigation) and mutually acceptable.

Arbitration can be binding, with the decisions enforceable in court. Although arbitration has historically been promoted as less expensive than formal litigation, that is often not the case, as their standards for conducting arbitration, the rules of evidence, discovery, and other matters (that are well defined in the judicial process) can take significant time and energy to negotiate during the arbitration process. Arbitration does have the benefit of being a confidential process, which is usually desired by health care professionals. Lawsuits are generally available for public access and publicity in the media if deemed newsworthy by media outlets.

The location or venue for the forum of any dispute to be heard, whether judicial, arbitration, or mediation, can be preagreed if the parties to the dispute have an underlying written contractual arrangement. This may be irrelevant to audiology practices because patients customarily reside in the same jurisdiction as their audiologist and insurance payers usually are unwilling to negotiate to modify their standard contractual terms which includes having the venue and area of judicial proceedings in the location of their principal office.

Retirement and Other Exit Strategies

Attorneys, physicians, and other professionals often retire only with reluctance. It is perhaps the love of the practice; perhaps an inability to grasp the concept of "enough"; and/or perhaps the lack of alternative desired activities. Nevertheless, planning for retirement may be most effectively accomplished years in advance by anticipating postretirement financial needs in the context of investments (personal and deferred plans) and liquidity of ownership interest in the audiology practice. The liquidity of the ownership interest in the practice is also relevant if practicing with the practice group turns out to be unsatisfactory and a change in practice environment is desirable.

In circumstances where a practice has co-owners, it is logical and usual to have a buy-sell arrangement in a shareholder or operating agreement that contemplates triggers for retirement or other exit strategies from a practice, as well as valuation method and payment terms for the price. In a solo practice without a co-owner, similar transition on retirement arrangements can be made with a nonowner employee audiologist, or the owners of another practice.

To cover situations where the goal is not retirement, but rather voluntary or involuntary departure from an incongruous practice group, the same sort of buy-sell arrangement, or an employment agreement if one exists, can be used to address comparable issues associated with the departure. Customarily, this mechanism involves a sale of the equity interest directly or indirectly to the remaining owners (often via redemption by the practice entity), on some valuation basis that takes into account three major areas of interest:

- Existing cash and cash equivalents of the practice;
- Receivables associated with the departing professional;
- Existing debt of the practice incurred to facilitate generation of such receivables.

If the departing audiologist is a recent graduate leaving a group practice after a relatively brief period of time, the event can be more simply structured as a "walk-away" with no payment for the proportion of receivables, and no offset for existing pro-rata debt.

In any retirement transition, issues to be considered include accounts receivable attributable to the efforts of the retiring owner. Patient transition is a major issue as consideration needs to be given for the continuity of the patient's care, how best to retain the patient in the practice, and how the patients will be advised of the transition. Liabilities of the practice are also of significant concern. If the transition involves a sale

of assets, a buyer might assume known liabilities, but usually will not assume unknown liabilities. Liabilities not assumed by a buyer of assets will remain with the seller. If the practice is conducted within an entity with limited liability, the entity generally may be dissolved and remaining assets distributed to the owner(s), as long as sufficient assets are retained by the entity to cover all known liabilities.

Tax effects of any such transition must also be considered. General rules include that sale of a capital asset, such as shares of corporation or interest in an LLC yields capital gains, whereas the sale of an entity's assets yields tax consequences based on the nature of the assets sold. Note that assets sold by a "C Corporation" will be taxed at the corporate level and that any subsequent distribution to shareholders may be nondeductible to the corporation and taxable as ordinary income to the shareholders. Finally, payments to former owners may not be deductible to the entity, depending on the structure and terms of the buyout. This can leave the continuing owners with the burden of funding the buyout with after tax dollars.

The term "tail" malpractice insurance covers claims made after expiration of "claims made" insurance coverage, but which relate to events occurring during the coverage period. Alternatively, "occurrence" coverage by definition covers events occurring during the coverage period, regardless of when the resulting claims are ultimately made. As most currently sold malpractice policies are "claims made" rather than "occurrence" based, tail insurance is a meritorious idea and at least a relevant consideration whether simply leaving an existing practice or retiring from practice.

Record retention is another retirement consideration. This is less of a concern if the practice and associated obligations are assumed by co-owners or by a buyer of the practice. However, if practice-related obligations are not assumed by others at the time of retirement, and patients are simply referred to alternative providers, existing records should be retained as may then be required by previous contracts with payors, applicable law, and relevant professional standards.

One hopes by the time retirement ultimately arrives, the audiologist will have achieved most of the professional and personal goals established over the years, will have anticipated legal issues to minimize adverse consequences to the practice, and will have found the practice to be the gratifying, rewarding, and professionally satisfying experience that caused selection of this career path in the first place.

Suggested Reading and Reference

Miller, R. L., & Jentz, G. A. (2006). *Business law today: The essentials.* Thompson-West, Mason, OH: (http://www.westbuslaw.com).

3

Developing a Pricing Strategy for the Practice

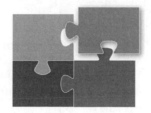

ROBERT M. TRAYNOR, Ed.D., M.B.A.

Even the most successful practitioners struggle with developing their pricing structure. Practitioners know that they must cover their costs, consider the competition, and the patient's willingness to pay, but the specific procedure for setting fees and product prices is somewhat of a mystery. Smith and Nagle (1994) indicate that arriving at the delicate balance between profitability and the patient's willingness to pay involves an integration of concerns for costs and value to the patients. In their opinion, pricing is not an exact science; it is a combination of educated guessing, real-

ity, and a bit of luck. As the prices practitioners charge for products and services are paramount to success and profitability, the purpose of this chapter is to present fundamental concepts and practical guidelines for pricing products and services.

Fundamental Concepts in Pricing

Pricing, as for other business fundamentals, can be done with the assistance of software programs. There are many pricing programs available on the Internet that can assist practitioners in conducting introspective and extropective market analysis and work toward establishment pricing in the practice. These programs are about $200 or so and offer an organized approach to pricing the products and services in the practice. These programs consider most or all of the concepts presented in this chapter and apply them to your practice to facilitate a pricing strategy that is based on sound data and sound business philosophy. These programs are highly recommended.

Although the price of a product is generally based on product utility, longevity, and the maintenance required, the use and utility of these products to the patient must be continually evaluated in terms of technology, status, and benefit delivered. As technology changes prices need to be modified accordingly to the relative capability of the products. For example, for electronic products such as hearing instruments, automatic digital instruments are generally perceived to be better than those that are simply amplifying the sound without changing according to environmental input and command a higher price, but when most hearing aid products change to automatically adjust to the environment, then the pricing must be modified to reflect that just being automatic is not worth a premium price.

The key to price determination is a basic knowledge of fundamental pricing concepts:

■ Costs
■ Product demand and price elasticity
■ Vertical and horizontal pricing
■ Cost-plus or mark-up pricing
■ Customer-driven or value-based pricing
■ Competition pricing.

Costs

There are numerous costs associated with doing business and the price for a product or service must cover **all** of these costs. Costs that must be covered when considering the price to charge for a product or service include:

■ Opportunity costs
■ Fixed costs
■ Incremental or variable costs
■ Avoidable costs
■ Sunk costs.

Opportunity Costs

Hall and Lieberman (2002) discuss the fundamental economics of opportunity costs as that which is given up when the choice is made to offer a service or product in the practice. As there is a limited amount of assets in the practice there are a finite number of procedures and activities that can be accomplished profitably. Decisions to offer a particular procedure in the practice can sometimes generate a tradeoff involving financial resources, personnel, or other assets within the practice. The efficient use of these assets to generate income becomes the question. What profitability will not be realized if the opportunity is not seized and the procedure(s) is/are not offered? Consider the decision to offer a new procedure in the practice, such as Videonystagmography (VNG) (Sidebar 3-1). There are overhead costs if the procedure is offered in the practice and opportunity cost that is part of the conscious decision not to offer VNG examinations in the practice. If the choice is **not** to offer VNG in the clinic there will be income lost (opportunity cost), but also the overhead of the equipment purchase, personnel to conduct the exami-

---

Sidebar 3–1
THE OPPORTUNITY COST OF VESTIBULAR ASSESSMENT

A good example of opportunity cost is in the offering of vestibular assessment in the practice. It is important to estimate the number of procedures that will be conducted per month to arrive at the appropriate decision as to the use of the assets required to conduct the procedure. Basically the concern is if a larger profit can be made by doing another procedure or if it costs more to conduct the procedure than the opportunity for profit. Consider that if the practice will do 7 VNGs per month at $300 each the practice would forfeit $2100 (7 × 300) per month or $25,200 per year in income. If the practice chooses ***not*** to pursue the VNG opportunity, the expense of $23,000 for equipment and payment of the audiologist (someone else or the practitioner) to provide the service would not be necessary. If the personnel costs per month would be $850 and the equipment costs were $500 per month the total costs of doing VNG business (the cost of the opportunity in overhead) would be $1,350 per month. When the income of $2,100 per month is considered against the expenses of $1,350 each month; then the opportunity cost of ***not*** offering VNGs would be $750 per month ($2,100–$1,350) or $9,000 gross profit year. Although there is an attractive opportunity to add an extra $25,200 of gross income into the practice each year, the question of if the opportunity is worth the assets required to acquire the additional income remains. It is possible that a more profitable service can be added to the practice which will generate more profit with the same asset investment.

On the other hand, if the VNG procedure is offered and there were 14 referrals per month with an income of $4,200 per month or $50,400 annually there could be substantial income opportunity lost. Even with the doubled personnel time of $1,700 and the $500 equipment payments there would be a substantial gross profit each month of $4,200–$2,200 or $2,000 per month or $24,000 each year.

---

nations, and space allocations will not be necessary. As presented in Sidebar 3–1, the decision is not how much it costs to offer or not to offer VNGs, but if the finite assets of the practice could be utilized more efficiently to make a profit for the practice by using them elsewhere.

Fixed Costs

Fixed costs are those incurred each month. Examples of fixed costs include bank loans, rent, telephone, utilities, salaries, payroll taxes, and other expenses that must be paid even if there is no business conducted. These expenses are a "hurdle" that must be cleared each month before any profit is created. In the break-even analysis presented in Figure 3–1, the practice must dispense 10 hearing instruments to cover fixed expenses each month, before reaching profitability. High fixed expenses commonly generate cash flow issues that can, if left unchecked, become a primary cause of financial collapse resulting in failure of the practice.

Incremental or Variable Costs

Variable costs are those that are incremental to the amount of business conducted. The greater amount of business transacted, the higher the incremental/variable costs. Incremental/variable costs include the costs of hearing instruments, commissions to employees, warranty support, materials costs (electrodes, probe tips, earmold impression material), and other items which will vary relative to the numbers of services provided or hearing instruments dispensed: The more business conducted, the higher the incremental/variable costs.

Some examples of methods to control incremental/variable costs include: observing and taking advantage of supplier discounts, modification of supplier arrangements, offering less warranty for hearing instruments with less profit margin, modification of employee relationships, credit card merchant fees, and

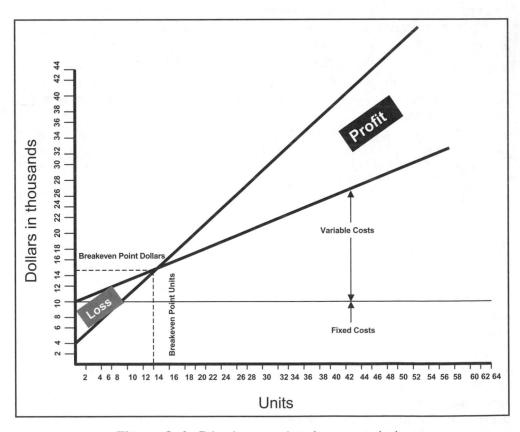

Figure 3–1. Price increase break-even analysis.

insurance discounts. If a supplier offers a discount of 12% for two hearing aids per month, but offers 25% if four are ordered each month, it might make sense to consider ordering at least four instruments each month as this reduces the variable costs for the next sale and adds to the profit. Another example of variable cost reduction is when credit is necessary to dispense instruments and a 12-month "same as cash" financing is utilized. To obtain the 12 month financing program the cost to the merchant (the practice) is 10% of the sales price, but costs for a 6-month program is only 4%. It may make sense to use the 6-month program and not use the 12-month program unless absolutely necessary.

Fixed and Incremental (Variable) Costs and Pricing

Accountants argue that **all** costs should be considered when establishing realistic pricing structures. Dolan and Simon (1996), however, indicate that the primary concern should focus on **relevant** incremental/variable costs. Relevant incremental/variable costs arc those that actually impact the profit of the practice and vary with the services and products offered, pricing philosophy, competition, and other factors specific to each location. Previous models for pricing in audiology practices have recommended averaging relevant incremental/variable costs as a basis for product pricing (Hosford-Dunn et al., 1995). The use of average costs to determine pricing masks the real price point and leads to over or underpricing services and products offered by the practice (Nagle & Holden, 2004). In principle, the identification of costs relevant to pricing is straightforward but in practice it is often difficult to identify all relevant costs. Smith and Nagle (1994) describe incremental costs that are associated with changes in pricing and sales volume. The distinction between incremental costs and nonincremental costs parallels closely, but not exactly. Sometimes this incremental/nonincremental cost differentiation is a bit confusing in the business literature. A distinction more familiar to clinical practitioners is the difference between *variable* and *fixed* costs commonly involved in the operation of any business. Variable costs, of course, are those that vary with sales volume, such as product acquisition, direct labor, telephone, power, supplies, commissions, and so forth. As pricing decisions affect the amount of business that will be conducted, variable costs are always incremental for pricing. Additionally, *fixed costs* such as marketing, advertising, leasehold costs, taxes, insurance, represent static operational costs incurred in the normal course of doing business.

Avoidable Costs

Avoidable costs are those that have not yet been incurred or can be reversed. Avoidable costs are true business costs that could be avoided. In all businesses there are methods to reduce costs by simply incurring less expense. Sometimes it is better to have the employees clean the office than to hire a janitorial service, to use less expensive equipment that allows the same procedures to be completed as the expensive brands, to have employees pay a significant percentage of their insurance costs, and by carefully observing the opportunity costs involved in offering new procedures and products. Although these are only a few examples of how to cut costs, more inventive methods may be practical for a variety of practice venues. Grima and Grima (2004) suggest that avoidable costs can be reduced or eliminated with the exclusion of a service or with a significant change in the size of the practice or its scope of work. In their opinion, it is easy to overestimate the amounts that can be saved through attempts to reduce avoidable costs. For example, it may be possible to reduce the professional employee compensation, but malpractice insurance, continuing education and benefits do not change that much unless the position is completely eliminated.

Sunk Costs

Sunk costs, according to Nagle and Holden (2004) are those costs that a practice is irreversibly committed to bear with no method of recovering the expense. In audiology practices these are costs for equipment, such as the ABR/OAE unit, VNG unit, computers, and peripheral systems. Although it can be argued that when systems such as an audiometers, ABR units, or computer systems are incorporated into the practice for a significant period past their costs, then some recovery of their sunk costs can be incurred, but they are still substantially reduced in value to others that will be interested in their purchase. The classic example of a sunk cost is a new neon sign for the office that marks and brands the practice. It is a good sign and can be used for years, but it is not likely that another audiology practice will want to purchase a sign that has been custom designed for your clinic. Similar to other business expenses, once the sign is obtained, it is a sunk cost that will never be recovered.

Price Elasticity and Product Demand

Price elasticity is a basic concept of pricing that refers to the amount patient demand for a product or service fluctuates according to increases or reductions in price. For example, if the price of a hearing instrument is raised, how much will the sales volume go down and with price reductions how much will sales increase. Amlani (2007) summarized price elasticity as the sensitivity of the consumer to the price of a product. Figure 3–2 demonstrates consumer price sensitivity in that sales volume or demand

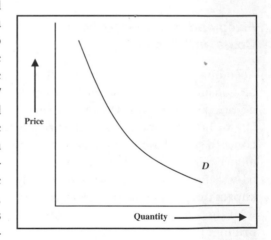

Figure 3–2. The relationship between price and quantity for a hypothetical demand function (*D*). (Amlani, A. M. [2007, Jan. 29]. Impact of Elasticity of Demand on Price in the Hearing Aid Market. *Audiology Online, Article 1757*. Direct URL: http://www.audiologyonline.com/articles/article_detail.asp?article_id=1757 Retrieved August 17, 2007, from the Articles Archive on http://www.audiologyonline.com. Reprinted with permission from Audiology Online—http://www.audiology online.com).

(*D*) is reduced as the price of the product is increased. Price elasticity (*E*), according to Dolan and Simon (1996), is figured as a ratio of the percentage change in sales volume (*SV*) to the percentage change in price (*P*) as expressed in the formula below:

$$E = \frac{\% \text{ Change SV}}{\% \text{ Change P}}$$

Nagle and Holden (2004) indicate that price elasticity (*E*) is usually a negative number, as positive changes in price (price increases) produce sales declines and negative changes in price (price cuts) generally produce sales increases. Thus, the greater the absolute value of *E* (usually >1), the greater the "elasticity" or change in the demand (sales volume), whereas the smaller the value of *E* (usually <1), the more "inelastic" or the less fluctuation of demand (sales volume). The slope of the demand curve presented in Figure 3–2 is directly related to the elasticity of a product. Practitioners should realize that their product sales are subject to some fluctuation relative to price elasticity. If the price elasticity is known for a specific type of product then the practitioner can make an intelligent decision as how to price these products, which ones to be discounted, and those that should be discontinued. Price elasticity can assist in predicting how many sales will reasonably occur if prices are modified by 10, 20, or 30%, and the demand for stock items such as assistive listening devices, open-fit hearing instruments, and other popular items, thereby reducing over- or understocking situations.

Demand can be estimated by three general methods. First, if the practice has been in place for a substantial period of time, demand can be reviewed historically. A historical demand analysis reviews the number of specific products, evaluations (often by CPT code), and other specific procedures that were completed over a specified period, usually 1 year. The historical review is a reliable method of evaluating demand throughout the year unless there are substantial changes in market or economic conditions. Second, demand can also be estimated by direct experimentation, purposely increasing the price and reducing the price to determine the price elasticity as suggested by Bennett and Wilkinson (1974). For example, raising and lowering the price of hearing instrument batteries and carefully observing the percentage that sales drop with the price increase and the percentage that sales go up with price reduction. Once the elasticity is known, prices may be modified according to knowledge of demand that is generated by the experimentation. This is, however, a dangerous method as it compromises profit to obtain information. Weiner (1994) offers a third method of predicting demand by asking the patients what they would pay for a specific service or product. Although this is a well-known method of predicting demand for products and services, Kotler (2001) cautions its use as buyers often underestimate what services or products they will purchase at higher prices (Sidebar 3–2, Figure 3–A).

Horizontal/Vertical Pricing

This concept applies primarily to products, such a hearing instruments, ALDs, or other accessories rather than services and is fundamental to achieving the correct price in the market. In the past, virtually all hearing instruments were *horizontal* product lines. These conventional products were only linear or compression instruments that looked and performed essentially the same so differentiation among the products was primarily by brand. As there were no circuitry differences among hearing instruments from one brand to another, product differentiation was simply determined by instrument size and brand packaging. The result was that the cost of these hearing instruments were essentially the same but differed slightly for some styles of the same product over others. In other words, a completely in-the-canal (CIC)

instrument, was more costly than an in-the-ear (ITE), but there was not much difference in the circuits between them. Thus, there was not much vertical difference among brands or models, only a horizontal difference within the product model for a particular brand.

It is fashionable in today's hearing health care market place for manufacturers to price their digital hearing instruments both *vertically* and *horizontally* (Figure 3–3). Manufacturers now differentiate products by available features to generate both levels of dispenser interest and to enable tiered pricing structures. Hearing instruments can be offered in tiers that include low-cost, mid-range, and high-end or premium levels. Within

---

Sidebar 3–2
PRODUCT PRICE ELASTICITY IN THE AUDIOLOGY PRACTICE

There are situations that tend to create high price elasticity. Dolan (1995) indicates with some degree of caution that businesses dealing with specific conditions have tendencies toward high price elasticity. In audiology practice, high price elasticity is created by most hearing instruments looking similar to the patients that purchase them. This creates a low product differentiation and the feeling that the patient can obtain essentially the same product elsewhere possibly at a lower price. Additionally, the more aware patients are of the substitute products, by competitive advertisements or "word of mouth," the more price sensitivity there will be in the hearing instrument market.

Inelasticity (or low demand variability) in the hearing instrument market is created when patients rely on the practitioner's professional guidance in suggesting the optimal solution for their hearing difficulties. Realistically, patients cannot easily compare the quality of the substitutes as they must obtain the products from a professional. To compare different providers is not usual and often there are other factors that cause patients to choose a particular provider over others. Amlani (2007) presents some determinants of price elasticity and suggests specific principles that should be considered when prices are modified (Figure 3–A).

Determinant	Demand	
	Elastic (High Demand)	*Inelastic (Low Demand)*
Many substitutes available	X	
Perceived as necessity by consumer		X
Item has unique features important to consumer		X
Consumer can easily compare item with products of competitors	X	
Item's price represents a substantial percentage of consumer's budget	X	
Consumer is paying only a small portion of the total price		X
Product has low switching costs	X	
Price is an indicator of quality by consumer		X

Figure 3–A. Determinants of elasticity. (Amlani, A. M. [2007, Jan. 29]. Impact of Elasticity of Demand on Price in the Hearing Aid Market. *Audiology Online, Article 1757*. Direct URL: http://www.audiologyonline.com/articles/article_detail.asp?article_id=1757. Retrieved August 17, 2007, from the Articles Archive on http://www.audiologyonline.com . Reprinted with permission from Audiology Online— http://www.audiologyonline.com)

each of these vertical product levels, prices are organized horizontally according to style and feature differences such as processing bands, directional microphones, noise reduction, and so forth. The instruments at the top of the vertical pricing structure are full featured and considered the highest premium and the highest cost. Those hearing instruments with progressively fewer features are lower on the vertical pricing hierarchy that descends from the highest cost premium to lowest cost entry level instruments. This vertical pricing system is common among most consumer products, such as appliances, automobiles, clothing, and

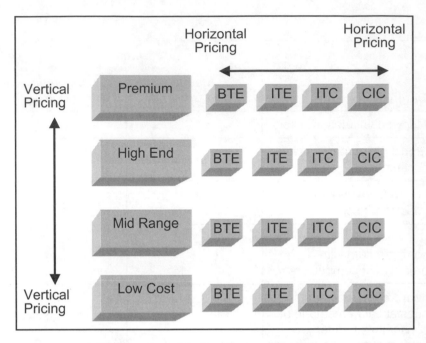

Figure 3–3. Vertical/horizontal pricing.

so forth. The best refrigerator will have an ice maker, water, and special features to keep food longer. The premium suit will feature special material, better tailoring, and a richer feel than at the entry level. Thus, the most premium hearing instruments will offer features with more possibility for the patient to achieve maximum benefit whereas the entry level products will simply offer amplification.

General Pricing Concepts

Price is often the centerpiece of strained relations with good customers and often the weapon competitors are use to steal market share. Pricing audiologic services and hearing instruments is typically a balance between the patient's desire for a good value and the practice's need to cover costs and earn a profit. Profit, according to Dolan and Simon (1996), is generated by the number of units of serv-

ice and products (volume) sold times the assigned price for which each unit sells minus operational costs incurred to secure the sale, as expressed in the formula below:

Profit = Sales Volume × Price – Costs

A look at hearing instrument dispensing would suggest that profit is dependent on the number of instruments dispensed times the price of the instruments to the patient minus the fixed and relevant incremental/variable costs. Although a simplistic concept, pricing is far more involved than arbitrarily assigning how much revenue the practice owner chooses to make, what the competition charges, or the suggested retail price offered by the instrument manufacturer. In addition to understanding the costs in the practice, accurate and effective pricing requires a full perspective of how the patient views the value of the services provided, products dispensed, and a reasonable understanding of what price points the targeted market segment will withstand.

Nagle and Holden (2004) present three fundamental pricing strategies incorporated routinely in general business:

- Cost-plus or markup pricing
- Customer-driven or value-based pricing
- Competition pricing

As the practice is a business, these methods can be used to generate pricing for products and services. To some degree, combinations of these methods are those that are employed by practitioners to set the fees and product prices. As these procedures are in use consistently throughout audiology practices it is fundamental to understand the advantages and limitations of their use.

Cost-Plus or Markup Pricing

Cost-plus or mark-up pricing is the most common method for products as it offers an aura of financial prudence to practitioners. Financial prudence, according to the cost-plus theory, is achieved by pricing every product or service to yield a fair return to the practitioner relative to the overall fixed and incremental costs that are fully and fairly covered by the markup of the product. Kotler (2001) feels that this is a popular method of pricing in business because it is easier for practitioners to determine their costs than the patient's capability and willingness to pay a particular price. As the actual determination of the patient's willingness and their price ceiling involves expensive sophisticated market research that is often beyond the reach of most

private practice audiology clinics, this is considered to be a method of pricing that is fair to both the practice and the patients. Cost-plus pricing typically works best when all the practices in the area use this system as it tends to minimize price competition and essentially allows practitioners to simplify the pricing task (Dolan & Simon, 1996) while concentrating on other differences among the practices, such as location, service, and so forth. Even though cost-plus or markup pricing is the most popular method of pricing for products and services, Staab (2000) considers cost-plus pricing strategies in audiology practices the least rewarding. Pricing professionals, such as Nagle and Holden (2004) even state that cost-plus or markup pricing is a blueprint for mediocre financial performance.

A review of the problems with cost-plus pricing begins with an assessment of costs. Generally, in cost-plus pricing there is a problem in finding a product's real unit cost before determining its price. That is, product costs usually change relative to the number of units sold. For example, if you order one or two hearing instruments per month there is a minimal discount, but if you order 20 or 30 per month a much larger discount is realized. If a true cost-plus or markup pricing system is instituted, there is one price for products that have a marginal discount and another price for those that have a major discount based on volume sales. If patient demand goes down, then the price goes up, if patient demand goes up the price goes down. Thus, true cost-plus pricing is difficult to achieve and leads to overpricing in weak markets and underpricing in strong markets. Audiology practices can use buying groups and other methods to reduce this patient demand/price difficulty but problems still arise in keeping up with actual costs. Costs for products, not only rise and fall across manufacturers, but some clinicians take more time, and some points of product and service delivery (locations) are higher cost than others. Thus, the literature suggests that if cost plus pricing is used at all, it should only be used as the minimum price to charge (Dolan & Simon, 1996; Nagle & Holden, 2004, Staab, 2000).

Cost-plus or markup pricing is not a recommended process as the procedure ignores such issues as current demand, perceived value, and competition components of the pricing equation; it remains, however, the most used pricing system among audiology practitioners (Sidebar 3–3; Figures 3–B and 3–C).

Sidebar 3–3
FIGURING COST-PLUS OR MARKUP PRICES

Five Times Cost Rule of Thumb Pricing Scheme

In the old days of hearing aid sales, the commercial hearing aid dealers would mark up a hearing instrument five times the unit cost from the manufacturer. Although this is the simplest form of cost-plus or markup pricing, this tended to ensure cost coverage and profitability with a simple calculation, presented below:

$$\text{Cost} \times 5 = \text{Retail Price}$$

In the days of analog conventional instruments when costs for these products were $79, retail prices were $395. These were high for the times, considering the value of money, but still affordable and practitioner could be assured that they were compensated very well for warranty service and follow-up using this simple mark-up procedure. If this simple rule is applied to current digital products it becomes useless as the cost of the products become prohibitive when the five times cost rule is considered. For example, if the cost of an entry level hearing instrument is 295.00, then the retail price is $1,475 each or $2,950 for the binaural set, hardly entry level. Similarly, if the cost of a high-end hearing instrument is $1,350, then the retail price would be $6,750 each or $13,500 bianually, totally outrageous in most markets. Although these may be ridiculous prices, versions of the scheme such as 2.5, 3, 3.5, or 4 times cost can be used to simply calculate retail prices.

Percentage of Profit Over Cost Scheme

Percentage mark-up strategies are also utilized to provide a more accurate calculation of real cost coverage and a margin that will bring profitability with an eye toward competitive retail pricing. The use of percentage mark-up requires that the practitioner establish a percentage mark-up for the products that will ensure cost coverage and profit on everything sold. In the percentage scheme, the practitioner should have knowledge of about how many products will be sold each month. To cover fixed costs, the number of expected instruments to be sold each month is divided into the monthly fixed expenses to arrive at the per unit fixed expense costs. These fixed costs are added to the purchase price of each unit as part of the purchase price when it is sold. Additionally, the known incremental costs are also added into the retail price to offset the known costs that vary by the number of units sold each month. Once the costs are added into the price, then the profitability is added to arrive at the final retail price of the device. For example, consider the situation presented below in Figure 3–B where the practitioner's goal is to make a 50% profit over the fixed and incremental costs. In this example, the cost of the instrument is $1000 including shipping and handling, the incremental or variable costs to dispense the device are $500 per unit, and the fixed costs are $500 per unit. At this point, there are $2,000 in costs that must be made up before the 50% profit is added into the equation. Marking up the costs of $2,000 by 50% or $1,000 gives us a retail price of $3,000 which will be charged to the patient for the instrument.

Cost-Plus or Mark-up Pricing Example – 50% Over Cost	
Cost of Instrument... Including Shipping/Handling	$1,000.
Cost of Dispensing Instrument (Incremental Costs) .... Time, Variable Costs, Warranty Costs	$500.
Fixed Costs..	$500.
Desired Profit (50% over costs).................................	$1,000.
Total Retail Sales (Price)	$3,000.

Figure 3–B. Cost-plus or markup pricing–percentage pricing.

Target-Return Pricing Scheme

Target pricing involves obtaining a price for products that will yield a certain return on investment (ROI). This method is often used by large corporations that manufacture automobiles and toasters that look for a return on their investment of 15 to 20%. Although this is often good enough if the corporation sells 50,000 units of a product, it is not very applicable to the audiology practice unless the percentage of return is greater. An ROI 120% is more reasonable for the audiology practice as the number procedures or products is usually extremely low in comparison to looking at the return on investment for a manufacturing process and provides a target pricing scheme that will give the practitioner reasonable profit for the investment that has been made in the practice. To utilize the target return method for pricing the formula is:

$$TRP = \text{Total Unit Cost} + \frac{DR \times IC}{\text{Unit Sales}}$$

Where the Target Return Price (*TRP*) is equal to the Total Unit Cost (including acquisition, incremental, and fixed costs) plus the profit which consists of the desired return (*DR*) times the invested capital (*IC*) divided by the unit sales. If the target return pricing concept is considered for pricing an auditory brainstem response (ABR) procedure the estimated cost to provide each procedure must first be calculated and then that sum must be added to the desired profit.

When using the target return method of pricing all costs must be figured per unit. For pricing purposes, all costs are added together including, acquisition, fixed, and incremental/variable and figured as a factor of each unit produced. Although conducting an ABR does not necessarily incur real acquisition costs, there are fixed and incremental costs that must be considered. The real costs of conducting the ABR procedure include an employee cost to cover time conducting and reporting the examination of $6,000 per year ($500 per month), lease payments on the equipment of $6,000 per year ($500 per month), material costs of $300 per year (electrodes, paste, paper, etc.), and allocated space costs of $1,200 per year. Other costs that must be included in the initial cost calculation are $2,000 for marketing, $1,000 for continuing education, and $5,000 for insurance discounts. As presented in Figure 3–C, the total estimated unit cost, if 180 procedures are conducted per year is $21,500 and when calculated per procedure (180 procedures per year), $119.44 of the total retail price is required simply to cover costs. To arrive at the total retail price of the ABR

$6,000...Employee time to conduct the procedure
$6,000...Payments of the Equipment
$ 300...Materials
$1,200...Space Costs
$2,000...Marketing Costs
$1,000...Continuing Education
$5,000...Insurance Discount

$21,500 Costs to Conduct ABR for 1 Year

Figure 3–C. Yearly break-even analysis for ABR example.

procedure the practitioner's goals for profit must be considered as $119.44 simply covers the cost of performing the evaluation.

$$\frac{\Sigma \text{ Costs}}{\text{N Procedures per year}} = \text{Total Unit Cost}$$

$$\frac{21,500}{180 \text{ Procedures per year}} = 119.44$$

Although this covers the costs, the profit component must be added in to allow the return on investment (ROI) necessary to meet the practitioner's goals. In this example, the practitioner's goal is to achieve a 125% ROI on the $25,000 instrument that it took to implement the procedure into the clinic. The formula for obtaining the profit component of the total retail price (TRP) is presented below:

$$\frac{\text{DR} \times \text{IC}}{\text{Unit (Procedure) Sales}} = \text{ROI}$$

Where, the ROI is equal to the desired return (*DR*) times the invested capital (*IC*) divided by the unit or procedure sales per year. In this case, the practitioner's desired return on the capital investment of $25,000 is 125%, or $31,250 and will require obtaining $31,250 per year in profit. Using the formula above, the calculation of the total retail price of the ABR becomes simple arithmetic.

$$25,000 \times 1.25 = \frac{31,250 \times 25,000}{180} = 173.61 \text{ ROI}$$

The ROI component of the price for each of the 180 ABR procedures per year is $31,250/180 or $173.33 per procedure. By rounding the costs per procedure to $120 and the ROI per procedure to $175 per, these two figures are added together to obtain the total retail (TRP) price of the ABR procedure at $295, covering both the costs necessary to conduct the procedure and the desired return on investment necessary to meet the practitioner's goals.

If the practice performs 180 ABR procedures per year, then the return on the investment, or profit would be 1.25% at the end of the year. If, however there were not 180 ABR procedures conducted, it might be beneficial to use a break-even analysis to determine how many procedures it would take, given the practitioner's costs, to not make a profit, but simply recover costs. It is possible to determine these figures from a break-even analysis which reveals how many units it takes to break even and, thus, at what number of procedures profit begins.

In times before programmable and digital hearing instruments, commercial hearing aid dealers had a "rule of thumb" where the retail price of a hearing instrument was five times its cost. Although the five times cost rule does not work these days as costs have substantially increased, many audiologists use some version of this simple system, such as three or four times cost to price their products. Although this is the most popular method of incorporating cost-plus or markup pricing strategy, percentage markups are often used as well to allow for cost coverage and profitability. Percentage methods are essentially the same but add a percentage markup to the cost of an item rather than a set amount. A percentage markup may be computed by taking the cost of the instrument, ALD, or other product and adding a percentage to the cost, such as 50%. If the cost is $100 then the retail price in the practice would be $150.

Other than the straight markup procedures there are some other philosophies that can be utilized. First, the practitioner can obtain a price for products that ensures a certain "return on investment" (ROI) often referred to in the pricing literature as a target-return philosophy. Most businesses price products to ensure an expected return of about 15 to 25% which provides a target pricing scheme that allows the practitioner a profit for the investment that has been made in the practice.

Another method of pricing according the cost-plus or markup strategy uses the break-even analysis. The break-even analysis considers the fixed, variable, and total operational costs and determines the number of units or amount of revenue necessary for the practice to reach a break-even point—where the practice costs equals total revenue (Parkin, 2005) (Sidebar 3–4; Figure 3–D). Staab (2000) indicates that once this point is exceeded, profits increase in direct proportion to the level of sales achieved beyond this point. The break-even analysis for the practice can be put into spreadsheet form and various "what if" scenarios can be exercised to determine the necessary prices to cover expenses and to achieve profit goals.

Sidebar 3–4
BREAK-EVEN ANALYSIS PRICING

In an audiology practice, ideally, there are both service and product contributions to the break-even analysis, but to keep the calculation simple consider the ABR example demonstrated above. Sometimes it is easier to see this break-even point when it is graphically presented as in Figure 3–D

The break-even analysis offers a simple explanation for the calculation of a break-even point (BEP) with the formula:

$$BEP = \frac{F}{(S\text{-}V)}$$

Where, *BEP* = break-even point; *F* = total fixed costs; *S* = selling price; and *V* = variable or incremental cost/unit. For the break-even analysis the costs are split into fixed and variable or incremental costs. In the ABR example (Sidebar 3–3), the total costs to provide 180 procedures per year were $21,500 and fixed costs were $7,500 of that total leaving 14,000 as fixed costs. Until the practice has conducted (and collected on) about 80 proce-

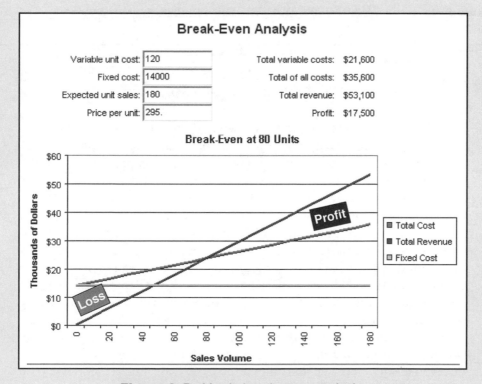

Figure 3–D. Yearly break-even analysis.

dures at the price of $295 they are losing money on this examination when the fixed and variable costs are considered. After 80 procedures profit begins and continues slowly to the 125% profit point and beyond, as the numbers increase beyond, 180 considered in the target retail price example. Note that the total revenue, $53, minus costs of $215, are equal to or exceed the practitioner's goal of 125% ROI. Review of the break-even analysis in Figures 3–D makes it easy to graphically depict the business necessary to cover all the costs, make the desired profit, and see what might happen if more procedures were conducted than originally estimated.

Customer-Driven Pricing or Value-Based Pricing

Commonly used in audiology practices to create tiered pricing structures, hearing instruments are categorized by price; entry level, medium, high end, and premium price points. These tiered pricing structures offer patients a menu of instruments to be considered based on meaningful features and price points (Sidebar 3–5; Figure 3–E). The patient's purchase decision will include the critical product features, recommendations offered by the audiologist, and their personal budgetary constraints.

Sidebar 3–5
TIERED PRICING SCHEDULE

Tiered pricing involves the patient in critical decision making and enables a practice marketing strategy that includes a "something-available-for-everyone" approach. It also affords greater laterality in counseling patients during the initial stages of their aural rehabilitation process. By discussing the benefits of each instrument group, the patient's clinical status will, by necessity, become a significant point of focus of the discussion. Severity of the patient's loss, speech recognition capabilities, and loudness tolerance issues will become more important in the process of selecting a tier of instruments best suited for the patient's particular needs. Those patients with poor cochlear reserve will likely require greater processing capabilities that may be available only in mid-range and upper tiered instruments. Tiered pricing structures enable a patient to incorporate both benefit and value in their decision-making. If the instruments within each tier are appropriately priced, adequate margins can be expected to favorably accommodate decision-making between and among the tiers. The clinician's focus can be

appropriately placed on maximizing benefit to the patient without disproportionate emphasis being placed on a set price point nor shifting the
patient from one tier to another based solely on fiscal parameters. Tiered
pricing forces the patient to be involved in important decision-making and
reinforces the practitioner-patient partnership where both parties are working together to generate an optimal outcome.

From a business principle standpoint a practice will lose many patients
without a tiered system. Dolan and Simon (1996) state that very heteroge-
neous customers warrant the cost of administrating multiple classes and differing price relationships. In business it is always better to sell something
at a profit, than to sell nothing as demonstrated in Figures 3-EA and 3-EB.
These figures, adapted from Dolan and Simon (1996), present the fact that
with a single price for products, such as hearing instruments there will be
sales limited to about 50% of the patients that present themselves for
treatment as many may have difficulty affording the services or products,
Figure 3-EA. Figure 3-EB considers a two-tiered system demonstrating
that if there are two pricing structures more of the patients that present
for treatment can be accommodated as they can afford the products and
services. Although some of the sales from the higher priced tier are compromised, the overall profit to the practice will be greater as more of the
population presenting for treatment can afford a treatment program. If
the numbers of tiers are increased to three and four tiers the same type of
increase happens, although the percentage of increased sales for each added
tier becomes smaller.

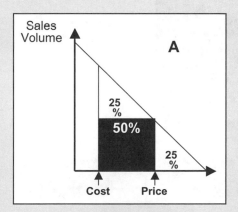 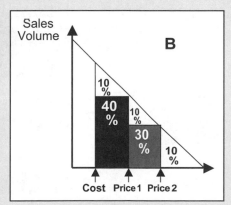

Figure 3–E. Effects of price tiering. (Adapted from *Power Pricing*, by R.
Dolan and H. Simon, 1996, New York: Free Press. Copyright 1996 by Free
Press. Adapted with permission.)

Value pricing process as outlined in Figure 3–4 depicts a process offered by Dolan and Simon (1996) where a practitioner can determine the profitability of services or products dispensed relative to patient's perceptions, offerings by the competition, product costs, and pricing. The correct price for the services and products of the practice lies in the value consumers attach to them. Once the patient understands and accepts the value of services or products dispensed their natural opposition to the price points for services or products declines. Additionally price becomes less a factor in bolstering patient satisfaction and long-term patient loyalty. Satisfied patients will return as long as value is appreciated— no matter the tier of the instrument purchased or cost of the services provided. In Figure 3–4, Dolan and Simon (1996) describe an essential exercise to arrive at the correct pricing scheme for a practice. The initial analysis of both consumer and competition is seen at the top of Figure 3–4. Analyzing the competition creates an opportunity to assess the level of sophistication the competitor brings to the market. By necessity, analyzing the competition comes down to a differentiation of available products in the marketplace. The analysis should produce information about what consumers find uniquely valuable in the competition's

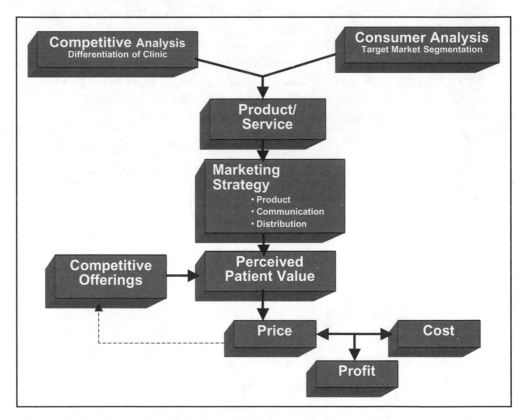

Figure 3–4. Value pricing process. (Adapted from *Power Pricing*, by R. Dolan and H. Simon, 1996, New York: Free Press. Copyright 1996 by Free Press. Adapted with permission.)

particular brand of audiologic care relative to the other practices or stores that might offer similar services or products. Although there may be many reasons for instituting price cuts in an audiology practice, a declining market share may be at the top of the list. Although the professional marketers, such as Berry and Wilson (2001) and Kotler (2001), suggest that a declining market share is not necessarily a problem. As the number of audiology practices increase and the availability of hearing care products from other sources (Internet, Costco, or Wal-Mart, etc.), it is possible that the increased competition may cause a reduction in the number patients seen in the practice and, consequently, fewer hearing instrument or service sales will be conducted at current prices, reducing the practice's overall profitability. One strategy to fight this new competition can be to reduce prices. Theoretically, the practitioner can see more patients at lower price and offset the competitive forces in the market. By reducing prices, the practitioner can attempt to dominate the market by offering "more for less." This "more for less" strategy can be successful in gaining market share for the practice but there are concerns that must be considered on its initiation.

Kotler (2001) states that when considering price cutting practitioners must be aware of three possible traps. First, patients may assume that lower priced products have lower quality. This could be especially true for hearing instruments as most patients do not know the brand of the products that are sold in audiology practices. It would be easy for them to assume that the products were changed to lower quality rather than prices lowered to offer value. Second, lower prices buy market share but not market loyalty. As products are available at a number of practices for about the same price, practitioners may need to carefully choose if they want market share at the expense of patient loyalty. Often patients that are very price sensitive are not very loyal because the next time they require products or services, they often go to the least expensive provider. Third, once the practice has cut its prices, it may be that higher priced competitors will also cut their prices. If they have more cash reserves they may be able to keep their prices lower for a longer time and be in business longer with a lower profit margin. This problem would, of course, offset the purpose of reducing the prices. The problem with hearing instrument pricing is that some patients require more services than others. Typically, audiologists make each patient pay whether they use those services or not, called bundled pricing. Here the patient is allowed no-charge follow-up services, usually through the warranty of the instrument, sometimes for life. There may even be other things bundled into the price, such as batteries and accessories. By charging for the instrument separately from the services, Gans (2006) feels that her patients actually pay for what they receive not for services that they do not use, as in the bundled approach. This unbundling of product charges from the fees and service charges can also be a method of reducing costs to patients (Sidebar 3–6).

Price increases can raise profitability substantially. Another strategy for the practice that is losing market share in a competitive market is to raise their fee substantially and only see patients that are willing to pay more than the going rate for products and services. Later, this concept will be presented as a market

Sidebar 3–6
BUNDLING AND UNBUNDLING OF PRICES

There is much discussion in the literature and at conferences about another method of reducing prices for products. As there is more to hearing instrument use than the product itself, most hearing instruments are sold with many services bundled into the costs. Ross (2005) indicates that the selection and fitting process takes time and audiologists may spend 4 contact hours or more with each new hearing aid user. Of course, audiologists still need to interview the person, conduct appropriate audiometric and other tests, take ear impressions, select and fit the aids, reprogramming when necessary, schedule several follow-up appointments, provide all necessary information, and deal with drop-ins when problems occur. Ross views these kinds of services as intrinsic to the hearing aid selection process. Without these services, patients could easily purchase hearing aids through mail order catalogues.

As our professional services are time consuming "unbundling" the hearing aid selection and follow-up process is proposed. In this concept of hearing instrument delivery the device is sold as a distinct product and every evaluation, clinical activity, and follow-up visit are charged separately. The proponents of unbundling point out that some patients take an inordinate amount of the audiologist's time, returning often for troubleshooting visits, whereas others take relatively little time, but that both pay the same price for the hearing aid. Thus, some patients can be said to be subsidizing the visits of other patients. The unbundling approach makes each patient pay only for the services that they receive whereas the opponents of unbundling are convinced that many people would not return for necessary follow-up services, and/or would not contact the audiologist when problems occur. Often patients require extra assistance with amplification products that repeated visits can give them, but unless these services are part of the original purchase deal they are unable or unwilling to pay for them, or simply unaware of the frequent necessity for follow-up visits. Bundled pricing means that the patient not only purchases the hearing instrument, but also receives services on the instrument for a period of time, often for the warranty period, sometimes for life.

Gans (2006) feels that patients actually respond positively to the unbundling of fees and services from the product costs and when payment was requested for services required, they did not question the charges. The unbundling or separation of product price from the fees and follow-up services can also be a strategy for competition in price sensitive markets. This strategy can allow the practitioner to reduce their price for products while maintaining their services separate keeping the cost of the products competitive. Although this appears to be a price cut, it is actually diverting the higher costs to those that use the extra services.

skimming strategy where only those that choose to spend a higher price than customary will come to the practice. A skimming strategy requires top quality products and services delivered according to the patient's convenience. High-end patients expect upscale special services at special times delivered in a high-quality environment. Although these patients are more demanding and require substantial attention; higher pricing can offer great financial benefits to the practice. Generally, patients are sensitive to price changes and the practitioner must be careful not to change them too often as modification of the overall pricing strategy is part of their practice image.

Consumer analysis should be geared to determining what types of services, levels of care, and other factors consumers find critically important such that they will choose to come to your practice rather than the alternatives within the geographical area. Once these critical evaluations of competition and consumers are completed, the information is incorporated to evaluate the product/service positioning, and select the target market and the value-creating elements of the marketing mix.

Competition Pricing

Competition pricing, sometimes called "strategic pricing" is also referred to as the "tail wagging the dog" or "follow the leader" pricing (Hosford-Dunn et al., 1995). This concept is often erroneously used by practices attempting to increase their market share as increased market share is often mistaken as an avenue to produce increased profit. Sometimes practitioners will lower their prices to gain market share with the idea that

the increased volume in sales will offset the lowered prices. Nagle and Holden (2004) hold that prices should be lowered only when they are no longer justified by the value offered in comparison to the value offered by the competition. Although price cutting is probably the quickest, most effective method to achieve a sales objective, it is usually a poor financial decision. As a price cut can be so easily matched by the competition, it offers only a short-term competitive advantage at the expense of permanently lower margins (Sidebar 3–7; Figure 3–F). Although product differentiation, advertising, and improved distribution do not increase sales as quickly as price cuts, their benefit is more sustainable and therefore usually more cost effective. Hosford-Dunn et al. (1995) indicate that looking to the competition is a dangerous method of selecting pricing as the competition may have unrealistic prices for their products relative to their business costs which may be drastically different than costs associated with your practice. Although it is necessary to be aware of competitive prices within the immediate demographic area of the practice, using prices set by your competitors is not sound business strategy.

Positioning the Practice by Price

Positioning is a process that solidifies the practice in the market segment targeted as the optimal segment of the demographic area. An effective positioning plan will require communication with the entire market and the target market specifically. Positioning the practice appropriately will ultimately establish the perception of the practice in the

Sidebar 3–7
THE CHANGING OF PRICE TO MEET THE COMPETITION

In the example offered in Figure 3–F a practitioner must decide whether to lower prices due to a new discount store that has just moved in across the street. The practitioner must decide to meet the prices of the new competitor or to leave prices the same offering a private service in a more comfortable environment than the discount store.

The practitioner has a regular price of $3950.00 for a set of binaural open-fit hearing instruments. As part of the fitting the practitioner offers a 2-year warranty, including follow-up audiologic support services for reprogramming, counseling, and other follow-up services such as cleaning and routine cerumen removal during the warranty period. As the practitioner considers the pricing modification to meet the competition, the thought process would include that the product acquisition cost is $1,400 for both instruments in the binaural fitting including shipping and a 2-year warranty. The fixed costs for space, employees, and other monthly overhead expenses have been calculated to be $500 per fitting at the current demand levels. The practitioner is making a gross profit of $2,050 per binaural fitting, but incremental costs incurred with each sale, must be figured in as well (see

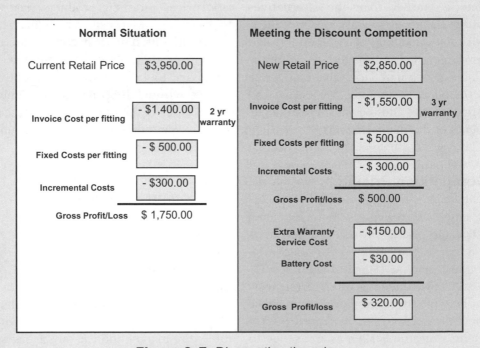

Figure 3–F. Discounting the price.

Figure 3–F). The practitioner considers that the incremental cost of warranty follow-up (clinic time for reprogramming, cleaning, and other services) and materials (tubes, tips, cleaning material) on this binaural fitting for the 2-year period of service is $300. Thus, the actual gross profit with all incremental costs included is $1,750.00 per binaural fitting. This is a very competitive price in the current market and one that works to meet incremental/variable costs, fixed expenses, and the goals for practice profitability.

The new discount store has a hearing aid sales center offering hearing instruments in a warehouse setting using exactly the same binaural open fit for a price of $2,850 with a warranty of 3 years and a 1-year supply of free batteries. As the practitioner considers the new price an additional $75.00 per unit ($150 per fitting) for the extra year of warranty must be added to the acquisition cost increasing the acquisition cost to $1,550 and another $30 must be added for the free battery offer. Not only does the acquisition cost increase by $150, but the practitioner must add an additional $150 to the cost of each fitting for the extra year of warranty (increase from 2 years to 3 years of service) to offer the "free" follow-up service.

If the practitioner chooses to match this competitive offer, the practice would need to conduct almost 5.5 times as many binaural open fittings to even come close to the same profit enjoyed before the price cuts. Competitive price cuts from new systems like discount stores can be frustrating and should be carefully considered to determine whether or not the practice chooses to compete on price alone or on credentials, environment, and other marketing variables.

market place. That perception will be held by potential patients and referral sources alike. The price of services and instruments dispensed in the practice will determine the position of the practice among the audiologists, otolaryngologists, and commercial hearing aid dealers in the geographic area. The practice's position, though ultimately determined by the patients in the marketplace, is greatly influenced by the strategy utilized to differentiate it from the competition. Once the pricing method is chosen, however, there may be psychological modifications to the assigned prices to facilitate fine tuning according to the type of patients that the practice hopes to attract.

Erickson and Johansson (1985) feel that many patients will use price as an indicator of quality as high prices sometimes indicate quality or a high level image. It can be an advantage or a disadvantage to be thought of as the high-priced practice. On the one hand, it can be part of the positioning strategy to place the practice's brand at a higher level than the competition. Other times, by being the highest priced practice in the community, high prices can win a nice image, but if the patients cannot afford the goods and services offered, then the high price will reduce profitability. Part of price tweaking is the consideration of the patients that will be purchasing the products and services. Thus, the specifics of their socioeconomic status, attitudes toward purchase, needs, and value are essential to the final price of an item.

Patients also have a reference price in their minds for products and services that are planted by discussions with friends, relatives, and the competition. For example, patients in the market for hearing instruments have a rough idea of what the costs will be based on competitive presentations of current prices, past prices, and the image of the practice where the purchase is contemplated. The prestige of being a patient in the highest priced place in town or the value received by seeking services and products in a practice where prices are low or services are offered for "free," serve different groups of patients, sometimes within the same geographic area. Rajendran and Tellis (1994) indicate that these reference prices can be significantly manipulated by practitioner sales presentations that explain the benefits of a product over another and that there is value to offset the higher price, or substantially less paid for what is perceived to be a higher quality product than is offered by the competition.

A patient's perception of value rests firmly in the maximum price he or she will pay for audiologic services and hearing instruments. Knowing these values for members of the target market demonstrates the essential trade off between pricing and sales volume and determines the position of the practice within the market.

Developing Practice Pricing Policies

Tiered pricing systems are quite popular in audiology practices and elemental to quality and price positioning of products in the practice. Kotler (2001) has nine price-quality considerations that can be used to develop pricing strategies. Figure 3–5 is adapted from Kotler (2001) and presents a product quality pricing chart that is useful in the development of pricing strategy. Both Quality and Price can be tiered in a high, medium, and low hierarchy. For example, a high-quality, high-priced product should have the performance and quality expected for the high price similar to other high-quality, high-priced products. Anything less than high quality for the high price is considered unsatisfactory.

A medium-value pricing strategy suggests that there are better products, priced higher and lower quality products priced lower. Figure 3–5 also suggests that if a medium price is charged for a high-end product, the pricing strategy is *high-value*, whereas a medium price for lower quality product would indicate a *false economy strategy*. Low-cost products are expected to be of lower quality than medium or high-cost products. Paying a low price for a medium-quality product is considered a *good value strategy* and paying a low price for a high quality product would be a *supervalue strategy* (Sidebar 3–8).

Most audiology practices follow Figure 3–5 from the upper left to the lower right, offering appropriate products for the correct price. In this appropriate pricing strategy, following Figure 3–5 the practice would offer high-end products at a high price, medium products at a medium price, and low-end products at a low price.

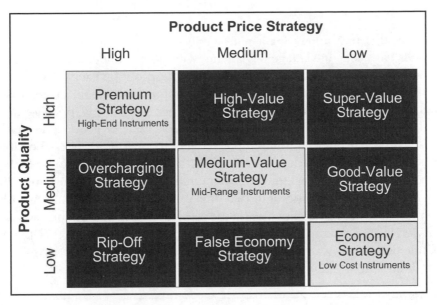

Figure 3–5. Pricing strategies. (Adapted from P. Kotler, 2001, *Marketing Management*, Upper Saddle River, NJ: Prentice Hall. Copyright 2001. Adapted with permission.)

Sidebar 3–8
ETHICAL OR PROFITABILITY COMPROMISES IN PRICING

When the practitioner is making pricing decisions about pricing it is necessary to make some ethical decisions. Figure 3–5 in the text presents a number of pricing philosophies that can be incorporated into the pricing decision, including the path chosen by most practitioners where high quality is high priced, medium quality is medium priced, and low quality is low priced. Departures from this model may cause either ethical concerns or profitability problems.

The challenge to ethics is when the practitioner chooses the high price for medium or low-quality products. Figure 3–5 presents a possibility to charge a high price (such as that normally charged for a high-end digital instrument) for a medium quality or low-quality product. Charging the high price for medium quality is simply considered as an overcharging strategy, whereas Kotler (2001) considered a high price for low quality to be a rip-off strategy. Although this may be part of the overall practice positioning, there are some ethical questions that arise with either of these strategies. The problem is that with either the overcharging or rip-off strategies, the patient could acquire the exact same technology to provide the assistance necessary for much less cost and it is the audiologist's responsibility to provide this technology for a reasonable cost. To the ethics purist, this "smells" of taking advantage of patients who do not understand the products they are purchasing while maximizing the profit on each product.

On the other side of Figure 3–5, is the opposite situation. In this case, high-quality products are presented to the public at a very low price for marketing what Kotler (2001) presents as the supervalue or good value strategies. This strategy compromises profitability to provide the best possible products for a minimal amount of cost. Although this appears to be highly altruistic and a good deal for the patient, it can drastically compromise the profitability of the practice. Ethically this can also be a problem in that the compromise of profitability may be the reason that the practitioner will not survive in the marketplace and leave the patient to look for another practitioner before the warranty and other provider responsibilities have been conducted fully.

A recommended pricing procedure is offered in Figure 3–6. This pyramidal pricing technique considers all of the fundamentals presented earlier and assists the practitioner in the development of price for products and services.

Developing the Pricing Strategy

Establishing pricing objectives in an Audiology practice involves setting profit objectives. It is one of the most important basics in pricing for the practice. Setting the proper strategic goals and pricing strategy will often make the difference between significant profitability and minimal profit. Staab (2000) feels that to set price objectives, the objectives of the practice must be clear and the type of pricing necessary for success, that is, high-priced, low-volume, low-priced, high-volume, and so forth must correspond to the goals and objectives. Additionally, the practitioner must understand the fundamental conflict between buyer

and seller. Staab (2000) feels that dispensers view price as (a) expected revenue, (b) an accumulation of costs, and (c) a marketing feature (high prices indicate quality—low prices provide a marketing advantage). In contrast, patients view the purchasing decision on the basis of perceived value of the product and on its price compared to the competition.

Pricing Objectives

Depending on the market conditions and the philosophy of the practitioner, the approach to pricing should be based on marketing objectives. The following objectives are philosophies that can be incorporated into the overall business plan:

- Maximizing current profit
- Maximizing market share
- Market skimming
- Product quality leadership.

Maximizing current profit relates to an immediate, positive change in prof-

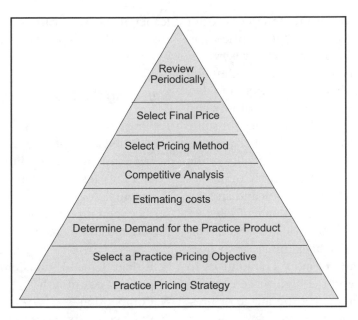

Figure 3–6. Setting practice pricing policy.

itability. This pricing objective involves estimating patient demand and costs associated with the alternative prices then choosing a price that maximizes immediate profit, cash flow, or return on investment (Dolan & Simon, 1996; Kotler, 2001). In essence, the profit maximization philosophy is to charge "whatever the market will bear" to keep the profit at his highest level. Although creating high profits in the short term, this method overlooks patient reactions to price and competitive market reactions causing difficulty in sustaining these profits over time, and costing the practice in the long term. An objective that maximizes profit may involve selling lower level products for more than they are worth and not only compromises the long-run performance of the practice, but ethics as well.

Some markets are highly price sensitive and offer opportunities to tune the practice for maximum market share. The vision of a large market share is extremely

attractive, particularly to a new practice. Low prices using the super-value strategy or the good value strategy presented in the right side of Figure 3–5 is one method of obtaining market share as these low prices tend to stimulate market growth, and discourage competition. This strategy of increasing market share, according to Dolan and Simon (1996), often compromises the practice profitability to gain market share and is discouraged as a practice-pricing objective. The use of this pricing alternative can compromise the profitability to the degree that the practice has significant difficulty meeting expenses and seriously reduce the practitioner's capability to meet product warranty responsibilities.

Some practices, especially those in exclusive markets, use a market skimming approach to their pricing strategy. In this strategy the practitioner sets fees for services and prices for products to "skim" the market. Skimming is setting a price objective for the practice to cater to those willing to pay a higher price than most for the same products or services. Kotler (2001) indicates that skimming works when there is a sufficient number of patients that have the capability and are willing to pay a higher price for some reason, such as status, atmosphere or location of the place provided, quality of the practitioner, and other factors. In market skimming, high current demand and the unit costs of a smaller volume of sales are offset by the higher prices charged. This philosophy of a high initial price does not usually attract more competitors to the market, and the high price communicates to the market the image or prestige of a superior product. For example, an audiology practice in Beverly Hills on Rodeo Drive or an exclusive part of the any city might be a good candidate for the market skimming strategy.

Another strategy is product quality leadership which may be represented in a number of products offered by the practice. The practice could be in a medical center of stature (i.e., Mayo clinic) and, therefore, quality is ensured simply by association. In this situation, quality leadership of the practice is the association with a specific entity or group in that patients assume that if you are good enough to be part of the famous clinic or health care group, then you and your practice must be high quality. Quality association can also be driven by the products carried in the practice. Hearing instruments known for quality and reputation are recognized by patients to provide quality association by virtue of the brand. Other forms of quality leadership in audiology practices include physically locating in a medical office building or a building associated with a hospital or health care center. Prospective patients have identified your practice as a quality leader in hearing care and as the destination they have chosen for their hearing care.

Selecting the Pricing Objectives

Pricing experts suggest that charges established for professional services and hearing instruments are influenced by a number of factors as seen in Figure 3–7. When audiologists establish charges for services and products dispensed, the following must be considered:

- Patient demand (units of service or product per month)
- Competition
- Price elasticity (how much sales volume changes when prices are raised or lowered)
- Net price to the patient after special offers, coupons, and other incentives.
- Incremental (variable) and fixed costs
- Expected profit
- Product life cycle.

These issues must be considered in the development of a pricing strategy that is fair to patients, the practice owner, and employees. Although a fair pricing strategy is the key to success, which one do we use? Which one is best for a particular practice and their patients? Does it work where I live? Do I need an accountant to calculate it? These questions are all components of the pricing strategy that is used to communicate with the market. Volume of sales is the most important component of profitability; however, pricing holds the key to the profitability of the practice. Marn and Rosiello (1992) determined that the correct pricing strategy will have three to four times the effect on profitability when they suggest that pricing objectives are as critical to

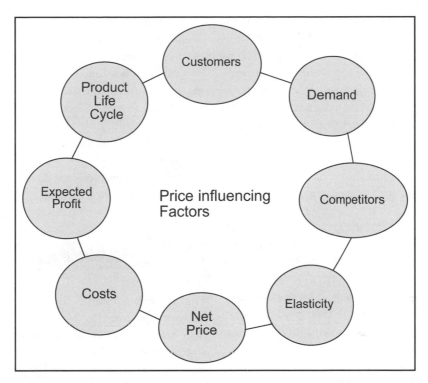

Figure 3–7. Price-influencing factors. (From Marketing Principles, by W. Staab, 2000, *Audiology Practice Management.* Copyright 2000 by Thieme. Reprinted with permission.)

the success of the practice as are objectives that determine how the practice will approach the market.

Determining Demand for Practice Product

The practitioner needs to conduct a market survey to determine where the practice fits into the marketplace and to predict demand for the services and products. This can be done by reviewing the historical demand for the services and products. If there is no history for this product, then experiments can be conducted or by asking patients what they would pay for these products. Demand must be predicted so that accurate fixed costs, and incremental/variable costs can be computed and figured into

the price along with the profitability goals of the practitioner.

Estimating Costs

The practitioner must estimate the costs of doing business and figure them into the basic cost factors including all fixed and relevant incremental/variable costs. This step is essential as all prices must cover costs.

Competitive Analysis

Although competitive analysis should never be utilized as the sole means for arriving at the final price, it is necessary to conduct a survey to determine what the competition charges for certain products and services. In arriving at the correct price it is always strategic to know your competition and what they offer for the prices charged. This competitive analysis allows the practitioner to know where they are relative to their eventual pricing and where their pricing is relative to competition. Knowledge of what the competition is doing for what prices is a competitive edge.

Selecting the Pricing Method

At this point on the pyramid, the practitioner has a strategy, objectives, product demand estimates, cost estimates, and a competitive analysis. At this step in the pyramidal pricing scheme it is necessary to choose among the cost-plus or markup, value pricing, or competitive pricing methods outlined earlier.

Selecting a Final Price

Selecting the final price is based on using the judgment and analysis of the market situation. It is often the practitioner's best judgment that patients will react to the prices as they have been set based on the data available as well as the goals and objective of the practice.

Reviewing Periodically

The market place will change rapidly and a review of prices must be considered and possibly recalculated as market conditions react to the economic and competitive situation.

Seven Principles of Pricing

1. All costs must be covered.
2. The market dictates the changes in prices.
3. Charge the maximum price the patient will pay.
4. Check the price continuously and adjust accordingly.
5. Prices must be established that will ensure sales.
6. If the public perceives a product has significant value they will pay more.
7. Patients purchase products based on benefits, not features.

Summary

The price we charge for our products and services are the financial remuneration for our hard work in school, a reward for putting off the earning in income while learning our profession, as well as for the risks taken by offering these products and services in a private practice environment. Often there is no discussion of pricing and where these figures come from in audiology clinics and training programs. Most audiologists forget that the price we charge for a product or service in the practice is simply the economic payback that the patient makes to acquire the product or have us apply our hard learned expertise to their hearing problem. This chapter attempts to provide the practitioner with the tools to price products and services fairly, but at a level that pays appropriately for their expertise. It presents what is meant by various costs, such as fixed costs and incremental or variable costs and other significant costs associated with maintaining an audiology practice. Sidebars for specific methodologies of pricing add details of how accurate pricing is achieved. Basic pricing concepts such as cost-plus or markup, value-based, and competition pricing are presented to provide a foundation to develop the practitioner's pricing strategy.

In essence, a patient purchases a product or service only if that product or service's perceived value, in terms of money, is greater than the price. This chapter provides a foundation for practitioners to develop the skills to present that delicate perceived value, fairly, to their patients and themselves.

References

Amlani, A. (2007, February). Impact of elasticity of demand on price in the hearing aid market. *Audiology Online.*

Bennett, S., & Wilkinson, J. (1974, January). Price-quality relationships and price elasticity under in-store experimentation. *Journal of Business Research*, pp. 30–34.

Berry, T., & Wilson, D. *On target: The book on marketing plans.* Eugene, OR: Palo Alto Software.

Dolan, R. (1995, September-October). How do you know when the price is right? *Harvard Business Review*, p. 178.

Dolan, R., & Simon, H. (1996). *Power pricing.* New York: Free Press.

Erickson, G., & Johansson, J. (1985). The role of multi-attribute product evaluations. *Journal of Consumer Research, 5*, 195–199.

Gans, P. (2006). *Professional dispensing model: Differentiating goods from services,* Lecture from R. Traynor (Professor) CAS 7308 Business and Professional Issues, University of Florida Working Professional Doctor of Audiology Program, Gainesville, FL.

Grima, S., & Grima, J. (2004). Understanding the cost of providing services. In B. Keagy & M. Thomas (Eds.), *Essentials of physician practice management.* San Francisco: Josse-Bass.

Hall, R., & Lieberman, M. (2002). ECO 533: *Introduction to economics* [custom text prepared for University of Phoenix]. Mason, OH: Southwestern College Publishing/Thompson Learning.

Hosford-Dunn, H., Dunn, D., & Harford, E. (1995). *Audiology business and practice management,* San Diego, CA: Singular.

Kotler, P. (2001). *Marketing management.* Upper Saddle River, NJ: Prentice-Hall.

Kortge, D., & Okonkwo, P. (1993). Perceived value approach to pricing. *Industrial Marketing Management, 22*(3), pp. 133–140.

Marn, M., & Rosiello, R. (1992). Managing price, gaining profit. *Harvard Business Review, 70*, pp 84–94.

Nagle, T., & Holden, R. (2004). *Strategy and tactics of pricing: A guide to profitable decision making* (3rd ed.). Upper Saddle River, NJ: Prentice-Hall.

Parkin, M. (2005). *Microeconomics.* Boston: Addison-Wesley.

Rajendran, K., & Tellis, G. (1994). Contextual and temporal components of reference price. *Journal of Marketing, 58*, pp. 22–34.

Ross, M. (2005). Why do hearing aids cost so much? *Hearing loss. Self Help for the Hard of Hearing, 26* (1).

Smith, T., & Nagle, T. (1994). Financial analysis for profit-driven pricing. *Sloan Management Review, 35*(3), 22–31.

Staab, W., (2000). Marketing principles. In H. Hosford-Dunn, R. Roeser, & M. Valente. (Eds.), *Audiology practice management.* New York: Thieme.

Weiner, J. (1994). Forecasting demand: Consumer electronics marketer uses a conjoint approach to configure its new product and set the right price. *Marketing Research, 4*, 6–11.

4

Fiscal Monitoring;
Cash Flow Analysis

ROBERT M. TRAYNOR, Ed.D., M.B.A.

Introduction

I Am an Audiologist,
Not an Accountant

Audiologists are practitioners, not accountants. Accountants establish and monitor procedures to ensure proper financial reporting of taxes, tax preparation, and other regulatory compliance reporting. Accountants develop bookkeeping procedures specific to the needs of the practice and establish internal controls that monitor the office staff in their bookkeeping efforts. They provide the practitioner with internal and external methods of monitoring theft and perform internal audits should theft be suspected. In addition to general accounting responsibilities they offer personal financial planning services and provide business valuations.

Just as audiologists are licensed to practice in their respective states, accountants are licensed by State Boards of Accountancy. Similar to audiologists that choose to seek certification from the American Board of Audiology (ABA), accountants may seek certification from the American Institute of Certified Public Accountants (AICPA: http://www.aicpa.org). Their certification title is Certified Public Accountant (CPA). All CPAs are accountants, but all accountants are not CPAs. Just as ABA certification is voluntary, so too is the certification process for accountants.

Audiologists have specialty certification opportunities through the ABA. CPAs have specialty certification available to those seeking advanced credentials as well. There is a specialty certification for CPAs important to practice owners who are considering merging or selling his or her practice. The AICPA offers specialty certification in business valuations. The Accreditation in Business Valuation (ABV) identifies those CPAs with advanced training and certification in assessing and issuing valuations of various businesses including health care practices.

Practitioners should have knowledge of the vocabulary, and language of accounting to effectively communicate with the accounting professionals who manage their practices, and protect their assets (Dunn, 2000; Tracy, 2001). It may seem to audiologists that dealing with a newborn for follow-up hearing assessment, or fitting sophisticated, digital hearing instruments constitute particular challenges in the day-to-day operations of their practice. The real challenge of audiology practice is staying in business over a long period of time and the more a practitioner knows about appropriate accounting methods, the better their capability to adjust practice procedures and policies to ensure profitability (Sidebar 4-1).

Sidebar 4–1
AN OVERVIEW OF ECONOMIC EXCHANGES IN AN AUDIOLOGY PRACTICE

In a perfect world a transaction would simply be between the patient and the audiologist. Tracy (2001) describes six basic types of economic exchanges for which accountants ensure correct business interaction. Generally, these economic exchanges involve many others who are part of necessary interactions in daily operations of the practice:

- Patients
- Government
- Equity sources of capital
- Debt sources of capital
- Suppliers and vendors
- Employees

These basic exchanges are how the practice interacts with the real world of daily operations. The practice deals with the patients through employees, office, and clinical supplies as well as hearing instruments and support items are purchased from suppliers, vendors, and hearing instrument manufacturers and repair facilities (Figure 4–1).

If cash reserves are unavailable to purchase these products or pay the employees and other expenses, the practitioner may have to obtain an interest-bearing loan or establish a credit line through their banker. Another option available to the practice owner is to add partners or stockholders who can bring additional financial opportunities in exchange for shares in the practice. These partners or stockholders will own a percentage of the practice and appropriately expect a return on their investment. Additionally, as they are financial stakeholders in the practice; they will likely want a say in the day-to-day operations and management of the business segment of the practice. The attorney for the practice will be involved in document preparation to establish the most appropriate method for adding partner/stockholders. The accountant for the practice will reconfigure the books to include allowances for the partner/stockholders and to make sure the practice meets its financial obligations to them.

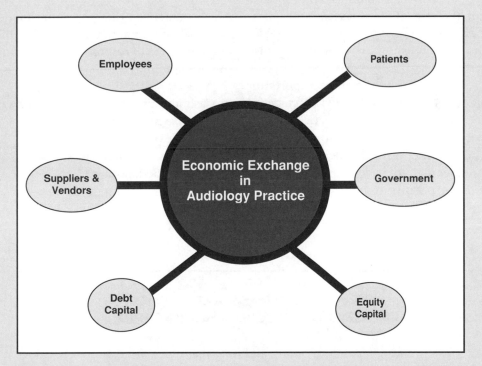

Figure 4–1. Economic exchanges of an audiology practice. (Adapted from *Accounting for Dummies* [2nd ed.], by J. Tracy, 2001, Hoboken: Wiley Publish-

Accountants—What They Do Best for Your Practice

Accountants not only ensure funds are deposited in the appropriate accounts, they advise the practitioner about the fiscal health of the practice. They provide information about cash flow and retained earnings relative to the adequacy of funding required to conduct day-to-day business transactions. It is also the responsibility of the accountant (in association with the bookkeeper, Sidebar 4–2) to make sure that expenses are paid on time and that transactions for these payments are recorded properly. In addition, property such as sound rooms, audiometers, VNG equipment, paper, printers, pens, and all other property are also accounted for so as to control the use of these assets and assess their real value for property tax purposes and in establishing appropriate expense deductions.

Accountants can prepare reports for practitioners to assist in evidence-based decisions about the success or failure of daily operations, a specific procedure, or a new market offering. These reports are fundamental to understanding the reasons for positive or negative changes in the bottom-line performance of the practice. Such accounting reports are prepared according to internationally accepted accounting rules called the Generally Accepted Accounting Principles (GAAP), a universal method of valuing profit and measuring assets and liabilities. Although they vary slightly from one country to another, GAAP rules are used to conduct accounting in all businesses. GAAP describes how transactions for costs, profit, inventory, sales, and other business specifics are recorded and allows a comparison of one practice to another as businesses all use the same procedures for accounting.

The Accountant's Primary Responsibilities to Your Practice

An accountant's primary responsibilities vary from one practice to another. Most common areas of responsibilities include, but are not limited to:

■ Cash into the practice (receivables)
■ Cash payments from the practice (payables)
■ Inventory and purchases
■ Property accounting
■ Tax accounting methods: cash or accrual
■ Payroll preparation.

Sidebar 4–2
KEY QUALITIES IN A BOOKKEEPER

As accounting for the incoming and outgoing funds are essential to a successful practice, special attention must be given to the person that handles the money. Bookkeepers are not accountants, but should be knowledgeable of business with a basic understanding of the essential differences between the five basic types of accounts (assets, liabilities, equity, income, and expenses) so that transactions are organized properly. As the practitioner has patient, management, supervisory, marketing, and other responsibilities, there is no time to "babysit" the bookkeeper so they must be capable of taking charge of basic financial operations. The practice owner or CEO is ultimately responsible for all that happens with the books, but a good bookkeeper should be able to work accurately and independently with assistance and occasional consultation with an accountant. Communication about the business of the practice is critical and good bookkeeping can foster understanding of what is taking place in the office without the practitioner having to record the day-to-day transactions. The bookkeeper should also have a clear understanding of the three basic financial statements, including the balance sheet, the income statement (profit/loss statement), and the cash flow statements that are fundamental to tracking the costs by item and procedural detail.

The days of manual bookkeeping systems are gone forever making it essential to find a bookkeeper with a knowledge of the basics of bookkeeping software, Word, Excel, E-mail, and the Internet. They should be committed to enhancing their skills with additional classes or self-study to ensure that they are staying up to date with the accounting skills your business demands. If hiring a part-time bookkeeper, the practitioner should find someone who will make your business a priority, not allowing a part-time bookkeeper to "squeeze" their bookkeeping responsibilities into their personal life as this puts the practice at a low priority.

In addition to being an honest and hard working individual, Newman (2006) suggests an 11-factor check list that should be considered when hiring a bookkeeper; they must possess:

- a basic understanding of bookkeeping/accounting terms.
- be detail oriented.
- an understanding of the big picture.
- a willingness to follow through on projects.
- the capability to have monthly financial statements available by the 10th of the following month.
- an understanding of how to do proper job costing.
- a basic understanding of your industry.
- good communication skills.
- good computer skills.
- an interest in continuing their education.
- a willingness to make a strong commitment to your business.

Receivables and Payables

The accountant will set up a chart of accounts depicting all transactions necessary to record incoming revenue (e.g., payments from patients or third party payors) and pay bills necessary to satisfy vendors, landlords, and other providers of services or goods to the practice (e.g., rent, hearing instrument manufacturer). The chart of accounts represents an exhaustive list of important accounts which must be monitored and carefully followed as it is the basis for the general ledger for the practice. The general ledger for the practice is the nuts and bolts of the financial monitoring system. It includes every account on the chart of accounts and contains information about monies received in the practice and money that must be paid to suppliers, vendors, federal, state, and local taxing agencies. The method of recording this information includes two significant items; debits and credits. It is, therefore, referred to as "double entry" method of bookkeeping.

Inventory Control and Property Tax Accounting

Recording purchases and related acquisition costs of items necessary for daily practice operations is important for a variety of reasons, not the least of which is to establish appropriate tax preparations and deductions. The accountant will establish appropriate guidelines to record all transactions that are important to your practice and works with the office manager/bookkeeper to optimize tax reporting, credits, and deductions. Although accountants can issue quarterly reports, semiannual reporting is less costly. As long as the practitioner is attending to fiscal details, semiannual reporting is usually adequate. A single, end-of-the-year report is not adequate to monitor the overall fiscal health of any health care practice. It is one thing to make up for an error or initiate needed changes in reporting at the mid-year point; it is another to have to retread the path of a full year of business transactions.

Cash and Accrual Methods of Accounting

The core of the cash method of accounting is based on the flow of cash in and out of the practice. Income is recorded when received and expenses are paid when they occur. Both income and expenses are put on the books and charged to the period in which they are received and taxes are paid based on actual revenue-in-hand. Historically, accountants have recommended the cash basis for small businesses with minimal inventory, less complex business structure, and only one or two partner/owners involved. From a tax perspective, it is sometimes beneficial for a new business to use the cash basis of accounting so that recording income can be put off until the next tax year, when expenses can be claimed immediately.

The accrual basis of accounting requires that income and expenses are entered into the ledger when a transaction occurs regardless of whether monies have been received for the services or products provided. Expenses are deductible when the practice is billed, not when the expenses are paid. Taxes are paid on the revenue on the ledger with or without revenue-in-hand. The obvious downside to this method resides in the fact that the practice might have to pay income taxes on monies that have not been collected in part or in full. The owner or manager of the practice can minimize the downside of the accrual method by collecting revenue for services and hearing instruments as soon as possible, preferably at the time of service. That may not be such a problem for hearing instruments; however, most patients rely on their insurance carriers to pay their medical bills, including diagnostic studies common to the practice of audiology. Third party payors who reimburse in a timely fashion (a dwindling lot to be sure) will aid in reducing the tax impact inherent in the accrual method of accounting.

Whether you are inclined to go with the cash or the accrual basis, the accountant of record for your practice must be involved in the decision process. He or she can clarify the two accounting methods and recommend the best course of action for your particular practice circumstance and venue.

Payroll Preparation

Preparing payroll is extremely important as all employees, including the practice owner or manager, must be paid for their services in a timely fashion. Appropriate federal, state, and local payroll taxes such as Social Security, Medicare, city taxes, and other deductions from their salary must be accurately calculated, applied, and recorded. These deductions must be deposited at the practice's bank each month in a special account reserved for government tax collection. Failure to deduct and deposit these taxes has severe penalties for the practice owner and possible liabilities for the individual within the practice designated responsible for developing the payroll and depositing the taxes. It is the practice owner who

bears the ultimate responsibility of making sure all taxes are deducted and that the funds have been directed to the appropriate depository.

It is cost prohibitive for most practices to have the accountant of record complete the payroll. A reasonable solution is to secure the services of a payroll company. There are a number of companies operating on a national basis that specialize in payroll preparation. Their clients include large and small companies and a variety of health care providers. They follow specific tax guidelines for state (varies from state to state) and federal reporting. Payroll companies will cause deductions to occur as directed, issue payroll documentation, and print payroll checks drawn on the practice bank account. Consult with your accountant about payroll services available in your area. He or she should suggest establishing levels of deductions relative to your specific needs and should review the first two or three sets of payroll checks and documentation to ensure appropriate deductions and documentation have been issued and recorded.

Financial Statements

There are two primary objectives of every business, including health care practices; profitability and solvency. Unless a practice can produce satisfactory earnings and pay its debt obligations in a timely manner, all other objectives will never be realized because the practice will not survive. Financial statements that reflect a practice's solvency (the balance sheet), its profitability (the income statement), and a view of its financial health (the cash-flow statement) provide the practitioner substantive information on which to make well-informed decisions about the operations of the practice.

Financial statements are so important that bankers and other lenders depend on them to support their decisions to grant credit opportunities. Additionally, the figures on financial statements are the bases of the calculations for business ratios that offer important, informative metrics about activity, liquidity, profitability, and debt of the practice.

The Balance Sheet

The balance sheet contains the elemental fiscal components of the practice: information about assets, liabilities, and owner's equity. It presents a snapshot of the financial condition of the practice at a specific moment in time, usually at the close of an accounting period such as the end of the month, quarter, or year (Brealey et al., 2002). Businesstown.com (2003a) indicates that its purpose is to quickly view the financial strength and capabilities of the business as well as answer important questions such as:

- Is the business in a position to expand?
- Can the business easily withstand the normal financial ebbs and flows of revenues and expenses?
- Or should the business take immediate steps to strengthen cash reserves?

The balance sheet gets its name from the fact that the two sides of the statement must numerically balance. Assets are recorded on left side of the balance sheet and Liabilities and Owner's Equity are recorded on the right side of the balance sheet, as presented in Table 4-1. Total Assets are set to equal 100%, with all other assets listed as a percentage of the total assets. On the right side of the balance sheet, Total Liabilities and Equity is also set equal to 100%. Entries of all liabilities and owner's equity accounts are also represented as the appropriate percent of the total liabilities and equity. The balance sheet must contain all of the practice's financial accounts and should be generated at least once a month. Monthly review of the balance sheet provides a comprehensive overview of the practice's overall financial position at that specific point in time.

Assets

Assets listed on the balance sheet are items of value and represent the financial resources of the practice. Accounts listed on the balance sheet are placed in order of their relative degree of liquidity (ease of convertibility to cash)—therefore Cash is always listed first as it does not require an action or an agent to convert cash into cash. Accounts Receivable is listed second as it represents Cash but must be "converted" into cash by collection. Assets are commonly differentiated into two classes; Current Assets and Fixed or Long-Term Assets, (see Table 4-1). Current Assets are short-lived and expected to be converted into cash or to be used up in the operations of the practice within a short period of time, usually within a fiscal year. Current Assets include cash, accounts receivable, hearing instrument and assistive listening device inventory, and prepaid expenses, such as insurance.

Long-Term or Fixed Assets are assets that will not be turned into cash within the practice's fiscal year. Examples of

Table 4–1. Sample Balance Sheet

Audiology Associates INC. Balance Sheet December 31, 2006	
Assets	**Liabilities & Owners' Equity**
Current Assets:	Current Liabilities:
Cash . . . . 34,000.	Short-Term Debt . . . . 20,000.
Accounts Receivable . . . . 80,000.	Accounts Payable . . . . 35,000.
Merchandise Inventory . . 170,000.	Other Accrued Liabilities . . 12,000.
Total Current Assets . . 284,000.	Total Current Liabilities . . 67,000.
Property, Plant, and Equipment (Fixed Assets):	Long-Term Debt . . . . 50,000.
Equipment . . . . 40,000.	Total Liabilities . . . . 117,000.
Less Accumulated	Owners' Equity . . . . 203,000.
Depreciation . . . . (4,000.)	Total liabilities and
Total Assets . . . . **320,000.**	Owners' Equity . . . . **320,000.**

Source: Adapted from *Accounting: What the Numbers Mean*, (6th ed., pp. 238–247) by D. H. Marshall, 2004, New York: McGraw-Hill.

Long-Term or Fixed Assets include audiometric and other equipment used in the practice, office equipment, and computers, purchased vehicles, purchased buildings, leasehold improvements, and telephone systems. These assets are found in the balance sheet (see Table 4–1) listed as "Property, Plant, and Equipment" or as "Fixed Assets." To best conceptualize Long-Term or Fixed Assets, consider that most fixed assets are purchased over time and must be in place over a long period of time to foster the day-to-day clinical and business operations of the practice. As equipment ages, it is said to depreciate. This depreciation of the equipment is an expense and can be claimed as a tax deduction. The accountant for the practice will evaluate the appropriate method for calculation and the extent of deductions available for every fixed asset listed on the balance sheet.

The following formula depicts the interactions described above to derive the Assets of the practice:

Assets = (Liabilities + Owner's Equity)
+ (Revenue – Expenses)

Liabilities

Liabilities include all obligations the practice has acquired through daily operations of the practice. Liabilities include accounts payable (e.g., hearing instrument acquisition costs), accrued business expenses, interest owed on loans, and other obligations incurred in the daily operations of the practice. Owner's or shareholder's equity includes financial investment by the owner or shareholders and the earned profits that are retained in the business. Presented on the right side of the balance sheet (see Table 4–1), current liabilities are listed as amounts owed to lenders and suppliers and are usually separated by those that are due in the short term and long term. As with the asset categories, current liabilities are delineated into subcategories such as short-term debt, accounts payable, and accrued liabilities. These are referred to as current liabilities as they are due to be paid in a short period of time, usually within the fiscal year. A separate category is for long-term debt, such as bank or other loans payable over a much longer period, usually longer than the fiscal year. All current and long-term liability amounts are then totaled collectively to reflect the total liability of the practice (see Table 4–1).

Owner/Shareholder equity is also listed on the right side of the balance sheet. This represents funds that were initially invested by the owner as well as the profit that was earned and retained in the practice.

The Income Statement

Income statements, sometimes called profit and loss statements or "P and L" statements depict the status of overall profits. McNamara (2007) indicates that income statements simply include how much money that has been earned (revenue) and subtracts how much has been spent (expenses), resulting in how much money has been made (profits) or losses (deficits). Basically, the statement includes total sales minus total expenses. It presents the nature of the practice's overall profit and loss over a period of time. Therefore, the Income Statement

gives you a sense for how well the business is operating.

In accounting, the practice's profitability is measured by comparing the revenues generated in a given period with the expenses incurred to produce those revenues. The difference between the revenue generated and the expenses created during the generation of the revenue is the profit (or loss) of the practice. In an audiology practice, revenues are defined as the inflow of revenue from providing patient care or the dispensing of products. Expenses can be considered the sacrifices made or the costs incurred to produce these revenues. If revenues exceed expenses, net earnings result whereas if expenses exceed net revenue, a loss is recorded.

As with other financial statements, the income statement, presented in Table 4–2, may be prepared for any financial reporting period and is used to track revenues and expenses for the evaluation of the operating performance of the practice. Businesstown.com (2003b) suggests that managers can use income statements to find areas of the practice that are overbudget or underbudget and identify those areas that cause unexpected expenditures. Additionally, income statements track increases or decreases in product returns; cost of goods sold as a percentage of sales, and offer some indication of the extent of income tax liability. As it is very important to format an income statement appropriate to the type of business being conducted, the structure of income statements may vary from one practice to another, depending on the particular mix of business conducted in diagnostics, hearing products, and rehabilitative services.

Net sales on the income statement consist of sales figures representing the actual revenue generated by the busi-

Table 4–2. Sample Income Statement

Audiology Associates Inc. Income Statement Year Ended December 31, 2006	
Net sales	1,200,000.
Costs of goods sold	850,000.
Net profit	350,000.
Selling, general, and administrative expenses . . .	311,000.
Income from operations	39,000.
Interest expense	9,000.
Income before taxes	30,000.
Income taxes	12,000.
Net Income	**18,000.**

Source: Adapted from *Accounting: What the Numbers Mean* (6th ed., pp. 238–247) by D. H. Marshall, 2004, New York: McGraw-Hill.

ness. Marshall (2004) states that the net sales entry on the income statement represents the total amount of all sales less product returns and sales discounts. Directly below the net sales in Table 4–2, is the cost of goods sold (COGS). COGS are costs directly associated with making and/or acquiring the products. These costs include the acquisition of products, such as hearing aids or assistive devices provided by outside suppliers. If hearing instruments are repaired or manufactured by the practice, COGS could also be materials, parts, and internal expenses related to the manufacturing or repair process, such as faceplates, shells, microphones, receivers, and components. Net profit, sometimes called gross profit, is derived by subtracting the cost of goods sold from net sales. Net profit, however, does not include any operating, interest, or income tax expenses. Just below the net profit entry in Table

4–2 is a category for Selling and General Administrative expenses. This subcategory is described by Tracy (2001) and Marshall (2004) as a broad "catch-all" category for all expenses except those reported elsewhere in the income statement. Examples of selling and general administrative expenses that are recorded here are legal expenses, the owner's salary, advertising, travel and entertainment, and other similar costs. The actual income from operations, sometimes called earnings before interest and taxes (EBIT), is the result of deducting the selling and general administrative expenses from the net profit. The earnings before taxes (EBIT) is the net revenue generated by the practice but there are still interest expenses and taxes that must be recorded. At this point, the interest expense is deducted and then the tax amounts are subtracted to arrive at the net income (or loss).

Account Balancing

Account balancing is primarily for the bookkeepers in the practice, but it is beneficial for the practitioner to know how the procedure works. Simple accounting programs specifically designed for small businesses, such as Quick Books, have revolutionized bookkeeping tasks. These relatively inexpensive programs substantially reduce or virtually eliminate many of the common accounting mistakes that have plagued bookkeepers for decades.

One of the common bookkeeping tasks is the trial balance. The trial balance of the books is usually conducted at the end of the month, quarter, or year, but could be done at any time. The purpose of the trial balance is to determine the total debits and the total credits balance for all of the asset and liability accounts. Occasionally, these accounts do not balance and it is necessary to find errors and determine how to reverse them. Although accounting software programs have safeguards and special routines that will assist in finding these errors it may be necessary to check for the following common causes of trial balance errors:

- Errors in the recording of a transaction
- Posting errors
- Computation of account balances
- Copying balances to the trial balance.

The Statement of Cash Flows

The cash flow statement reflects the cash position of the practice as well as the sources and uses of cash in the prac-tice during a specified business cycle. It presents how cash flows in and out of the practice. Monthly cash flow statements are useful but quarterly statements of cash flow provide look at trends that might be developing in the overall cash-flow picture. Financially successful practices manage both profit and cash flow well.

Profit and cash flow are intimately related. A practice can be highly profitable yet on the verge of bankruptcy if the profits are sequestered in accounts receivables—*high profit, low cash flow*. This situation results in limited cash to pay the practitioner and other employees and to service the accounts payable. Conversely, if there is substantial cash inflow to a practice with excessive overhead costs strangling profitability, financial difficulties will ensue—*low profit, high cash flow*. This is a situation wherein the practice owner has overextended available resources with ill-conceived equipment purchases, exceptional leasehold costs, or extraneous staff salaries and other questionable business decisions. To illustrate how cash flows in and out of the practice, Marshall (2004) indicates that the statement of cash flows is used to identify the sources and uses of cash over time and can be compared to the current period for analysis. In Table 4-3, the cash flow statement is divided into three general sections, cash flow from operating activities, cash flow from investment activities, and cash flow from financing activities. The operating activity section begins with the net income (taken from the income statement, see Table 4-2) and includes all transactions and events that are normally entered to determine the operating income. These entries include cash receipts from selling goods or providing services, as well as income from income earned as interest

Table 4–3. Sample Statement of Cash Flows

Audiology Associates, Inc. Statement of Cash Flows Year Ended December 31, 2006	
Cash Flows from Operating	
Net income	$ 18,000.
Add (deduct) items not affecting cash:	
Depreciation expense	4,000.
Increase in accounts receivable	(80,000.)
Increase in merchandise	(170,000.)
Increase in current liabilities	67,000.
Net cash used by operating activities	$(161,000.)
Cash Flows from Investment	
Cash paid	$ (40,000.)
Cash Flows from Financing	
Cash received from issues of long-term debt . .	$ 50,000.
Cash received from sale of common stock	190,000.
Net cash provided by financing	$ 240,000.
Net cash increase	**$ 39,000.**

Source: Adapted from *Accounting: What the Numbers Mean* (6th ed., pp. 238–247) by D. H. Marshall, 2004, New York: McGraw-Hill.

and dividends, if the practice has investments. Cash flow from operating activities also includes cash payments such as inventory, payroll, taxes, interest, utilities, and rent. The net amount of cash provided (or used) by practice operating activities is the key figure on a statement of cash flows. The operations section is of the most interest as it presents the specific areas of the practice where cash was consumed.

The second section of a statement of cash flows reviews income generated from investing activities. This section includes transactions and events involving the purchase and sale of securities, land, buildings, equipment, and other assets not generally held in the practice for resale. This area of the statement also covers the making and collecting of loans, if the practice internally finances products and services these loans to consumers internally. Investing activities are not classified as operating activities as they have an indirect relationship to the central, ongoing operation of the practice.

Transactions in the third section record cash flows from financing activities and deal with the flow of cash between the practice, the owners (stockholders), and creditors as well as the cash proceeds from issuing capital stock or bonds. For example, if there was a need to transfer profit from the practice to the owners or from the owners (or creditors) into the practice, it would be reflected in the financing activities section.

Careful review of the Statement of Cash Flows can present valuable information to the practitioner with valuable information as to where the cash generated actually goes and presents an invaluable opportunity to make adjustments in practice operations for management purposes.

Financial Accounting Ratios

Until the financial data is actually used to track information about the practice, the Balance Sheet, Income Statement, and the Statement of Cash Flows are just numbers. These numbers, however, are totals of practice performance in various categories during a particular period of time and have valuable information for the management of the practice. To unlock the real information in these statements, it is necessary to conduct some simple calculations on the balance sheet and income statement data that can allow the practitioner to track specific information for management purposes.

Performance Comparison

These calculations, called Financial Accounting Ratios, are used in business to compare the practice to other practices or to compare the practice to itself at different points in time. Freeman, Barimo, and Fox (2000) describe Cross-Sectional Analysis and Time Series Analysis as two methods for the comparison of practice performance using these financial ratios.

Cross-Sectional Analysis

Cross-sectional analysis involves the calculation of financial ratios and comparing them to an industry standard usually compiled by a trade organization. A cross-sectional analysis offers an industry standard for financial performance that facilitates comparison of a specific practice to the industry standard. These ratios are calculations on the totals (from the Balance Sheet, see Table 4-1; Income Statement, see Table 4-2; and the Statement of Cash Flows, see Table 4-3). Although cross-sectional analysis facilitates a comparison of a small two-person practice with a large corporate conglomerate in many areas, these cross-sectional analyses are not readily available to practices in audiology. Within the field of audiology, these industry standards are not readily available, except possibly to a few practice appraisers and large corporate audiology chains, such as Sonus, Hear USA, and others.

Time Series Analysis

As it is difficult to obtain the data to conduct a realistic comparison of practice performance to an industry standard, the time series analysis is usually of the most value to the practitioners. A time series analysis compares the practice's performance to itself over various periods of time, usually month to month, quarter to quarter, or year to year. This type of analysis involves conducting calculations on financial statements to determine financial ratios, which by themselves, simply present how the practice performed at a particular point in time and have minimal significance in isolation. Although the various statement totals and calculated ratios give some indication of how the practice has performed, the real information in financial statements is unlocked by a comparison of the practice to itself across other financial periods. Although only somewhat informative in isolation, comparing the current totals and calculated financial ratios to those conducted at other points in time, such as monthly, quarterly, or yearly intervals, they come alive with informative data that paints a true picture of success or failure. For example, comparing the totals and calculated ratios of the first quarter of 2005 with the first quarter of 2006, or Year Ending December 31, 2005 totals and calculations with Year Ending December 31, 2006, or year to date for this year and last year can reveal a wealth of information to the practitioner or other stakeholders. More specifically, Marshall (2004) offers that these ratio calculations can assist in the determination of a practice's financial position as well as the result of overall practice operations in terms of liquidity, activity, debt, and profitability. These relatively simple measures can be calculated and tracked by spreadsheets to be reviewed over time to demonstrate the health of the practice for obtaining loans, supplier credit, reviewing success and failure for management decisions, or simply general information. Ratios calculated on these statements also provide information regarding the practice's capability to meet its obligations regarding supplier expenses, employee salaries, product returns, loans, leases, and a multitude of other miscellaneous expenses that become apparent in the balance sheet calculations.

Monitoring the Practice with Ratio Calculation

Although there are interesting calculations on the other statements, most of the important ratios are mostly performed on the balance sheet.

There are three general types of financial ratios that are used to analyze the balance sheet. These ratios demonstrate the strengths and weaknesses of a practice for:

- Liquidity
- Activity
- Debt or leverage
- Profitability.

Although liquidity ratios are used to measure the short-term ability of a practice to generate enough cash to pay currently maturing obligations, activity ratios measure how effectively the organization is using its assets by specifically analyzing how quickly some assets can be turned into cash. Debt or leverage ratios reflect the long-term solvency or overall liquidity of the practice and are typically of interest to the investors and/or the bankers that have loaned money to the practice. Profitability ratios are an indication of practice performance and look at the adequacy of the practice's net income, the rate of return, and profit margin as a percentage of sales.

Liquidity Ratios

Current Ratio and Quick Ratios

A common liquidity ratio is the Current Ratio (CR), sometimes called a Working Capital Ratio. The CR is a calculation of how many times the practice's current assets cover its current liabilities. Put another way, the Current Ratio asks the question; can the practice pay its bills? The Current Ratio is figured as follows:

$$\text{Current Ratio} = \frac{\text{Current Assets}}{\text{Current Liabilities}}$$

If the result of a CR calculation is less than 1, the practice will not be able to meet its current liabilities, whereas if the CR is 2 or more, the practice can pay its bills with money left over. Usually most bankers and practice managers like to see this ratio between at least 1 and 2. The CR calculation includes prepaid expenses, such as insurance and inventory, and sometimes presents an overly optimistic view of the real capability to meet expenses.

If the inventory and other prepaid expenses are included in the calculation, it increases the CR offering a higher ratio than if these prepaid expenses are not included. Thus, the Current Ratio can sometimes offer an unrealistic picture of the practices capability to pay its expenses. This may be especially true as audiology practices move from mostly ordering hearing instruments to stocking open-fit products. To figure activity without considering the inventory and prepaid expenses calculation of the Quick Ratio (QR) also know as the Acid Test Ratio (ATR) can be calculated. The QR or ATR evaluates the practice's liquidity without considering the inventory and prepaid expenses and, in doing so, often presents a more accurate indication of the liquidity of an audiology practice. The QR is figured as follows:

$$\text{Quick Ratio} = \frac{\text{Cash + Marketable Securities + Accounts Receivable}}{\text{Current Liabilities}}$$

As with the CR, Quick Ratio values less than 1 demonstrate that the practice has serious difficulty meeting everyday expenses. Creditors and practice managers also prefer to see this ratio between 1 and 2 (Sidebar 4–3).

Defensive Interval Measure

Another useful liquidity calculation is the Defensive Interval Measure (DIM). The DIM is a ratio that measures the time for which a practice can operate without any external cash flow or simply, how long the practice can operate if there is no business. The DIM is determined by the amount of cash or assets that can be used to keep an otherwise healthy practice open if there are unforeseen problems, such as hurricanes, major snow storms, or other situations where business ceases or drastically slows down. In accounting, these emergency funds are called Defensive Assets (DA). By definition, the DA are those assets that can be turned into cash within 3 months or less, such as cash (savings), marketable securities, or accounts receivable. In order to figure the DIM, based on a specific amount of DA, it is first necessary to know the Projected Daily Operating Expenses (PDOE) of the practice or how much it costs to keep the practice open each day. To find the PDOE, simply go to the income statement and find the selling and administrative expenses for the year and divide by 365:

$$\text{Projected Daily Operating Expenses} = \frac{\text{Total Yearly Expenses}}{365}$$

Sidebar 4–3
COMPUTATION OF THE CURRENT RATIO AND QUICK RATIO (ACID TEST RATIO)

The current ratio and quick ratios are activity ratios calculated on balance sheet totals useful in the determination if the practice can pay its expenses. The current ratio formula is as follows:

$$\text{Current Ratio} = \frac{\text{Current Assets}}{\text{Current Liabilities}}$$

Referring to Table 4–1, find the total current assets of $284,000 and the current liabilities of $67,000. Once these figures are found then put them into the formula as presented below:

$$\text{Current Ratio} = \frac{\$284,000}{\$67,000} = 4.2$$

In this example, this practice has 4.2 times the amount of funds necessary to pay its expenses. Stocked items, or inventory, included in the CR can often present an overestimate of the practices expense-paying capability. If the inventory is included in the calculation it increases the CR offering a higher ratio than if the inventory is not included. To correct for this the quick ratio is used and calculated with following formula:

$$\text{Quick Ratio} = \frac{\text{Cash + Marketable Securities + Accounts Receivable}}{\text{Current Liabilities}}$$

To compute the quick ratio from the balance sheet offered in Table 4–1, add the cash to the accounts receivable to obtain the current assets (there are no marketable securities) to obtain the total current assets of $114,000.

$$\text{Quick Ratio} = \frac{\$114,000}{\$67,000} = 1.7$$

Once obtained, divide $114,000 by the total current liabilities of $67,000 and obtain a quick ratio of 1.7. As the quick ratio must be over 1 to pay its bills, this practice has enough funds to pay their current expenses. In this example the quick ratio offers a more realistic picture of the practice's capability to pay expenses.

Once the daily operating expenses (PDOE) are known, the DIM is found by dividing the DA by the PDOE:

$$\text{Defense Interval Measure} = \frac{\text{Defensive Assets}}{\text{Projected Daily Operating Expenses}}$$

The DIM calculation gives the practice manager the length of time the business could survive if revenue was substantially reduced or absent (Sidebar 4-4).

Activity Ratios

Activity Ratios are calculations that allow the manager to review how efficiently the practice uses its assets to generate cash. Although there are a number of Activity Ratios that can present the efficiency of the practice, the Accounts Receivable Turnover Ratio (ART), the Inventory Turnover Ratio (IT), and the Total Assets Turnover Ratio (TAT) are quite useful to practice managers (Sidebars 4-5, 4-6, and 4-7 highlight calculation examples).

Accounts Receivable Turnover Ratio (ART)

Ideally all patients need to pay when services are delivered but reality is that insurance companies pay slowly, sometimes 60 to 120 days after the services are rendered, or may often not even pay the first time the claim is submitted. Additionally, some patients need credit to pay for goods and services they require such as hearing aids, batteries, repairs, and other goods or services. Managers need to monitor the Accounts Receivable to determine how much is due to the practice and how long, on the average, it takes to collect these credit sales. The Accounts Receivable Turnover Ratio (ART) reveals how many times the receivable account is turned into cash each year. To obtain the ART ratio it is necessary to first find the average amount that is due the practice from the receivable account or Average Accounts Receivable (AR) balance. This is obtained by adding the accounts receivable balance at the end of last year (or other period) to the balance of the accounts receivable at the end of the current year (or other period) and divide by 2 (see Sidebar 4-5):

$$\text{Average Accounts Receivable} = \frac{\text{AR (Year 1)} + \text{AR (Year 2)}}{2}$$

Once the average AR is computed, the ART ratio, or the time it takes to convert this account into cash, can be obtained by taking the Net Sales from the income statement (sales after returns and discounts are subtracted) and dividing that amount by the average accounts receivable balance:

$$\text{Accounts Receivable Turnover Ratio} = \frac{\text{Net Sales}}{\text{Average Accounts Receivable}}$$

Once known, the ART can tell the manager how long it takes, on average, to collect the amounts in the accounts receivable. In this calculation, the higher the ratio the better; for example, if the ART ratio is = 5.3, the practice turns over the accounts receivable 5.3 times per year or every 2.26 months which is about average.

Sidebar 4–4
CALCULATION OF THE DEFENSE INTERVAL MEASURE

The Defense Interval Measure (DIM) is a ratio that determines the time for which a practice can operate without any external cash flow or how long the practice can operate if there is no business. The DIM is determined by the amount of cash or assets that can be liquidated to keep the practice open if there are problems, such as hurricanes, major snow storms or other uncontrollable situations where business ceases or drastically slows down. To compute the DIM, however, there are some things that must be known. First, the amount of funds that can be used for defense purposes. In accounting these funds are called Defensive Assets (DA) and can consist of many different assets, but they must, by definition, have the capability to be turned into cash within 3 months. The amount of the DA will vary from practice to practice, bit it is suggested that somewhere between a 90- and 120-day capability should be available. To calculate the DIM to determine the length of time that the practice can open its doors in an emergency, it is necessary to consider the Projected Daily Operating Expenses (PDOE). The PDOE is calculated by the following formula:

$$\text{Projected Daily Operating Expenses} = \frac{\text{Total Yearly Expenses}}{365}$$

To arrive at the PDOE, simply go to the selling, general, and administrative expenses located on the income statement in Table 4–2 and find the total yearly expenses of $311,000. Then divide the total yearly expenses of $311,000 by 365 as presented below:

$$\text{Projected Daily Operating Expenses} = \frac{\$311,000}{365} = \$852.00$$

In this example, it costs the practitioner $852 per day to stay open each day. This is if the practice is open 365 days per year; most practices are only open Monday through Friday and, thus, the divisor should be much less, on the order of (365-104 [days closed]) or 261 and in this case the PDOE would be much higher at about $1,191 per day. If the practitioner has $50,000 available for Defensive Assets, then the practice's Defensive Interval Measure would be 58.6 days, or with the more conservative measure, 41.9 days. To meet the recommended DIM of a minimum of 90 days the practitioner in this example would need $76,680 for the first example or $107,190 for the more conservative example.

Sidebar 4–5
AVERAGE ACCOUNTS RECEIVABLE (AAR) AND ACCOUNTS RECEIVABLE TURNOVER RATIO (ART)

Managers need to monitor the accounts receivable to determine how much is due to the practice and how long, on average, it takes to collect these credit sales. The accounts receivable turnover ratio (ART) reveals how many times the receivable account is turned into cash each year. To obtain the ART ratio it is necessary to first find the average amount that is due the practice from the receivable account or average accounts receivable (AAR) balance. This is obtained by adding the accounts receivable balance at the end of last period to the balance of the accounts receivable at the end of the current period and divide by 2. In this example, our interest is in the average accounts receivable balance from the past 2 years. To calculate this AAR use the following formula:

$$\text{Average Accounts Receivable} = \frac{\text{AR (Year 1)} + \text{AR (Year 2)}}{2}$$

The calculation of the average accounts receivable balance comes from the balance sheet. Referring to Table 4-1 (Balance Sheet), find the current AR balance of $80,000 and assume that last year's AR balance from last year's balance sheet was $31,000. Using these figures the AAR would calculate as follows:

$$\text{Average Accounts Receivable} = \frac{\$31,000 + \$80,000}{2} = \$55,000$$

Once the AAR is determined then the ART can be calculated using the formula presented below:

$$\text{Accounts Receivable Turnover Ratio} = \frac{\text{Net Sales}}{\text{Average Accounts Receivable}}$$

From the Income Statement (Table 4-2) the net sales are $1,200,000 which is divided by the $55,000, the average accounts receivable is as follows:

$$\text{Accounts Receivable Turnover Ratio} = \frac{\$1,200,000}{\$55,000} = 21$$

The example above demonstrates that the accounts receivable turns over about 21 times per year or about every 17 days.

Sidebar 4–6
AVERAGE INVENTORY AND INVENTORY TURNOVER RATIO

The inventory turnover (IT) ratio is a calculation that measures how fast the inventory is sold. As in the measurement of the accounts receivable turnover ratio, before figuring the inventory turnover ratio, it is necessary to obtain the value of the average inventory on hand in the practice. Thus, the average inventory (AI) is found by adding the beginning inventory for the period to the ending inventory of the previous period and dividing by 2.

$$\text{Average Inventory} = \frac{\text{Beginning Inventory} + \text{Ending Inventory}}{2}$$

The calculation of the AI balance comes from the Balance Sheet. Although the practitioner could look at any period, in this case, the practitioner is interested in looking at how many times the inventory will turn each year. Referring to Table 4–1 (Balance Sheet), find the current merchandise inventory balance of $170,000 and assume that last year's merchandise inventory from last year's Balance Sheet was $111,000. Using these Balance Sheet figures the AI would calculate as follows:

$$\text{Average Inventory} = \frac{\$170,000 + \$111,000}{2} = \$140,000$$

Once the AI is determined the inventory turnover ratio can be calculated to determine how many times the stock will turn during the year. Inventory Turnover Ratio is calculated as follows:

$$\text{Inventory Turnover Ratio} = \frac{\text{Cost of Goods Sold}}{\text{Average Inventory}}$$

To arrive at the Inventory Turnover Ratio, it is necessary to refer to the Income Statement, Table 4–2 and find the Cost of Goods Sold, $850,000. This is the total amount of goods that were sold during this 1-year period. The $850,000 cost of goods sold is divided by the average inventory of $140,000 obtained earlier to present a calculated Inventory Turnover Ratio of 6.

$$\text{Inventory Turnover Ratio} = \frac{\$850,000}{\$140,000} = 6$$

An IT of 6 indicates that the inventory in this practice turns over 6 times per year, that is, every 2 months, or 60 days. This calculation is useful in ordering stock, such as batteries or open-fit hearing instruments in that it is necessary to have a 60-day supply of goods on hand to ensure that the goods will not sell out before another shipment can be obtained.

Sidebar 4–7
TOTAL ASSETS TURNOVER RATIO

An activity measure that presents how effectively the practice assets are turned into cash is the Total Assets Turnover (TAT) Ratio. The TAT ratio looks at the sales for goods and services and divides by the total assets to arrive at how many times the practices assets turn over per year.

$$\text{Total Asset Turnover Ratio} = \frac{\text{Net Sales}}{\text{Total Assets}}$$

To calculate the Total Assets Turnover Ratio it is necessary to obtain information from both the Balance Sheet (Table 4-1) and the Income Statement (Table 4-2). From the Balance Sheet the total assets are obtained at $320,000 whereas the Net Sales of 1,200,000 is obtained from the Income Statement.

$$\text{Total Asset Turnover Ratio} = \frac{\$1,200,000}{\$320,000} = 3.75$$

The calculation is simply dividing the Total Assets into the Net Sales to determine how many times the practice assets are turned into cash each year. A Total Asset Turnover Ratio of 3.75 offered in this example suggests that this practice is efficient in that it will turn its assets into cash 3.75 times per year, or about every 94 days.

To obtain more detail, the calculation of the number of days it takes to turn the accounts receivable can be obtained by simply dividing 365 by the average accounts receivable, in this case 68.86 days. Sidebar 4-5 offers a calculation example where the accounts receivable is turned 21 times per year, about every 17 days.

In the above example the accounts receivable turnover time is very short, but it can often take much longer to receive cash from those that you have extended credit. If the accounts receivable only turns two or three times per year it may make some sense to consider factoring your accounts receivable. Factoring is a process specially designed to turn over the accounts receivable and is used in many other professions, including, medicine, dentistry, chiropractic, and optometry. Factoring companies can give the practice quick cash infusion by purchasing the receivables at a discount. Although this process is a way to increase cash flow without increasing debt, it largely depends on the credit worthiness of your patients and the insurance companies with which you interact as well as the amount of your monthly invoices.

For example, if the monthly Accounts Receivable regularly totals at least $8,000 to $10,000 factoring firms will act as a collection agency for your practice. Although some of these companies have some upfront fees, shop around, as many simply take a percentage of the receivables and often immediately advance as much as 80 to 90% or more of the confirmed amount of the receivables. The factoring firm later collects from patients and companies that owed you when the account is due. If your Accounts Receivable totals $60,000 or more and it runs 90 to 120 days, it may make sense to pay factoring company to collect it. If there is a 10% fee on the $60,000 it would cost $6,000. In this situation, they would pay the practice $54,000 in cash immediately. If the fee is more than the costs then the benefits of factoring need to be weighed by the practitioner. Certainly, the accounts receivable is a tremendous source of cash and if handled correctly can keep the practice from actually needing a loan during business downturns.

Inventory Turnover Ratio

Generally, audiology practices do not have much inventory: a few loaners, some demonstration instruments, batteries, accessories, and some assistive devices. Although there is not much of an inventory for most practices, there is a new trend for practitioners to stock open-fit devices. When inventory exists in the practice it is important to understand how fast the inventory turns so that plans can be made for restocking. The Inventory Turnover (IT) Ratio is a calculation that measures how fast the inventory is sold. As in the measurement of the Accounts Receivable Turnover

Ratio, before figuring the Inventory Turnover Ratio, it is necessary to obtain the value of the average inventory on hand in the practice. Thus, the Average Inventory is found by adding the beginning inventory for the year (or period) to the ending inventory of the previous year (or period) period and dividing by 2 (see Sidebar 4–6).

$$\text{Average Inventory} = \frac{\text{Beginning Inventory} + \text{Ending Inventory}}{2}$$

Once the average inventory is known, the IT ratio is computed by dividing the cost of the goods sold by the average inventory. If, for the year, the IT ratio was 5.9, the inventory will turn almost 6 times each year.

$$\text{Inventory Turnover Ratio} = \frac{\text{Cost of Goods Sold}}{\text{Average Inventory}}$$

As with other activity ratios, the turning of the inventory can be further delineated to reflect how long it takes the inventory to sell out in days by simply dividing 365 by the IT ratio. In this example, if the inventory turns about 6 times per year, then it takes about 61 days for the inventory to sell out. These data assist the manager in planning product orders efficiently throughout the year, ensuring that there is always a fresh, sufficient supply as well as taking advantage of discounts (see Sidebar 4–6).

Total Assets Turnover Ratio

An activity measure that presents how effectively the practice assets are turned into cash is the Total Assets Turnover (TAT) Ratio. In practice the TAT ratio looks at the use of the assets, such as employees, materials, space, equipment, and other assets calculating how effectively these assets were turned into cash for the practice the practice. The TAT ratio looks at the sales for goods and services and divides by the total assets to arrive at how many times the practices assets turn over per year.

$$\text{Total Asset Turnover Ratio} = \frac{\text{Sales}}{\text{Total Assets}}$$

Of course, the higher the TAT value the better as this is an indication that the assets of the practice turn over more times during the year and suggests that the assets are used efficiently (see Sidebar 4-7).

Debt or Leverage Ratios

Two ratios that are beneficial to the practitioner in presenting how much debt the practice has relative to its assets are the Debt to Assets (DA) Ratio and the Times Interest Earned (TIE) Ratio. These ratios give indications whether the practice has the capability to support more debt for the purpose of loans, adding equipment, opening another location, or other activities (Sidebar 4-8).

The Debt to Assets Ratio

The Debt to Assets Ratio (DA) is expressed in percent and offers an indication of how much liability the practice has for every dollar of assets. Creditors can review the debt to assets ratio and obtain insight as to the ability of the practice to withstand losses without impairing the interest of the creditors. Although good and bad Debt to Asset ratios are different for each industry the general goal for most practices should be to keep the

percentage as low as possible. A low Debt to Assets ratio is a goal for the practitioner as the higher the number indicates that the practice is more dependent on borrowed money to sustain itself. Similar to the personal debt to asset ratios familiar for personal loans, Edmonds et al. (2006) indicates that business lenders are concerned if the DA is high, as this suggests that small changes in cash flow might cause serious difficulties in the capability to repay debt. The DA computation is simply the Total Liabilities divided by the Total Assets (also presented in Sidebar 4-8):

$$\text{Debt to Assets Ratio} = \frac{\text{Total Liabilities}}{\text{Total Assets}}$$

Times Interest Earned Ratio (TIE)

Edmonds et al. (2006) indicate that the Times Interest Earned (TIE) ratio is an indication of how many times the practice would be able to pay its interest using earnings. The TIE provides lenders with more information as to the success of the company and its capability to repay loans for expansion projects, or other activities. The TIE is computed by taking the earnings before interest and taxes (EBIT) and dividing it by the interest charges.

$$\text{Times Interest Earned Ratio} = \frac{\text{Earning Before Interest and Taxes}}{\text{Interest Charges}}$$

Freeman et al. (2000) indicate that in audiology practices the TIE should be somewhere between three and five, indicating that the earnings are at least three to five times greater than the interest payments. A TIE that is less than 1 is evidence that the practice cannot pay its interest commitments (see Sidebar 4-8).

Sidebar 4–8
DEBT TO ASSETS (DA) AND THE TIMES INTEREST EARNED (TIE) RATIOS

The DA presents how much liability the practice has for every dollar of assets and provides the creditors with information about the ability of the practice to withstand losses. The DA is simply the total liabilities divided by the total assets from the Balance Sheet. In this example review of the Balance Sheet

$$\text{Debt to Assets Ratio} = \frac{\text{Total Liabilities}}{\text{Total Assets}}$$

Table 4–1 shows Total Liabilities of $117,000 and Total Assets of $320,000.

$$\text{Debt to Assets Ratio} = \frac{\$117,000}{\$320,000} = 36.5\%$$

Dividing the Total Liabilities by the Total Assets yields 36.5%, suggesting that for every dollar of assets the practice has 36.5 cents of debt. Although not serious debt, in practice the debt to assets ratio should be as low as possible.

The times interest earned (TIE) ratio is an indication of how many times the practice earns the amount of interest charged on the money that it has borrowed. The TIE is computed by taking the earnings before interest and taxes (EBIT), and dividing it by the interest expense; both values are obtained from the Income Statement (see Table 4–2).

$$\text{Times Interest Earned Ratio} = \frac{\$39,000}{\$9,000} = 4.3$$

In the example, the EBIT is $39,000, divided by the Interest Expense of $9,000 for a Times Interest Earned Ratio of 4.3 and these ratios should be, according to Freeman et al. (2000), between 3 and 5, and a TIE less than 1 is an indication that the practice cannot pay its bills.

Profitability Ratios

Although most routine calculations presented so far are conducted on the balance sheet, sometimes the ratios that may tell the most about a practice are the profitability ratios. These profitability ratios are clues as to how well the practice has performed and look at whether the practice's net income is adequate, what rate of return was achieved, and profit margin as a percentage of sales. The ratios routinely considered in this group are the Profit Margin on Sales (PMOS) using information from the income statement and the Asset Turnover (AT) Ratio that uses information from both the income statement and the balance sheet discussed earlier in this chapter.

Profit Margin on Sales

The Profit Margin on Sales (PMOS) presents the profit margin achieved after all of the expenses are subtracted and calculates how much of every dollar of sales are profit (Sidebar 4-9). The PMOS is important as it can give you an indication of how much margin there is on each sale or service provided. This calculation can establish if the margins are adequate from period to another so as to sustain the practice. To compute the PMOS, Net Profit is divided by Sales:

$$\text{Profit Margin On Sales} = \frac{\text{Net Profit}}{\text{Sales}}$$

PMOS results are represented in a percentage that reflects the amount of each dollar that is profit. For example, if the calculation yields 20% then $0.20 cents of every dollar collected is profit. These values can be tracked to determine if there are either up or down changes in the ratios that occur during the year (see Sidebar 4-9).

Tying It Together

Unless there is so much cash in the practice that there is never a concern about where it goes, and this is extremely rare, a fundamental monitoring of the health of the practice is essential. The above ratios are certainly not an exhaustive list and the practice accountant may recom-

---

Sidebar 4–9
PROFIT MARGIN ON SALES

The profit margin on sales (PMOS) presents the profit margin achieved after all the expenses are subtracted and presents how much of every dollar of sales are profit. To compute the profit margin on sales, net profit is divided by the net sales. For example, refer to Table 4-2 and find the Net Profit of $350,000 and

$$\text{Profit Margin On Sales} = \frac{\$350,000}{\$1,200,000} = .29$$

the Net Sales of $1,200,00. To arrive at the PMOS simply divide the Net Profit by the Net Sales and obtain .29. This figure means that 29 cents of every dollar is profit from this practice; this figure can be tracked to determine if there are changes that require attention.

mend that other ratios be monitored in addition for special purposes. The ratios presented here should be considered fundamental calculations essential to an overview of financial health. The practitioner should know if the practice is capable of paying the bills and if not, why? Knowledge of how fast the accounts receivable turns into cash is important to the cash flow into the practice and fundamental to paying the bills. Why not know when the inventory will need to be reordered so that cash allocations can be made to facilitate payment? A look at the debt structure, operating costs, and profitability offers a simultaneous sense of reality and security to the practitioner rather than "seat of the pants management."

Just knowledge of these ratios and what they are today, however, does not present the opportunity to make changes in management decisions to modify the health of the practice. Ratios must be tracked and compared to other months, quarters, or years before these calculations unlock the important information essential for management modifications in the practice. Before you can alter an upward or downward trend you need

all the information to make the correct managerial adjustments. By simply creating a spreadsheet and entering data each month, ratio data can be analyzed to manage the practice. Tracking or monitoring ratios allows the practitioner to evaluate the liquidity, activity, debt, and profitability over time to investigate the reasons for successes or failures.

A classic example of how tracking can be of assistance in the explanation of difficulties in the practice is presented in Figure 4-2. Figure 4-2 presents Quick Ratios for Audiology Associates, Inc. for the years 2000 to 2004. A review of the Quick Ratio histograms for the years, 2000, 2001, 2003, and 2004 demonstrates that the Quick ratios are greater than 1 indicating that the practice could pay its bills and even with money left over in 2003 and 2004. In 2002, however, the Quick Ratio was less than 1 suggesting that there were problems paying business bills. In 2002, the practice was having difficulty meeting expenses and even had to borrow funds to meet expenses that year.

Although this information is of great benefit, it must be remembered that all financial statements and the subsequent

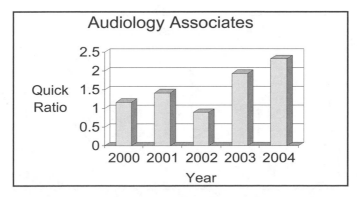

Figure 4–2. Quick ratio for Audiology Associates— 2000–2004.

ratios generated represent specific informational snapshots in a specified window of time. These data reflect how business has been in the past and, due to competition, market pressures, and other significant factors, may or may not be predictors of the health of the business in the future. Ratios can be very helpful in the evaluation of a practice; however, Freeman et al., (2000), Tracy (2001), and Marshall (2004) offer cautions on the use of ratio analyses. They indicate the best information about a company's financial health is determined from comparisons and analyses of a group of ratios, not a single ratio, and that these comparisons need to be made at similar times of the year to arrive at accurate data on the practice's performance. In the example presented in Figure 4-2 simply tracking the Quick Ratio across the years provided information as to what the Quick Ratio was during the good and bad years but it is necessary to review other ratios to explain *why* the Quick Ratio was less than 1 during 2002. Tracking a number of ratios allows the practitioner to search further for differences between 2002 and the other years to ensure that these difficulties are not repeated. By tracking other ratios and comparing them to the Quick Ratios from 2000 to 2004, the answer to the problem experienced by Audiology Associates, Inc. becomes evident. Figure 4-3 presents the tracking of the Accounts Receivable Turnover Ratio (ART) for Audiology Associates, Inc. for the same period 2000 to 2004. Recall that the ART presents how long (in days) it takes for the practice to turn the accounts receivable or credit sales into cash. Figure 4-3 demonstrates that in most years it only takes 40 to 50 days to turn the accounts receivable into cash. In 2002, however, it took over 90 days to clear the accounts receivable.

By reviewing Figures 4-2 and 4-3 together, the practitioner can see at a glance, one possible reason for the problems in 2002. In 2002, when the Quick Ratio documented that it was difficult to pay the bills, the Accounts Receivable Turnover Ratio indicated that it took over 90 days to turn credit sales into cash. When compared to the other years, it took almost twice as long to be paid for products and services in 2002 than the other years, offering a possible explanation for the financial difficulties. Obviously, tracking the various ratios and

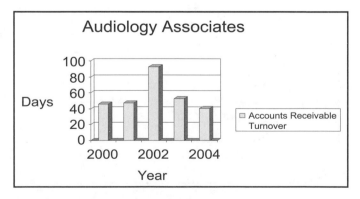

Figure 4–3. Accounts receivable turnover ratio for Audiology Associates—2000 to 2004.

reviewing them over time greatly eases the management burden on practitioners and provides a mirror to reflect the problems in the practice and to fix them before they have had too much impact.

The development of an assessment technique most appropriate to the venue and demographics of a particular practice should be generated to track various important components that should be developed with the guidance of the practice's accountant. Once established, these calculations and others discussed below can be easily monitored on readily available spreadsheets. Managing your practice with the clarity that data provides represents the highest form of evidence-based practice management.

Finance for Audiologists

Generally defined, finance is a discipline that studies and addresses the ways in which individuals, businesses, and organizations raise, allocate, and use monetary resources over time, taking into account the risks entailed in projects that create wealth. Finance is used by individuals (personal finance), by governments (public finance), by businesses (corporate finance), and so forth, as well as by a wide variety of organizations including schools and nonprofit organizations. The goals of each of the above activities are achieved through the use of appropriate financial instruments, with special consideration to their institutional setting. Finance is one of the most important aspects of practice management for without proper financial planning, a new practice cannot even start, let alone be successful. As cash is the single most powerful liquid asset, managing cash is

essential to ensure a secure future, developing wealth for both for an individual practitioner as well as the practice.

For audiology practice management purposes, the term finance incorporates:

- The management and control of assets.
- Profiling and managing project risks.
- Finding funds for the generation and maintenance of business.

When considering financial operations of the practice a special set of techniques are used to manage financial affairs, particularly the differences between income and expenditure while monitoring the risks of their investments. In a profitable practice where income exceeds expenditure, the practitioner can lend or invest the excess income. Excess profit must be invested to build Defensive Assets for the practice or for funding expansions, equipment, or other projects that led to more profit. On the other hand, in an unprofitable practice where income is less than expenditure the practitioner may need to raise capital by borrowing, selling shares in the company, decreasing its expenses, or increasing its income.

Investing the Profit

When the practice is profitable, the profit should be invested to provide a secure background for the practice when business is slow. These savings and investments for the practice are, as presented above, called Defensive Assets to be used when times are difficult to pay employees, accounts payable, and other expenses. Typically, a certain portion of these assets will be kept in a place where they can be rather liquid such as a Certificate of Deposit or a Mutual Fund that allows for transfers to the business account as necessary. The best method of securing and sustaining the investments for the practice is to consult with the practice's accountant and/or an experienced financial planner.

Borrowing Money for the Practice

All businesses have ups and downs in their lifetime. Although the practitioner would rather not need to borrow money, there is usually a time when this is necessary to pay suppliers, employees, and other monthly expenses. Most practitioners know of borrowing from various personal loans, auto loans, educational loans, and other borrowing experiences and loans for the practice work very much the same.

One of the three most important individuals to the practice is a good banker. Without the financial advice and assistance of an experienced financial advisor the practice will have difficulties. Do not just shop for a bank, shop for the *banker*, an individual that knows you, your practice, and your business plan. The correct banker can help with the investment of profits or supply cash infusions as necessary, but it is the individual relationship that makes the difference.

There are always risks involved in borrowing money, so you should carefully analyze your need for it first. Bankrate.com (2007) indicates that the practice's place in the business life cycle will help determine the type of loan you need. There are three basic phases in a company's early years: seed, start-up, and growth.

■ *Seed money* is used for initial planning. These funds sustain during the time that market research is conducted and are also used to

create a business plan. Few small-business owners require a lot of cash for organizing and planning, so this step is typically self-funded.

■ *Start-up funds* are used to get going in business and can vary greatly. This phase may be financed by the owner or a commercial lender. The credibility for the lenders is based on the practitioner's Business Plan (see Chapter 1). Even though the practitioner is a doctor, banks and commercial finance companies are less likely to lend money to start-ups unless there is a significant amount of collateral pledged by the owner. If your collateral does not meet the standards of a conventional loan offered by a bank, the next consideration should be the Small Business Administration (http://www.sba.gov). Your bank may even be a preferred lender with the SBA, and can give you a loan under the SBA-guaranteed loan program where the bank's risk is minimized because the government guarantees payment.

■ *Growth financing* is used when the practitioner has a successful practice and wants or needs to expand. This growth point is when practitioners look to banks or large investors for cash to fund new locations, equipment, and other cash need during a growth phase of the practice.

When money is borrowed for a company, the lender (the bank) receives interest and the practice will pay a higher interest rate than the lender (the bank) pays for the money from the Federal Reserve, and pockets the profit. The bank charges the interest at a rate that reflects their risk in the transaction. Thus, if a loan is considered for a start-up practice with little or no track record the practitioner will usually pay a higher rate than an established practice that has an established clientele and solid financial history. The purpose of the Business Plan (outlined in Chapter 1) is to convince the lenders that the risk for this specific practice is minimal so that the correct amount of funds can be obtained at a reasonable interest rate.

As borrowing money is expensive, Bankrate.com (2007) suggests some points to consider when deciding whether you really need a loan:

- Make sure it is capital you lack, not good cash-flow management.
- Borrow in expectation of needs, not in desperation—or due to the risk, you may have to accept expensive terms.
- If your business is in transition to its next life stage, you probably do have a need for cash to foster growth.
- Have a specific purpose in mind, and be prepared to tell a lender exactly how the money will be used, preferably in a solid business plan.
- Gauge the health of your industry in your business plan; it will make a difference in how favorably your loan proposal is viewed.
- Consider establishing a good credit relationship with a banker by opening accounts or taking out small lines of credit, but don't get into debt without a plan for paying it back.

There are two basic kinds of loans available, *short-term* and *long-term*. Short-term loans generally reach maturity in 1 year or less and can carry you through the doldrum months in a seasonal practice. For example, if your practice is in Arizona and there are no patients in the summer or in northern Minnesota and there are no patients in the winter, lines of credit, working capital loans, and accounts-receivable loans that are repaid in a short term can be essential to survival. Long-term loans usually mature in 1 to 7 years, but can be longer for real estate or equipment. These loans are used for major business expenses such as vehicles, purchasing facilities, construction, and furnishings. They also can be used to carry the practice through a depressed business cycle.

Recently graduated Doctors of Audiology that want to create a start-up practice on their own will have an uphill struggle, despite the accuracy of their well-developed business plan and accurate projections for profitability. Traditional lending institutions will consider the practice, the demographics, and letters of recommendation then, in the end, likely not fund the venture completely. The bank might provide start-up funding and create a flexible line of credit at specific times in the practice's first 3 years but even that is a weak assumption. Glaser (2006) refers to the realities of securing conventional financing for new Au.D. graduates with substantial debt from their education. He states that the note (bank loan) must be secured with assets, not promises of future income, or the note must be cosigned by an individual with the means to repay the note. Debt load (the amount of indebtedness) plays heavily in determining loan eligibility.

Couple the above with the fact that bankers are conservative and skeptical by nature of practitioners with little or no track record or experience in managing a practice. Bankers are in business to lend money but are well aware that often start-up businesses are unsuccessful, especially when those requesting these start-up funds have little training or experience in practice management.

Basic Financial Management

Budgeting

A major error in the financial management of a practice is not planning for the future. One such plan may involve building a budget to use a guideline for the expenditure of funds. Budgeting is the process of developing and adopting a profit and financial plan with definite goals for the coming period. Budgets are financial plans that include forecasting expenses, revenues, assets, liabilities, and cash flows based on a plan that is guided by the goals of the practice manager for a particular period, usually a year. Once the budget is determined, the actual performance of the practice can be compared to the budgeted goals to determine progress or the lack of it.

Tracy (2001) indicates that budgeting in business provides some important advantages. First, the budget facilitates an understanding of the profit dynamics and financial structure of the practice, and second, it becomes the plan for changes in the coming period. The preparation of a budget forces the practice manager to focus on the factors that must improve to increase profit. In most practices, however, it is rare to see a budget planned for more than a year in advance. Although budget preparation can be time consuming and frustrating, it is simply not enough to live day to day in a practice, paying the payables, collecting the receipts, and hoping for enough profit to make it next month. In the absence of a budget or a plan for the future it is possible to end up paying higher taxes, overpay for products, and/or make bad investment choices in equipment and/or in office expansions.

Although budgets for major corporations can be quite complex and take months to complete, for a small Audiology practice the process is relatively simple and can be a painless process if the accounting is conducted accurately. Before beginning the budget, the practice manager needs to make some assumptions about the industry, the local economy, and other factors affecting the business (and audiologic) climate as well as the practices' strategy for the particular period in question. These decisions will drive the budget for its optimism, or conservatism, depending upon the outlook. Although the budgeting process should be conducted with the assistance of an accountant or other business professional, it may be a complex conservative estimate of expenditure if a new practice in the first year or simply a look at the expenditure from the previous year and allotting an amount for each category based on your expected increase or decrease in revenue. Whatever the specific procedure budgeting is well worth the process as it provides a spending plan that is based on a substantial consideration of the practice and the economic climate.

Lease Versus Purchase

As practitioners are involved in learning how to take care of their patients, the idea that money is worth more today than tomorrow may only be a peripheral concept. As money is worth less tomorrow than today the practitioner's hope is that by laying out the capital today, there will be business in the future that will more than offset the expenses. The purchase of items that appreciate make sense because as the dollar is worth less each day, the appreciation usually more than makes up for the devaluation that occurs over time. Items that depreciate are paid for with today's dollars and continue to devalue from the date of purchase until the value finally goes to nothing over time. Thus, it may be wise financial management to purchase your office space, as it does not usually depreciate but to simply pay to use (rent, lease) equipment and avoid the use of working capital to pay for a depreciating asset, such as a new VNG or ABR unit.

Leases often have a lower investment at the beginning, as compared to loans that usually require a down payment of 10 to 20%; however, at the end of the lease payment program you will not own the equipment. It must be turned in or you may choose to purchase it at fair market value, sometimes only $1.00. For office equipment or audiologic equipment with its constant changes, leasing simply makes good sense. As the equipment technology is constantly evolving the capability of the instrument that was purchased today will change over the next 3 to 4 years, possibly outdating it—why own it? The goal then for rapidly changing equipment is to simply have the right

to use it for a specified period of time as it will be worthless in 3 or 4 years.

On the other hand, if the equipment is a sound room that is less sensitive to technology changes, it makes sense to purchase it and then use the room as long as the practice exists without a monthly expense. Business Spreadsheets (2007) and other companies offer pre-prepared Excel spreadsheets that assist in the calculation of the lease purchase decision. These preprepared analysis systems can assist practitioners when the decision is not obvious (Figure 4–4).

Types of Leases

There are a number of different lease products on the market that apply to various situations and types of equipment. Two types that are often used in audiology practices are the Operating Lease and the Financial Lease.

Operating leases, according to Business Victoria (2007), are relatively short-term

Purchase Versus Lease

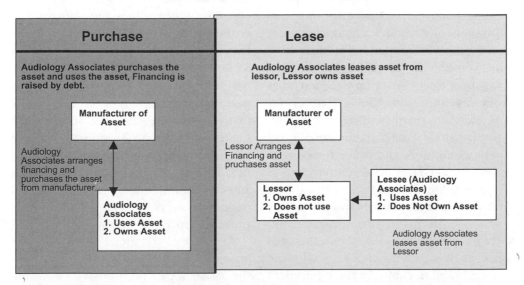

Figure 4–4. Purchase versus lease. (Adapted from *Fundamentals of Corporate Finance*, [p. 549], by R. Brealy, S. Myers, and A. Marcus, 2002, New York: McGraw-Hill.).

contracts for the use of an item. As the term of the contract is relatively short and the payments are lower, the payments made to the leasing company usually are not enough to allow the lessor to fully recover the cost of the asset. As the term of the lease may be less than the economic life of the asset, the remaining value of the item is called a residual value. For example, if you lease a car for 2 years, the car will have a substantial residual value (or leftover value) at the end of the lease, and the lease payments you make will pay off only a fraction of the original cost of the car. The lessor, in an operating lease, expects the lessee to either lease the car again or purchase it for the residual value, or turn it in to the lessor. If turned in the lessor will either lease or sell the item again. Sometimes in operating leases the lessor is responsible for taxes, insurance, and maintenance of the item, which is usually passed on to the lessee in the form of higher payments. Another defining characteristic of the operating lease is that the lessee may have the right to cancel the lease with very short notice by turning in the item and ceasing payments, although this option usually requires a higher payment for the option. Although practices have these operating leases for the automobiles, hearing conservation vans, and other very large items that they will never pay off, there are other types of leases more appropriate to leasing audiometric equipment, computers, and office furniture.

Financial Leases are also referred to as Capital Leases, Lease Purchase, $1 Buyout, or Full Payout Leases and are usually for longer terms involving equipment. Stratus.com (2005), describes a financial lease as being similar to a loan, with the lessee building equity in the equipment as they make each payment. Because of this, the lessee has to account for the asset as a conditional sale and must depreciate the equipment as a capital asset. At lease termination, the lessee may purchase the item at fair market value, fixed price, or for some items, such as equipment or software, or a $1 purchase option is usually available for higher payment. The term for these financial leases must exceed 75% of the estimated economic life of the leased property and the value of all the lease payments must be equal to 90% or more of the cost of the leased property.

Leasing of equipment for an audiology practice can have significant advantages as there are usually major changes in the equipment over a short time. Audiology is traditionally an "equipment poor" discipline in that our profession is extremely sensitive to changes in technology. For example, it took almost 10 years to replace the 1982 Nicolet CA 1000 ABR unit in our practice. The old beast was a workhorse remembered very fondly as a rugged, reliable, and accurate device used for years after its lease was fully paid. The Biologics Traveler that replaced it, however, was replaced in 3 to 4 years due to the changes in software, transducers, and other technologic changes that ensued during that time. By the time the lease was fully paid, it was purchased for $1.00 and used occasionally, but it was basically out of date. Obsolescence is part of our profession just as it is part of many other professions that utilize equipment for analysis and rehabilitative treatment of various physiologic difficulties. Leasing of audiometric equipment and computers that support the clinical operation supports the practitioner as presented in Table 4–4.

As with all financial decisions, the lease/purchase should be considered with the assistance of the practice's accountant who appreciates the balance sheet implications of each option.

Capital Investment Projects— Rates of Return

In audiology there is often the need to open a new location to expand the practice into another lucrative market. As the expansion will not likely be funded internally, it is necessary to go to the bank for a loan to secure appropriate space, develop needed leasehold improvements, and obtain requisite business and clinical equipment for the new office. Although this seems simple enough, the banker wants to know, "How long will it take you to 'break even' on this project; or, "Is the Net Present Value on this project positive or negative?" The question the banker is really asking is, will it be profitable, and if not, how long until the project pays for itself.

The banker needs to make certain there is a high likelihood for success in this new venture. After all, they will be providing funding and the bank wants to ensure they can receive consistent payments on the loan. In every business

Table 4–4. Equipment Acquisition—Leasing Versus Purchase

Lease	Purchase
Conserves Capital No down payment	**Consumes Capital** Down payment required
Flexibility of Payments Lease payments are fixed and do not change with interest rate fluctuation	**Specified Payments** According to Interest rate, term of loan may change with interest rate fluctuation
Convenience On the spot financing and immediate delivery	**Inconvenience** Apply for loan, credit application, counts against debt of the practice
Protection Against Obsolescence a lease can be structured to include upgrades and partial or complete equipment swaps either at mid-term or at lease-end.	**Cannot Turn in for Updates** What you bought is what you get . . . forever
Eliminates Risk At the end of the lease it is turned in or bought for $1.00	**More Risk** Must junk it, use it, or sell it at the end of the loan
Off-Balance Sheet Financing Can potentially increase borrowing capacity while easing the budgeting process and preserving key financial ratios	**On-Balance Sheet Financing** Uses up precious capital and causes debt ratio to be higher
Improved Return on Assets (ROA)	**Less Return on Assets (ROA)**
Paid with BEFORE-Tax Dollars	**Paid with AFTER-Tax Dollars**

venture, there must be a solid plan that realistically forecasts profitability for a proposed expansion. As presented in Chapter 1, with a sound Business Plan and realistic financial projections in hand, the bank is more likely to loan the funds for the project at a favorable interest rate. There are a number of methods that can be used to figure the rate of return on your project, however, two methods commonly used; are the Break-Even Analysis (BA) and/or the Net Present Value (NPV).

Break-Even Analysis (BA)

According to Kasewurm (2000), the break-even analysis provides a sales objective, expressed in either dollar or unit sales, at which the business will be breaking even (also discussed in Chapter 3). Described more technically by Brealey et al. (2002), the break-even analysis is the level of sales at which profits are zero or the point at which total revenues equal total costs. The calculation of a break-even analysis involves the use of the formula:

$$\text{Break-Even (B)} = \frac{\text{Fixed}}{(\text{Gross Profit per Unit} - \text{Variable Costs})}$$

In the calculation of a break-even analysis, the fixed expenses are simply divided by the gross profit minus expenses to come up with the number of sales (or audiometric procedures or hearing aids) that it costs to break even. Of course, the practitioner is in business to make a profit and hopes to see many more procedures sold than to simply enough to break even (Sidebar 4–10).

Moser (2006) indicates that any expenditure made in the hope of generating more cash later can be called a Capital Investment Project. For these large capital investment projects it is best to incorporate a calculation that considers the initial investment, everyday operation expenses, and the interest rate at which the funds for the project were borrowed. Although there are a number of financial calculations that attempt to predict the success of capital investment projects, a relatively simple calculation is the Net Present Value (NPV) (Sidebar 4–11). The key to understanding the NPV calculation is, as indicated previously, the concept that the value of money is less tomorrow than it is today. This is why banks and other financial institutions charge interest. The value of the money may be less tomorrow but also the use of this money means that it cannot be used for another purpose if it is used in your particular project.

In capital investment projects it is often necessary to know if there is a possibility that the project will be successful while still in the planning stages. This allows the practitioner to choose the most successful project among a number of proposals based on the calculated NPV. The chosen project is the one that has the highest return and a positive NPV value. Moser (2006) make a straightforward statement about negative NPV that all projects that carry a negative NPV are losers and should not be attempted. The rules for the use of NPV indicate that the value of the practice will be increased by conducting those capital investment projects that are worth more than they cost—projects with a positive NPV.

Capital investment calculations, such as NPV and other project evaluations, should be conducted with the assistance of the practice accountant to ensure accuracy of the cash flow predictions.

Sidebar 4–10
BREAK-EVEN ANALYSIS

Described more technically by Brealey et al. (2002), the break-even analysis is the level of sales at which profits are zero or the point at which total revenues equal total costs. The calculation of a break-even analysis involves the use of the formula:

$$\text{Break-even (B)} = \frac{\text{Fixed}}{(\text{Gross Profit per Unit} - \text{Variable Costs})}$$

For example, Audiology Associates wants to open a new location for its diagnostic evaluations at the local hospital. At this alternative location, the practice will receive referrals from local physicians for routine audiometric evaluations, otoacoustic emission evaluations, videonystagmography, and auditory brainstem response evaluations. In the example offered in Table 4-5, the variable costs for items to conduct the tests, such as electrodes, forms, and insurance discounts are an average of $78.00 per patient and the fixed costs for the new center are $4,500 per month to keep the clinic open. These fixed costs include an audiologist's salary, receptionist salary, rent, phone, and lease payments for equipment. For the full diagnostic services each patient is billed an average of $350.00.

Therefore, the question to the practitioner that owns Audiology Associates is how many units of service must be provided each month to break even? Using the break-even analysis calculation, simply take the fixed expenses of $4,500 divided by the gross profit per unit ($350) minus the variable costs ($78).

$$\text{Break-even (B)} = \frac{\$4,500}{(\$350 - \$78)}$$

$$\text{Break-even (B)} = \frac{\$4,500}{(\$272)} \text{ BA } = 16.54$$

Table 4–5. Costs for the Diagnostic Center Break-Even Analysis

Audiology Associates, Inc.		
Diagnostic Center		
Fixed Costs per month	Personnel, lease payments, space, phone, etc.	$4,500
Variable costs @100 Units	Insurance discount, forms, supplies, etc.	$ 78
Average Fee	Billed per patient	$ 350

From this analysis, the clinic must bill for 16.54 or 17 procedures each month to just break even. Of course, as this is only the point where the clinic breaks even, one hopes there will be substantially more than 17 units of service each month so that the new diagnostic center can stay in business.

Sidebar 4–11
NET PRESENT VALUE (NPV) CALCULATION

Probably the most accurate technique to use in the estimation of the payoff for a remodeling or expansion project is one that actually considers the initial investment in addition to the everyday operational expenses and the interest rate at which the funds were borrowed. One method is to look at a calculation of the Net Present Value or NPV often used by corporations to describe a number of project proposals allowing the manager to choose the project that will have the highest return and a positive NPV value. All projects, according to Brealey et al. (2002) that carry a negative NPV are losers and should not be attempted. A simple definition of the Net Present Value (NPV) of a project or investment is that it presents the sum of the present values of the annual cash flows minus the initial investment. In a new clinic site these annual cash flows are the Net Benefits (revenues minus costs) generated from the new clinic site during its lifetime. In the NPV calculation these cash flows are discounted or adjusted by incorporating the uncertainty or risk of the success of the clinic and time value of money. In financial literature, the NPV offers the most robust financial evaluation to estimate the overall value of an investment.

Basically, the NPV calculation is to determine the time required and the projected cash fow to repay the capital outlay (Co) for the project. Although there are Internet calculators for NPV, Odellion (2005) states that the calculation of NPV involves three simple yet nontrivial steps. The first step is to identify the size and timing of the expected future cash flows generated by the project or investment. The second step is to determine the discount rate or the estimated rate of return for the project. The third step is to calculate the NPV using the equations shown below:

$$NPV = Co + \frac{\text{Cash Flow Year 1}}{(1 + r)} + \frac{\text{Cash Flow Year 2}}{(1 + r)^2} + \frac{\text{Cash Flow Year 3}}{(1 + r)^3}$$

Consider the example in Table 4–6, where the cost to remodel the space for the new diagnostic Audiology center at the hospital is $27,000. The clinic can borrow the funds for this project at 6.5% for the project. This $27,000 includes items such as furniture, carpet, lighting, creating treatment rooms, reception area, wall coverings, art, and other appointments. The clinic also has some extra equipment that will be used in the new facility

Table 4–6. Costs for Diagnostic Center NPV

Audiology Associates, Inc.
Diagnostic Center
Initial Investment
Remodel Space (Borrowed at 6.5% Interest Rate) $27,000
Estimated Cash Flows
Year 1 .... $25,000
Year 2 .... $40,000
Year 3 .... $75,000
Future Value of Practice if Successful $75,000

so there is no equipment cost. Cash flow estimates have been estimated by the accountant with input from the practitioner at $20,000 for year 1, $40,000 for year 2, and $75,000 at year 3. It is expected that after 3 years of operation; the new clinic could be worth $75,000.

$$NPV = \$27,000 + \frac{\$25,000}{1.065} + \frac{\$40,000}{1.134} + \frac{\$75,000}{1.207}$$

$$NPV = \$27,000 + \$23,474.17 + \$35,273.36 + \$62,137.53$$

$$NPV = \$93,885.06$$

As this is a highly positive NPV, the project should be conducted.

Epilogue

Fiscal management is fundamentally the practitioner's accountability for the practice. A fiscally responsible practitioner not only knows where the funds are, who needs payment, and when they need to be paid, but also is current on ever changing costs and how to adjust to them. By reviewing financial statements and ratios regularly and tracking comparisons with other periods for monthly, quarterly, or yearly comparisons, the changes in the landscape of the practice are evident. Knowledge of how to manage a fiscally responsible practice opens up many new horizons for the practitioner as to how to adjust to the external and internal changes in the environment.

Finance is an area where most audiologists have no interest or background. A chief financial officer (CFO) is the chief financial policymaker in the company with duties often extending into many other areas including accounting, budgeting, and capital investment. Wise practice CFOs borrow smartly, expand cautiously, and invest in sound projects that will bring future success to the practice. Good financial investment may even counteract business problems, such as equipment breakdowns, slow business, or other unforeseen emergencies; providing a source of unencumbered cash to augment income as the situation changes. As the audiologist is usually the CFO of their own practice, it is necessary to understand the accounting process, and know how to review and track financial statements, prepare budgets to plan for the efficient use of funds, and calculate the benefits and realities of expenditure projects in our unrelenting quest for the unencumbered cash. Our goal with this chapter was to introduce the new practitioner to fiscal management, offer specific management points for increase efficiency to those that have been in practice for some time, and present the case that it is no longer safe and prudent to manage practices by the "seat of the pants." In today's competitive market, where most of us are doctors, these "seat of the pants" managers will fall by the wayside, victims of their own ignorance of the numbers and their valuable insight.

References

Bankrate.com . (2007). *Small business basics*. Retrieved April 3, 2007, from http://www.bankrate.com/brm/news/biz/green/19990823b.asp

Brealey, R., Myers, S., & Marcus, A. (2002). *Fundamentals of corporate finance*. New York: McGraw-Hill.

Business Spreadsheets. (2007). *Lease versus purchase decisions*. Retrieved April 6, 2007, from http://www.business-spreadsheets.com/solutions.asp?prod=91

Businesstown. (2003a). *The balance sheet*. Retrieved March 25, 2005, from http://www.businesstown.com/accounting/basic-sheets.asp

Businesstown. (2003b). *The income statement*. Retrieved March 25, 2005, from http://www.businesstown.com/accounting/basic-sheets.asp

Business Victoria. (2007). *Types of leases*. Business Victoria, Victoria, Australia, Retrieved April 6, 2007, from http://www.business.vic.gov.au/BUSVIC/STANDARD/1001/PC_50080.html

Dunn, D. (2000). *Managerial accounting for daily and long-term practice success*. In H. Hosford-Dunn, R. Roeser, & M. Valente (Eds.), *Audiology practice management* (pp. 337–349). New York: Thieme.

Edmonds, T., Edmonds, C., McNair, F., Olds, P., & Schneider, N. (2006). *Fundamental financial accounting concepts* (pp. 124–125). New York: McGraw-Hill.

Freeman, B., Barimo, J., & Fox, G. (2000). Financial management of audiology practices and clinics. In H. Hosford-Dunn, R. Roeser, & M. Valente (Eds.), *Audiology practice management* (pp. 351–362). New York: Thieme.

Glaser, R. (2006). Point/counterpoint on issues in ethics. *Hearing Journal, 59*(10), 44.

Kasewurm, G. (2000). Business plan and practice accounting. In H. Hosford-Dunn, R. Roeser, & M. Valente (Eds.), *Audiology practice management* (pp. 313–336). New York: Thieme.

Marshall, D. H. (2004). *Accounting: What the numbers mean* (6th ed., pp. 238–247). New York: McGraw-Hill.

McNamara, C. (2007). *Profit and loss statements*. Authenticity Consulting, LLC. Retrieved April 7, 2007, from: http://www.managementhelp.org/finance/fp_fnce/fp_fnce.htm#anchor561785

Moser, K. (2006). *Lecture notes from Finance 544*. Phoenix, AZ: University of Phoenix.

Newman, P. (2006). *11 expectations to be set for your bookkeeper*. Entrepeneur.com: Retrieved August 2, 2006, from http://smallbusiness.aol.com/manage/managing/article/_a/11-expectations-to-set-for-your/20060801161009990001

Odellion. (2005). *NPV equation*. Odellion Research Group. Retrieved July 24, 2005, from: http://www.odellion.com/pages/financial%20models/NPV/financialmodels_npv_equations.htm

Stratus.com. (2005). *Advantages of leasing*. Stratus Technologies Bermuda, Ltd., Retrieved July 27, 2005, from http://www.stratus.com/leasing/advant.htm

Tracy, J. (2001). *Accounting for dummies*. (2nd ed.). Hoboken, NJ: Wiley.

5

Coding, Billing, and Reimbursement Capture

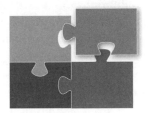

DEBRA ABEL, Au.D. AND ROBERT G. GLASER, Ph.D.

Introduction

As audiologists, we have historically experienced road bumps with coding, reimbursement, and the recognition by third party payors for the work we do. We have had a long, arduous road of educating those third party payors as to that work as well as defining "audiology" on a national as well as grass roots level. Consequently, this education has also been conducted within the hallowed halls of the Center for Medicare and Medicaid Services, otherwise known as CMS. Many third party payors look to CMS, the Resource-Based Relative Value Scale (RBRVS), and the Medicare Physician Fee Schedule (MPFS) as the benchmark for establishing fee schedules, thereby perpetuating this flawed, inefficient system. The RBRVS and the MPFS are discussed on the next pages of this chapter. It is critical to understand the process of where we have been and where we are going in terms of autonomy and professionalism.

In addition to the reimbursement side, there are a plethora of issues and concerns to consider when contemplating the foray into independent practice, some legal and some practical.

At the time of the publication of this book, CMS has recognition for audiologists only as diagnosticians and not providers for the treatment of hearing and balance disorders such as rehabilitation of hearing loss, tinnitus management, and the management of the patient experiencing dysequilibrium. Unfortunately, many of the third party payors with whom we interact look to Medicare for these standards that have been imposed.

With the advent of the Au.D. and the advancement of the profession of Audiology to a doctoring profession, evolutionary change has occurred with some third party payors as well as with managed care and likely will continue. It is incumbent on us to educate these third party payors as to who we are, what we do, and what the services are that we can provide to their subscribers. If a Medical Director of an insurance company does not recognize audiologists as health care providers, local audiologists are encouraged to meet with him or her and embark on a mission of education. In your armament, you will want to have the American Academy of Audiology's scope of practice and redacted copies of several Explanations of Benefits (EOBs) from competitors providing reimbursement for audiologic services. The intent of this meeting is not only to educate the Medical Director about audiology but to provide information regarding the cost-savings benefits with the expertise we can provide to those patients in need of our services.

The Code Valuation Process

To understand coding, one needs to know how a code is valued and the formula that it is based on for reimbursement. Medicare bases payments on the Resource-Based Relative Value Scale (RBRVS). There are three components that establish the relative value unit (RVU). The first component is the practice expense (PE). This includes the overhead of operating and maintaining an office: the rent, the office's physical liability coverage, staff expenses, and the disposables needed for the equipment you have, for example.

The second component is work or cognition. Codes that historically have had the professional work component are auditory brainstem response (92585), the ENG family of codes (92541-92546 and 92548), and also comprehensive or diagnostic evaluation [comparison of transient and/or distortion product otoacoustic emissions at multiple levels and frequencies] (92588). These codes have the TC or technical component and also the professional component or—26. This enables an audiologist to bill the code globally which means the audiologist completed the procedure and the interpretation. If one only does the procedure, then the technical component is billed. If one only does the interpretation, then the professional code is billed. This enables another professional to bill the other component of what they performed.

Beginning in 2008, nine additional CPT codes will have the professional work component. The five diagnostic codes are comprehensive audiometry threshold evaluation (92557), Tympanometry (92567), Acoustic Reflex Threshold Testing (92568), Reflex Decay

(92569), and Visual Reinforcement Audiometry (92579). The 4 cochlear implant programming codes are Diagnostic analysis of cochlear implant, patient under 7 years of age; with programming (92601), subsequent reprogramming (92602), Diagnostic analysis of cochlear implant, age 7 years or older; with programming (92603) and subsequent reprogramming (92604).

The third component of the RVU is liability or malpractice. "Work" comprises 50% of the total payment. Practice expense accounts for 45% and the professional liability/malpractice accounts for the remaining 5% of the total payment.

Coding Formula Components

Each of the three components including PE, work, and liability are multiplied by a geographic index (GI) for the specific area of the country in which the provider practices. For example, the costs of a metropolitan office will be higher in California than in a rural area in Arkansas. This segment of the formula is multiplied by a conversion factor determined annually by Medicare (CF). The formula is expressed below:

$$RVU = (Work \times GI) + (Practice\ Expense \times GI) + (Liability \times GI) \times CF$$

The Evolution of the Current Procedural Terminology (CPT) Codes

As we open our new CPT manuals every fall to see if there are any new CPT codes that we can implement in our practices,

it is helpful to know the process involved in the development of the codes. The American Medical Association (AMA) has owned the 8,000 plus CPT codes since 1966, about the same time Medicare was developed as a health care entity. The intent was to standardize codes for procedures performed and submitted to third party payors for reimbursement and for health care related data collection. CPT codes comprise one of the components of the transaction and code sets of the Health Insurance Portability and Accountability Act (HIPAA) which also includes the International Classification of Diseases-9-CM codes (ICD-9-CM, the diseases/diagnoses codes), and the Healthcare Common Procedures Coding System (HCPCS) that includes ancillary services and supplies including hearing instrument related expenses not addressed by CPT codes. CPT code usage is tracked and included in the database of the AMA Specialty Society Relative Value Scale Update Committee (RUC). As each health care provider is identified by their unique, National Provider Identifier (NPI), audiologists will be more accurately portrayed relative to the CPT codes used and tracked. For example, audiologists will likely be recognized as the leading provider billing CPT code 92557, comprehensive audiometry threshold evaluation and speech recognition (92553 and 92556 combined).

Initiating a New CPT Code

A code request can be initiated by anyone. The majority of requests emanate from interested parties such as professional organizations. When a potential code will be utilized by several interested organizations, they will often submit a code request together. There are several requirements in submitting a code request. The request must be accompanied by five articles peer reviewed in the United States and an extensive vignette detailing the utility of the procedure for a "typical patient."

The CPT Editorial Panel is responsible for revising or updating the CPT codes. This 17-member panel is composed of 11 physicians representing the AMA, one each from Blue Cross and Blue Shield Association, the Health Insurance Association of America, The American Hospital Association, and the Centers for Medicare and Medicaid Services (CMS), and the co-chair and a representative of the Health Care Professionals Advisory Committee (HCPAC) (AMA, 2004). There are term limits of a maximum of two 4-year terms for seven members. The remaining four members have one term of four years. This allows different specialties to "sit at the table."

There are two other groups involved in this process: the CPT HCPAC and the RUC HCPAC. The CPT HCPAC reviews the code requests. The HCPAC is vital to Audiology as this group is composed of limited licensed practitioners and other allied health professionals (AMA, 2004). The HCPAC reviews the two higher weighted components of the RVU, the work and practice expense components. The RUC HCPAC reviews recommendations on the RVU's for nonphysician specialties' work and practice expenses. The Performance Measures Advisory Committee (PMAC) represents the professional organizations who are concerned with performance measures (AMA, 2004).

The CPT Editorial Panel meets three times per calendar year to consider new code requests or revision of existing codes. Code requests can be tabled or rejected: If accepted, the new code will appear in the next printing of the CPT Manual. There are three categories of codes that reflect usage (Category I), performance measurements (Category II), and performance of emerging technologies (Category III). The American Academy of Audiology and related professional organizations submit new code requests under Category I. A Category I code must show that there are no other procedures with existing codes that might be reportable; that peer-reviewed literature establishes the clinical efficacy of the procedure; and that the procedure can be performed by qualified practitioners throughout the United States (AMA, 2004).

Billing Practices: Third Party Payors

Audiologists will use all three coding systems in the course of their practice: CPT, ICD-9-CM, and HCPCS. Current manuals should be in every audiology office regardless of practice venue. The five-digit CPT codes contain and describe the procedures that audiologists commonly perform. The ICD-9 codes delineate underlying pathology and are intimately related to appropriate procedural codes. HCPCS codes are the supply codes that specify styles of hearing instruments, assistive listening devices, and related items.

Patients coming to your office for services have a specific contract with their insurance plans. These insurance plans, often referred to as the "third party payors," specify the procedures and products covered under the terms of the policy. The policy will establish a payment schedule for services rendered or for hearing instruments or other devices necessary to complete the treatment regimen of the insured. The terms of the policy specify their discounted rate at which they will reimburse each procedural code. Some payors will pay 80%, some 50%, and all will establish payment ceilings for each procedural code. If you submit a code with a fee that is less than the ceiling amount, the payor will pay you the amount you have submitted. If you submit a code with a fee that exceeds the ceiling amount, you will be reimbursed at the established ceiling amount. As a participating provider in that particular health care plan, you have agreed to accept assignment and, therefore, you must accept the reimbursement you receive.

Important Third Party Payor Issues to Be Considered

In the event that you have submitted fees that exceed the ceiling amounts to be paid, the patient will have an unpaid balance on his or her account. Many third party payors prohibit billing the patient for that balance and expect the practice to write off the remaining charges on the patient's account. A few third party payors will permit balance billing of the patient; however, the trend has been to prohibit such billing tactics. Practitioners must consider the advice of Pessis and Williams (2005) when dealing with third party payors: Insurance is a *mechanism* for reimbursement, not a form of payment (Pessis & Williams, 2005).

It should be quite clear that the practitioner must review each contract carefully so that he or she experiences no surprises when the check arrives. Unfortunately, audiologists have not had a great track record when it comes to turning down an opportunity to become a participating provider in a health care plan. Many have signed on to plans that offer little more than break-even revenue just to be recognized as a provider. Perhaps this rush to join will diminish as audiologists become more discerning about health care plan schedules of reimbursement and policies that affect the bottom line of their practices. There is no excuse for anything less than careful scrutiny of all relevant documents that describe the levels of participation in the plan, the reimbursement and expected discounts, and their usual payment turnaround times from submission of a claim to receiving the check. Every practitioner must ask the tough question; what if I do not participate in this particular plan? If it is the only game in town, you may have little choice: If it is a plan that reimburses less than 50% of the other plans in which the practice participates, it may not be worthwhile to spend the same amount of time on this patient as it would to spend the time on patients with better reimbursement opportunities.

Unfortunately, some third party payors offer reimbursement levels that are simply cost prohibitive. If you are in doubt about the reimbursement levels or the language in the plan, have a representative of the plan come to your office for clarification. Prior to the meeting, generate a list of questions based on the levels of reimbursement and other policy-related issues that seem unclear to you or your office staff. Have your accountant review the plan. He or she will provide insight based on cash flow, reasonability of reimbursement rates and specific sections that might prohibit successful integration of the plan into your established lineup of third party payors.

The representative of the health care plan should address each of your questions and concerns and reference the specific language in the provider agreement relative to your inquiries. You should receive answers that are in concert with the language in the plan. If not, ask the representative to put their interpretation in writing so that should questions arise in the future, you can produce the interpretation of their employee rather than relying on your own interpretation of their reimbursement policies. If he or she is unable to commit to writing what is offered as an interpretation of their policy, consider asking their superior for written clarification or simply withdraw your application to become a participating provider. If you are already a participating provider in the plan, you may choose to disengage from your commitment as a participating provider. Some plans will indicate that as you have signed on as a participating provider that you, therefore, must see patients covered by their plan for the duration of the length of the contract. Should this situation arise, you will need to consult your attorney to determine the best way to remove yourself from their roster of providers. Had your attorney reviewed the documents prior to your signing, he or she would have likely pointed out the implied or real level of your commitment and offered suggestions to adjust, lessen, or perhaps pass on the opportunity. Just as it is a good idea to have your accountant review participating provider agreements relative to the fiscal impact, it is recommended that the attorney for the practice review the agreement as well. It is money well spent.

Types of Third Party Payors

There are many types of third party payors: federally supported Medicare; federal- and state-supported Medicaid; Tricare (government benefits for active duty, retired military, and their dependents); private carriers such as United Health Care, Blue Cross/Blue Shield, and Aetna; Health Maintenance Organizations (HMO); Preferred Provider Organizations (PPO); Point of Service (POS) and Fee for Service (FFS) organizations.

Medicare

The Medicare supplementary health insurance programs for those 65 years and older was signed into law by President Lyndon Johnson on July 30, 1965. Medicare covers 43 million beneficiaries and provides health insurance for those who are blind, those who have been on disability for at least 2 years, and individuals with end-stage renal disease (ESRD) (CMS Web site, 2005). Medicare is often their primary insurance, but with more people over age 65 remaining in the workforce, Medicare may be secondary to their employers' health care benefit.

Medicare's Definition of an Audiologist as a Diagnostician

CMS Program Memorandum AB-02-080 states that " . . . diagnostic testing, including hearing and balance assessment services, performed by a qualified audiologist is paid for as 'other diagnostic tests' under §1861 (s)(3) of the Social Security Act (the Act) when a physician orders testing to obtain information as part of his/her diagnostic evaluation or to deter-mine the appropriate medical or surgical treatment of a hearing deficit or related medical problem" (CMS, 2002). It further states that services are excluded by virtue of §1862 (a)(7) of the Act when the diagnostic information is already known to the physician, or the diagnostic services are performed only to deter-mine the need for or the appropriate type of hearing instrument" (CMS, 2002) (Sidebar 5–1).

Sidebar 5–1
CMS PROGRAM MEMORANDUM AB-02-080

(Rev. 1, 10-01-03)
B3-2070.3, PM-B-01-34, B-02-004, PM AB-02-080

Diagnostic testing, including hearing and balance assessment services, per-formed by a qualified audiologist is covered as "other diagnostic tests" under §1861(s)(3) of the Act when a physician orders such testing for the pur-poses of obtaining information necessary for the physician's diagnostic eval-uation or to determine the appropriate medical or surgical treatment of a hearing deficit or related medical problem. Services are excluded by virtue of §1862(a)(7) of the Act when the diagnostic information required to deter-mine the appropriate medical or surgical treatment is already known to the physician, or the diagnostic services are performed only to determine the need for or the appropriate type of hearing aid.

Diagnostic services performed by a qualified audiologist and meeting the above requirements are payable as "other diagnostic tests." The payment for these services is determined by the reason the tests were performed, rather than the diagnosis or the patient's condition. Payment for these services is based on the physician fee schedule amount except for audiology services furnished in a hospital outpatient department which are paid under the Out-patient Prospective Payment System. Nonhospital entities billing for the audiologist's services may accept assignment under the usual procedure or, if not accepting assignment, may charge the patient and submit a non-assigned claim on their behalf.

If a physician refers a beneficiary to an audiologist for evaluation of signs or symptoms associated with hearing loss or ear injury, the audiologist's diagnostic services should be covered even if the only outcome is the prescription of a hearing aid. If a beneficiary undergoes diagnostic testing performed by an audiologist without a physician referral, the tests are not covered even if the audiologist discovers a pathologic condition.

80.3.1—Definition of Qualified Audiologist

(Rev. 1, 10-01-03)
B3-2070.3

<u>Section 1861(11)(3)</u> of the Act, provides that a qualified audiologist is an individual with a master's or doctoral degree in audiology and who:

- Is licensed as an audiologist by the State in which the individual furnishes; such services; or
- In the case of an individual who furnishes services in a State which does not license audiologists has:
  - Successfully completed 350 clock hours of supervised clinical practicum (or is in the process of accumulating such supervised clinical experience),
  - Performed not less than nine months of supervised full-time audiology services after obtaining a master's or doctoral degree in audiology or a related field, and
  - Successfully completed a national examination in audiology approved by the Secretary.

CMS Recognition of Audiologists and the Primary Care Provider

Since 2005, Medicare beneficiaries who are new to Medicare (within the first 6 months of enrollment) are entitled to an initial physical examination by their physician. Hearing and balance disorders are addressed by screening questionnaires approved by the American Academy of Audiology and the American Speech-Language-Hearing Association. This represents a distinct opportunity for audiologists in that hearing and balance difficulties may become the focus of further study based on the screening questionnaires. As the role of audiologists as participants in the diagnosis of hearing and balance disorders has been clarified by CMS, audiologists can advise primary care and other health care providers that CMS recognizes audiologists as participating providers in the clinical evaluation of hearing and balance disorders.

Additionally, it provides an opportunity to educate other health care providers and their respective clinical and administrative staffs about the limiting effects of hearing loss. Despite the fact that Medicare does not cover hearing instruments, contemporary treatment options including hearing instruments can and should be discussed as an effective treatment option. Physicians and their clinical staffs should also be informed about appropriate evaluation of their patients with dysequilibrium. Beyond diagnostic vestibular studies, methods of assessing fall risk, and providing appropriate fall avoidance training for patients with balance difficulties should be discussed as an available and important treatment option in their continuing medical management of their patients.

Medicare Regions and Fiscal Intermediaries

Medicare currently has 10 regions administered by assigned fiscal intermediaries and carriers. In the next few years, these 10 regions will be reconfigured to 15 regional jurisdictions to balance the allocation of workloads, promote competition, account for integration of claims processing activities, and mitigate the risk to the Medicare program during the transition to the new contractors (http://www.cms.hhs.gov, 2007). The new jurisdictions will reasonably balance the number of fee-for-service beneficiaries and providers. These jurisdictions will be substantially more alike in size than the existing fiscal intermediary and carrier jurisdictions, and will promote much greater efficiency in processing Medicare's billion plus claims a year (http://www.cms.hhs.gov, 2007).

As each region has the authority to interpret the Medicare statute independently, Medicare regulations may not be the same or consistent from region to region. You will want to have at your disposal the local coverage determination (LCD) policy for your region as well as the Medicare Physician Fee Schedule (MPFS), updated annually, for your region (http://www.cms.hhs.gov, 2007). Embedded in the LCD policies are the CPT and ICD-9-CM codes accepted for patient care when submitting billing for services provided to Medicare beneficiaries. The Medicare regional carrier is responsible for reviewing and paying those claims. As this fee schedule changes annually, each practice should review the schedule and make adjustments to the practice's fees accordingly. Medicare regional carriers welcome inquiries and calls about clarification of coverage. Regional offices will, from time to time, offer no-charge courses to familiarize providers with Medicare requirements. Those responsible for billing and reimbursement capture in the practice should attend whenever possible.

The Four Segments of Medicare: A, B, C, D

Medicare is composed of four parts: Part A (hospital-based services), Part B (typically outpatient services), Part C (Medicare HMO's, often having audiologic benefits for diagnosis, annual monitoring and, in some local areas, hearing instrument benefits), and Part D (prescription drugs).

Part A. Hospital-Based Services

The following components comprise Medicare Part A: Hospitalization, Home Health Care, Hospice Care, and Skilled Nursing Care after hospital discharge. As audiologists providing services in hospital settings are operating under Part A, those who bill as independent practitioners must be appropriately contracted with the hospital. The hospital will reimburse the independent audiologist for services provided as part of the patient's Diagnostic Related Group (DRG). The

Joint Commission for Accreditation of Healthcare Organizations (JCAHO) credentials hospitals and only those hospitals with this accreditation will be reimbursed by Medicare. Part A Medicare is funded by payroll taxes, self-employed individual contributions, and contributions from railroad workers and their employers (Hobot, Medicare New Provider Training, 2006).

Part B. Outpatient Services

Medicare recipients with Part B coverage are eligible for reimbursement of outpatient services. This coverage includes all physician office visits as well as visits to audiologists in independent private practices, community speech and hearing centers, and to those audiologists in ENT-audiology practices, Part B lists the following general categories wherein expenses will likely be covered: Outpatient medical services, ambulatory surgical services, home health care, and laboratory services. Each Medicare region has a local coverage determination (LCD) policy. This describes in detail what functionally constitutes the procedure, which CPT and ICD-9-CM codes that may be utilized, and other parameters that each Medicare provider needs to be familiar with. LCDs can be obtained online at http://www.cms.hhs.gov. Part B Medicare is funded by Medicare premium payments, contributions from general revenues, and interest earned on the Part B Trust Fund (Hobot, Medicare New Provider Training, 2006).

Part B providers have several categories in which to provide services. Participating Provider (Par provider) status is the most common category in which audiologists participate in Medicare. The other categories, Non-participating Provider and Limiting Provider, are not as common for audiologists and are not considered in this chapter.

Patients covered by Medicare likely comprise a significant portion of your practice. Even if that group is not the primary demographic for your practice, patients will appreciate your participation in Medicare. Medicare will pay the provider 80% of the Medicare Physician Fee Schedule for the procedures performed. The patient pays their 20% co-insurance at the time of their visit to the audiologist. The 20% co-insurance payment must be paid at the time of service, unless a secondary insurance benefit is in effect. If so, Medicare will automatically forward the claim to the secondary insurer which will likely cover the 20% co-insurance.

Participating providers may choose to "opt out" or disengage from Medicare. They will no longer accept Medicare reimbursement for services provided to those covered under the Medicare system. Despite opting out of Medicare, providers will not remain untouched by a Medicare decision as most third party payors look to the Medicare Physician Fee Schedule to set their reimbursement rates. If a practitioner decides to opt out of Medicare, he or she must understand that the minimum period to lapse before reapplying as a participating provider in the Medicare system is 2 years. Additionally, a written contract between the provider and a patient eligible for Medicare benefits must be issued before services are provided. The contract must include four components: That the provider will not submit a claim to Medicare; that the patient agrees to pay the provider for the services performed at the rate the provider has stipulated; that the patient's secondary insurance may not reimburse as Medicare is not applicable; that the patient may seek services from a Medicare provider who will accept reimbursement for those services at any time (AAA, Capturing Reimbursement, 2006).

Part C. Health Care Plans and Systems

Medicare Advantage Plans were created in the 1997 Balance Budget Act to enable Medicare beneficiaries to participate in choosing their health care plan. This is accomplished via a coverage plan, typically local, which provides services not traditionally covered by Medicare. Annual audiograms and hearing instruments which are statutorily excluded in the traditional Part B segment, may be included in Part C. It may take the form of a Preferred Provider Organization (PPO), a Health Maintenance Organization (HMO), a Point of Service (POS), or Fee For Service (FFS) plan.

Consider the example of a local hospital that has created a Medicare Part C plan. The patient enrolls in this plan and is no longer on the traditional Medicare plan. They pay an additional premium amount greater per month than the traditional plan, but also have greater benefits that are not covered by Medicare. These additional benefits may include hearing instrument coverage at varied rates and amounts, depending on how the plan has allocated the benefit. The hearing instrument benefit commonly covers a specific amount to be distributed every 36 months, regardless of whether one or two instruments are dispensed. Balance billing is permitted and the patient would be responsible for paying the balance owed on their account after the Part C reimbursement has been received.

Part D. Prescription Drug Benefit

The Medicare Modernization Act was signed into law by President George W. Bush on December 8, 2003. This legislation enables everyone with Medicare, regardless of income, health status or prescriptions drugs to get prescription drug coverage (http://www.cms.hhs.gov/History/). It has no effect on hearing instruments nor other items relatable to those patients with hearing or balance disorders beyond medications that may be prescribed by their physician.

Medicare Beneficiary Notification

There are two alerting notices for Medicare beneficiaries that are components of the Beneficiary Notices Initiative (BNI). These notices are to ensure the patient understands that all of their health care may not be a statutorily covered service, advises them of their expected out-of-pocket payment, and enables them to be more active participants in their health care decisions. They may choose not to pursue that service at that time, a right they have to exercise. If the patient proceeds with the suggested procedures, they have been advised that they may be responsible to pay the provider.

Advanced Beneficiary Notice (ABN)

The Advanced Beneficiary Notice informs the patient that their procedure(s) may be denied by Medicare as "not being medically reasonable and necessary" and is downloadable from http://www.cms.hhs.gov/BNI/Downloads/CMSR131G.pdf. The participating provider is bound to secure an ABN if that provider suspects that the procedure(s) may not be reimbursed by Medicare. The patient is expected to pay for those services listed on the ABN if Medicare fails to provide reimbursement to the practice. The patient must be given a dated copy of the ABN with the procedure(s) to be performed and the reason the procedure(s). may be denied or partially paid before the completion of those procedures(s). On receipt of the Explanation of Benefits which indicates denial or partial payment and the reason for their adjudication, the patient may be billed for the balance owed on the account.

There are two important items to consider regarding the ABN. First, the ABN may not be issued for noncovered services such as hearing instruments or annual hearing assessments. Second, although you may want to protect your patients and your practice, it is ill advised to have every patient complete the ABN. This is considered blanket utilization by Medicare and is not a recommended policy (Palmetto, 2007).

Notice of Exclusions from Medicare Benefits (NEMB)

Annual hearing studies to monitor a patient's hearing status are excluded by Medicare. If the patient's visit is scheduled as an annual study for monitoring purposes, the patient must be issued an NEMB *before* any services are provided as it notifies them that Medicare will *not* pay for that particular service. The NEMB would also be given to the patient if the visit was due to anything related to hearing instruments, because of its statutory exclusion. Medicare is not billed for any of these services; therefore, the patient is advised of their personal financial responsibility. You will need to contact *your* Medicare carrier as local policies differ and therefore may differ in their guidance. The NEMB can be downloaded from the CMS Web site at (http://cms.hhs. gov/BNI/Downloads/CMS20007English. pdf). The ABN is form number CMS-R-131-G and the NEMB is CMS-20007.

Billing as "Incident To"

"Incident to" has been utilized for many years by otolaryngologists billing for the services provided by audiologists employed in their medical practice; they are not services the otolaryngologist has personally provided; the services are performed "incident to" the services provided by the otolaryngologist. The implication is that the services are performed under the supervision of the otolaryngologist. None of the codes commonly used by audiologists require physician supervision. Medicare defines "incident to" as "separate, but related, services provided to a Medicare patient subsequent to a physician's evaluation." These "incident to" services can be rendered if the services are within the person's scope of practice (Pessis, Williams, & Freint, 2006). If billings are done as "incident to," the physician must be within the facility at the time the services are rendered and there must be an indication of supervision. If the services of an audiologist are billed as "incident to," the work of the audiologist is credited to the otolaryngologist and does not credit the audiologist for any work value. As audiologists have qualified provider status within Medicare, audiologists should bill for their services under their identification number and for the services they render to the patients. This is, in no small way, related directly to the professional autonomy of every audiologist billing for services provided to patients in all settings. CMS has established the following requirements in order to bill "incident to":

■ A procedure or service must be furnished by a physician initiating the course of treatment,

■ the service is billed secondary to the medical visit, or "incident to" the visit,

■ services are furnished in a noninstitutional setting to noninstitutional patients,

■ the services are of a type commonly furnished in the office of a physician,

■ services are provided under the direct supervision of the physician,

■ services are furnished by a physician, other practitioner, or auxiliary personnel and only for services that do not have their own benefit category.

As audiologists are recognized providers by CMS, the last bulleted point is the primary reason why audiologists should not be considered in an "incident to" billing scenario. Billings generated by audiologists should not be submitted as "incident to" no matter the practice venue (Pessis, Williams, & Freint, 2006).

Other Third Party Payors

Although many third party payors look to Medicare to set their standards and fee schedules, there are other health care entities and licensed agencies engaged in reimbursement for services rendered by audiologists. This virtual alphabet soup of HMO, PPO, FFS, and POS groups have

been operating for many years and will likely continue to be an important segment of health care delivery options in the future.

Health Maintenance Organizations (HMO)

Health Maintenance Organizations (HMO): The gatekeeper or primary care physician (PCP) is the coordinator of health care for the patient. The goal of an HMO is to control utilization and, therefore, to keep the cost of health care at a minimum. Primary care physicians include the family practitioner or generalist, pediatricians, internal medicine physicians, gerontologists, and obstetrician/ gynecologists. Referrals to other health care providers, including audiologists, must be sanctioned by one of the primary care physicians listed above. There will be no reimbursement for services rendered unless a referral was obtained and is present in the audiologist's chart signed by the referral source.

Preferred Provider Organization (PPO)

Preferred Provider Organizations (PPO) are preferred by patients as they are free to choose a provider within the specified PPO network without a referral. If they seek care from an out-of-network provider (a provider not contracted with the PPO), the patient will incur greater cost and higher copayment rates. Patient costs are minimized and incentivized with an in-network provider as the copays are less and the reimbursement percentages (90% of the costs reimbursed, for example, patient pays the remaining 10%) versus out-of-network that may have a higher copay as well as greater exposure (70% of the costs reimbursed for example, patient pays the remaining 30%).

Point of Service Networks

Point of Service (POS) is a step-down from an HMO. Patients have more out-of-network options, but there are greater financial benefits for staying in-network as is the case for most of these health care structures. Higher copays or co-insurances are disincentives used to discourage use of out-of-network providers.

Fee-for-Service (FFS)

Fee-for-service enables health care plan enrollees to choose their own health care provider. It is the oldest hybridized reimbursement model as patients paid for their services in cash and, in some cases, eggs, chickens, or for services in kind. It involves an annual deductible to be met and a discounted pay rate to the provider, usually 80% of the usual and customary fee for each service provided. The patient is responsible for paying the remaining 20% after the deductible has been met.

Workers' Compensation

The Department of Labor's Office of Workers' Compensation Programs (OWCP) administers four major disability compensation programs which provide wage replacement benefits, medical treatment, vocational rehabilitation, and other benefits to federal workers or their dependents who are injured at work or acquire an occupational disease (DOL, 2007). Depending on the needs of the injured worker, hearing examinations and rehabilitation intervention including hearing

instruments and follow-up care may be covered in full or in part. The Energy Employees Occupational Illness Compensation Program, the Federal Employees' Compensation Program, the Longshore and Harbor Worker's Compensation Program, and the Black Lung Benefits Program serve the specific employee groups covered under the relevant statutes and regulations by mitigating the financial burden resulting from workplace injury (Department of Labor, 2007). Those who are injured and employed by a private employee or by state or local governments are served by their state Workers' Compensation Board(s). These state funded boards provide compensation for those injured in the workplace. Not only are injuries compensated on a short- and long-term basis, but it is the intent to provide rehabilitative services for that employee to return to the work force or a job related to one for which they have the training and skills.

Disability

Administered by the Social Security Administration (SSA), those who are disabled are funded for disability and/or Social Security Income (SSI). Application for medical disability commences at the local Social Security level. Physician and other applicable health care provider reports are assessed to determine eligibility. Once eligibility is established, payments are adjusted as to longevity of being in the work force in addition to other factors.

Social Security pays benefits to people who cannot work because they have a medical condition that is expected to last at least one year or result in death. Federal law requires this very strict definition of disability. Although some programs give money to people with partial disability or short-term disability, Social Security does not (SSA, 2007). For those on disability for two or more years, Part A and/or Part B Medicare benefits are available.

Specific Coding Considerations

In order to optimize reimbursement capture, CPT codes must be appropriate for the selected ICD-9 Codes. The patient's symptom(s) or chief complaint is the reason they have been referred or present to the practice. As an example, if they present with the symptom of tinnitus, 388.31 (tinnitus, subjective) should be listed. If the hearing examination results in the diagnosis of severe sensorineural hearing loss, 389.12 (neural hearing loss, bilateral) should be listed. Third party payors will often accept multiple diagnoses codes per CPT code. The most specific five-digit codes applicable for the ICD-9-CM's are the most advantageous and are less likely to result in a denial. For example, 389.10 (sensorineural hearing loss, unspecified) is not the best choice for sensorineural hearing loss due to lack of specificity even though it is a five-digit code. It is best to avoid those ICD-9-CM codes ending with a zero as they have the least specificity. An unwritten rule is to always code for specificity. In the immediate example above, selecting a more specific code 389.12 (neural hearing loss, bilateral) will have greater chances for approval as it specifically identifies the type of hearing loss and that it is occurring bilaterally. Greater specificity could be assigned by using the code for neural hearing loss based on the patient's otoacoustic emissions data.

Greater specificity increases the likelihood of approved reimbursement.

Consider the following example of a patient referred for evaluation of aural fullness and hearing loss following an airplane flight. Audiometric studies are completed including air, bone, speech reception thresholds, and evaluation of word recognition (CPT 92557) with tympanometry (CPT 92567) and acoustic reflex threshold measures (CPT 92568), Medicare will allow one diagnosis per CPT, so you may elect to utilize ICD-9 code 389.03 (conductive hearing loss, middle ear) for all three procedures. If the patient indicates the onset of tinnitus was related to the original complaint, ICD-9 code 388.31 (subjective tinnitus) could be used for 92557 and ICD-9 code 389.03 (conductive hearing loss, middle ear) for the tympanometry and acoustic reflex threshold codes. Documentation of the patient's complaint in his or her audiologic records must include comprehensive descriptions of the history of the event, the effects described by the patient, and information about the patient's complaints from onset to the current visit. Following the diagnostic studies, results and recommendations including treatment or referral for additional assessment or treatment must be clearly documented in the patient's record.

There Is No ICD-9 Code for Normal Hearing

When a patient is referred for an audiologic assessment based on presenting symptoms offered to the primary care provider, the patient may be referred to your practice for a hearing evaluation or vestibular assessment or both. The referring health care provider expects you to assess the patient, develop a diagnosis, and advise him or her about the patient and options for treatment. Those options may include further medical or surgical evaluation by other specialists, consideration for additional medical or audiologic tests or a recommendation to undergo interventional rehabilitative management in your practice.

Your examination of the patient establishes normal hearing sensitivity and word recognition scores, normal otoacoustic emissions, and normal middle ear function. You check the appropriate CPT codes on the billing form and now what do you do with the diagnosis of normal hearing as there is no ICD-9 code for normal hearing? According to the CMS Program Memorandum AB-01-144 (CMS, 2001) the correct coding of a patient with normal hearing is to code the signs, symptoms, or chief complaint presented by the patient and on which the referring physician based his or her referral for audiologic assessment. The memorandum specifically states: "If the diagnostic test did not provide a diagnosis or was normal, the interpreting physician (audiologists are recognized as acting as if a 'physician') should code the sign(s) or symptom(s) that prompted the treating physician to order the study."

Co-Pays and Co-Insurance

A co-pay is a specific amount that is to be collected from a patient at the time of service. The amount of co-pay to be collected typically ranges from $10.00 to $35.00 depending on the insurance plan. A co-insurance is the collectible percentage of the cost of the services completed during the patient's visit. It is that per-

centage of the charges incurred that is to be paid by the patient. Co-insurance payment plans are commonly used by PPO systems and in FFS situations. Those patients seen as part of a Medicare Part B visit are subject to paying the co-insurance percentage at the time of service (CMS, 2003). *The Medicare Resident and New Physician Guide* offers this guidance: "Co-insurance is the amount that Medicare will not pay; the beneficiary or the beneficiary's supplemental insurance company is responsible for paying coinsurance to the physician . . . physicians must collect the unmet coinsurance from the beneficiary." Consider the following example for a PPO patient: The sum of the charges for procedures performed during the visit to your practice is $250.00. The co-insurance payment is listed as 20%. The patient would pay $50.00 to the provider before they leave the office. If the patient would have gone to a provider who is not in the PPO network, they can expect to pay a higher co-insurance, in some plans 40% or higher instead of the 20% levied for seeing an in-network provider.

Deductibles

Deductibles constitute the annual financial responsibility a patient is required to pay before their health care benefits begin to cover medically relatable expenses. Deductibles vary with health care plans. They may range from $250.00 to as much as $5000.00. The patient is responsible for paying for all charges incurred up to the specified level of their deductible. If the deductible is $500.00 per annum, the patient is to pay the first $500.00 of their medical bills with the remainder covered by the insurer for that particular year of coverage. If a patient comes in to see you in the early part of the year, barring any health care issues or visits, it is likely they have not met their deductible and they will need to pay the entire amount of the charges for the visit, up to the amount of their deductible. This amount will then be applied to their deductible.

Balance Billing

As mentioned previously, if the patient's insurance carrier has agreed to pay 80% of all charges for services rendered, there remains an unpaid balance of 20% of the charges for the services. Logically, the patient would be responsible for paying the 20% not covered by their insurance as the patient has contracted with you directly to provide the services—your practice has not contracted with the insurance carrier. Many insurance carriers and health care systems such as PPOs require that your practice accept the 80% as payment-in-full and they will not permit the patient to be billed for the unpaid balance. That is a point in each contract that should be carefully weighed when making the decision to join any health care plan or other third party payor group as a participating provider. If there is no prohibition on balance billing, the patient will be expected to pay for all services provided and is personally responsible for paying the remaining balance on their account.

Third party payors commonly provide an Explanation of Benefits (EOB) with payments provided on behalf of their insured subscriber, your patient. The patient also receives an EOB and will thus be notified as to what was paid and what may be their fiscal responsibility.

EOBs should be carefully scrutinized and billings for each patient should be adjusted accordingly. If you are just beginning an independent private practice, you should set up a spreadsheet to monitor each third party payor, what each pays for each procedure, and whether you can bill the patient for the unpaid balance. This monitoring technique allows you to observe trends in payment schedules and amounts reimbursed for specific CPT codes and to help determine whether or not your practice should continue to participate as a provider. Balances not payable by the patient as agreed on in your contract as a participating provider must be written "off the books." These are not considered tax deductions, but is revenue lost due to contract adjustments.

Bundling Versus Unbundling Service Fees and Instrument Costs

There has been considerable angst for many years as to whether billing for hearing instrument fittings should be "bundled" as one price on the patient's billing statement or "unbundled" wherein the cost of the instruments, associated professional service fees, and ancillary costs are itemized. Under some third party payor situations, this may be a nonissue in that there is a directed billing format for itemization. In the instances where insurance coverage is not involved, the practice may bundle or unbundle as appropriate according to the business philosophy, state insurance laws and what the community will support (Abel & Hahn, 2006, p. 69). Bundling versus unbundling is a moot point for commercial hearing instrument dealers in that state laws prohibit them from charging for diagnostic studies reserved for those licensed or registered as audiologists.

Strom (2000) sets forth a forward-thinking treatise on bundling and unbundling hearing services and hearing instruments: "Audiological and aural rehab services have a monetary value usually commensurate to the time spent and/or equipment used in performing those services. They should not be 'lumped in' with the cost of a hearing instrument for the sake of simplicity . . . hearing health care professionals don't just dispense a product; they dispense hearing care. Hearing care services come at a price to the dispensing office, they are effective for the consumer, and they have a value that should not remain hidden by bundling prices." Despite the accuracy and appropriateness of Strom's forecast (Strom, 2000), Amlani (2006) indicates that " . . . most audiologists and hearing instrument specialists combine (i.e. bundle) the costs of professional services with the cost of hearing instruments." Why is it that audiologists persist in giving many of their professional services away in bundled pricing? This is an especially troubling question when the roots of bundled pricing for hearing instruments derives from commercial hearing instrument dealers who had but one commodity and that was the instrument (Metz, 2006, p. 45).

If the hearing examination, fitting fee, counseling, and follow-up care is lumped together in one charge that is inexorably linked to the hearing instrument, the services appear to the patient to have no value; only the instrument has value. Professional services are worth what the patient pays for them. If the professional service fees are masked by embedding

them within a single price, the patient will likely see little value in the services provided. Patients have been subjected to fee-for-service health care and, as such, have come to place value on professional services when delineated for specific services. In an itemized statement, which should be reviewed with each patient, fees for professional services provided during the course of the patient's hearing (re)habilitation will establish value and merit for the services rendered. It more than implies that your professional time is worth the money spent.

Despite the fact that much of the literature since 2000 supports the case for unbundling, there are compelling reasons to maintain or consider a single price for the hearing instruments dispensed. Many patients like to pay one price for one service or clinical process: One payment, one price; done. Proponents of bundling suggest that a single price puts money out of the picture and enables the patient to focus on the total rehabilitation process. Patients do not mind coming for follow-up visits that are considered paid. If the patient must pay for postfitting visits, continuity of care may be interrupted and the patient may not return if they feel they can get by without what might be a necessary adjustment to the instrument(s). Additionally, one price, one payment is far less confusing for many of our patients. They, like many of their depression-era family members and friends, have a comfort level in knowing the payment process has been completed and that no bills will follow.

There are additional favorable considerations in unbundled pricing. Depending on the agreement in place between you as the clinician and the patient, the charges for the hearing examination and fees for fitting and follow-up visits would be (properly) retained if the instrument(s) is/are returned if not prohibited by state licensure laws. If the patient decides to keep only one instrument, the cost of that instrument will be returned and the charges for related professional services will be retained again, if not prohibited by state licensure laws.

There will be occasional patients who come to your office for in-office repairs or adjustments while vacationing or visiting the area. A well-developed fee schedule for services should be reviewed with that patient and anticipated charges discussed. This is especially true in cases where an active instrument warranty is in place. If your practice is not a participant in the original warranty associated with the instrument presented for repair or adjustment, the patient should be charged for any service rendered including an evaluation and sending the instrument in for repair under the warranty. By advising the patient of the anticipated charges, they can decide whether to take the instrument back to the original instrument fitter for warranted repair considerations.

CPT Code Modifiers

Modifiers are used to clarify the status of the particular CPT code to which it is appended. They are added to indicate that a service was more or less complex than expected, to indicate that a service was repeated or discontinued and to eliminate the appearance of multiple or duplicated billing. The most common modifiers used by audiologists are listed below.

—22 Unusual Procedural Service

This modifier is appended when a procedure takes a longer time or is more complex than for the "typical patient." An example would be obtaining a comprehensive audiogram on a patient with dementia or a child who needs reminding of the task in order to complete the evaluation. Documentation addressing why the test took longer must accompany the billing; therefore, it will need to be submitted via hard copy and not electronically.

—26 Professional Component

Three family of codes, otoacoustic emissions (OAE), electronystagmography (ENG), and auditory brainstem response (ABR) are to be billed globally when the procedure was performed as well as interpreted by the same provider. The professional component (-26) is to be used with Otoacoustic Emissions, comprehensive (92588), the ENG family of codes (92531–92546), and with Auditory Brainstem Response, comprehensive (92585) when you only interpreted the test and did not perform it. If you interpreted OAEs without performing the test, it would be appended as 92588-26. If you perform and interpret one of the above tests, you would bill it globally as 92588.

—TC Technical Component

This is the counterpart to the professional component if an audiologist only performs 92588, 92531–92546, and 92585 and another provider does the interpretation. If you only performed an otoacoustic emission test and another provider did the interpretation, it would be appended as 92588-TC. If you performed and interpreted 92588, it would be billed globally and no modifier would be necessary.

—51 Multiple Procedures During Same Encounter

This is when multiple procedures are performed on the same day at the same session. An example employed by audiologists would be a pre- and postoperative air and bone conduction study with PE tube insertion to document the improvement. This would be appended as 92553-51 for this example.

—52 Reduced Service

This is the partial completion of the procedure or reduced services. The most common audiologic implementation is when testing is completed unilaterally. All of our codes are binaural and if the entire procedure was not completed for both ears, it will need to be appended to reflect that only one ear was tested. If air conduction was done on one ear, possibly after a tube insertion, it would be appended as 92552-52.

—53 Discontinued Procedure

This signifies that the procedure was stopped by the provider due to the patient becoming ill during that procedure. An application for audiology would be if a patient became very ill during caloric testing. In this example, it would be appended as 92543-53.

—76 Repeat Procedure by Same Provider

This modifier is utilized when the same procedure is performed on the same day by the same provider. Audiologic applications may include a baseline and another comprehensive assessment post administration of an ototoxic agent. This would be appended as 92557-76.

—77 Repeat Procedure by Other Provider

This is when the same procedure is performed on the same day by a different provider. An application for audiologists could be when an outpatient sees an audiologist for a baseline audiogram pre-administration of a neoplastic or amino-glycocide agent. The patient is then seen postadministration by another audiologist as the first may have gone to lunch at the time of the second evaluation. This would be appended as 92557-77.

—99 Multiple Modifiers

The intent is to inform the insurance carrier that there will be multiple modifiers appended to the same code such as with the example: 92557-99-22-GY (Grider, 2004). This would indicate that a comprehensive audiologic assessment was performed, taking longer than it does for the "typical patient" and needing a denial by Medicare to be sent to the patient's secondary for his hearing instrument coverage to be implemented.

GY, GA, GZ Modifiers

Modifiers that pertain to medical necessity and the use of the ABN include GY, GA, and GZ. GY is when the procedure is statutorily excluded and does not meet the definition of a Medicare benefit, such as hearing instruments. Many third party payors require a denial from Medicare for them to provide the patient their hearing instrument benefit. In this case on line 19 of the CMS 1500 form, you would indicate that this is for denial by Medicare by appending 92590-GY (hearing instrument examination) and the applicable hearing instrument codes such as V5160 (dispensing fee, bilateral) and V5261 (hearing instrument, digital, binaural, BTE), thereby removing the onus of billing fraudulently for a procedure that is statutorily excluded. The use of this modifier will incur an automatic denial and will then be forwarded to the secondary insurance.

GA indicates that the patient has a signature on file by way of their signed ABN and the procedure may not be a covered service due to it not being medically reasonable and/or necessary. In the event it is not reimbursed, the patient can then be billed for that service. If a patient has 92557, comprehensive audiometry, performed and Medicare denies it, the patient will have been told of their responsibility by signing the ABN. They can now be billed for that service upon the denial.

GZ is utilized when the procedure is expected to be denied, an ABN was not completed, therefore a signature is not on file and the patient cannot be billed. The same code scenario would be 92557-GZ in this example.

Collections

Some patients do not pay their bills. The agreement the patient signs when engaging the practice for services must clearly state that every patient is responsible for paying the bills generated as a result of services rendered or instrument(s) supplied. Additionally, consequences of nonpayment should be set forth in the agreement. Exceeding billing cycles—going beyond acceptable dates of payment—should have consequences including turning the account over to a collection agent. Beyond being subjected to the actions of the collection agent, the patient's credit rating is jeopardized. Other actions may be considered including filing legal action or entering small claims court to rectify the unpaid balance on the account—both costly actions in terms of time spent, legal fees, and lost revenue. The major solution to having patients owing considerable amounts on their unpaid balance is to collect payment for services or instruments provided at the time of service. The more collected up front, the less will be lost.

Many offices avoid this problem with credit card payments that are confirmed in real time and there is no issue of nonpayment. There are several health care credit cards available in order for the credit card company to pay you and the patient in turn pays them. This eliminates your office having to bill monthly, something that can only add to the cost of doing business. Of course, these also come at a cost and some audiologists find them not to be cost effective. Patients may find them prohibitive with inflated monthly percentages levied.

Having an office policy in place detailing the amount or balance due and the time it is due avoids many pitfalls in nonpayment. Many audiologists have adopted a financial policy that requires the patient pay 50% of the fee at the time the hearing instruments are ordered, leading to payment in full when the instruments are dispensed. For those instruments that are fit the same day, payment in full is expected at the time of service. This is detailed with the patient in their hearing instrument contract in order for them to be aware of their fiscal responsibility before the instruments leave the office. Signage in the waiting room and/or at the cashier station of your office signaling the policy of "payment due at the time of service" certainly apprises your patients of what is financially expected of them and when.

Superbills or Encounter Forms

A superbill or encounter form is a listing of the applicable and most widely utilized codes in that particular facility. It is a mechanism to alert the front office of the services provided in order for them to be billed to the patient and/or a third party payor. Relevant identifying information including the patient's name, date of service, provider's name, CPT codes, and ICD-9 codes commonly appear to delineate the services provided at the patient visit. If hearing instruments or related supplies were issued, appropriate HCPCS codes should be indicated.

If you are considering private practice or need to update your current superbill or encounter form, the American Academy of Audiology (http://www.audiology.org) has two superbills on the Web site, one for diagnostics and the other for hearing instrument related fees that also includes assistive listening devices. These superbills may be downloaded and modified for implementation in your office.

Practice Audits

CMS has the right to audit any patient record wherein services were delivered and claims were filed—whether the claims were or were not paid. CMS may issue fines for noncompliance or charge you with fraudulent billing practice which can result in fines and imprisonment depending on the extent of involvement and infraction. Beyond fines, they may demand repayment of funds issued to the practice within a specific time period and for long forgotten dates of service. Charges and fines are to be paid as they indicate. Fraudulent billing involving patients participating in CMS programs is a federal offense and not to be taken lightly. Bill only for services that are necessary in the quest of determining the diagnosis. The Office of the Inspector General, in their pursuit of fraud and abuse, are on the lookout for false claims, especially submitting claims for services not rendered.

Private insurance carriers may also audit charts as stipulated in most provider agreements. They have the right to file civil actions for fraud and abuse which may lead to civil, and in some cases, criminal penalties. This is not about making honest mistakes; this is about intentionally manipulating the system with intent to fraudulently obtain funds.

Medicare audits (also known as a Comprehensive Medical Review) as well as private insurance carrier audits look for similar indicators. Although this list is not exhaustive, it was generated based on discussions with an individual who was an auditor for CMS:

- Record documentation and accuracy —how terms are used, completeness of notes, verification of coverage and patient's eligibility for services. Lack of documentation can be considered fraud and abuse (Nigro,1998).
- Appropriate patient identification numbers including Social Security number and policyholder number(s) must be accurate and current.
- Privacy concerns must be met in written and electronic records.
- CPT codes must match and support diagnosis codes.
- Billing codes and documentation must be appropriate, accurate and reflect those that are "medically necessary."
- Services rendered must be appropriate to provider status.
- Physician order must be signed, dated, and indicate medical necessity.
- Patient records must include complaint, relevant medical and family history, diagnostic tests used, diagnosis, and plan of care.
- Patient records demonstrate logical decisions in the diagnostic process relative to the conclusions reached.
- Plan of care must be appropriate to clinical findings or diagnosis.
- Plan of care must be appropriate to the physician's order.
- Services provided must match the physician's order.

- Progress notes must document outcomes and indicate education provided.
- Annual hearing re-evaluation or periodic assessment not ordered by physician should not have been billed to Medicare.
- Services billed must have been completed in support of the records.
- Multiple billing errors may be viewed as insurance fraud.

Documentation

If an item or event is not documented in the chart, that item or event is considered nonexistent. Practice auditors cover a wide-ranging list of possible chart deficiencies. Basic compliance requires that documentation in the patient's audiologic records include the patient's demographic information, insurance information, the referral source with the reason for the referral, working and established medical diagnoses, family history of hearing loss and related issues, extensive clinical history, and information about onset of the complaint including allergies, surgeries, hospitalizations, medications, and all information relating to the patient's continuum of health care.

All audiologic data must be signed and dated by the audiologist completing the studies. Findings should be based on the information obtained with all evaluative procedures listed in the text of the report. Diagnostic conclusions must be supported by the procedures used and the results obtained. If the data obtained fail to support the history or reason for the referral, appropriate justifications are necessary. If there is a lack of consistency in the patient's response behaviors or a lack of consistency across the data generated, repeat studies to monitor stability of the findings should be recommended. Follow-up care and recommendations for further study should be specific and straightforward. Specificity is important in recommending further studies or additional referral to other health care specialists. If mistakes are made in the charting process, several guidelines need to be followed: Do not destroy, rewrite, or replace what you have written. Correction fluid should not be used. Strike out what you want to eliminate; initial it with your three initials, and place the date near those initials. Addendum notes may also be attached, depending on the software of the electronic record. If using a hard copy, this will be sufficient with the date of the addendum added with your signature.

In hospital settings, the chart may be reviewed for quality assurance issues by Quality Assurance (QA) or Continuous Quality Improvement (CQI) committees. These committees are generally comprised of medical staff, hospital board members, hospital executives, and ancillary hospital staff. The proceedings of these committee meetings are highly confidential and the offending practitioner will be notified of documentation issues and the mechanism on how to repair those issues. Sanctions, fines, and withdrawal of hospital privileges may be levied against noncompliant practitioners including audiologists.

Records Management

HIPAA requires that HIPAA forms be retained for 6 years. It is suggested you search the Web site of state governmental offices or contact your state's insurance commission for a copy of state record retention laws. Typically, records of minors are to be retained for 7 years after reaching the age of 21. Records for adults should be retained for 7 years following the date of their last visit. For those patients who are deceased, charts need to be retained for 3 years after the date of death.

Patients have the right to review their chart and amend anything with which they are not in agreement. The chart is to be maintained by the facility who "owns" it according to the Medical Board of California (http://www.mbc.ca.gov) and the Yale-New Haven Hospital and Yale University School of Medicine (http://www.med.yale.edu). Under most state laws, the originator/creator of a medical record generally owns the record (Manning, 2007) and the patient is allowed to review and retain a nonoriginal copy. If the chart is subpoenaed, the subpoena will specify if the original chart has to be submitted or whether a copy will suffice. A copy of the chart as requested by the patient, attorneys, or another third party should be issued in a timely manner by the facility that maintains the chart. Chart requests may be due to a litigated case, a workers' compensation case, or the patient needs the record for another health care provider. The patient may be charged for the copy of their chart and state insurance laws commonly dictate what that charge may be on a per page basis.

Electronic Medical Records (EMR)

In 2004, President George W. Bush envisioned Electronic Medical Records (EMR) being a reality by 2014 (CMS, 2007). An

EMR is a paperless medical record. It is completely computerized and stored within specific databases. The bulleted information above will be the core information of the EMR. Signatures will be electronically encrypted for specific dates of service, demographic information, progress notes, medications, history and physical findings, diagnoses and treatment regimen, and outcomes will be available to all with access to the EMR (CMS, 2007). The benefit of an EMR is the rapidity and completeness of the medical records available to health care facilities. Real-time access can be critical in emergency situations and when the patient is in the hospital. EMRs must be retained on the same schedules as hard copy records.

Negotiating Contracts to Provide Services

The health care landscape has changed dramatically over the years. Although still driven primarily by physicians and physician groups, audiologists have come to be recognized by licensure, advanced education, and the quality and outcomes of their care as valued participants in the contemporary health care arena.

Third party payors paying for the services provided to patients in your practice do so under specific guidelines of coverage outlined in the patient's schedule of benefits. The provider agreement stipulates the services to be provided and operational issues covering billing procedures, referral requirements, and other parameters required by the third party payor. Failure to comply with the tenets of the provider agreement can result in removal of the practice from the list of participating providers and discharge from the plan.

There are a number of questions a practitioner must answer before he or she decides to become a participating provider in a health care plan. If too many of these questions are answered in the negative, appropriate consideration should be given and inquiries made for clarification. If a health care plan pursues your practice to become a participating provider, consider the realities of the plan and make the decision based on how the plan will benefit your practice—not because it appears that the practice *should* be listed on every health care plan list of providers. Reimbursement opportunities must be in line with the practice fee schedule as well as the other plans in which the practice participates. Key questions to consider:

- Are audiologists credentialed? What does that process entail and how long does it take to be credentialed?
- Is there a credentialing fee at the time of application?
- What is the fee schedule and how often is it revised?
- Is the fee schedule commensurate with the time that will be spent with patients?
- Is balance billing allowed?
- What is their discounted fee schedule?
- When can payment be expected?
- What is the denial process?
- How much liability insurance do I need to carry?
- Length of the contract? Is it renewed automatically?
- How can the contract be terminated and by whom? What is the required time frame for advance notice?
- Can the contract be changed unilaterally by the third party such as

with a unilateral change in the fee schedule?

■ Are there "withholds" in effect where a percentage of the patient's billed services are retained by the third party payor for administrative costs?

■ Will this secure a demographic area?

■ Ease of verification of patient enrollment?

■ Are prior authorizations required?

The decision to join a plan as a provider is multifaceted. Once the questions are answered, a decision needs to be made. It is best not to make the decision in isolation. Involve the front office staff, the accountant, and attorney for the practice. Each will add important perspectives to the decision.

Independent Practice Associations and Managed Care

Recall the expression, "safety in numbers." It has a place in negotiating contracts for services with third party payors. Historically, audiologists have banded together to create a unique legal identity, an Independent Practice Association (IPA). This affords audiologists the ability to contract with insurers that you may not have access to as a single practice yet allows you to maintain the autonomy of your own practice and may be created on a local or state level. This may afford you a larger geographic area and other economies of scale as well as sharing some expenses for a contract negotiator whose responsibility includes obtaining desired contracts. There are several national audiology related IPA's which provide an exclusive contract enrollment of your practice as a benefit of your IPA membership.

When an IPA is established, each practice or participating practitioner is expected to provide a sizable contribution to cover start-up costs which commonly include hiring an attorney to draft articles of incorporation and various papers defining participation in the plan. An accountant should be considered to establish and maintain appropriate accounting, payroll, and tax records. Most important to the success of the IPA will be the hiring of a knowledgeable contract negotiator responsible for securing contracts for the group. A management team of IPA participants must be created to follow the guidelines of operation set forth in the documents outlining operations and management. Establishing an IPA can be an expensive business. The rewards of isolating contracts under exclusive coverage must outweigh the start up and maintenance costs.

Health Care Practice Laws

As health care providers, we are required to comply with a number of laws that include the Stark Laws, the Antikickback Statutes, Safe Harbors, False Claims Act, and the Health Insurance Portability and Accountability Act (HIPAA). These laws are to protect patients, and insurers, as well as federal government health care programs from fraudulent practices. Each of these are examined in detail individually and their applications to audiology specified.

The Antikickback Statute (AKS)

The Antikickback Statute (42 U.S.C. §1320a-7b) was enacted to prohibit transactions that are intentionally designed to exploit federal health care programs. It is a felony for anyone to be involved in the soliciting and receiving of kickbacks in return for referrals of patients whose items or services are reimbursable under federal health care programs. It prohibits any person from "knowingly and willfully soliciting or receiving any remuneration (including any kickback, bribe, or rebate) directly or indirectly, overtly or covertly, in cash or in kind," to induce someone to refer an individual for "any item or service for which payment may be made in whole or in part under a Federal health care program" (except the Federal Employees Health Benefits Program [FEHBP]). In addition, it is also felonious to recommend, purchase, lease, or order an item or service payable, in whole or in part, under a federal health care program except for FEHBP (Abel & Hahn, 2006).

Stringency of compliance will vary from audiology practice to practice. Many hospitals and otolaryngology offices have adopted policies of no gifts, including pens, note pads, or anything of substantive value as it may be considered as remuneration as well as being construed as buying loyalty.

The Ethical Practice Committee of the American Academy of Audiology has advised that gifts of minimal value ($100.00 or less) related to the audiologist's work may be accepted (http://www.audiology.org) and that no "strings" should be attached to any accepted gift. This may change as those in business and professional arenas look inward in the wake of ongoing headlines. In 2002, the Pharmaceutical Research and Manufacturers of America adopted voluntary rules limiting the value of gifts to $100.00 or less and banning free entertainment tickets (CBS News, 2007).

AKS Prohibitions and Punishments

The AKS prohibits kickbacks, because (1) they create an incentive to overutilize reimbursable services, increasing costs to Medicare and other federal health care programs; (2) they distort medical decision making; and (3) they result in unfair competition by freezing out qualified providers who are unwilling to pay kickbacks (Abel & Hahn, 2006).

The AKS is a criminal statute. Violation of the AKS is a felony punishable by imprisonment, heavy fines, and/or exclusion from federal health care program participation. Unlike the Stark Law, which is a civil law, intent is a critical element that must be proved by the prosecutor. However, although intent to induce or reward referrals or purchases of reimbursable items or service must be proven, it is not required to be the only purpose of the transaction. The AKS is enforced by the Department of Health and Human Services' Office of Inspector General (OIG), not CMS. Thus, the elements of an AKS violation are the following:

- Intent: acting knowingly and willfully
- Offering, giving, soliciting, or receiving remuneration which is broadly defined to include anything of value;
- Either (1) referral of patients for the furnishing of any item or service reimbursable under a federal health care program (except FEHBP); or (2) the purchase, lease. or ordering of (or recommending or arranging the purchase, lease, or ordering of) any item or service reimbursable under a federal health care program, except FEHBP; and

- Doing so with the knowledge and intent that at least one purpose of the remuneration is to induce or reward such referrals, purchases, leases, or orders (R. Hahn, personal communication, May 2, 2007).

Here are a few examples of possible arrangements between audiologists and physicians that may initiate the AKS:

- An audiologist furnishes diagnostic tests to a physician's patients at no or reduced charge in return for hearing instrument referrals, where hearing instruments are covered by the state Medicaid plan. The audiologist is giving the physician remuneration (i.e., free or reduced price diagnostic tests) in return for referrals of hearing instrument business reimbursable by Medicaid.
- An audiologist rents office space from a physician and pays rental based on the number of referrals of Medicare/Medicaid patients received from the physician. The audiologist is giving the physician remuneration (i.e., above-market rent) in return for referrals of Medicare/Medicaid business.
- An audiologist accepts remuneration (in the form of gifts, entertainment, loans, cooperative marketing funds, or other benefits) from a hearing instrument manufacturer in return for prescribing the manufacturer's hearing instruments, where the hearing instruments are covered by Medicaid or another federal program (other than Federal Employees Health Benefits Program). The audiologist is receiving remuneration in return for recommending purchase

of hearing instruments reimbursable by Medicaid (Abel & Hahn, 2006).

The above paragraph is the very core of the dilemma most audiologists encounter. Whereas the military and Veteran's Administration have had very stringent guidelines for nonacceptance of any items for many years, many hospitals now have adopted the same policies. Some of those hospitals require vendors to sign agreements establishing a no gifts rule.

Although manufacturers continue to offer trips, they are not the entity who is being reimbursed by federal government monies, it is the audiologist. If an audiologist is accepting equipment or a loan with "strings attached" with a requirement to purchase hearing instruments from a manufacturer to fulfill a payback obligation and is also billing Medicaid or Vocational Rehabilitation, for example, this is a clear violation of the AKS and the practitioner will be subject to the penalties of the AKS if convicted.

The Ethical Practice Guidelines on Financial Incentives for Hearing Instruments position statement adopted by the American Academy of Audiology (Academy) (http://www.audiology.org) and the Academy of Dispensing Audiologists (ADA) (http://www.audiologist.org) in 2003 educates the members of these organizations about the ethics and legality of the acceptance of trips, cash, and other gifts in exchange for recommending items that may be paid for by a federal health care program. Abiding by these guidelines protects the audiologist from inadvertent violations of the Anti-kickback Statute. It is recommended that all audiologists read these guidelines (Abel & Hahn, 2006) as well as adopt them in their clinical practices.

Safe Harbors

To avoid criminalizing innocent conduct, OIG has created a number of "safe harbors" to the AKS. If a transaction meets all the requirements of a safe harbor, it is protected from prosecution. However, failure to qualify for a safe harbor does not automatically mean a transaction is not in violation of the AKS.

The safe harbors include arm's-length agreements for the rental of office space or equipment, discounts, waivers of beneficiary copayments, and remuneration given to bona fide employees. Arm's-length agreements are when involved parties do not have a close relationship. Although a complete discussion of the AKS safe harbors is beyond the scope of this chapter, one of the safe harbors is worth mentioning because of its widespread use (Abel & Hahn, 2006).

To qualify for safe harbor protection, a discount must be "a reduction in the amount a buyer (who buys either directly or through a wholesaler or a group purchasing organization) is charged for an item or service based on an arms-length transaction" (42 C.F.R. §1001.952[h][5]). The discount must be made at the time of sale (or, if a rebate, the terms of the rebate must be fixed and disclosed in writing to the buyer at the time of sale). The buyer receiving the discount must, on request of the OIG or state regulators, provide certain information provided to it by the seller. In addition, the discount must be accurately disclosed and reflected in any charges billed to a federal health care program paying for the item or service (R. Hahn, personal communication, May 2, 2007). Thus, the discount must inure to benefit the Medicare or Medicaid program. The discount must be earned in the same fiscal year as the purchase of the applicable item or service. The safe harbor does not protect discounts in the form of cash payments (or cash equivalents) (Abel & Hahn, 2006).

The application of this interpretation for most audiology practices are the invoice cost discounts listed on manufacturer invoices. These are to be honored when billing third party federal programs. In the event of an audit, that invoice will be requested and what was billed to the patient should be reflected in the charges.

Safe Harbor Rental Agreements

To qualify for the office rental safe harbor, an audiologist must ensure that rental payments are not disguised kickbacks to induce referrals by the physician-landlord. Specifically:

- The rental agreement must be in writing and signed by the parties;
- The rental agreement must cover all premises rented by the parties and specify the premises;
- The term of the agreement must be at least one year;
- If the audiologist is renting space for periodic intervals, the agreement must specify the exact schedule of usage;
- The aggregate rental amount must be set in advance, consistent with fair market value, and may not take into account the volume or value of referrals; and
- The aggregate space rented may not exceed what is reasonably necessary to accomplish a commercially reasonable business purpose.

For more detail, refer to the OIG Special Fraud Alert: Rental of Office Space in Physician Offices by Persons or Entities to Which Physicians Refer (OIG, 2000). Many states have their own antikickback and Stark laws, which may differ from the federal AKS and may be more stringent. When there is doubt concerning a potential or particular transaction, legal counsel well versed in both federal and state antikickback laws should be obtained (Abel & Hahn, 2006).

The Stark Law

Audiologists should be aware of the federal antifraud laws (as well as any relevant state antifraud laws). The Stark Law and the Antikickback Statute should be considered separately; activities or arrangements that are acceptable under one may violate the other (Abel & Hahn, 2006). As such, it is recommended that contracts to provide services involving a physician or physician group be reviewed by legal counsel familiar with health care fraud and abuse laws.

The Stark Law (42 U.S.C. §1395nn) prohibits physician "self-referrals" (Abel & Hamill, 2004). That is, it prohibits a physician (or a physician's immediate family member) from referring patients for designated health services to an entity in which the physician (or his or her immediate family member) has a financial relationship, unless a specific exception applies. The law also prohibits the entity receiving the prohibited referral from billing for those designated health services (Abel & Hahn, 2006).

The Stark Law is a civil, not a criminal law. Violations may result in denial of reimbursement, mandatory refunds of federal payments, civil money penalties, and/or exclusion from federal and state health care programs. The Centers for Medicare and Medicaid Services (CMS) has issued regulations (42 C.F.R. Part 411) implementing the Stark Law in two phases over a period of several years, and there will be a third phase in December 2007. (Abel & Hahn, 2006).

To violate Stark, there must be a *referral* by a physician (or his or her immediate family member) to an *entity* in which the physician (or his or her immediate family member) has a *financial interest* for the furnishing of *designated health services* (DHS).

Stark Law and How it Applies to Audiology

Because of this narrow definition of DHS, the Stark Law has limited application to audiologists as audiologists are not considered "physicians" and the Stark Law generally does not apply to referrals by audiologists to other providers. Audiologist and audiology practices may run afoul of Stark, however, if they receive a prohibited referral from a physician. A violation occurs only if the prohibited referral is for the furnishing of DHS (R. Hahn, personal communication, May 2, 2007). The only audiology services that fall within the definition of DHS are audiology services furnished as hospital inpatient or outpatient services. However, as the entity furnishing DHS is the entity that receives payment from CMS, and as CMS reimburses the hospital for inpatient and outpatient services, it is the hospital (not the audiologist) that must comply with the Stark Law.

Other Eligible Services Under Stark

Other eligible services include CPT codes 92507 and 92508 (treatment of speech, language, voice, communication, or auditory processing; individual and group, respectively). CMS considers these procedures to be speech-language pathology services, and therefore DHS. Because DHS must be payable by Medicare, these procedures are arguably DHS when furnished by an audiologist "incident to" a physician's services. However, even if an audiologist were to perform these services pursuant to a prohibited referral, they would in most cases be exempt from the Stark Law under the "in-office ancillary services" exception (Abel & Hahn, 2006). .

How the Stark Laws pertain to audiology is applicable to specific diagnostic tests, including cochlear implant mapping and reprogramming (CPT codes 92601 through 92604), as they are not DHS. In addition, CMS has clarified that hearing instruments are not DHS. The Stark Law is not applicable to physician referrals for diagnostic tests or hearing instruments.

The Stark Law and CMS

The Stark Law and implementing CMS regulations provide a number of exceptions. These include bona fide employment relationships, arm's-length agreements, those that involve parties who do not have a close relationship for the rental of office space or equipment, and "in-office ancillary services." To qualify for an exception, a transaction or arrangement must meet specific requirements. For example, to qualify for the in-office ancillary services exception, the services must meet a supervision requirement (e.g., furnished by an individual under the supervision of the referring physician), a building requirement (e.g., furnished in the same building in which the referring physician normally furnishes services to patients), and a billing requirement (e.g., billed by the supervising physician, the group practice, an entity wholly owned by the physician or group practice, or an independent third-party billing company acting as agent of the physician, group practice, or entity).

The False Claims Act

Under the False Claims Act (18 U.S.C. §287) it is a criminal offense to submit false claims to the federal government. A separate law (31 U.S.C. §3729 et seq.) also known as the False Claims Act, provides a civil cause of action against anyone making a false claim to the federal government (R. Hahn, personal communication, May 2, 2007). Violations include these ill-advised actions:

■ Submitting claims for services that were not rendered;
■ Submitting claims for services not medically necessary;
■ Not billing with the appropriate provider number;
■ Billing for services known to be noncovered;
■ Falsifying a patient's diagnosis;
■ "Upcoding" or billing for a service at a higher rate;
■ "Unbundling" bundled codes (such as 92557's components, per the Correct Coding Initiative Edit).

In addition to criminal and civil penalties, violations may result in the revocation of privileges to provide services to a private insurer, and revocation of state license(s). Bill only for services that are necessary in the quest to determine the diagnosis. The Office of the Inspector General, in its pursuit of fraud and abuse, is on the lookout for false claims, especially claims submitted for services not rendered.

Health Insurance Portability and Accountability Act (HIPAA)

In 1996 the Health Insurance Portability and Accountability Act (HIPAA), Public Law 104-191 was promulgated by Congress to "improve portability and continuity of health care when there was a change of jobs, to combat waste, fraud and abuse in health insurance and health care delivery . . . to simplify the administration of health insurance, and for other purposes" (American Academy of Audiology, 2006). There were several titles that comprised the Act that are pertinent to audiologists: Transaction and Code Sets, Privacy, and Security.

Treatment, Payment and Operations (TPO) Parameters

HIPAA addresses the importance of disseminating the minimum information necessary for Treatment, Payment, and Operations (TPO) in dealing with patient care and privacy issues. Casual discussions about specific patients are inappropriate and violate HIPAA rules as it is not considered under the parameters of TPO. When a journal article is submitted or when academic or clinical information is presented, the patient's privacy must be preserved and all identifying information that relates to the discussed patient(s)must be deleted.

Authorizations are needed for a one-time, date-specific event for information and are required for purposes other than health care treatment, payment, or operations. An example of an application that pertains to audiology would be a clinical audiologist and an educational audiologist exchanging information on a mutual patient. The Family Educational Rights and Privacy Act (FERPA) is the pervading law for those in educational settings and is their version of HIPAA, promulgated to protect student education records. You need to specify the patient's name, address, date of birth, the name of your facility, what information/test results are requested, the expiration date of the authorization request, and the name/address of the recipient. The patient's right to revoke the authorization as well as notification if the PHI may be redisclosed by the recipient need to be addressed in the authorization.

Permission to Evaluate and Treat

We have all encountered the patient who does not seek audiologic treatment under their own volition, but by that of a well-meaning relative or friend. The patient has the ultimate right of determining treatment. When that patient is incapacitated and unable to make their own decisions, it is recommended that a power of attorney (POA) act on their behalf. It is suggested you include a place for the patient or their POA's signature on your practice registration form, indicating the patient or their POA is granting you permission to provide the necessary audiologic diagnosis and treatment options. For those 18 years or younger, a note granting permission to evaluate and treat is required from the parent or guardian to provide audiologic services in that parent or guardian's absence (Abel & Hahn, 2006).

Privacy Officer

Every office providing health care in compliance with HIPAA has specified on their Notice of Privacy Practices (NPP) the name of their privacy officer. This is to be used if a patient has a complaint which can then be addressed in-house. According to HIPAA rules, a privacy officer must be designated by each health care facility. Should a patient wish to exercise their right to review their chart and request a change or otherwise amend their records, they will do so in accord with the designated privacy officer. The change or amendment to the record will be accepted or rejected by the privacy officer who will document the full transaction in the record. The patient may file a complaint if they disagree with the ruling of the privacy officer.

Privacy Exceptions

In daily clinical operations, audiologists will see evidence of child abuse or neglect and domestic violence. These situations require careful consideration and appropriate action. Referral to appropriate authorities in cases where abuse, neglect, or domestic violence is seen or suspected may be mandated by state licensing laws governing the practice of audiology or in other sections of laws pertaining to health care practitioners. Privacy concerns are effectively suspended in these cases; these patients need to be reported to the appropriate authorities immediately which may include law enforcement, children's services and/or domestic violence shelters. This should be addressed in your Notice of Privacy Practices (NPP).

Sign-in Sheets

Early in the process, there were many myths about what was allowed within the confines of HIPAA, some of which have persisted. The patient may sign in

on a sign-in sheet, but should not specify the reason for the visit. Many offices who utilize the sign-in process have a sticker on which the patient signs his or her name and is then peeled off after their visit is noted. Charts and computer monitors must not face the patient or be in a highly trafficked area.

Collection Calls

Collection calls, informing patients of any test results, or discussing recommendations should be completed in an area where one will not be overheard. You should only speak to the patient about such issues and not anyone else unless it is specified in their NPP.

Reminder Cards and Office Newsletters

Reminder cards sent to the patient need to be in envelopes so that Personal Health Information (PHI) cannot be viewed. A newsletter or other form of mass mailing that provides general information is permissible as long as it does not include PHI or promote a specific product and/ or brand that could impart information about the PHI (Pessis, 2003).

Security and Information Protection

The intent of the security component of HIPAA is to protect data integrity, confidentiality and accessibility as part of an overall privacy strategy. It was implemented on April 21, 2005. The security section is composed of four categories: Administrative procedures, physical safeguards, technical data security services, and technical security mechanisms (Pessis & Williams, 2005):

- Administrative procedures covers documentation, how staff protects the data, the selection and execution of information. Assessment and review of information security procedures, manuals, and records is required.
- Physical safeguards address the actual computer system from theft, fire, intrusion, and other environmental hazards.
- Technical data security services safeguards the processes used to protect, control, and monitor information access. Computer passwords are included in this component as well as biometrics, smart cards, and electronic signatures.
- Technical security mechanisms are geared to prevent the intrusion of an unauthorized, uninvited outside source into your data. Firewalls and encryption apply to this component.

HIPAA Penalties

Violations of the Administrative Simplification Regulations can result in civil monetary penalties of $100 per violation, up to $25,000 per year. In 2005, the U.S. Department of Justice (DOJ) clarified who can be held criminally liable under HIPAA. Covered Entities (CE) and specified individuals, as explained below, who "knowingly" obtain or disclose individually identifiable health information in violation of the Administrative Simplification Regulations face a fine of up to $50,000, as well as imprisonment up to 1 year. Offenses committed under false pretenses allow penalties to be increased to a $100,000 fine, with up to 5 years in prison. Finally, offenses committed with the intent to sell, transfer, or use individually identifiable health information for

commercial advantage, personal gain, or malicious harm permit fines of $250,000, and imprisonment for up to 10 years (AMA, 2005).

National Identification Numbers

National Provider Identifier (NPI)

As of May 23, 2007 all health care providers are required to have secured their 10-digit NPI. The NPI is now the standard, unique number identifying each health care provider throughout the entire health care system in this country (Federal Register, 2004). This single provider number replaces all previous identifier numbers including the Medicare Provider Identifier Number (PIN). The NPI will be the only number a health care provider will use for their entire professional career. On-line application may be made at http://www.nppes.cms.hhs.gov/NPPES .

National Employer Identifier (NEI)

The National Employer Identifier (NEI) became effective on August 1, 2005 for small health plans and all other covered entities. This nine-digit number is assigned by the Internal Revenue Service to all health care facilities and employers. All practice venues are required to have this number for billing purposes. The NEI is required on every CMS 1500 billing form. It is also required by other third party payors on requests for reimbursement. If the practice has multiple offices, only one NEI is required and each office is also required to have an NPI number.

State Regulations and Licensure

Audiologists are regulated by state licensure or registration in all 50 states. Licensure and registration is mandated for the purpose of consumer protection. These laws and administrative rules set forth minimum qualifications, competencies, and continuing education requirements to practice audiology. It is incumbent on every licensed or registered health care practitioner to understand their respective laws and rules. Ignorance is not an adequate defense; if you are registered or licensed as a health care practitioner, you are burdened with the implied acceptance that you have read and understand all tenets of the laws and rules governing your professional involvement with patients under your care. Should a licensee or registrant violate the laws or rules, the consequences may include restriction or loss of the license to practice. This also applies to those who come under your direct supervision in the practice. Licenses and registration certificates carry the weight of law: Billing for services performed without a license is fraud and subject to criminal penalties.

Certification

There is a significant difference between obtaining and maintaining a license to practice and being a participant in a pro-gram of certification. State laws require health care practitioners to be licensed to practice their specialty within the broad range of opportunities that comprise the delivery of health care in their respective states. Certification is voluntary. By submitting to a process of certification, usually offered in accord with a professional organization, the applicant indicates their specific credentials and preparation to meet the requirements for the certificate. Certification is an affirmation awarded to an individual by a body of his or her peers. It recognizes specific accomplishments and may define an area of specialty preparation or advanced study. The American Academy of Audiology endorses and supports board certification and specialty certification through the American Board of Audiology (ABA). The ABA has a Managing Director and an elected Board of Directors that manages the certification process from application to granting of general board certification and recently developed opportunities for specialty certification. To date, no third party payor requires board certification for reimbursement. Specialty certification for those with recognized, advanced academic preparation and clinical training may, at some point in time, stand as the only provider to be reimbursed for services provided under their specialty certification.

Summary

The importance of compliance with state and federal laws and Medicare guidelines cannot be understated. Notices to be provided to patients such as the ABN and NEMB must be completed at the right time and for appropriate reasons. Correct billing procedures must be followed to avoid unpleasant entanglements with regulatory and third party payors alike.

This chapter aimed to describe coding and billing mechanisms and to illustrate other practice management and compliance issues vital to the success of the practice. Submitting proper CPT and ICD-9 codes to optimize the likelihood of reimbursement is a minor operational consideration in the grand scheme of reimbursement capture. In order to maintain compliance, a host of actions must be considered including appending appropriate modifiers, following guidelines for referrals, issuing alerting notices when needed and securing prior authorizations for services when required. Equally vital is the knowledge of whether balance billing the patient is permitted after the insurance benefits have been paid: maintaining a steady cash flow for services provided by private pay patients and third party payors is required as well.

HIPAA compliance requires careful and consistent activities within the practice as does compliance with Antikickback and Stark Laws when working with various suppliers and vendors.

The path to a successful practice involves a multiplicity of rules and compliance requirements. The philosophical mantra for the practice must be "*insurance is a mechanism for reimbursement, not a form of payment*" (Pessis & Williams, 2005). As respected care providers in today's demanding health care arena, audiologists must recognize the value their intervention and management of patients brings to the marketplace. Those valued services, when carefully considered and thoughtfully managed, will provide both professional and personal fulfillment, regardless of the practice setting.

References

Abel, D., & Hahn, R. (2006). Ethical issues in practice management. In T. Hamill (Ed.), *Ethics in audiology: Guidelines for ethical conduct in clinical, educational, and research setting* (pp. 61–74). Reston, VA: American Academy of Audiology.

Abel, D., & Hamill, T. (2004). Don't "fall" into hazardous practice. *Audiology Today*, *16(4)*, 30.

American Academy of Audiology's Coding and Practice Management Committee. (2006). *Capturing reimbursement: A guide for audiologists* (pp. 1.4–2.4, 3.1–8.6). Reston, VA: American Academy of Audiology.

American Academy of Audiology. (2007). *2007 Audiology superbill template*. Retrieved on April 2, 2007 from http://www.audiology.org/NR/rdonlyres/6A7E2DA8

American Academy of Audiology. (2007). *2007 Hearing aid superbill template*. Retrieved on April 2, 2007 from http:www.audiology.org/rdonlyres/A1547924

American Medical Association. (2004). *CPT process* (pp. 3–14). Chicago: Author.

American Medical Association. (2005). *HIPAA Violations and Enforcement*. Retrieved March 29, 2007 from http://www.amaassn.org/ama/pub/category/11805.html

Amlani, A. M. (2006). Study finds payment method may limit dispenser's fitting options. *Hearing Journal, 59*(3), 48–54.

CBS News. (2007). *Survey: Docs wined, dined by drug makers*. Retrieved April 26, 2007 from http://www.cbsnews.com/stories/2007/04/26/health/printable273050

Centers for Medicare and Medicaid Services. (2001). *Program Memorandum AB-01-144. ICD-9-CM coding for diagnostic tests*. Retrieved March 31, 2007 from http://www.cms.hhs.gov/transmittals/downloads/AB01144.pdf

Centers for Medicare and Medicaid Services. (2002). *Program memorandum AB-02-080. Audiologists-payment for services fur-*

nished. Retrieved June 3, 2002 from http://www.noridianmedicare.com/cgibin/coranto/viewnews.cgi?id

Centers for Medicare and Medicaid Services. (2003). *Medicare resident and new physician guide: Helping health care professionals navigate medicare.* Baltimore: Author.

Centers for Medicare and Medicaid Services. (2005). *History overview.* Retrieved April 30, 2007 from http://www.cms.hhs./History

Centers for Medicare and Medicaid Services. (2007). *Advanced beneficiary notice.* Retrieved April 1, 2007 from http://www.cms.hhs.gov/BNI/Downloads/CMSR131G.pdf

Centers for Medicare and Medicaid Services. (2007). *Electronic records overview.* Retrieved April 26, 2007 from http://www.cms.hhs.gov/EHealthRecords

Centers for Medicare and Medicaid Services. (2007). *Notice of exclusions of medicare benefits.* Retrieved April 1, 2007 from http://www.cms.hhs.gov/BNI/Downloads/CMS20007English.pdf

Centers for Medicare and Medicaid Services. (2007). *Pay for performance.* Retrieved April 26, 2007 from http://www.cms.hhs.gov/apps/media/press/release

Centers for Medicare and Medicaid Services. (2007). *Specialty MAC jurisdictions.* Retrieved April 30, 2007 from http://www.cms.hhs.gov/MedicareContractingReform/06_SpecialtyMACJurisdictions.asp#

Department of Labor. (2007). *About office of workers' compensation programs.* Retrieved April 26, 2007 from http://www.dol.gov

Grider, D. J. (2004). *Coding with modifiers.* Chicago: American Medical Association.

Hobot, R. (2006). Wisconsin Physician Services, *Medicare new provider training.* American Academy of Audiology, Minneapolis, MN, April, 2006.

Manning, W. L. (2007). Privacy and confidentiality in clinical data management systems: Why you should guard the safe. *Health Law Resource.* Retrieved April 21, 2007 from http://www.netreach.net/wmanning/cdm.htm

Medical Board of California. (2007). *Patient access to medical records.* Retrieved April 29, 2007 from http://www.mbc.ca.gov/Medical_Records_Access.htm

Metz, M. (2006). Ethics of professional communication. In T. Hamill (Ed.), *Ethics in audiology: Guide for ethical conduct in clinical, educational, and research settings,* (p. 45). Reston, VA: American Academy of Audiology.

Nigro, S. (1998). *Comments concerning a Medicare audit: Making peace with medicare.* Association of American Physicians and Surgeons, Inc. Retrieved April 29, 2007 from http://www.aapsonline.org/fraud/nigro.htm

Office of Inspector General. (2000). *Special fraud alert: Rental of space in physician offices by persons or entities to which physicians refer.* Retrieved May 28, 2006 from http://www.oig.hhs.gov/fraud/docsalertsandbulletins/office%20space.htm

Palmetto, G. B. A. (2007). *When and how do I use an advanced beneficiary notice (ABN)?* Retrieved April 1, 2007 from http://www.palmettogba.com/palmetto/providers.net

Pessis, P,. (2003, October). *Reimbursement: Am I playing by all of the rules?* Presentation at the Academy of Dispensing Audiologists Convention, Ft. Myers, FL.

Pessis, P., & Williams, K. (2005, March). *We're near the capitol so let's increase your capital!* American Academy of Audiology 17th Annual Convention Pre-Convention Seminar, Washington DC.

Pessis, P., Williams, K., & Freint, A. (2006, April). *Cracking the reimbursement code.* American Academy of Audiology Audiology NOW! 2006 Learning Lab, Minneapolis, MN.

Social Security Administration. (2007). *Disability benefits.* Retrieved April 29, 2007 from http://www.ssa.gov/pubs/10029.html#part11

Strom, K. (2000, Sept.). Valuable services. *The Hearing Review.* Retrieved April 10, 2007 from www.hearingreview.com/issues/articles/2000-09_07.asp

Yale-New Haven Hospital and Yale University School of Medicine. (1997). Frequently asked questions about medical records. *Risk management handbook.* Retrieved May 9, 2007 from www.med.yale.edu/caim/risk/handbook/rmh_medical_record 2html

6

Referral Source Management

ROBERT G. GLASER, Ph.D.

Referral Source Acquisition

Acquiring referral sources is important to ensure the long-term success of your practice. A creative blend of consistent, professional marketing strategies is necessary to populate the practice referral base. Besides satisfied patients, referral sources will most likely include primary care and internal medicine physicians, neurologists, physiatrists, psychologists, optometrists, podiatrists, speech-language pathologists, nurses, a variety of other health care professionals, front office personnel and practice administrators.

A benchmark of the reputation of a practice within the professional community is the productivity of its referral base. It is an index of confidence and trust in the quality and consistency of services provided to their patients while in your practice. A productive referral base indicates confidence that your reports will contain important information that contributes to the overall care of the patient. A referral from the patient's primary care provider or other trusted, health care professional sets the stage for the initial patient encounter. It immediately develops a positive mind set about your services well in advance of the patient's arrival at the receptionist's window.

There is no harm in making the referring professional shine in the eyes of their patients. Recognizing the referral source for his or her insight into the patient's particular set of communication difficulties bolsters the patient's perception of the quality of care provided by the referring health care provider. Patients like to hear that those providing their health care are interested, insightful, and knowledgeable about when to refer to the proper professional to help with their hearing or balance difficulties. Just as the referral to your practice is a statement of your credibility as a provider, positive comments about the referring practitioner will boost their image in the patient's eyes. Consumer loyalty is as important to referring professionals as it is to the success of your practice. Physicians and other health care providers are interested in keeping their patients satisfied as much as keeping them healthy and functioning well in their daily life activities. Anything you do to bolster patient attitude and loyalty to the practitioner who referred them to your practice will help retain that provider as a productive member of your referral base.

Referral Source Retention

High patient satisfaction is elemental in retaining referral sources. It must be the foremost goal of every practice and a pervasive force that drives each member of the professional and support staffs. Patient satisfaction is not just about the patient. It includes encounters with family members, friends, and others interested in the patient's communication difficulties.

Family and concerned friends will also provide impetus to those with hearing loss to come to your practice. They are interested in the outcome of your clinical intervention and have a vested interest in the patient's success as they also stand to benefit by the patient's improved communication capabilities: As such, family and friends should be included in the process at every opportunity.

Patients and a family member or friend should be invited into the examination or fitting room to observe. They should be included in the question and answer segments of the process and during counseling. Of course, this must be in compliance with the patient's wishes. With individuals other than the patient in the examination or fitting room, care must be taken to focus on the patient and his or her needs primarily. The patient must never be left out of the conversation nor become less than the center of attention of all involved. Having family or friends involved in the patient's evaluation and rehabilitation is a welcomed benefit for the clinician. They provide insight into the effects the patient's communication difficulties are having in their relationship and can serve as strong supporters for the patient after the fitting. Additionally, they may serve as keen observers of the patient's compliance, successes, and circumstances of poor performance. Most family and friends are pleased to be included in the process and have the patient's best interest at heart.

Patients returning to the referring practitioner commonly report on their visit to your practice. The practitioner will likely discuss the findings and recommendations in your report. That prompts the patient to share specific information about their perception of their visit to your office. If your practice has succeeded in its goal to develop high patient satisfaction, the patient will sing praises about the hospitality of the office staff from initial phone call and appointment making to their experience at checkout—and every step in between.

Satisfied patients will tell the referring practitioner exactly what he or she thought of your demeanor, your skills, and the completeness of your examination. Not much gets by patients and they readily advise their physicians (as well as their friends) about the positives and negatives of a practitioner. After all, your practice was entrusted to participate in a segment of their health care and as a result, your practice has become an integral link to both the referral source and their patient.

Despite the fact that the patient had positive feelings prior to getting to your practice and as they trust their health care practitioner to send them to someone who is honest, fair, courteous, and above all, professional, all of this can unravel rapidly at the reception desk or if the patient is left waiting beyond their scheduled appointment time. If a patient thinks the practitioner or his staff cares little about the importance of their time or if the receptionist meets them with a terse greeting, the likelihood of losing a referral source increases.

There are other important ways to retain your referral sources. Serving as a readily available resource by phone or E-mail, providing in-office seminars about how staff should approach those with hearing impairment, and talking to the referral source's civic group are a few activities to maintain a good relationship with your referral sources. Occasionally there will be patients referred by family or friends or who respond to your mar-

keting efforts but do not have a family physician for one reason or another. Should they ask for a referral to a primary care provider, choose an appropriate health care provider from your referral base. Have your staff contact the office to make sure they are taking new patients and that they know your practice is referring the patient to them. Consider the value a new referral is to your practice and the impact will be similar to the practitioner to whom you have made the referral.

Clinical excellence and high patient satisfaction are essential to retaining valued referral sources. On-time arrival for scheduled visits, having a sincere interest in their patient's well-being, and sending a reciprocal referral from time to time will go far to sustain the need for your referral sources to continue to send patients to your practice.

Communicating with Referral Sources

Reporting Findings: Turnaround Time; Format and Content; Recommendations

Report Turnaround Time

Though content may reign supreme when it comes to reporting clinical findings, report turnaround time from patient visit to the referring health care practitioner, will separate your practice from others. In this day of tomorrow-is-too-late information exchanges, consistently slow report turnaround time could result in your referral source searching for other providers to rely on for consistency and better accountability to their practice.

How slow is "too slow" depends on each referring practitioner's needs and practice pattern. Every setting providing clinical services should strive for 24 hour turnaround time on reports of findings and follow-up visits or progress notes. At least a 48-hour turnaround time should be the longest period from completion of services to faxing or mailing clinical findings or reports of follow-up visits.

Establishing a habit of writing your clinical reports immediately following each patient encounter, fosters a fresh perspective on important information obtained during the visit. Dictation used to be the method of choice to expedite documentation and create reports. With the advent of electronic medical records (EMR) and word processing programs loaded with prewritten report segments, it is far more efficient to compile reports for mailing or fax transmission before the patient leaves the office—a lofty but attainable goal.

Although there will be special cases and forms to be completed that will require more time and attention after the patient has left your office, if you get into the habit of completing clinical reports and progress notes immediately, specialized reporting will require less time and attention. You will have far less of a stack of reports to complete at the end the day, and will be better able to remember the details of each patient visit.

Referral sources take careful note of reports that are missing when the patient returns to their office. The worst-case scenario for the referral source is the patient in the exam room with the practitioner trying to explain why your report is not in their chart. Although the report may be languishing in the practitioner's to-be-filed basket, calls can be expected from the practitioner or a member of the practice's clerical staff for an immediate phone report, an admonishment, or both.

A good strategy to optimize turnaround time and create a record of report transmission is to list the details of the transmission in the chart. Develop an internal sheet for the chart or use the left side of the chart jacket to record the date, time, description of the document, and where it was sent. Should the referring practitioner call your practice to inquire why they do not have a report in their file, your staff will have a complete record of the transmission. If it was not sent, an apology and/or immediate fax or E-mail must be sent: If it was sent, the referring practitioner's staff "should" rummage through their piles of reports-to-be filed to locate the appropriate document. Your practice will, occasionally, be asked to resend a report because their staff person is too lazy or overworked to take the time to search through the pile for your report. If this becomes a consistent pattern, a call to the office manager must be considered to rectify the situation.

Report Format and Content

Good clinical reporting characterizes the symbiotic relationship of content and brevity. Content reigns supreme when it comes to reporting clinical findings: Brevity is equally important. Health care practitioners sending patients to your practice do not have time to wade through three pages of discourse and data to get to the critical message that their patient has normal hearing. For the most part, they have no interest in looking at the waveforms of a brainstem response and may not have time to review the audiogram and tympanograms. They are interested in your findings and opinions about their patient's status.

The information provided by your practice will help solidify the diagnostic classification of their patient. Including a title or line segment in your report entitled "*DIAGNOSIS*" offers the reader an opportunity to move directly to the most important line in the report. An example of the written section of a brief format report is presented in Figure 6–1. The audiogram, speech threshold, and recognition score as well as other clinical information are immediately above the report language on the same page. Middle ear findings and otoacoustic emissions data are on the reverse side of the report.

In this recommended format, diagnostic classifications are listed followed by their respective ICD code numbers on the "*Diagnosis*" line. The referring practitioner will use these codes to support their documentation about the patient's ongoing health care and diagnostic classification for a variety of reasons including reimbursement. An active medical record in a physician's office commonly contains a patient's current diagnostic codes. These codes are present whether specific treatment is underway even if they are not likely to change as in sensorineural hearing loss.

When a patient has been referred to your practice or clinical area for an extensive evaluation, the reporting structure must be modified. The most efficient way to handle a great deal of information is to send relevant data along with a letter or cover sheet summarizing the results, diagnostic classifications, and listing recommendations.

REFERRAL: Dr. Smith   **AUDIOLOGIST:** Robert G. Glaser, Ph.D.

HISTORY: Pt. describes increasing difficulty understanding speech in a variety of communication settings. Wife & family concurs. He reports long-standing, nondisruptive, nonpulsatile, high-pitched tinnitus at each ear. He denies dysequilibrium, familial history of hearing loss and takes no medicine. He has worked as a toolmaker without hearing protection for >25 yrs.

HEARING: Severe, high-frequency, sensorineural loss occurring symmetrically with distinctive "noise notch" and moderately reduced speech recognition at each ear.

MIDDLE EAR FUNCTION: Normal middle ear function, bilaterally.

DIAGNOSIS: Noise-induced hearing loss 388.12; Impaired auditory discrimination 388.43; Tinnitus 388.31.

PLAN/TREATMENT: Pt. and wife counseled with findings. Recommendations include consistent use of hearing protection devices and suggestions to improve communication efficiency. Advised candidacy for high-frequency emphasis amplification; information provided. To return to Dr. Smith as planned.

Figure 6–1. Example of brief format report.

The referring practitioner should be able to easily and quickly locate important diagnostic information and your recommendation(s) for treatment. A letter or cover sheet with a "quick look" summary will increase efficiency for the referring physician and increase the likelihood of future referrals to your practice as well and allow the referring physician to make their diagnoses easily. Sending reports littered with multiple pages of information that the referring practitioner does not need or may not understand, defeats the purpose of the summary page. For example, if the patient has undergone a tinnitus evaluation, the results of tinnitus mapping procedures, brainstem response data, and severity inventories will be meaningful to you as a clinician but not to the referring physician and should not be included.

On the other hand, a patient who has been in an accident wherein he sustained a fracture of the temporal bone resulting in unilateral deafness, all clinical data obtained should be included with the summary as they are important to the patient's ongoing care and critical for comprehensive, medicolegal documentation.

Recommendations

When a health care practitioner sends a patient to your practice for an evaluation, they do so because they are interested in your findings as well as your recommendations. They have invited you to become a participant in their patient's care and management. They expect recommendations; they do not have to agree with them nor act on them. If your findings support a high index of suspicion of a retrocochlear lesion, it is reasonable for you to suggest they consider an MRI of the posterior fossa. A recommendation couched as a suggestion gives the referring practitioner an option rather than an apparent order.

Although most physicians will pay attention to such a suggestion, some may choose to ignore it and pursue other diagnostic options or referrals. A direct recommendation for an MRI, however, puts the referring physician in a situation where he is compelled by your direction to have the patient undergo an MRI. If your direct recommendation includes a statement such as " further studies are indicated including an MRI " the referring physician has little choice but to comply with your recommendation. It is always better to offer suggestions that have ample room for the selection of medical diagnostic procedures by the patient's physician. It is not the audiologist's choice to make despite the knowledge that a specific medical diagnostic study has the necessary value in making the differential diagnosis. If there is a particular patient with a high index of suspicion of a retrocochlear lesion based on audiologic and vestibular test findings, a telephone conversation with the managing physician will afford the opportunity to offer comments that will not appear in the records of your report of findings.

When recommending treatment involving hearing instruments, state your suggestions with clarity. Do not overwhelm the referring physician with unnecessary information in an effort to demonstrate your knowledge or clinical prowess. If the patient is a candidate for binaural placement, indicate that despite the fact that the patient has issued protests indicating his interest in a monaural placement. You must issue recommendations that will optimize your patient's outcome. If the patient chooses to wear only one hearing instrument, it becomes a choice beyond your clinical judgment and recommendation.

Indicate expected limitations and specific needs relative to the patient's hearing loss, speech recognition, and tolerance issues. If you foresee several options, or a lack of options, include that information in your recommendations. If you anticipate difficulties during the fitting and adjustment process, they should be stated in detail appropriate to the issue(s).

Reporting Interactions with Difficult Patients

Individuals with hearing impairment can, at times, become angry and explosive in the office. Diminished communication capabilities foster these outbursts and frustrations. The cost of the instruments and unrealistic expectations versus actual performance can set the stage for reduced patient satisfaction (Faiers & McCarthy, 2004). Anger is a common situational response during the assessment, fitting, and adjustment process. It is often displaced and the professional managing the patient's hearing care is a common target for the expression of anger (Hawkins, 2005). Despite appropriate strategies to provide evidence of value and effectiveness prior to and during the fitting process, anger and aggressive behaviors can sometimes escalate to a point where the patient may be asked to leave the office.

If the patient exhibits aggressive or threatening behaviors, they need to be documented in the record precisely as the events happened. Note who was an observer at the time and how staff reacted to the patient's behaviors. Immediately after the episode has been documented, the referring practitioner or primary care provider should be called and advised of the situation. That telephone conversation should be followed by written correspondence confirming the call and how you plan to address the situation with the patient in the long term. Depending on the extent of the outburst and the effects on you and your staff, you may be unwilling to see the patient again. If that is the decision, it must be so indicated in written correspondence to the referring practitioner. Also, depending on the severity and circumstances of the situation, a certified letter may be sent to the patient confirming that you will no longer participate in his or her care with an alphabetical listing of area providers. It is advisable to discuss this matter with your attorney prior to contacting the patient.

Practice-to-Practice Marketing to Retain Referral Sources

There is an old adage that is appropriate when considering your relationship with a referring practitioner and his or her office staff: "*Nothing succeeds like success.*" Consistent and timely report turnaround, concise and accurate reporting of your findings, unequivocal diagnoses with associated ICD-9 codes, and clear recommendations and suggestions for continued care or assessment characterize items and actions that should be in place on a routine basis. No gold stars should be issued for compliance with a practice standard of excellence. Adherence to clinical details, accurate results, and reporting enables a referring professional to rely on your participation in the care of their patients. And the successes you establish with the patients you serve as well as the response to the referring practitioners will likely enhance their level of care as well as their patient's loyalty.

In Chapter 12 to come, marketing strategies are considered in the basics of marketing of your practice. Beyond those basic strategies, other opportunities arise to continue marketing on a different, more specific level. An often overlooked opportunity for marketing to referral sources within the practitioner's office includes their office staff—receptionist, billing and coding personnel, office managers, and the clinical staff—nurses, physician's assistants, and nursing assistants. When a patient calls the office to inquire about having their hearing evaluated, the front office staff might make the referral to your practice immediately by issuing your practice name, address, and phone number. If the call is passed on to the clinical staff, the nurse, for example, will likely triage the request to determine if the patient needs to come in or can be referred to your office for assessment. If you have developed a positive reputation with the front office and clinical staff in a referring provider's office, you will likely enjoy the luxury of direct referrals for your services. Some primary care physicians require seeing their patient before granting a referral to another health care provider's office for assessment or consultation. If that is the rule, and you have developed a positive reputation for consistent and reliable service provision with that physician, you will likely get a referral for that patient as quickly as you did from the front office or clinical staff in another office without physician requirement.

Image Management

Image management is crucial to your success. It is most important that you foster and maintain a good, professional image within the medical community and as well in the community at large. If you are viewed as a colleague in the give-and-take realm of professional referrals in health care, your future will be bright and your practice will be populated with a stream of patients. There are two simple ways to enhance your image by increasing your local professional visibility. Providing lectures at professional functions such as meetings of departments of family practice or pediatrics at the local medical school or during specialty group meetings of medical societies in your practice demographic will go far to establish your credentials and clinical offerings in your practice.

Another way to bolster your professional image in the health care arena is to advertise in the local medical society membership directory. These advertisements must maintain a minimalist attitude while establishing your office and location(s) as the best source of care available in the community. Call the local medical society to check out advertising possibilities and rates. They will be pleased to help you in your efforts to access their members.

Excellent services sell themselves. If you are receiving referrals from an individual health care practitioner within a practice group, that particular referring practitioner will likely inform the other practitioners or their respective clinical staff about the level of care and interest your practice has afforded his or her patients. These "internal referral systems" will, in effect, link your practice with theirs when it comes to the services available in your practice.

The more opportunities created to maintain good will and a good, professional image for you and your practice, the more patients you will see in your practice. Making it easy for the front office and clinical staffs of referring health care providers cannot be overstated. Taking over the appointment so that their office staff has less involvement in the booking is a small but important strategy. Get the patients off their plate and put them on yours. When your front office staff takes charge of the appointment, efficiency increases and the likelihood of booking errors that can result in patient frustrations are reduced—good for the patient and for both offices.

Image management also includes your reports of findings and informational and practice-related brochures. If your letterhead or reporting form has a list of services available on the left margin or elsewhere, all segments of the referring practitioner's office personnel will be reminded each time a letter or report is read or is to be filed or comes across the nurse's desk preparing the chart for the patient's visit. Helpful brochures about speech and language development, the damaging effects of excessive or unprotected noise exposure, and information about tinnitus are a few examples of informational brochures used by primary care physicians as waiting room items or when counseling their patients. It is best to tailor these brochures and have them printed locally. As for linking the brochures to your office, subtle listing on the reverse side of the brochure will increase the likelihood they will be accepted and used in their office. If it appears to be a commercial for your practice, it will limit use in medical practice offices.

Who Are Your Clients?

Your clients will vary depending on the professional circumstance. For a primary health care provider, patients may come from the entire population in a specific demographic area surrounding the office. The demographic area can be defined by drive times to the office, specific counties or municipalities, or by other markers of interest to that particular practice. As generalists in medicine see the young and the old, the urgent and the routine, their potential client base is truly the entire population in a particular area (Rainer, 2004). For specialty care physicians, the population of patients narrows and dependency on referrals from primary care providers increases. Specialists, therefore, see those who refer patients to their practices as their clients.

Audiologists providing comprehensive diagnostic and rehabilitative care will have patients coming to their practice from their own advertising efforts, word-of-mouth referrals based on successful evaluation and treatment of other patients, and as walk-ins. Patients coming to the practice in this fashion become the clients of the audiologist. Those referred to the audiologist by another health care practitioner are certainly patients to be cared for in the practice; however, the client in this case is the referring health care practitioner.

Why does it matter how the patient arrives at your door? It matters in the sense of the dynamics of the referral including how information is to be issued and under what conditions of care the patient enters the audiology practice. It is an axiom of good practice that every patient should receive the same level of excellent care. When a patient comes to the practice without another health care provider's referral, their care from assessment to rehabilitative care is a matter of your management. That does not lessen the burden of communicating with their primary care provider as a matter of professional courtesy, a common occurrence in the medical community at large.

Medical Records and the Primary Care Provider

As the repository of medical records, primary care providers should receive reports of findings and recommendations as if they had referred the patient to your practice. If the patient has no primary care provider, recommend a provider or group that will most likely meet their needs within the community. Matching the patient to the right practice is important and the better you know your referral sources and their front office and clinical staffs, the better you can match the patient to the practice. Write a letter of introduction for the patient to the primary care provider after you have contacted their practice to ensure they are seeing new patients. It is best to make these connections prior to the patient leaving your office. Everyone wins when you match your patient with the right primary care provider. These referrals are appreciated and do not go unnoticed in the primary care practice. Think of the opportunity for both the patient and the physician to make a long-term commitment to a good patient-provider relationship. Not only is it a good fiscal benefit to the primary care provider, the patient will thank you for the referral for many years to come.

When another health care provider sends a patient to your practice for evaluation, you are bound to transmit your findings, diagnoses, and recommendations relative to your findings. As the referral came to your office, it is inappropriate for you to make referrals to other health care providers without involving the patient's physician directly. When asked to provide your diagnostic assessment and input, you are asked to do so with the unwritten knowledge that authority for referrals to other practitioners rests solely with the attending physician who sent the patient to your office.

For example, if your findings support the need for a referral to an ENT physician, a patient who walked into your office for an appointment on his own accord may be referred directly to the ENT physician. That same patient, when referred to your office by a primary care provider, should be returned to the primary care provider with your reasons and recommendations that he or she be referred to the ENT physician: Referring a patient to another provider without notifying or consulting with the original health care practitioner who sent the patient to your office, is the fastest way to lose a valued, medical referral source.

Strategic Assessment of Referral Sources

Once your relationship with other health care providers in the community is established and referrals are coming in on a regular basis, you will want to learn how your practice can better facilitate their patient's care. Are you meeting their expectations for the patients referred to your practice? Knowing that each referring practice will have different needs and perceptions about how you are (or should be) servicing their patients, responses to these inquiries will vary greatly (Levoy, 2002). Assessment can be as simple as a phone call to the referring practitioner's office manager or clinical staff manager. Ask questions about their views on your practice's efficiency, turn-around time on reports, patient's perceptions of your services or office staff, whether your reports provide adequate information in a succinct fashion. The call need only take a few minutes to get to the heart of the questions. Expect truthful answers, and if they are negative, seek their input on a solution or ask if you might call back with a resolution based on a staff meeting or conversation with other members of your practice. If the negative response is coupled with a noted decline in referrals from their practice, it may be time to make an appointment to talk to their clinical staff or with the physician(s) in the practice to further explore the situation and to develop an equitable resolution. Another way to get feedback about the effectiveness of your practice and a referral source is to send a brief questionnaire about your services. It should contain no more than eight to ten items in a check-off format. A franked, return envelope addressed to your practice must be included. The idea is to make it as easy as possible to complete the task and put it in the outgoing mail basket. Address the envelope to specific individuals in the office. The office manager and members of the clinical staff are the most likely personnel to complete the task.

Evidence-Based Assessment of Referral Source Activity

Assessing the numbers of referrals made from specific health care providers can be a relatively simple matter. There must be a section on the patient information sheet to list the person who made the referral to your practice. That person may be different from their primary care physician; therefore, an additional line must be designated specifically for their primary care provider. These two opportunities will enable accurate tabulation of the referral source whether they are the primary care provider, another health care practitioner, or a friend or relative.

Numbers of patients referred to the practice should be tallied for each referral source. To consider referral patterns, these data can be listed monthly or by each quarter of the fiscal year to determine trends that may develop to guide your marketing efforts. If referrals for a particular provider decline in a certain period, marketing efforts should be directed immediately prior to that time period next year in an attempt at "smoothing" the referral pattern. If the referral source is a group of health care practitioners, it is best to tally the referrals by each practitioner within the group. Each practitioner may develop his or her own pattern depending on their level of participation within the group. Those practitioners who fall significantly behind in referrals in that group should receive more attention when marketing to the group at large.

Taking the pulse of your referral sources can lead to valuable introspective assessment of your practice and how it is interacting with a specific practice as well as the health care community at large. If a particular referring group or individual practitioner has fallen off their usual pace of referrals, it could signal dissatisfaction with your services or the availability of another provider in the area. A review of patient charts from that practice within the time period when referrals have declined might lend insight into the decline. One dissatisfied, vocal patient can affect the referral patterns of a physician or his or her clinical staff members who are also responsible for referring patients. Their response to the patient's complaints may seem punitive, and in some cases they are just that, but without your vigilance you may never have the opportunity of initiating a phone call to inquire about the decline in referrals. Straightforward inquiries usually get straightforward answers which can lead to dialogue and resolution of the problem, real or imagined. Taking the time to analyze drops in referral rates will provide information critical to both the short- and long-term success of your practice.

Once a collegial relationship has been developed with referring health care practitioners, you can expect direct communication when patients provide information (real or imagined) about a topic or situation that may have arisen from a recent trip to your office.

An example drawn from practice records describes a patient returning to the referring physician after a hearing assessment advising their physician that the practice no longer accepted Medicare patients. That was a surprise to the physician who promptly called the office to validate their patient's claim. Medicare patients have always been welcomed in the practice despite the fact that coverage includes only the hearing examination without coverage of hearing instruments or related items or activities. In further discussions with the referring physician it became clear that the patient had confused statements regarding coverage by Medicaid versus Medicare. The physician was advised that the practice was unable to accept Medicaid patients in the practice unless the patients are enrolled in the local Medicaid HMO system. This particular patient was covered by Medicaid but was not enrolled in the local HMO system. As such, the patient was not eligible for aural rehabilitation services through the practice. After the patient enrolled in the Medicaid HMO, the practice continued to provide services to that patient and many more referred by that physician who took the time and trouble to get to the bottom of a dilemma that did not seem to agree with past actions of the practice. He cared not just about his patient but also about the practice wherein his patients had received excellent care for many years.

References

Faiers, G., & McCarthy, P. (2004). Study explores how paying effects hearing aid users' satisfaction. *Hearing Journal*, 57(12), 25–32.

Hawkins, D. (2005). When you're attacked: Fight, flight, or what? *Hearing Journal*, 58(4), 76.

Levoy, B. (2002). *201 Secrets of a high-performance optometric practice*. Woburn, MA: Elsevier Science.

Rainer, C. (2004). *Practice management: A practical guide to running a medical office*. Lima, OH: Wyndham Hall Press.

7

Patient Management

ROBERT G. GLASER, Ph.D.

The Importance of Nonclinical Activities in Your Practice

Successful patient management is not solely about assessment, therapeutic intervention, and clinical technique. There are a surprising number of nonclinical activities that can significantly affect the continuum of a patient's care. This chapter explores how nonclinical activities affect your ability to provide quality care, increase patient satisfaction, and develop patient loyalty to your practice.

Patient care begins when a member of the front office staff schedules an appointment. The person on the other end of the line moves from caller to patient in a matter of minutes. The caller, now patient, will be arriving at your office expecting a high degree of professionalism, timely service, attentive staff, and caregivers sensitive to their particular needs. Every patient must experience seamless transitions from the waiting area to exam room, from exam room to payment window, and from departure to promised follow-up care. Seamless transitions in any health care setting depends on the synchrony of the front office and professional staffs and how well they take care of patients at the center of their coordinated efforts.

Developing Patient Loyalty

"The best customers, we're told, are loyal ones. They cost less to serve, they are usually willing to pay more than other customers, and they often act as word-of-mouth marketers for your company" (Reinartz & Kumar, 2002). In their extensive study of critical business relationships, Reinartz and Kumar (2002) establish several factual statements based on customer loyalty that are directly applicable to the services provided in everyday clinical practice:

■ Customer satisfaction is the key to customer loyalty. (Satisfied patients will likely return for repeat services.)
■ Loyal customers expect tangible benefits for their loyalty. (Patients expect cost breaks on batteries, special "tune ups," etc.)
■ Loyal customers become more price sensitive. (Second or third set of aids expected to cost "reasonably" more than the last set.)
■ Loyal customers may not be less expensive to maintain. (Consistent marketing necessary to obtain as well as retain patients.)
■ Loyal customers provide effective word-of-mouth marketing. (Satisfied patients will recommend your services to others.)

Building "patient loyalty" can be expensive in both time and capital. It is, however, a task that both front office and professional staff alike must continuously and consistently strive to develop. Each patient encounter is an opportunity to foster patient loyalty: It is, as well, an opportunity to derail patient loyalty. Patient loyalty must be considered in the diagnostic phase as much as the rehabilitative segment of a patient's journey through your practice. All forms of communication with your patients must focus on developing and maintaining patient loyalty; telephone conversations, newsletters, reminder letters, special offers, and other advertising medium used to communicate with your existing database of patients.

Patient loyalty begins and ends with highly satisfied patients. According to Wong Hickson, and McPherson (2003), satisfaction ratings are likely influenced more by how well patients are treated than by the sound quality and improved speech intelligibility that their hearing aids provide. Satisfied patients are more likely to seek your guidance and care for the long term. If you are seeing the majority of your patient base annually, providing meaningful services delivered in a sincere and patient centric manner, your patients will likely continue with your care and return to you for new hearing instruments when needed. It does not, however, take much to move a loyal patient in your database to one seeking an alternative location for their hearing care. The Research Institute of America reported on just how costly it is for businesses to be apathetic toward customer service. To underscore the point of importance to all in the business of providing professional services, we have inserted the word "patient" for "customer":

■ The average practice will hear nothing from 96% of unhappy patients who receive rude or discourteous treatment.
■ 90% of patients who are dissatisfied with the services they receive will not come back or buy again from the offending practice.

- Each unhappy patient tells his or her story to an average of nine other people.
- Only 4% of unhappy patients bother to complain to your office—they will complain to the referral source and will do so loudly and vociferously.
- Of those patients voicing a complaint, between 54 and 70% will do business again with the organization if their complaint is resolved—-that figure rises to 95% if the patient feels the complaint is resolved quickly.
- 68% of patients who refuse to return to a practice do so because of the perception that the practice is "indifferent."

With conventional wisdom putting the average life span of contemporary hearing instruments at 5 to 7 years, it becomes crucial to the long-term success of your practice to have patients return consistently for their hearing care. Hopkins (2006), while highlighting the importance in developing close, clinical relationships with patients, points out another reason to maintain a loyal patient database: "Even if your product has a long life span and people shouldn't need to replace it for a long time, you still want to work on keeping those clients (patients) loyal to you. The reason: They'll tell their friends, relatives and even strangers about what a great experience they had with you. They'll be your biggest fans and provide free advertising for your services with their testimonials and referrals."

Marketers refer to three stages of the customer/patient life cycle, each with critical points of contact with the practice: First-time customers, repeat customers, and customer advocates (Marsh, 2005). Creating a group of customer advocates who voluntarily function as true "cheer-leaders" is, without doubt, the greatest form of marketing and stands as a great tribute to any professional practice.

Patient loyalty should be considered an outcome of the practice's dedication and diligence in developing and maintaining patient satisfaction. Long-term, loyal patients will be the desired outcome if they are well satisfied, and treated with respect, dignity, and technical excellence by every member of the practice team. To maintain patient loyalty, each patient must be absolutely delighted with your services; being satisfied is no longer sufficient. Patients dissatisfied with your services for whatever reason, real or imagined, are likely to be lost forever.

Figure 7–1 depicts the interrelationship and importance of patients classified in one of three, distinct categories: Dissatisfied, Simply Satisfied, and Absolutely Delighted. Dissatisfied patients are in an Area of Discord. They are, for whatever reason, dissatisfied with services or personnel in the practice: They are unhappy and when asked about their experiences in the practice will probably issue strongly negative comments. Negative word-of mouth comments can be damaging to the reputation of a practice. Positive word-of-mouth comments also have impact on the reputation of a practice. To illustrate the impact of word-of-mouth comments, consider a restaurant you went to recently for the first time. Chances are high that you decided to try the restaurant based on a word-of-mouth recommendation. And if you valued the person's opinion because he or she is a good cook or an ardent gastronome, the value of that recommendation will have added credibility and increased the likelihood of your acting on the recommendation. Consider the same scenario for

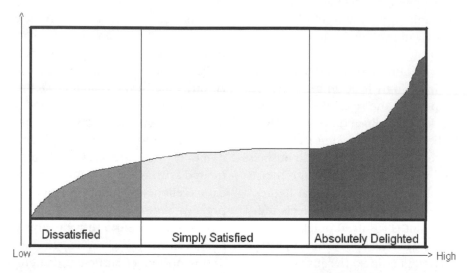

Figure 7–1. Levels of patient satisfaction and effect on loyalty to the practice.

negative word-of-mouth comments. If the comment about the restaurant was negative from that same, credible source, the likelihood that you would not visit the restaurant would likely be higher than going to the restaurant based on a positive comment.

The same holds true for health care practices. Positive word-of-mouth testimonials may not ensure a new patient appointment in your practice; however, negative word-of-mouth statements, will likely derail many more potential appointments than you can imagine.

Study after study in business journals and textbooks confirm that more people will be influenced by negative comments about a business or a practice than positive comments. The enduring folklore about the relative efficacy of positive and negative word-of-mouth "reputations" suggests that a well-satisfied patient typically talks to 3 or 5 people whereas a disgruntled patient will replay a discordant event to as many as 10 or more individuals. Add that to the "word-of-mouse" world of Internet-bolstered communica-

tion and the potential numbers of contacts a determined, dissatisfied patient can reach in your local practice area expands at an alarming rate. Improving patient satisfaction will decrease the likelihood of negative word-of-mouth comments about your practice. Nevertheless, it is best to always offer your patients accessibility to communicate their dissatisfaction with any member of the practice team. Better those patients complain to personnel within the practice who can intervene and remedy a bad situation than to issue complaints and dissatisfaction to their family and friends.

Practices with even a few patients in the Area of Discord depicted in Figure 7-1 are operating suboptimally. Dissatisfied patients will leave the practice to reduce existing discord and avoid future conflict. Retrieving these patients requires a frank assessment of their discord and an immediate, personal response to eliminate the source of the disharmony. Once the source of the discord is identified and an affirmative plan to resolve the situation is set into motion for the individual and his or her family, the patient is likely to move quickly to Area of Simply Satisfied. It may not take much to achieve this shift. An acknowledgment of an error, an apology, an indication of your sincere appreciation of their being a patient in the practice, and perhaps a reasonable token of appreciation for their willingness to readjust their thinking could, potentially, move them to the Area of the Absolutely Delighted.

Patients in the Area of the Simply Satisfied may not be the best asset to your practice as they are susceptible to competitor outreach in advertising or direct solicitation offering technical advances, simplicity of operation, or compelling pricing strategies. As a group, these patients pay little attention to efforts to foster patient loyalty and many demonstrate the attitude of "what-have-you-done-for-me-lately?" at each visit to the practice. They are less concerned about the practice and more concerned about price than most patients. They rarely recommend the practice or comment about their experiences at the referring practitioner's office. Practices dedicated to simply maintaining good, yet basic care, dwelling on avoiding mistakes, just meeting patient needs, maintaining staff members with appropriate, yet limited enthusiasm will have a large section of their patient database falling in the Area of Simply Satisfied.

Patient-centric practices that value each patient as an engaged partner in their program of hearing or balance rehabilitation will generate a substantial number of patients in the Area of the Absolutely Delighted. These patients frequently become cheerleaders for the practice, recommending your services to family, friends, and strangers in casual conversations. They will thank the referral source

for his or her wisdom in recommending they seek their hearing care in your practice and will continue to sing your praises at every opportunity; bridge club, church group, or social gathering. These patients are worth far more to the practice than the revenue generated by their diagnostic studies, office visits, and hearing instruments.

Several key elements that must be present to elevate a person to the ranks of the Absolutely Delighted or increase the likelihood that a new patient will be initiated into the ranks of the Absolutely Delighted from the onset of their care include:

- Patient-centric practice
- No barriers to getting an appointment —ease of access to the practice
- Professionalism of each member of the practice team
- High technical expertise of professional staff
- Engaging, welcoming, and empowered front office staff
- Outstanding office space, accessible to all
- Referral sources positive about the practice and service to their patients
- Consistent follow-up care and follow-through on promises issued
- Easily accessible complaint system— ease of venting
- Prompt resolution of conflict or errors
- Interested, prompt, and attentive follow-up during resolution of complaint
- Never repeating the same error with the same patient-—or any other!

There is little doubt that negative word-of-mouth comments can destroy the reputation of a practice. Providing a patient with an avenue to express their dissatisfaction, and gain resolution of their problem, and an opportunity to stay in the practice that cares enough to resolve issues of discord will create increased patient satisfaction. Retrieving those patients lost to internal errors gives hope to all in the practice, patients, and staff, that even the most egregious errors can be rectified to everyone's satisfaction and benefit.

The Provider-Patient Relationship: Verbal and Nonverbal Communication

The manner in which a clinician communicates information to a patient is as important as the information being communicated. Patients, who understand their care providers are more likely to acknowledge their health problems, understand their treatment options and modify their behavior accordingly (Travaline, Ruchinskas, & D'Alonzo, 2005).

Beck, Dautridge, and Sloane (2004) reviewed an extensive body of published evidence linking specific verbal and nonverbal behaviors to short, intermediate, and long-term outcomes in interactions between primary care providers and their patients seen in their office practices. A total of 36 verbal and 16 nonverbal behaviors were considered from the 22 studies included in their meta-analysis. Despite the fact that these behaviors were included in controlled or descriptive studies involving primary care providers, the consistency of impact noted throughout the studies between the provider and the patient enables an appropriate extrapolation to health care providers in general and audiologists specifically. Many of the behaviors fostering positive

clinical outcomes (better patient compliance; improved response to various treatments; improved overall health status) describe a list of patient-centric behaviors necessary to develop patient comfort within the practice and to increase the likelihood of satisfaction with both professional and front office staffs. The list of behaviors linked to negative outcomes provides a guideline of behaviors to be avoided. Verbal behaviors associated with significant, positive patient outcomes are included in Figure 7–2.

Behaviors associated with significantly negative patient outcomes include those listed in Figure 7–3. These behaviors were found to consistently promote negative feelings and disenfranchisement to the extent that patients did not return to the providers studied. Although not reported, the literature on the topic of verbal and nonverbal behaviors likely to develop negative attitudes, loss of confidence, and patient exits from practices appear to be those that can easily permeate the atmosphere of any practice. This is especially true of those practices that fail to focus on the patients, their integration into the practice, and the levels of their satisfaction with all members of the practice staff.

Beck et al. (2004) describe 16 specific nonverbal behaviors found in one or more studies that were significantly associated with patient outcomes. Behaviors of interest to audiologists which were associated with positive clinical outcomes included: Less mutual gaze; positive head nodding of the provider; forward lean toward the patient; direct body orientation of the provider (shoulders squared to patient); uncrossed arms and legs by the provider. Nonverbal behaviors that were associated with unfavorable clinical outcomes included: More patient gaze by the provider; provider body orientation

- Empathy—intellectual appreciation of a patient's situation

- Provider statements of reassurance or support

- Encouraging patient questions

- Allowing the patient's point of view to guide the visit

- High proportion of objective statements by provider (explanation)

- Provider's expression of approval related to positive patient actions

- Laughing and joking from the provider's side (tension release)

- Provider addressing patient problems of daily living, relationships, and emotions (psychosocial issues)

- Provider asking about and providing counseling for psychosocial issues

- Increased time spent on health education and sharing clinical data

- Provider fosters discussion of treatment parameters

- Friendliness and courtesy of the provider

- Receptivity to patient questions and statements (listening behaviors)

- Provider talking at the patient's level

- Provider ready to clarify and educate patient

- More time spent on history taking

- Increased encounter length

Figure 7–2. Verbal behaviors of health care providers linked to significant, positive patient outcomes.

45 to 90 degrees away from the patient; backward lean away from the patient; crossed arms by the provider; frequent touch by the provider.

Selected Verbal Behaviors to Improve Patient Satisfaction

Professional and front office staff should be aware of both verbal and nonverbal statements and behaviors that can effect patient satisfaction and clinical outcomes.

Beck et al. (2004) suggest that health care providers should focus on the following verbal behaviors linked statistically to patient satisfaction, compliance, comprehension, and positive perception of their provider: Empathy, courtesy, friendliness, reassurance, support, encouragement of patient's questions, giving explanations, and positive reinforcement or good feelings of positive patient actions or compliance in their treatment.

Many of the findings reported in their analysis were common sense; for example,

√

- Negative social-emotional interactions

- Passive acceptance of information provided by patient to the provider

- Antagonism and passive rejection of the patient by the provider

- Formal, directive behaviors on the part of the provider

- High rates of biomedical questioning by the provider

- Interruptions issued by the provider

- One-way information flow from patient to provider without response

- Lack of attentiveness on the part of the provider (disengaged listening)

- Provider directives issued with apparent irritation, nervousness, or tension

- Dominance and verbal directness on the part of the provider

- Provider issuing opinions prior to completion of the evaluation

Figure 7–3. Behaviors of health care providers linked to significant, negative patient outcomes.

empathic patient-centered verbal styles were associated with high patient satisfaction. Participatory decision making was found to be a strong provider-partner interaction issuing significantly better clinical outcomes. Additionally, extensive sharing of clinical information and patient education about potential effects of treatment were found to consistently improve patient comprehension and satisfaction contributing to an overall improvement in clinical outcomes.

The extensive meta-analysis by Beck et al. (2004) indicates the strong impact of verbal and nonverbal behaviors in the development of the interrelationship between clinicians and their patients. Content, method of delivery, body positioning as well as visual contact and other physical and nonverbal postures have been shown to significantly impact clinical outcomes. The importance and impact of these findings on daily clinical practice cannot be underestimated nor discounted. Practice owners and managers should include discussions and training about these opportunities for success as well as negative imagery and messaging to be avoided when interacting with patients in the practice.

Critical Points of Patient Contact: Office Staff

The first line of patient care begins with the front office staff. They may be called the office assistant, the receptionist, front office staff coordinator or they might even be called a spouse or the owner of the practice (from this point forward in this text, we use the term "receptionist"). It all depends on who answers the phone.

The true value of the receptionist lies not solely in his or her abilities to organize and care for patients logistically and in a timely fashion but in abilities to quickly and accurately assess patient distress and respond with a solution to their problem. An invaluable asset, the best receptionists are part mechanic, part counselor, part customer service specialist, part magician, always dressed appropriately, and, above all else, great listeners dedicated to the patient and their success in the practice.

They create the first and, often, most lasting impression on the patient. They are responsible for explaining financial policies, obtaining insurance information, and collecting copays. Not only must they be efficient in practice operations, they must also possess excellent interpersonal communication skills and a thorough knowledge of clinical procedures and treatment options available in the practice. Time spent instructing a receptionist to be a good listener; a good gatherer of information, and an excellent communicator, and host or hostess will contribute immensely to consistently high patient satisfaction ratings. Taylor (2006) reports that the interaction with the audiologist is the most important driver of patient satisfaction, but the interaction with the receptionist had significant impact on overall patient satisfaction with the practice.

Fostering Patient Confidence

It is no easy task to have telephones ringing, people at the payment window, and make a caller and prospective patient know that the office he or she has chosen or has been referred to will be a comfortable place to receive the type of care they need. The patient must know from the initial contact with your practice that the care they will receive will be comprehensive and excellent in every way. High patient confidence at the first patient visit is the responsibility of the receptionist. Confidence in the practice during and after the first visit is the responsibility of all members of the team; front office and professional staff alike.

The Receptionist as an Informational Source and Anxiety Reducer

The receptionist must be well trained and understand not only office procedures, specifics about billing, coding, and collection, and how to successfully guide a patient to the office from across town, but must also know and understand the clinical aspects of the office. A good way to train a receptionist about what goes on in the practice is to have them become a "patient." Undergoing a comprehensive hearing evaluation, a vestibular assessment with recording, or watching a hearing instrument fitting provides lasting impressions and increases sensitivity to what patients experience during their visits.

The insight gained by the receptionist-as-patient will translate into valid experiential depictions of what to expect, how the patient might feel during the procedures, and what to expect on being fitted with hearing instruments for the first time. Patients respond favorably to having prior knowledge of the clinical situation. Reduced fears and increased confidence will set the stage for a comfortable visit and a far less anxious patient.

We learn well by what we experience. A receptionist who has undergone a vestibular study can immediately reduce a patient's anxiety about the procedure because she has "gone through it and lived to tell about it." With first-hand experience, the receptionist will be better able to answer patient questions and resolve concerns that might otherwise result in a missed or cancelled appointment. Receptionists are critical, frontline members of the team and have as much duty to the patient on the front end of the appointment as does the professional involved in the clinical assessment, counseling, and rehabilitation on the back end of the appointment. The frontline must be a strong line. Patient comfort and satisfaction is, after all, about outcomes and receptionists own a large part of setting the patient up for consistent, positive patient outcomes. Reduced fears and increased patient confidence sets the stage for a successful office visit for the patient and professional alike.

When the patient arrives for the appointment, the receptionist once again becomes the first point of contact. The approach to each patient should vary with the patient's personal needs and anxiety level. Making the patients feel welcome and comfortable in the office should be a seamless transition from the booking conversation on the telephone to the greeting at the reception room window. These patient interactions are crucial junctures prior to the actual patient-professional interaction. As a part of the team, the receptionist will develop observations and opinions on the patient's emotional status and perhaps a view of their expectations as well. By engaging the patient in conversation as they are about to fill out forms or as they are escorted to the examination room, the receptionist has the first opportunity to observe the patient's behaviors. Even with hearing instrument repairs, the receptionist should foster discussions about how the instrument is working, what the patient's observations have been, and when the problems began.

These informal discussions serve to cue the patient about questions to ask during the visit. They also provide the patient with an opportunity to vent frustrations about their particular situation or difficulties that have driven them back to the office. The more inquiries the patient hears about their particular situation, the more the patient develops a secure sense that everyone in the practice is interested in solving their problems. When every member of the practice team shows sincere interest and issues an empathetic response, a sincere smile, or an encouraging statement, however brief, the probability of a positive outcome during the visit is enhanced.

The Patient's Perspective

The receptionist should be viewed as an interested, caring person, fully engaged in the best interests of the patient. The patient must have confidence that the receptionist will serve, at least to some extent, as an in-office advocate, who will get them to the appropriate member of the professional staff in a timely manner. In that sense, a receptionist is as much a care provider as any member of the clinical staff. No license is needed to be involved in fostering a patient's well being. The ultimate goal in all patient care is to have every member of the practice working toward a positive and comprehensive outcome for the patient.

This goal is established on behalf of the patient as well as his or her family and the professional who referred the patient to the practice.

Long-term patients value the receptionist. They expect to hear her or his voice on the telephone when they call with questions, to order hearing aid-related items, or to schedule a visit to the office. Relationship building is as important at the front desk as it is in the fitting room. The patient-receptionist relationship is important and should not be discounted in the continuum of care provided by the practice. Low turnover rate in the receptionist position is critical. Should the receptionist leave the practice, it is important to have the replacement spend adequate time integrating patient information and front office operations beyond the expected orientation with procedural and policy information contained in the receptionist's job description.

After-Care Duties: Thank-You Notes and Follow-Up Calls

The receptionist should be assigned the duty to contact patients after they have left the office, and should be responsible for sending each new patient an after-care thank-you card in which the patient is encouraged to call if there are questions about billing, setting up another appointment, or to review what the next step might be after the initial appointment. Patients remember these efforts and they are likely to tell their friends and families about the note and the excellent service they received in your practice. Building patient loyalty is critically important to the long term health of the practice. Every member of the team must have a strong commitment to

this effort and contribute to building patient loyalty on a daily basis.

Follow-up phone calls a few days after a hearing instrument fitting (preferably by the audiologist) or after replacing a repaired instrument are just as important as a thank-you note to a new patient. Checking on their progress with their new or repaired instruments is an effective way to show interest in their response to your treatment regimen and to provide a spot check on the adequacy of the fitting and the stability of the repair. If the caller suspects the patient is struggling with adjusting to their new instruments or if the patient is concerned about the effectiveness of the repair, the patient should be scheduled for a return visit at the patient's earliest convenience. Waiting for their next scheduled visit simply prolongs the anxiety and promotes a loss of confidence in the fitting or repair replacement.

Occasionally a patient may have a difficult time in response to segments of the vestibular evaluation. Patients who have a prolonged refractory period in response to caloric stimulation or who have a general weakness following the examination should be contacted by telephone the same day of the test. Inquiring about their status and suggesting that they return to the referring physician as scheduled and reiterating the findings will go far in assuring them that their response to the test was nothing extraordinary. Of course, if their response was beyond that which is usually anticipated, the patient should be directed to consult with their physician immediately. The referring physician should be contacted and a course of action should be agreed on.

Unfortunately, too few practices take the time to capitalize on easily managed opportunities like these to increase

patient satisfaction and loyalty. Little
time is involved in most patient management activities. Telephone calls can be
completed during lulls in activities in
the office or at the end of the day. If the
caller (front office or professional staff)
encounters the patient's voice mail, he
or she should leave a message that
imparts interest in their progress, reassuring them that all in the practice stand
ready to resolve any particular issues that
might have developed and issue an invi-
tation to call back to let the practice
know how they are doing.

Handling Challenges on the Telephone or at the Window

Challenging interactions with patients
occur on a regular basis. A variety of
factors contribute to these, sometimes
confrontational, episodes. Beyond instrument repair issues, errors on the part of
the practice staff and misinterpretation
of information issued to the patient by the
practitioner are two of the more common reasons for challenges by patients,
their spouse, or other family members.
Hearing loss, advancing cognitive deficits,
medications, misinformation provided
to family members by the patient, and
confusion about the "next steps" to be
taken in their care plan also contribute
to challenges.

The first responder to problem situations is usually the receptionist who must
be empowered to resolve and manage
as many challenges—usual and common;
angry and outrageous. Receptionists must
be great listeners and gatherers of information. Having a sense of humor is a
definitive prerequisite for the position.
They must have well-developed communication skills, patience, and commitment

to patient satisfaction above all else. They
must know when they cannot satisfy the
caller or person at the window and how
to deftly transfer the patient to the office
manager or practice owner in a manner
that appears to be part of the solution
versus a means to get the patient "out of
her hair." Receptionists must be tactful,
deft, and sensitive to the patient's concerns and be fluidly willing to apologize
for situations or circumstances over which
they have neither control nor contribution to the difficulty at hand. The Rules
of Patient Engagement (Figure 7–4) ori-
ents all staff members to necessary attitudes and actions to optimize patient
satisfaction in a patient-centric practice.

Every member of the practice team,
however, must be able to identify patient
concerns and immediately move to resolution. Prompt recovery when mistakes
or misperceptions on the part of the
patient occur, will make the difference
between a satisfied patient and a "former
patient" in the practice. The faster a situation is resolved, the better the likelihood the patient will be satisfied. All

---

- Patients are the priority
- We work for them
- Always with a smile
- Courtesy at all times
- Professional appearance is important
- Your boss is always on the phone
- Apologies are always appropriate
- Solutions not excuses
- Excellence at the speed of light

Figure 7–4. Rules of patient engagement.

staff must remember one of the key elements in the rules for patient engagement: "Excellence at the speed of light." Patients are, generally, uninterested in who is to blame, nor should they be bothered with details of how an error or oversight occurred. If they are interested in an explanation, they should receive as detailed an account as seems appropriate for the particular situation.

The most common clinically relatable complaints include; repeat repairs (defined as a second repair within 45 to 90 days of the first repair), costs of the instruments, battery consumption, too many follow-up visits, time to adjust to instruments is too long, instruments are too conspicuous, noise reduction features fail to meet expectations, and difficulty using instruments with telephone. Despite the fact that most of these issues are outside the purview of the receptionist, complaints must be addressed and the patient should be encouraged to realistically assess their complaints in view of their position in the continuum of the fitting process, the extent of their hearing loss, and the goals set forth prior to and during the assessment and counseling period. Reassurance and a quick willingness to have the patient return prior to a scheduled visit is usually adequate in stemming the tide of anxiety in the early stages of adjustment to new or recently repaired instruments.

If the patient is concerned about an inordinate turnaround time for a repair or in establishing their appointment for their fitting, the receptionist should check the dates of the order or repair submission and advise the patient of the appropriateness of the time frame in question. If the repair or new order is outside the customary period from order to arrival, one should immediately call and check on the order, promptly contacting the patient the same day of their inquiry.

Patients deserve an acknowledgment of an error, an apology, and prompt resolution of their problem with the assurance that the error will not happen again. They expect the person to whom they are talking to be empowered to resolve the situation and they expect the staff person to be solution-driven. Patient-centric practices embrace problem resolution without judgment and with one goal in mind: Total patient satisfaction. No blame, no excuse, no fault, just resolution to maintain long-term patient loyalty.

Challenges by Prospective Patients on the Telephone or at the Window

One of the most common sources of confusion and error when talking with prospective patients on the telephone rests with the unknown parameters of their hearing loss. Receptionists must be able to understand the reason for their call, make sure the patient has heard and integrated the appointment date and time, and determine that the patient understands the services to be provided during their upcoming visit. Asking the patient to repeat the appointment date and time is one way to confirm their reception of the information. If the patient is obviously severely hampered on the telephone, the receptionist should ask to talk to another family member or friend. In some cases, having a "designated talker" for severely hearing-impaired patients or those with known cognitive impairments will facilitate the process of issuing and confirming appointment dates and times. Family or friends are usually willing to call the office and exchange messages or confirm appointments for the patient.

Long-standing, well-known patients in your practice with developing cognitive impairments present a unique challenge. The staff may not be privy to their decline and expect responses to questions, inquiries, or remembering appointment dates and times as had been successfully negotiated prior to the onset of their cognitive issues. Recognizing difficulties involving memory issues compared to the relatively consistent problems associated with the patient's hearing loss takes an attentive ear and a good sense of the clinical presentation of memory-based difficulties. In this day of widely dispersed families, it is unwise to rely on family members to make a patient's developing cognitive issues known to the practice. By the same token, when cognitive decline is suspected, a call to the patient's physician may not only be informative to you and your office staff, it will likely be appreciated by the primary care provider and his or her staff as well.

When the appointment is made, the receptionist should advise each patient about items of importance to bring to their scheduled appointment—each appointment whether the initial visit or an annual hearing instrument inspection and cleaning. They should bring hearing instruments currently in use or any information describing the instrument, current instrument or repair warranties; information about their health care coverage; if a hearing examination is needed they should bring a medical concurrence form signed by their physician, depending on their particular insurance requirements.

New patients should be apprised of the extent of Medicare coverage or, if known, about their particular carrier's benefits for hearing assessment or, in some cases with private carriers, a hearing aid benefit. If your practice has specific policies about payment at the first visit or about missed appointments or other items of interest, that information should be issued on the telephone or in writing to the patient prior to the first visit.

Critical Points of Patient Contact: Difficult Patients/Families

There are several chairs in each exam or fitting room. One chair is for the patient and the other chairs are for those interested in the outcome of your professional intervention and care. These chairs are filled with family members, friends, parents, children, sons and daughters-in-law, or significant others. Each chair supports one person and each person is present at the visit because they are inexorably intertwined with the patient. As such, they are as much a part of the diagnostic and rehabilitative process as is the patient. Each has a vested interest in the patient's success. After all, it would be nice to be able to talk to Aunt Edna without the conversation being heard above the blaring of the neighbor's television. Aunt Edna just wants everyone to stop shouting. The younger children in the family would be more likely to engage her in conversation if they did not have to talk so loud it hurt their ears. Each person has accompanied the patient for specific reasons: None should be ignored nor considered less important than the patient. They deserve to be included in the information processing, the fitting process, and follow-up care. They will likely become care providers and will need assistance and guidance in proper insertion, cleaning and maintenance, and battery replacement. These are the family and friends we like to see in our offices. Their involvement can only enhance the patient's experience and serve to develop realistic expectations in the circle of their family and friends.

Noncompliant Patient/Family/ Extended Care Facility

Individuals able to comply with a rehabilitative plan and choose not to follow the recommended plan must be considered noncompliant. Each takes a volitional step not to proceed as advised. Some will do so to gain a passive-aggressive advantage: Others because of depression or disinterest in their living arrangements. Each will have a reason which is, more times than not, hidden from professional care providers, family, and friends. Noncompliant patients are not unique to the practice of audiology. Physicians, dentists, and other providers see them with surprising regularity.

Consider Mrs. Filbert who is returning to her cardiologist following a 3-month trial of a new medication for hypertension. During the office visit, the cardiologist notes that her blood pressure remains elevated and asks if she has been taking all of the five pills she is supposed to take each day. She replies that she decided it was too much trouble taking five pills so she cut it down to three a day. Concerned about the patient's obvious

noncompliance, the cardiologist stresses the need to take all five pills as prescribed. Mrs. Filbert responds by saying that she can only take three pills a day, not five. The cardiologist must now decide to either discharge the patient or increase the strength of the medication so that 3 pills will work or find another medicine that does not require 5 tablets a day.

Audiologists are faced with similar difficulties. Many practices require their new patients to begin wearing their hearing instruments with daily regularity, morning until night. Others may create a schedule for the first and second weeks. When the patient returns to the first postfitting visit and exclaims that he only needs to wear the hearing instruments when "he thinks he needs them regardless of what his wife says," the audiologist must determine the best method to convince the patient that he will be less likely to adjust to his instruments if he fails to wear them as recommended, especially during the initial fitting period. If this noncompliance continues into the second or third postfitting visit, there is an increasing chance the patient will return the instruments or keep them and become one of the dissatisfied patients who will complain how the practice and the professionals let him down and how hearing instruments simply do not work.

Much of the problem of noncompliance can be avoided by careful patient selection or at least having an idea of what a particular patient will be bringing to the overall clinical mix. Traynor (2003) suggests that although formal assessment with personality inventories like the Myers Briggs Type Indicator or the Kiersey Temperament Sorter would be an optimal approach to identifying difficult patients, this sort of assessment does not lend itself well to the rigors and time constraints of daily clinical practice. Informal assessment can be readily used to identify those patients in need of tailoring approaches to optimize outcomes. Observing and listening to how patients respond to questions or statements borrowed from these inventories will enable the clinician to localize each patient into one of four personality categories, each with its own characteristics to be addressed or considered during their assessment and treatment.

According to the characteristics outlined by Traynor (2003), noncompliant patients fall into the category of "Intuitive-Thinking Clients." Several of their characteristics outlined include:

- Can present as aloof, intimidating, argumentative, and arrogant
- Often impatient with the aural rehabilitation (fitting) process
- Complains about small problems
- When unsuccessful, may change program on their own
- Skeptical and often require lots of references and rational for A/R process
- Tend to overanalyze the problem and to fix it themselves.

Being able to identify a noncompliant patient early on in the clinical process can help in determining whether or not the difficulties the patient will likely bring to the practice will be more strain than benefit. If too many issue arise from his or her treatment and a point of decision is reached—prompted by patient or professional—to consider returning the hearing instruments, it may well be in the best interests of staff and patient alike to terminate the rehabilitative effort and issue a referral to another practice.

As Traynor (2003) indicates so eloquently, "Clinicians should be grateful that (these patients) make up only 4 to 5% of the general clinical population."

Despite the best efforts at identifying problem patients, some will slip through even the most vigilant audiologist's sensors. The key question is what can be done to retrieve the situation and move the patient to a satisfied or delighted hearing instrument wearer? As a matter of the usual course in dealing with patients, there may not be any conceivable adjustment or tactic to take to alter the situation. There are a few measures that should be considered. The first includes evaluating the extremes by having the patient and family or friends assess his relative performance with and without the instruments. By recommending this assessment, a discussion will begin in the office and continue into their respective homes or workplaces about how much better the patient performs with the instruments in his or her ears than with them in a drawer or on the dresser.

Another approach is to have the patient return to the office for follow-up visits until he is wearing the instruments with acceptable consistency based on the observations of the family or friends. The goal of this approach is to assist the patient in appreciating the benefits of consistent instrument use. If you can move these patients to an acceptable schedule of consistent instrument use, he or she will develop increasingly greater satisfaction as the benefits of usage become readily apparent to both the patient and those around him.

Patients in extended care facilities (ECF) present a different issue concerning compliant use of hearing instruments. In many of these facilities, the patient may not be able to insert the instruments and must rely on the staff of the ECF to provide the necessary and appropriate assistance to do so. If the staff fails to appropriately place the hearing instruments in or on the patient's ear or places the instruments appropriately and fails to turn them on, change the batteries, or rotate the volume control to ensure audibility, it is the staff of the ECF and not the patient who is creating a noncompliance situation at the patient's expense. Finding a nursing unit within an ECF that takes pride in the quality of care provided to their residents to the point that each patient wearing hearing instruments is functioning to their maximum hearing potential is a distinct rarity. Unfortunately, this seems to be the case no matter what the family is paying for their loved one's care in ECFs. Altering the course of this particular catastrophe will require intervention with the nursing supervisor and staff. Having the attending physician write specific orders of inserting, care, and cleaning might help. With orders written, oversight for appropriate hearing instrument placement and assessment of use becomes part of the medical record and is discussed during care conferences. The attending physician is now integrally linked to the quality of care provided under his or her medical management and adds a powerful ally to both the patient and family should disputes over the adequacy of care regarding hearing instrument usage develop in the care conferences. However, it is more likely that these simple but, time-consuming tasks will fall to the patient's family or friends. Following your patient to the ECF and providing instructional support to the staff will help. Nothing will supplant the watchful eye of demanding family members.

Angry or Disgruntled Patients

Anger fueled by health or concerns, frustrating encounters with insurance companies, other health care providers, or repeated, yet necessary follow-up visits, or the cost of hearing instruments are but a few items that can turn an otherwise kind and cooperative patient into a caustic, angry, and unsettled person at the receptionist's window.

Immediate steps must be taken to resolve his issues and to assure him that whatever it takes to reduce frustrations or change an irritating situation will be done. Every member of the front office and professional staffs of the practice is responsible for patient satisfaction and patient loyalty. Recall that 68% of patients refusing to return to a practice do so because they felt the practice was "indifferent" to their concerns and needs. No one wants to think they are unimportant. Recall also that if the patient's issues are delineated, discussed, and resolved quickly, the patient will likely stay with the practice and develop an odd sense of pride in generating what is perceived as much needed change.

Service recovery is not just about fixing a particular patient's problem. It is about listening to the patient and recognizing their dissatisfaction. It should never take two members of a practice to resolve an issue for one patient nor should two people be required to foster patient satisfaction and loyalty. There are patients in every practice that are consistently cranky. It should be the goal of every staff person to make his or her visit the best, friendliest, and pleasant visit on each and every visit to the practice. One patient who fit the bill for being consistently cranky had been coming to one of our offices for many years.

Every person in the office agreed to make his visits full of smiles and charm. One day the patient exclaimed, obviously peeved: "What is it with you people? I do nothing but moan and groan and you all stay so cheerful and upbeat no matter what!" The entire office staff celebrated this minor, yet important team victory with a celebratory pizza lunch the next day. They were determined to charm his socks off and they had succeeded. In a patient-centric practice, every patient is treated in that manner, every day the office is open for business.

Conflict Resolution and Staff Safety

Every member of the practice staff must be trained to resolve patient issues and calm patients down when they are agitated or overly concerned. In addition, each staff member must be able to recognize when a situation has gotten out of control and what steps to follow to resolve the issue. Patients can, at times, become highly agitated and, in some cases, combative. Just as the practice should have an exit plan in the event of a fire and a plan for calling 911 in the event of a medical emergency, so too should there be a plan in place to protect the staff from a potentially dangerous patient. Just about the time the office staff begins to think they have seen everything or that "our patients would never become physically abusive" a major eruption takes place at the payment window with the patient slamming his fist into the wall or tossing wall hangings on the floor in a frenzy.

In that event, an immediate 911 call summoning the police should be made. What about the time from the call to their arrival? What can be done to calm the situation and regain everyone's temperament and civility? Interventionists suggest that anything to defuse the situation should be done. Telling the patient not to worry about charges for the day and reassuring him that there has been no harm done as long as he begins to calm down will go far to lessen the tension of the situation. If the spouse or a friend is with him, ask for their intersession in the matter and have them help calm the situation. Conflict resolution needs calm more than focusing on immediate resolution in the early stages of an incident. Whatever it takes to calm the situation should be put into play. The goal is to have the patient leave the office without harming himself or others—or for the police to arrive and secure everyone's safety. Angry patient scenarios should be considered an important topic for discussion at staff meetings; just as important as fire safety or procedures for office closure for inclement weather (Sidebar 7-1).

Cool-down techniques to resolve conflict should be discussed and training should be completed at least annually. A procedural description of cool-down techniques to be used in the event of significant patient conflict should be developed with the help of mental health professionals. The basic components of cool-down techniques geared to mollify patient anger include; (1) engaging the assistance of the spouse or family member accompanying the patient to intervene; (2) if the interaction involves a member of the front office staff, immediately involve a member of the professional staff in the situation; (3) appropriate physical distance between the patient and staff members must be maintained; (4) immediate understanding and unequivocal agreement about the issue at the

Sidebar 7–1
BELLIGERENT PATIENT

Mr. H. came to the office on the referral of Dr. B, his primary care provider. During the history-taking, Mr. H. became obviously agitated and angry in response to common questions about the development, severity, and effects of his hearing loss in his daily living activities. His wife was in the exam room and noticed his agitation. At one point he stopped the questions and demanded to know why we needed to know so much about his hearing problems. He demanded that we " . . . just get on with the testing . . . " and that the " . . . rest of this stuff is none of your business." It was obvious by his breathing and the extension of his neck vessels that he was markedly angry. His wife tearfully urged him to calm down. His response to her suggestion was to decompensate into torrid remarks and movements that suggested he was about to escalate the situation into a physical confrontation. I stopped the conversation with an admonishment that he needed to "cool down," and that we were trying to get information that would figure into a plan to help him and his family. I announced that I would give him 5 minutes to regain composure and that I would return to decide our next step in his visit.

The patient remained agitated and angry when I returned to the exam room. He announced that " . . . you SOBs are only after the contents of my wallet so you might as well just open it up and take it now!" With that comment, he flung his wallet to the wall and his wife burst into tears. At that point, I asked him to leave the office. He refused and told me to " . . . just go on with your damn tests and let's get this over with." I informed him that we were finished for the day and reiterated my request that he leave the office immediately. He said nothing yet stayed in the exam chair. His wife begged him to leave. I had alerted the front office to be prepared to call the police if needed. I informed the patient that if he did not leave immediately, that I was going to call the police and have him removed from the property. He muttered under his breath, told his wife to get the car, and left the exam room. He left his wallet on the floor. I handed it to him before he left the office. It was empty. His insurance was billed for the visit and his primary care provider was called as soon as he exited the property.

The primary care provider indicated that the patient had a recent altercation with his billing staff, which he attributed to the patient's early stages of dementia. Organic brain syndromes including dementia do not lessen the dangers of physical confrontation with patients; indeed, we should be aware of the possibilities of aggressive behaviors from even those patient known to have been mild mannered over the many years of care provided in the practice. In any event, aggressive or threatening behaviors toward professional or front office staff must not be tolerated. Staff should be well trained to identify and handle these situations. Annual reviews of emergency measures within the office should be part of a routine effort to reduce patient-related violence in your practice.

core of the disturbance should be exhibited on the part of the staff; (5) encourage the patient to talk about the problem without being patronizing—talk, talk, talk; (6) staff members should avoid any statement or behavioral posture that could escalate the situation—listen, listen, listen; (7) assure the patient that resolution of the circumstance will be in his or her favor; (8) resolution must be rapid, outcome(s) clear, and assurance reiterated that all will be resolved to his or her satisfaction; (9) if the patient remains agitated despite best efforts to cool the situation to a tolerable level, the front office staff should be prepared to dial 911 Emergency to summon the police; (10) if there is no reduction in the intensity of the situation, the professional staff member must politely—yet-firmly—ask the patient to leave the office; (11) if he or she refuses, advise the patient that you intend to call the authorities; and (12) if there is refusal to leave, 911 should be called—"This is Dr. _____'s office at XYZ address, we have a combative patient situation and we need help immediately—the patient's name is _____ he is a _description_ .

For the safety of all concerned, the practice staff must remain calm and in control of the situation. Physical contact with the patient must be avoided at all costs. Police response is usually quite rapid due to the explosive nature of these situations and the potential for physical altercations. Most municipal police departments have a community relations officer who will come to the office to discuss emergency notification and response times with specific instructions about reporting and responding to an incident involving an angry or agitated patient. Immediately following an incident, the referring physician should be contacted to explain the situation and circumstances under which the patient became agitated with a full disclosure of the resolution—no matter the outcome of the situation. A detailed, factual report of the incident from onset to final outcome should be prepared by each staff member involved. The comments should be signed by the staff member and each report should be reviewed by the attorney of record for the practice. A follow-up letter should be sent to the referring physician to confirm the telephone conversation and the resolution of the situation. The report should be part of the patient's continuing medical record. The practice's attorney will advise how best to interact with the patient in the future. He may advise no further contact whatsoever or possibly sending a certified letter to the patient confirming the need for the patient to seek care elsewhere.

Statutory regulations governing the practice of medicine and dentistry commonly contain sections regarding patient abandonment. These sections usually stipulate the circumstances under which patients may be discharged from a practice and set forth guidelines or suggestions how best to advise a patient that he or she will no longer be seen for continuing care. Although required for physicians and dentists, it is not common to see these requirements in laws or other regulatory language governing the practice of audiology. A thorough reading of your state licensing law and administrative rules should clarify whether or not there are specifically proscribed requirements or necessary means to inform a patient that he or she will no longer be seen as a patient in your practice. If in doubt, contact your state licensing board with a written request for clarification. When corresponding with your state licensing board or registration department, always send the correspondence, no matter the topic, via certified mail with a return receipt requested. This creates a documented record of your submission or inquiry. Should there be no response from the licensing board in a reasonable time period; a phone call to the Executive Director of the board should be made to determine the status of your inquiry. If the Executive Director is unable to satisfy your request, contact the Chairman of the board or your elected state representative to make an inquiry on your behalf.

Follow-Up Care: Critical Element of Successful Long-Term Practices

Consistent follow-up care is a requirement in any health care practice. Follow-up care should be highly systematized and patient centric at the office staff level and engagingly personal at the provider-patient interface. Follow-up care is an operational method to increase patient satisfaction, foster patient loyalty, and another means to encourage patients to sing the praises of the practice, not just to their family and friends but to the health care provider responsible for their referral to your practice.

The Art of Personalization

The era of Sign in—Sit down—Shut up health care is swiftly coming to a close. Baby boomers will be between 43 and 61 years old in 2007 and they will by no means be accepting of anything less than full participation in their health care. The generation to follow them, Gen X, will be 29 to 43 and no less demanding than their older cohorts (Sidebar 7–2). Neither practice nor practitioner can prosper without creating an atmosphere of patient involvement and personalizing their particular segment of a health care market. That is true for medical specialists and generalists, dentists, optometrists, and audiologists as well. Personalizing your particular brand of health care will increase the likelihood of continued success and provide the elements necessary to maintain patient satisfaction while optimizing patient loyalty.

Some examples of personalization in the process of hearing care includes a handwritten note of appreciation following the initial patient encounter thanking them for either choosing the practice for their hearing examination or for following through on the recommendation of their primary care physician. A note or brochure encouraging the patient's participation with insightful information about what to expect at

Sidebar 7–2
THE BABY BOOMERS:
THE NEW POPULATION TO BE SERVED

Maintaining customer/patient loyalty is becoming more difficult regardless of your profession. That may be especially true of the primary population to be served over the next 20 years. Primary care physicians, dentists, optometrists, and audiologists are becoming acutely aware of the markedly reduced tensile strength of the ties that bind baby boomers to their respective practices. As the baby boomer generation begins to access the health care system, new demands will be placed on the health care system in general and the hearing instrument delivery system specifically.

Baby Boomers approach their health care like no other group. They enjoy almost unlimited access to medical and health care information through the Internet. When they go to their providers for assessment or care, they are commonly well armed with an expansive knowledge of their particular health care issues. Baby boomers seek the most qualified practitioners directly—frequently without referral by their primary care physician. They are more likely to schedule visits with practitioners having advanced degrees, specialty certification, or specific recognition as a specialist health care provider. They are abruptly critical of the quality of care provided and the surroundings in which the services are delivered. They are more likely to leave a health care provider to seek second opinions if they do not feel they are receiving accurate and appropriate information or care.

Baby boomers' trust and confidence in their health care providers develops from their perceptions of professionalism within the office, the efficiency and friendliness of the front office staff, and the important, yet ephemeral, doctor-to-patient relationship. They are less likely to accept mediocrity and less tolerant of problems arising from limited attention, common errors in billing, and items or issues in need of, what they consider to be, too much after-purchase attention.

Baby boomers are more likely to seek hearing care sooner than those in the previous generation and they readily accept well-credentialed, nonphysician practitioners as their health care provider for specific, well-defined health care needs. As a group, they are more likely to seek alternative providers to their current providers based on price, time to schedule services, convenience of service locations, time spent in the office, and, most importantly, their perception of the quality and outcome of each professional/patient encounter.

In the final report of the Clarity-Ear Foundation two-part survey focusing on the prevalence and impact of hearing loss on baby boomers, a number of interesting and important characteristics about this group came to light. The study began in 2004 with 437 randomly selected participants between 49 and 59 years of age. An initial on-line survey was completed followed by a telephone interview focusing on the prevalence of hearing loss. The second part of the study was completed in 2006. It focused on how Baby Boomers felt their lives were impacted by their hearing loss. A group of 458 randomly selected participants 41 to 60 years of age completed an on-line survey which was also followed by telephone interviews.

These findings should be of special interest to audiologists as the first, formal classes in audiology were begun in 1946 at Northwestern University—the same year the first batch of over 75 million Baby Boomers were born. The findings of the study confirmed many clinical observations and produced several interesting, and in some cases surprising findings selected below:

■ About one-half (53%) of baby boomers have at least a "mild" hearing loss.
■ Men were significantly more likely to report a hearing loss than were women (62 to 38%).
■ Three-fourths of those reporting a severe hearing loss were men.
■ 26% of those with hearing loss had their hearing loss formally diagnosed by a health care professional—37% had not had their hearing tested.
■ Only three out of four (73%) parents whose adult children say they have a hearing loss had their hearing tested (Boomers not well schooled by their parents).
■ One-forth said their hearing loss affected their work; handling phone calls and conversations with coworkers were the areas most impacted.
■ One-fourth said their hearing loss had an impact on their earning potential.
■ 97% of participants stated they were aware of hearing aids.
■ 78% indicated they were aware of amplified telephones that could help individuals with hearing loss.
■ Among those with severe hearing loss, only 42% wore hearing aids.

the fitting and during the instrument adjustment period has proven to be a well-appreciated informational bridge (Sidebar 7–3). Even the most seasoned hearing instrument wearer will admit to at least a bit of trepidation during the waiting period for their new hearing instruments.

Sidebar 7–3
PATIENT BROCHURE

BEFORE HEARING INSTRUMENTS . . .

Realistic Expectations

Hearing aids are just that, devices to aid your hearing. Hearing instruments will not return your hearing function to normal and they will not "cure" your hearing loss. If you use your hearing aids appropriately and wear them consistently, you can expect to hear better in almost all situations. There will be a few where you may experience difficulty, such as extremely noisy restaurants. But, for the most part, you and those around you can expect improved hearing and better communication.

Adjusting Takes Time

Realistic expectations are critically important. So too is the time it takes to get used to your new hearing instruments. Although periods of adjustment vary, many patients report continued hearing improvement and better speech understanding over a 3- to 6-month period. As the auditory centers in the brain have not been subjected to these sounds, processing remembered sounds gets noticeably easier day by day.

Everyday Sounds

There is also an adjustment period to everyday sounds in our environment. Many patients report they forgot how annoying certain sounds can be and would just as well do without hearing them again. Clocks ticking, noisy refrigerators, and emergency sirens are examples of noises that may not seem important, but each contributes to your environment. Modern, digital circuitry has been designed to reduce the negative effects of noise in your listening environment.

Background sounds are no longer the greatest hurdle a hearing instrument wearer needs to overcome. Better technology coupled with better fitting techniques add up to a tremendous outlook for a successful outcome—even in areas with background noise, you will likely benefit from your hearing aids and hear those people seated at your table. It may not be perfect, but it will be far better than with older hearing aids or by avoiding new instruments because you have heard they are so difficult to get accustomed to.

Keeping in touch with your environment is important. Enjoy all the sounds in your environment and recognize that even unwanted sounds have value. It's about taking a bit of the bad with all the good and staying in the everyday richness we call life. Welcome back to the world of all kinds of sounds!

Everyone Will Benefit from Your Hearing Instruments

Most of our patients come to us by referral from their family doctor. Others come to us by the "urgings" of their family or friends. They have a vested interest in your hearing. If you are hearing better, everyone benefits from easier and more accurate communication.

Good communication is a two-way street. If you persevere in wearing your hearing instruments, you and your family and friends will benefit from your willingness to improve your communication situation. Although it may be difficult at times, the more effort you put into adjusting to and wearing your hearing instruments, the more you will benefit from them.

Ultimately, better hearing is really up to you. You must wear your instruments consistently, maintain them well with regular cleaning, and have an extra battery on hand at all times. Improved hearing takes but a few minutes of your time and attention daily. Our office is dedicated to your success and we are here to assist you in any way to make your journey to better hearing the best it can be. We will be available to you as long as you need us!

Friends, Family, and Patient Referrals

Patients referring patients to your practice is the highest form of recognition for any health care practitioner. It sends a clear message to the incoming patient that the current patient has had a good experience with your practice, has been well served, and is confident enough to make a recommendation to a friend or another member of the immediate or extended family. The referring patient should be recognized in some way. A personal thank you note or a note and a certificate for a free pack of batteries provide recognition and appreciation. Although it is inappropriate and breaches a variety of organizational codes of ethics, actively seeking patient generated referrals must not be considered a part of marketing or practice promotion. Accepting the recognition of a referral by a satisfied patient in the practice is appropriate: Actively seeking these referrals is, beyond the issues of ethics, simply unprofessional.

Notes in the Margins and Photo ID

A handy way to personalize your relationship with your patients is to jot notes in the margins of the chart so that you can recall events or circumstances important to the patient at the next visit. Birthdays, weddings, retirements, and funerals, are items of great importance to your patients and if they feel comfortable sharing this information, you should take the time to listen and make an effort to inquire about it at the next or subsequent patient visits. Staff should consistently peruse the newspapers about these events and if the event involves one of the patients in the practice, an appropriate response will be greatly appreciated and remembered for many years. Birthdays can be programmed to come up in most management information systems and patient databases. Although some patients have stopped counting birthdays, everyone likes to be recognized on their birthday.

Patients appreciate your going an extra step and feel as though your interest in their well-being exceeds the services provided during the course of your providing their hearing care. Loyal patients are those with high comfort levels within the practice—both in the excellence in the professional care and in the interest paid to them as participating patients in your practice. Loyalty is directly related to comfort and confidence and a sense of the staff having a genuine interest in the patient as an individual, not just as a person with hearing impairment seeking and receiving professional services to improve their hearing.

One of the most effective tools for front office and professional staffs to improve patient recognition is to keep a photo of the patient at the back of the chart for reference. A good copy of their driver's license will do quite well. It is amazing how many times the practice staff will refer to a patient's photo to solidify their image with the name or to confirm they are dealing with a specific patient about a topic relevant to that particular patient's care or billing situation. Of course, having access to these photos can also clarify the patient's identity in a rogue's gallery sort of way. Every practice has difficult patients and making sure who is who can serve as a means of alerting staff about particular problems, likes or dislikes, or patients with specific needs.

Newsletters

Practice newsletters are not only appreciated by your patients, they are anticipated and a welcome update about the goings-on in your office. Loyal patients often feel a part of the practice and, as such, are interested in staff changes, training, and accomplishments. They want to know about academic training and attendance at seminars to improve technical and clinical skills. They like to read about new technology and will call and inquire about the need to consider "newer" technologies. Newsletters services are available. You send your database to them and they mail a newsletter at specified intervals. They are well written and contain a wealth of information. However, they lack the personal edge of a practice-generated newsletter. Practice newsletters are time consuming, should be formatted by a professional printing service, and carry both production and mailing costs. If you do not have the time, talent, and resources to develop and mail at least three newsletters per year, consider a commercial practice newsletter. Either way, practice newsletters provide an important opportunity to stay in the patient's interest range and to maintain visibility within the household.

Summary

There is no substitute for well-developed patient management skills. Not always something learned during clinical training, effective patient management skills arc usually learned from the best teachers—the patients themselves. An ability to communicate and readily develop rapport and comfort in patients and those accompanying them to their office visits will set your practice above those merely interested in numbers of patients, procedures, and instruments dispensed. Whether in an independent private practice, an ENT-audiology practice, or a nonprofit community speech and hearing center, capable patient management must be the cornerstone of excellence in your daily clinical schedule. Patients referred to or seeking the professional care of an audiologist are learning to expect clinical excellence and positive outcomes in their quality of life—anything less and not only are patients and their referring health care providers poorly served, the whole of the profession of audiology loses important standing in the arena of health care, one important patient at a time.

Every patient seen in your practice must know that their physician, friend, or relative issuing the referral to your practice has done so with great confidence in your patient management skills. They have made the referral knowing that audiologists are the professionals uniquely qualified to provide both diagnostic studies and appropriate treatment for patients with hearing and balance difficulties. They also refer knowing that patients will, after comprehensive assessment, be appropriately recommended for medical or surgical intervention when needed.

Each patient coming to the practice must expect professional, dedicated service from every member of the practice staff—at all times, every day the doors are open and the telephones are being answered. Anything less than the items found in the Patient Bill of Rights (Sidebar 7-4) and the practice is not serving patients nor referral sources well.

Sidebar 7–4
PATIENT BILL OF RIGHTS

As a patient in our practice you should

- Expect more from Audiology and Speech Associates than from any other provider.
- Know that you will be respected by everyone in our practice.
- Expect us to answer your phone call in a timely, friendly, and welcoming manner.
- Be greeted in a friendly and appreciative manner by every member of our practice.
- Know that we recognize the importance of your time.
- Expect a quick response and immediate action at all times by every member of the practice.
- Require excellent communication from us.
- Know that we will listen to you and understand your concerns.
- Expect quick and accurate resolution of questions or concerns about your account.
- Receive an apology if we are in error.

References

Beck, R. S., Dautridge, R., Sloane, P. D. (2004). Physician-patient communication in the primary care office: A systematic review. *Journal of the American Board of Family Practice, 15*(1), 25–38.

Hopkins, T. (2006). *Do your customers feel ignored?* Retrieved February 6, 2006, from Entrepreneur.com

Marsh, D. (2005). Turning patients into patient advocates. *Hearing Journal, 58*(2), 48.

Reinartz, W., & Kumar, V. (2002, July). The mis-management of customer loyalty. *Harvard Business Review*, pp. 86–94.

Taylor, B. (2006). How quality of service affects patient satisfaction with hearing aids. *Hearing Journal, 59*(9), 25–34.

Travaline, J. M., Ruchinskas, R., & D'Alonzo, G. E. (2005). Patient-physician communication: Why and how. *Journal of the American Osteopathic Association, 105*(1), 13–17.

Traynor, R. M. (2003, August). Personal style and hearing aid fitting. *Hearing Review*, pp. 16–22.

Wong, L., Hickson, L., & McPherson, B. (2003). Hearing aid satisfaction: What does research from the past 20 years say? *Trends in Amplification, 7*(4), 117–161.

8

Personnel Management

ROBERT G. GLASER, Ph.D.

"Management is nothing more than motivating other people."

Lee Iacocca

Introduction

Effective personnel management is the unifying force that establishes the tone and complexion of a practice. It begins when the practice owner hires an employee to complete specific tasks as directed. It is that "as directed" that forms the nucleus of personnel management. The owner/manager must be able to effectively impart what needs to be accomplished and how important that task is to the current and future status of the practice. He or she must make a commitment to the employee to establish what is expected in the position; to

evaluate and provide regular feedback to the employee regarding their performance; to establish parameters of appropriate demeanor with patients and fellow employees; to clarify the need for teamwork focusing on the common goals of patient and referral source satisfaction; and to understand that failure to fulfill the duties and expectations in the job description may result in termination of employment.

Personnel management will vary as a function of style and experience. Some managers will rule in a top-down, do-as-I-say fashion. Others will state the objectives and desired outcomes and let the employees figure out the best way to accomplish the task to get to the defined outcomes. Savvy personnel managers will optimize productivity by recognizing that each employee responds differently— what motivates one employee may not motivate another.

Effective personnel management will naturally develop a team pulling in the same direction with common goals where individuals step outside themselves to accomplish tasks in the best interests of the patients served in the practice.

Leadership and Personnel Management

Managing people requires leadership. The ability to lead is a collection of skills, nearly all of which can be learned and improved. Leadership has many facets; respect, experience, emotional strength, people skills, discipline, vision, momentum, and timing (Maxwell, 2002). It is about being the sort of person people will confidently follow and work diligently to gain your attention and approval. It is about becoming a person of influence and respect; each is earned by example and establishing model behaviors and developing an easily discerned attitude about the importance of patients and their success as a result of coming to the practice.

Leading a practice and managing a practice are different on several levels. Leadership is about influencing people to follow; management focuses on maintaining systems and processes which may or may not be effective. Maxwell (2002) believes there are fundamental differences in being the "boss" (manager) versus operating as the leader of a practice:

- The boss drives his workers; the leader coaches them.
- The boss depends on authority; the leader on goodwill.
- The boss inspires fear; the leader inspires enthusiasm.
- The boss says "I"; the leader, "we."
- The boss fixes blame for the breakdown; the leader fixes the breakdown.

An effective leader recognizes those working in the practice as critically important assets necessary to achieve high patient and referral source satisfaction. The leader intuitively understands the role that selection, training, trust, respect, and empowerment play in the transformation of an employee to an associate. An associate shares the vision and goals of the practice and works as a partner and colleague in joint pursuit of patient and referral source satisfaction.

From Employee to Associate

Practice leaders will doggedly pursue and find the most talented individual and provide the atmosphere for them to do their best work. No matter the position, a practice leader will find the person who best fulfills the preselection requirements based on the position description in the Policy and Procedures Manual. The process of selection may be time consuming and tedious; however, the more time spent, the more specific the preselection requirements and the greater the clarity of the position description, the better the outcome.

Be prepared for more than a few disappointments. Depending on the necessary skill level needed to fulfill the requirements of a position, the demographics of your area, and the competition offered by other job opportunities, you might become frustrated enough to take the next applicant walking through the door: neither a wise choice nor an investment in the practice. A large group of mediocre candidates is not as valuable as a small group of good candidates with most or all of the characteristics and skills to fill the available position (Sidebar 8–1).

Sidebar 8–1
VALUABLE CHARACTER TRAITS IN POTENTIAL CANDIDATES

attentive	hard-working	responsible
calm	honest	self-confident
cheerful	imaginative	self-motivated
common sense	independent	self-starter
conscientious	intelligent	sense of humor
courteous	interesting	sensitive
creative	kind	sincere
curious	likable	team player
dependable	likes challenge	tenacious
detail-oriented	loyal	thorough
eager to learn	patient	tolerant
eager to please	perceptive	tolerates pressure
empathetic	persistent	understanding
energetic	personable	unflappable
enthusiastic	polite	vibrant
flexible	productive	warm
focused	punctual	willing to stay late
friendly	resourceful	work ethic
goal-oriented	respectful	zestful

Recruiting: Getting the Best Group of Candidates Through the Door

Whether adding a front office staff person to assist in scheduling, billing, and patient information management or searching for an audiologist as a potential partner in the practice, recruiting talented candidates requires a great deal of planning and preparation. Once the decision to begin the search for an additional member of the staff has been established, both administrative and professional associates should be involved in the process. Concerns about how the new person will fit in, what their personality make up should be, what past experiences are important for the position, and other issues will surface. Most of the concerns will boil down to one, important factor; will the new person be a "good fit" for the existing team? The existing team, despite confidence in the practice leader's decision-making, will be at least a bit uncomfortable until they have had a chance to participate in part or all of the selection process.

If your practice has a number of associates, you could select an independent team of associates to review resumes to arrive at a nucleus of candidates to consider for further evaluation. Deciding who to bring in for an interview is often adequate to fulfill an associate's need to participate in the process. Others may wish to become more involved in the process. Including associate staff members in this process is important for office morale. It provides the staff with an opportunity to exert some level of control over the selection of the person who will be working with them in the practice. The goal is to develop a comfort level for both sides of the equation: When the selection has been made and the new hire walks into the practice on the first day of their employment, all members of the practice should be satisfied with their choice and provide an honest welcome to their new colleague. The newly hired associate should feel a part of the team on their first day of employment.

Establish a Recruiting Protocol and Stick to It—No Matter What

Developing a recruiting protocol to be followed consistently is important for a variety of reasons not the least of which includes fairness and consistency in hiring practices. Asking the same questions of each candidate provides the opportunity to compare answers. Though structured, the process need not discourage asking additional questions based on the applicant's responses. Remain flexible in your line of inquiry, but be sure that all interviewees respond to a core set of questions. By preparing those questions in advance, you can rest assured that all key points will be covered to get a sample of the candidate's views on topics important to the practice.

Whether adding a new staff member or filling a vacancy, it must be recognized as an opportunity to improve the practice. Fresh looks, new ideas, and patient-centric operational strategies brought into the practice by new associates can provide new ways to address old issues. If nothing else, new personnel will provide thought-provoking conversations about a variety of operational and patient care issues that may have been brushed under the table until that important catalyst comes along as an agent of important change.

The recruiting protocol (Sidebar 8–2) will differ from one practice to another. Each venue will need to consider specific items that may be part of a Human Resource Department requirement or otherwise be important to the specifics of the respective practice venue.

Resume Review

The posting of the position should include specific directions to apply for the position. The candidate should submit a resume and follow the directions listed in the posting. If the applicant cannot follow these directions or submits a resume that is ill-prepared or otherwise unacceptable, delete the application and continue the process. If the applicant does not convey the qualities deemed necessary for the position in their resume, eliminate the resume and seek those candidates with signs of achievement, established career goals, complementary experiences, and education commensurate with the position.

Candidates are selected for a telephone interview based on the information provided in their application. The application form should contain queries that

---

Sidebar 8–2
RECRUITING PROTOCOL

1. Post or advertise the position

2. Issue explicit directions about how to apply for the position; request resume

3. Resume screening develops pool of candidates

4. Candidates sent position application with return by date

5. Schedule telephone interview based on qualifications listed in application

6. Telephone interview to confirm candidate's qualifications; assess phone skills

7. Select candidates for face-to-face interview

8. Develop structured questions tied to decision-making criteria

9. Contact references by phone; verify experiences, strengths, and weaknesses

10. Contact licensing board for confirmation of license and status, if applicable

11. Review background check by local or state police provided by the candidate

12. Complete face-to-face interviews

13. Offer position to selected candidate

will help differentiate applicants in the selection process such as prior employment experience, licensing status, dates of availability, references, and desired salary range.

The Telephone Interview

The telephone interview is conducted to confirm the applicant's credentials, qualifications, assess their presence on the telephone, and gain additional, subjective impressions of the applicant: Did he or she return your call promptly or at the agreed on time? Was the applicant polite? Could this applicant interact well with the patient population in the practice? Based on the resume, the responses on the application, and a telephone interview, two or three candidates should be selected for face-to-face interviews.

The Face-to-Face Interview

Preparation for the face-to-face interviews should include contacting references by telephone to verify strengths and weaknesses and to get an idea of past performance; past performance is a strong indicator of future performance. If the position involves a licensed professional an inquiry should be made at the licensing board to confirm their status and to ask if there have been any complaints filed or adjudications levied. This information is a matter of public record. All applicants, regardless of the position they are applying for, should supply a copy of a current background check completed by state or local police. This is done for the protection of the practice and its staff as well as the patients to be served in the practice.

Questions should be prepared prior to the interview. The questions should be based on the job posting, tasks to be completed in the position, expected responsibilities, previous experiences, and accomplishments in prior employment. Ask the same questions of each candidate. "What if" questions or scenarios can be proposed to get an idea how each candidate would react or respond to specific situations that might arise in day-to-day operations of the practice. The interview should include those associates in the practice with vested interest in hiring the applicant as well those who will be working directly with the applicant chosen for the position.

Tendering an Offer

When the decision to hire has been made, contact the applicant by phone with a verbal offer. If they accept the offer, a formal letter should follow confirming the salary structure, the schedule for the first few weeks, documents or licensing information to bring to the practice on the first day, and other requirements that might be relevant to the particular venue of the practice. If the candidate is considering several offers, set a time frame to respond your position. If the candidate is exceptional, there is no harm in asking where your offer stands on the pile and what conflicting issues are hindering their decision. If it is based on wages alone, you must decide whether this candidate is worth the difference in dollars and qualifications over the number two or three choice in your final pool of selected applicants. It is strictly a business decision. If they cannot make up there minds in a reasonable period of time (defined by your needs, not theirs), move to the next qualified applicant and wish your first choice well.

Orientation and Training

An associate's orientation and training begins in the hiring process. The tone of the business and personnel should have become apparent through the various steps in the recruiting protocol. Why else would they have agreed to join the team? During orientation and training, the new employee should develop an understanding of practice operations, the importance of patients and referral sources, and the culture of the practice —written and unwritten philosophy and rules of the practice. The more time spent and the greater the quality of training, the greater the likelihood the associate will be satisfied in his or her position, and will work diligently and consistently as a team member on behalf of the patient and the referral source. The well-trained associate will have the confidence to make mistakes in the beginning, develop the skill set to reduce errors over time, and understand the rationale behind the policies and procedures which guide the actions of all who participate in the practice.

On-Boarding

The concept of "on-boarding" an employee was developed by large corporations to efficiently integrate and improve retention of new employees in top management. It is a systematic method of introducing the newly hired individual to the people they will work with and report to during the initial stages of employment. First impressions are important and that is especially true in the first 30 days of a new position. New hires should feel welcomed, valued, and well prepared for the demands of their position. Orientation and training should be personalized, simple, interesting, and focused. It should include information on both written and unwritten rules of operation, demeanor, dress code, and other obvious and not-so-obvious conventions that make up the "culture" of the practice.

All of the staff of the practice should be prepared to meet and greet their new coworker not as a set of job functions and duties but as a colleague and member of the team, regardless of the practice venue. An effective practice leader will guide and direct the on-boarding experience so that the new person in the practice is welcomed by the staff, well informed about their duties, and glad that they accepted the offer. Reviewing the position description, issuing keys and codes, orienting them to their work environment, and issuing a copy of the policies and procedures for the practice is a good list of first day accomplishments. Over the course of the first 90 days of employment, the new hire will continue his or her training. That training schedule should be prioritized based on input from incumbent members of the practice. Important tasks should be mastered first; those with less impact on patients, referral sources, and office operations should follow on the training schedule.

Health care systems such as HMOs and hospital-based audiology practices have a Human Resources Departments to issue information and details about health and disability insurance benefits, retirement plans, paid time-off and leave of absence policies, dress code and demeanor expectations, parking, personal cell phone use, and other issues and rules. An independent audiology practice with three employees, now adding a fourth, will have no less need for completeness. The on-boarding process should be as systematic and complete as it is in larger health care facilities. The desired outcomes are the same—employee development, satisfaction with their position, and retention. The more time spent on the front end of the position in orientation, training, and developing realistic views of their position, the higher employee satisfaction and retention. On-boarding is designed to optimize an employee's knowledge and skill base through systematic training geared to realistically developing necessary competencies in the first 90 to 120 days of employment. On-boarding in an audiology practice involves three distinct steps: meeting the players, teaching the tasks necessary to the job description, and evaluating performance.

Meeting the Players on the Team

Acceptance is important to all of us. That is never truer than on the first day of a new position. Meeting the other members of the team can be intimidating. A warm welcome issued by established members of the practice team should be extended to every new hire. Those who lend support in the practice on a part-time or occasional basis should be included in the introductions and welcoming activities as well. Every member of the practice team is an important asset and anyone doing business with the practice must understand that important fact.

The accountant and his or her associates who interact with the practice should be advised of the new person in the practice and encouraged to introduce themselves. Informing other vendors and hearing instrument manufacturer's field representatives and introducing them to the new person when they call on the practice will underscore the importance and value of the newest member of the practice team.

Teaching the Tasks

Training is best accomplished by a knowledgeable person in the practice who has been successful in that position or in a related capacity. The trainer must have the necessary patience to serve as a guide to the nuances of each segment of the position. Certain competency levels should be achieved before the new hire is expected to function independently. He or she should not be placed at the front desk to answer phones, book patients, and record billings until such time that the tasks can be handled with at least a modicum of efficiency and accuracy. It is important to optimize the chances for early success by providing adequate training to master the daily operations of the practice.

Objectives to be achieved over the first 90 to 120 days should be outlined and the training should be achieved so that the new hire can meet their objectives. For example, it would be foolhardy to expect a new hire to complete the billings for services provided on the same day of service during the first few weeks of employment. A goal could be established, however, wherein the new hire is expected to complete all billings for services rendered on the same day of within 6 to 8 weeks of the first day of employment. When realistic expectations and goals are set and not achieved, training may need to be repeated or modified and another assessment time frame should be established.

Empowering Associates

As the leader in the practice it falls to you to assist every associate in fulfilling the responsibilities in their respective job descriptions and to foster job satisfaction as they complete their tasks. Effective leaders develop a mutual respect; the associates respect the leader and the leader respects the associates. If the practice holds at its core the success of every patient and the satisfaction of every person who refers patients to the practice, every person in the practice must continuously try to exceed the wants and needs of both patients and referral sources at every encounter and opportunity. The practice leader must focus on the core of the practice, provide examples at every opportunity, and provide guidance, instruction, and praise to each associate pulling in the same direction.

The best way to make a commitment to an associate is to empower that person to make decisions based on the benefits of the patient, the referral source, and the practice. Their decisions should be made in that order. Empowerment is a strong drug. It implies trust and confidence. When the practice leader empowers an associate to make a decision, he or she is relying on the associate's assessment of the situation, their ability to come to a just and fair conclusion, and their confidence knowing that their decision will not be second-guessed nor otherwise undone. The practice leader, who enables his or her associates to make decisions about hearing instrument returns, repairs at no charge, or waiving charges for a situation that could use some salve on a wound caused by an error or misstep, demonstrates confidence and faith in their capabilities. *Practice owners* (or managers) readily delegate tasks to employees. *Practice leaders* empower others with decision-making capabilities to get things done. It takes a great deal of confidence, self-assurance, and security to transfer segments of authority to associates. By creating strong and effective associates who can work on behalf of the patient, the practice leader will have developed a group that can make the difference in the market place, a group that is known for competence and excellent care and patient satisfaction.

As you empower others, you will find that most aspects of your life will change for the better. Empowering others can free you personally to have more time for other matters in the practice, increase the effectiveness of your practice, and, best of all, and make an incredibly positive impact on the lives of the people you empower.

Performance Appraisal

McClain and Romaine (2007) state emphatically that despite the need for their existence, managers and employees inherently dislike evaluating performance. They contend that regular communication—daily or at least weekly—is the most effective way to both monitor and shape employee performance.

In practices with fewer than six to eight people involved in daily operations, there remains a need to complete formal evaluations although perhaps less critical than in larger practices. When an individual in a smaller practice fails to pull his or her weight, the work products of the team may suffer. Peer-generated appraisals are usually immediate and effective. In larger practices and those in corporate or health care settings, formal performance appraisals are necessary as a stipulation in hiring guidelines or for compliance with malpractice or malfeasance insurance coverage. The last thing a practice or a corporate entity wants to defend in a malfeasance case is why the individual involved had not had an appropriate performance appraisal in 2 or 3 years relative to the time the alleged malfeasance was to have taken place.

There are as many ways to develop a performance appraisal as there are authors with opinions about the topic. It should be viewed as an opportunity for an associate's continued success and improvement: It should be tied to the associate's efforts to maintain and advance patient and referral source satisfaction and retention. Performance appraisals should be considered a "formalized" part of a continuous program of recognition, on-the-run feedback, and positive modeling of behaviors in clinical service delivery in the practice. Nothing, therefore, should come as a surprise in an appraisal meeting.

Probably the most unnerving and counterproductive aspect of formalized performance appraisal rests in the fact that financial parameters are intimately involved in the process. Burrows (2006), indicates that promotions, pay raises, bonuses, and job assignments should be made on the basis of a formal evaluation. No wonder people view performance appraisals with such overwhelming trepidation when so much of the outcome is clouded by the threat of loss of promotions and other financial matters. Performance appraisals and financial incentives are undeniably tied; however, by disengaging the appraisal meeting from the time when promotions, pay raises, and bonuses are granted (or denied), the appraisal meeting becomes less of a threatening circumstance and a greater opportunity to concentrate on performance assessment and strategies to improve. The focus of the performance appraisal moves from financial issues to performance issues.

The goal of performance appraisal should be to improve the best asset of the practice—the people. If performance appraisals are completed in January, promotions, pay raises and bonuses will be issued in July. If the associate has made the necessary adjustments to improve identified deficiencies or has continued to provide excellent service to the practice, there will be no need for an additional meeting coincidental to the awarding of promotions, pay raises, and bonuses in July.

The key elements in a performance appraisal in an audiology practice should include at least the following:

■ A review of the position description, related duties, and responsibilities as the basis for the performance review (clinical in the case of an audiologist; operational in the case of office staff);

■ An assessment of the associate's contributions to patient and referral source satisfaction relative to their duties and responsibilities;

■ An assessment of the associate's competencies and deficiencies;

■ An assessment of the associate's abilities to take direction, to work cooperatively, to follow policy and procedures, and to work independently;

■ To establish a means and a time line to improvement of areas in need of improvement.

Employee Retention

Retaining associates is important for several distinct reasons: (1) it is expensive in time and capital to go through recruiting and evaluating potential candidates for the position; (2) there is a causal link between employee retention and high patient satisfaction; (3) continuity of care issue—even with the front office staff, patients like to see the same faces on a regular basis and (4) the practice loses an associate with knowledge and a skill set specific to the position—that skill set will have to be re-established with the new hire for the position.

The goal of any employee retention program in health care is to keep those who add value to the practice. Competition for good people is intense and the practice leader must commit to the realities of the marketplace. If he or she wants to hire good people who will, in turn, become sources of patient satisfaction and facilitate revenue for the practice, it is essential to develop a compensation package that validates an estimate of their worth. There are practice management gurus who preach that money and benefit packages are not that important to prospective employees. Do not buy into that theory. True, employees who become associates must have a sense of value in the practice and must be involved in aspects of daily operations as stakeholders. Much of that begins during the on-boarding process. However, the immediate decision to consider the practice as a possible employer in the first place centers on the financial opportunities.

The work environment contributes significantly to employee retention. Consistent interactions with members of the management team and access to the practice leader with the liberty to discuss practice policies and procedures are also points of appreciation important to retention. Having an employer who will listen, cares about their well-being, and is sympathetic yet fair in their requirements about the position contribute to retention. Well-trained, well-recognized, and empowered associates have pride in the practice and readily develop an allegiance that will likely transcend offers that might be attractive to those with less stature and unable to make a decision without permission. Trust is a critical element in retention. If an associate is trusted, they will work diligently to maintain that trust and the empowerment and positive self-image it brings.

Termination of Employment

Terminating an employment arrangement is never easy. It is probably one of the most difficult tasks a practice leader will face, regardless of the reason for the termination. In today's litigious society, justifiable terminations may be challenged by attorneys eager to gain a nuisance settlement in a wrongful termination suit. The advice of legal counsel to most health care practices is to reach a payout agreement rather than incur a lengthy and expensive engagement. If your ducks and documentation are in a row and the termination was appropriate, there is no reason (beyond the financial and time costs) to roll over and pay out the demands put on the table by your former associate's attorney. Indeed, if fewer would roll over, perhaps there would be fewer incidences of wrongful termination lawsuits threatened or filed. Evaluate the potential costs realistically, remove your emotionality from the situation, and make a decision in the best interests of the practice—and with the advice of your attorney

The Policy and Procedures Manual or employment contract should contain not only the associate's position description but clearly stated grounds for termination as well. In most instances of audiology practices, the employees are considered "at will" employees and may be terminated at any time. Despite this status, it is good to document performance appraisals, specific situations that constitute noncompliance in their position description or expected parameters of the workplace such as reporting on time, adhering to paid time-off policies, and other expectations that are required for continued employment in the practice. At every incidence of noncompliance where the practice leader has had to discuss an issue or situation with the associate, it should be described in writing, with a plan to resolve the situation and/or a clear depiction of the consequences if the infringement occurs again. It should be dated and signed by the associate and the practice leader. In any event, never let an employee or associate dictate the terms of his or her employment nor hold your actions hostage by the stated or implied threat of a wrongful discharge suit. The position would not be there if it were not for your starting the practice, managing the department, or otherwise serving as his or her superior. If the employee or associate meets the criteria for dismissal, take firm action on behalf of the practice, the patients, and the other members of the team who have been affected by the person's noncompliance as well.

Adding an Audiologist to the Professional Staff of the Practice

When adding a member to the professional staff of the practice, procedural contexts, diagnostic protocols specific to the practice, and a discussion of both philosophical and pragmatic approaches to patient evaluation, interpretation, and care management should be considered. Certainly if the audiologist has been practicing for several years and carries the valuable mantel of experience, there will be little required of the practice leader save working with the new colleague on report formats, getting to know the ins and outs of all the referral sources, and filling in clinical vacuums such that they might exist. Perhaps the audiologist had been in a dispensing practice that did not offer vestibular evaluation. If so, the audiologist will need to re-establish a knowledge and skill set to participate in the clinical assessment and, when applicable, treatment of patients with disequilibrium. The new audiologist may require directed readings as well as clinical instruction on vestibular assessment techniques, interpretation of data, and report writing.

Fourth-Year Au.D. Externships

Adding a fourth-year Au.D. student to the practice does not constitute adding an audiologist to the professional staff of the practice. When the Au.D. degree was first considered and earnest discussions about curriculum and clinical training preceded the first Au.D. program at Baylor, under the leadership of Dr. James Jerger, the fourth year was to stand as a beneficial circumstance for both extern and preceptor alike. The student was to enter the practice and "hit the ground running" compared to students in their clinical fellowship year (CFY) immediately following the Masters degree. The fourth-year Au.D. student was to have had comprehensive academic and clinical training such that the preceptor would do little more than round off the rough edges. The culmination of that effort was to have produced a competent audiologist, able to work independently within a few weeks of arrival at their externship site.

Unfortunately, at the time of this writing, a number of practitioners serving as preceptors express concerns that contemporary fourth-year students fall markedly short of an ability to work independently and require almost, if not as much, time and attention as did the CFYs of yesteryear. This is to be expected to some limited extent as fourth-year externships are in their relative infancy in the developing continuum that is the Au.D degree. One hopes the efforts of the Accreditation Commission for Audiology Education (ACAE) will (finally) establish a method to credential training programs so that both academic and clinical preparation will be stratified to the extent that fourth-year externs can indeed "hit the ground running" instead of needing to be brought up to speed to make up for limited clinical experience and, in some cases, less than stellar academic preparation.

These reports point to the need for an honest and open dialogue between universities and preceptors about the training program's strengths and weaknesses. Although the extern remains a tuition-paying student during their fourth-year rotation, the preceptor has, de facto,

accepted the role of mentor and guide in an important, pragmatic phase of the clinician's development. It is not, however, the task of the preceptor to shore up an extern's academic and clinical preparation. The preceptor should focus on providing an opportunity for the extern to be intimately involved in patient management and exposed to the operational pragmatics of independent practice. If the university fails to respond to the issues brought forth in discussions, the fourth-year externship will remain a catch-up time rather than the experiential opportunity it was intended to become.

This situation should not be taken lightly. The bedrock of any health care profession is the independent professional providing services and improving the quality of life for their patients. If we, as a profession, fail to produce practitioners able to hang a shingle and make a living by providing services as an audiologist, we have failed ourselves and future generations of audiologists who may be doomed to providing services directed by ENTs or working under the signature of a medical director in a corporate or hospital-based practice setting.

Summary

Successful personnel management, most importantly, requires strong leadership: An ability to lead and motivate and guide an individual's development from employee to associate. Every practice should develop uniform protocols for recruiting good people to provide the services outlined in a concise position description. Good people in the right positions will contribute significantly to the primary mission of any audiology practice: patient and referral source satisfaction.

Orientation and training formulates the important substrate that is the culture of the practice. It is the process by which all associates in the practice pull together as a unified team to optimize positive outcomes for every patient referred for services. Retaining good personnel is critical to the long-term health of the practice. The practice leader must conscientiously strive to maintain employee satisfaction as diligently as maintaining patient and referral source satisfaction. The success of a practice hinges on the capabilities and dynamic involvement of the practice leader. It is his or her duty to hire the best, focus on the mission of the practice, and keep patients, referral sources, and associates secure in the knowledge that by selecting their practice, they have made the right choice.

References

Burrows, D. L. (2006). Human resource issues: Managing, hiring, firing and evaluating employees. *Seminars in Hearing*, *27*(1), 5–17.

Maxwell, J. C. (2002). *Leadership 101: What every leader needs to know*. Nashville, TN: Thomas Nelson.

McClain, G. S., & Romaine, D. S. (2007). *The everything managing people book*. Avon, MA: Adams Media.

9

Policy and Procedures Manual

ROBERT G. GLASER, Ph.D.

Introduction

Policy and Procedures Manual, Employee Handbook, Employee Manual are titles to documents created to communicate the expectations of employers to their employees and what employees can expect from their employer. In some health care practice venues, there may be two sets of documents that serve as operational guides. The Policy and Procedures Manual will, in some practice venues, serve as the source of information to be included in an Employee Manual or

Handbook developed for a specific position or group of employees. Although the Policy and Procedures Manual serves as the basis for employee manuals or handbooks, it may also be reserved solely for the use of specific managers or directors within an organization. Employee Manuals or Handbooks may be developed from the Policy and Procedures Manual for specific employees depending on their informational needs. An Employee Manual or Handbook for an audiologist may differ greatly from those generated for administrative staff despite the fact that there will be operational issues common to all employees. No matter the title of the document, Employee Manuals or Handbooks are critically important to optimize consistent operations in both small and large practices.

Policies Versus Procedures

Policies establish the rules of the practice; procedures clarify operational issues. Policies provide the rules of engagement around which employees operate. They commonly include rules for paid time-off (PTO), sick leave, jury duty, covered holidays, dress code, confidentiality, and a host of other parameters that set forth the character and tone of the practice. For example, PTO must be readily delineated so that both new hires and long-term employees understand the rules of computation and acquisition of time-off, the nature and definition of various types of PTO—personal leave, military leave, sick leave—the process to request PTO, whether it is cumulative or needs to be used or lost, and so on.

Procedures prescribe and substantiate operational topics such as how the practice defines a comprehensive audiologic examination—delineating the acquisition of clinical information and data from the patient to come to an appropriate diagnosis. Although the procedure establishes the clinical components of what constitutes the examination in the practice, history, pure tone and speech threshold and recognition testing, otoacoustic emissions testing, and so forth, it should not be so detailed that it includes specific instructions of the technical components of the procedures. It is not so much how an audiologist gets to the data as much as the quality of the data

gleaned from the clinical test battery that has been chosen to constitute the comprehensive audiologic examination as a procedure for the practice. The decision to establish a procedure defining the comprehensive audiologic examination was determined based on the best methods to arrive at an accurate and valid diagnosis.

The Need for a Policy and Procedures Manual

For the purposes of this chapter, the term Policy and Procedures Manual (P&P Manual) will be used instead of Employee Manual or Handbook. As indicated above, in some practice venues, the Employee Manual or Handbook may be one and the same or the Employee Manual or Handbook may be derived from a P&P Manual that may have limited access relative to status within an organization such as a hospital or managed health care delivery system.

The P&P Manual establishes the operational characteristics necessary to provide professional services in accord with the Mission Statement of the practice. It enables the practice owner or manager to establish operational parameters in concert with his or her vision of how the practice operates and the manner and types of services to be provided.

Beyond systematizing administrative and operational aspects of the practice, the Policy and Procedures Manual provides rules and guidance for decision-making and appropriate actions throughout the practice at every level of involvement; owner, director, department head, and clinical and administrative staff. It should be considered the ultimate resource document for an audiology practice whether the venue of service delivery is an autonomous audiology practice, a hospital department, an educational resource center, an ENT Department in a medical school, or a private ENT-Audiology practice.

Each employee must agree with and abide by these "rules of engagement" which clarify what the employer should expect from the employee and what the employee should expect from the employer. An employee's acceptance of these rules and procedural guidelines is critical to their becoming "stakeholders" in the practice. Additionally, employees who fail to comply with the tenets and principles in the P&P Manual do so under a stipulated understanding that they are jeopardizing their continued employment. That stipulation is completed by the employee having signed and dated an acknowledgment form indicating his or her agreement to the tenets set forth in the P&P Manual as presented in Sidebar 9–1.

The P&P Manual can serve as a tutorial document for potential new hires and the basis for their orientation to the practice. Each person considered for employment must be able to follow the established rules and procedural guidelines. They should be encouraged to ask

---

Sidebar 9–1
POLICY AND PROCEDURES MANUAL

ACKNOWLEDGMENT FORM

I have read the Policy and Procedures Manual for *(insert the practice or specific practice venue)*. By acceptance of the Policy and Procedures Manual (P&P Manual), I acknowledge notice and agree to abide by and provide services or interact with patients, referral sources, and others in accord with all policies and procedures set forth in the P&P Manual. I recognize the need and agree to maintain patient health information in a secure fashion such that each patient's health information is protected and secured in accord with current HIPAA regulations. I understand that changes may be made from time to time and that *(insert the practice or specific practice venue)* has the right and authority to make any representations contrary to the statements set forth in the P&P Manual. I also acknowledge that no one employed by, or acting on behalf of *(insert the practice or specific practice venue)*, is authorized to make oral statements to change the at-will employment relationship between *(insert the practice or specific practice venue)* and its employees. I understand that *(insert the practice or specific practice venue)* or I may terminate my employment at any time for any reason.

Signature _____ Date _____

for clarification if they do not understand or have differing views on policies or procedures. If a potential employee is unable to agree with the tenets of the practice as set forth in the P&P Manual, they should seek employment elsewhere.

The P&P Manual sets the tone of the practice; how it feels and looks to patients and referral sources—employee dress and demeanor in the office or on the telephone, the structure, brevity, content, and turnaround time of reports, front office staff interactions with the referral source's office staff, and response to the number of rings on an incoming call. Many, if not all of the policies and procedures are geared to developing patient satisfaction which has been identified as the critical element in securing the long-term success of any practice.

Legal Considerations in Developing a Policy and Procedures Manual

As indicated in Chapter 2, a Policy and Procedures Manual is important no matter the numbers of employees. It establishes a basis for many otherwise unstated, ambiguous, and/or misunderstood aspects of the employment relationship. Critically important to that relationship is the confirmation of the "at-will" status of the employee and the right of the employer to terminate employment for any or no reason.

Some argue that a P&P Manual will not prevent an employee from filing a suit against the practice and its owner(s). In the final analysis, that is true. It will not prevent a legal encounter by an employee. However, having the rules of engagement set forth, and the terms of employment stipulated and agreed on

by the employee will serve as the best defense against employee-related legal claims. Burrows (2006) indicates that a well-written employee handbook (P&P Manual) will serve as a defense against employment lawsuits. A written document is the practice's best chance of not having a court case become the owner or manager's word against that of the employee. The remedy for that situation is to produce a well-written document that has been reviewed and approved by the attorney-of-record.

When preparing the P&P Manual it is best to assume that it may, right or wrong, be viewed as a legally binding contract. For that reason among many, the legal counsel for the practice must evaluate the entire document. He or she will ensure that appropriately worded disclaimers are in place and that the language in the document is in accord with the employer-employee relationship. Miller and Jentz (2006) aptly point out that employers have learned hard lessons from court decisions about what is said in P&P Manuals. They indicate that promises made in an employment manual may create an implied-in-fact contract. Miller and Jentz (2006) suggest that employers must make it clear to employees that the policies expressed in a P&P Manual must not be interpreted as a contractual promise and that the manual is not intended as a contract. They suggest the following disclaimer, appropriately adapted to the particular needs of the workplace venue, be set off and prominent from the surrounding text by the use of larger type, all capital letters, or some other device that calls the reader's attention to it:

This policy manual describes the basic personnel policies and practices of our Company. You should understand that the manual does not modify our Company's "at-will" employment doctrine or provide employees with any kind of contractual rights.

An All-Encompassing Compliance Document

In the ever appropriate and increasingly important arena of establishing the "rules of engagement" between an employer and an employee, consideration should be given to establishing a general compliance document. The employee signs the document upon employment. In this compliance document, the employee agrees to a variety of appropriate stipulations including records protection and confidentiality, proprietary information of the practice, forms, electronic and hard copy files, and so forth. The employee agrees to these stipulations on an a priori basis prior to his or her resignation or termination as an "at-will" employee (see Sidebar 9–1).

Overview of a P&P Manual for an Audiology Practice

There is little uniformity across the tables of content for P&P Manuals, Employee Handbooks, and Manuals. Content varies with the practice venue, with the practitioner/owner, and with the extent of clinical services offered in the practice. There is no set rule, order, or list that might signal completeness of information. The details of each section of P&P Manuals vary greatly. The spectrum of details ranges from minimalist statements to extensive descriptions of issues with definitions, footnotes, and comprehensive legal precedents. It is important

that the scope of issues in the P&P Manual be well met and adequately conveyed so that the document is clear and concise, leaving little question in the mind of the reader.

The best judge of completeness of information and topics covered relative to the venue of the practice is the attorney-of-record. He or she must review the document to ensure completeness, correctness, and accuracy relative to current laws established both in the state wherein the practice is located and according to federal guidelines. An attorney's view of the P&P Manual will be grounded in employment law and compliance as well as the best interests and protection of his or her employer—the practice owner.

Each practice venue has different needs. If the practice is in a hospital department, most of the P&P Manual will likely have been completed at the corporate level. It may be left to you as the Director or Head of Audiology to complete those sections pertaining specifically to the clinical services offered and the personnel delivering those services. The completed document will be reviewed by the hospital's legal staff as well as the administrator charged with oversight of your department or clinic. If you are in a university setting, clinical oversight as well as those with oversight of research activities will likely have to review the P&P Manual. As with corporate oversight in hospitals, universities may have even greater numbers of reviewers and personnel in oversight capacities with the final oversight commonly resting with the office of the Provost.

The outline that follows may not appear logical to some, incomplete to others, and overextended by those who adhere to the "less is better" philosophy. It is offered as a guiding outline more than an all inclusive document. Each section should be given weight appropriate to your particular needs. Selected examples will be offered for your consideration. In some cases more than one option will be proffered with suggestions. Developing a comprehensive P&P Manual is beyond the scope of this text; however, this outline should enable you to get a good start and come up with a document that can be reviewed and edited by your attorney, accountant, and others with experience and knowledge in developing similar documents. The proposed text of the P&P Manual appears in italics with commentary and suggestions, when issued, are in regular font.

Policy and Procedures Manual

Title of the Policy and Procedures Manual

POLICY AND PROCEDURES MANUAL FOR AUDIOLOGY ASSOCIATES

Introduction to the Policy and Procedures Manual

Introduction
This Policy and Procedures Manual (P&P Manual) contains the policies, practices, and procedures of Audiology Associates. This P&P Manual is not intended to be all inclusive. Audiology Associates reserves the right to make final decisions regarding the interpretation and application of its policies, practices and procedures, whether or not identified in the P&P Manual, and

to change or discontinue them at any time. The Manual also contains general information about the benefits that are available to you.

Audiology Associates is concerned not only with your job performance but also with you as an individual. If you have a question about work or any material in this Manual, contact Dr. Glaser or the Practice Manager. Remember that, a question can be answered only if it is raised, and conditions with which you are dissatisfied can be improved only if you bring the problem to management's attention.

Audiology Associates maintains an open, honest, and cooperative work environment. This work environment gives us an opportunity to get to know you and encourage you to understand and share the goals of Audiology Associates.

Finally, you should understand that this manual is not intended to create nor constitute an employment contract between you and Audiology Associates. Because the P&P Manual is not contractually binding, you have the right to terminate our employment relationship at anytime, with or without any notice or reason, and the Company, of course, retains the same right, unless specified differently by contract. In other words, our employment relationship can be defined as employment at will.

Purpose of the Policy and Procedures Manual

Purpose
The P&P Manual was developed to provide you with guidelines and policies regarding your employment with Audiology Associates. This manual is an important guidebook to be used as a

resource regarding policies, employee guidelines, and our practice standards. We hope that this manual will be beneficial in establishing the responsibilities of both the employer and employee to each other and eliminate any misunderstanding that may occur due to poor communication. These policies have been developed to serve the current needs and might need to be adjusted periodically. Both Audiology Associates and the employees are encouraged to recommend revisions they feel are appropriate.

The Mission of the Practice

Mission Statements
To always provide the best hearing and balance care for every patient at every encounter knowing that we are privileged to participate in an important portion of their health care.

To always make decisions in favor of our patient or referral source at every opportunity knowing that we cannot be wrong if we are trying to be right for those whom we serve

To provide the professional community with the best source of accurate, consistent, and responsive hearing and balance care available in our area.

Practice Philosophy: A Commitment to Patients

A Commitment to Our Patients
■ We pledge to always make decisions in favor of the patient and referral source at every opportunity knowing that we cannot be wrong if we are trying to be right for those whom we serve.

■ We are professionally, ethically, and personally committed to providing excellent care in a timely and caring manner to all members of the communities we serve.
■ Our Audiologists represent the finest professional resource for hearing and balance evaluations, tinnitus assessment and management, and hearing instrument evaluation, fitting, and follow-up care in the communities we serve.
■ The entire staff of Audiology Associates recognizes and appreciates the importance of all health care providers and their staff who refer patients to us for our specialized care and consideration. We will always strive to maintain their trust by issuing timely, concise, and accurate reports and by maintaining an active liaison between the referral source and their patients.
■ Each member of our practice subscribes to the following Patient's Bill of Rights:

Patients in Our Practice Should . . .
1. Expect more from Audiology Associates than from any other provider in our community.
2. Know that each patient will be respected by everyone in our practice.
3. Expect us to answer your phone call in a timely, friendly, and welcoming manner.
4. Expect to be greeted in a friendly and appreciative manner by everyone in our practice.
5. Know that we recognize the importance of their time.
6. Expect a quick response and immediate action at all times by every member of our practice.

7. *Require excellent communication from us.*
8. *Know that we will listen and understand their concerns.*
9. *Expect quick and accurate resolution of questions or concerns about your account.*
10. *Receive an apology if we are in error.*

Management Rights

It is important that any manual for employees have a clear statement of the rights of the management of the practice to conduct business in an appropriate and businesslike manner according to their terms. The statement need not be lengthy. It must clarify the roles, obligations, and expectations that management considers important to the continued operation of the practice as a business. Likewise, the employee should understand clearly where in the scheme of the practice he or she fits in relative to management. The wording is commonly straightforward and must leave little room for conjecture as to the roles of management and the intent to operate the practice as a business.

Rights of Management
Audiology Associates has and will always seek the opinions of every member of the practice about working conditions, ways and means to accomplish all tasks important to the success of our practice, and other matters that are of importance to each and every member of our team. From time to time, Audiology Associates must make decisions without the input from the members of the team. As such, Audiology Associates retains all managerial and administra-

tive rights referred to inherently and by law. These rights include, but are not limited to, the right to exercise judgment in establishing and administering policies, practices, and procedures, and to make changes in them; the right to take whatever action is necessary, in management's judgment, to operate the business, and the right to set standards of productivity and services to be rendered. The management of business and the direction of those working in the practice including, but not limited to, the responsibility to hire, promote, transfer, suspend, or discharge, and the responsibility to relieve employees from duty because of lack of work, or other reasons, are vested exclusively in the management of Audiology Associates. In addition, Audiology Associates has the right to amend, modify, or delete provisions of this manual with or without prior notice.

Acknowledgment Forms

Critically important to any P&P Manual is a statement, signed and dated by the employee indicating that he or she has read the document and agrees with its content and implied or actual actions which may be put into effect by the owner or manager of the practice. Any document that stipulates specific compliance, duties, rules, or expected actions or response by an employee must be signed and dated during the earliest stages of employment. It is difficult to get documents signed immediately prior to or after an employee has been discharged.

Two examples follow. The first is an acknowledgment form that commits the signer to the tenets of the P&P Manual. It underscores the need for confidentiality and compliance with HIPAA regulations. The second is an equally important acknowledgment document specifying the proprietary rights of the practice. Although it will not prevent theft of documents, forms, and the like, the courts have taken a dim view of individuals leaving a business or practice with proprietary or trade information after they have affixed their signature to a compliance document describing specific proprietary items and information that must be left at the workplace. Of course, these documents can be combined; however, by having two separate forms, the underlying reasons and differing content are made clearer. Each should be signed in the early stages of employment, after the P&P Manual has been read and orientation to the practice has been competed. The second form lets the employee know that, in the event he or she decides to leave the practice or is terminated, there are specific rules regarding confidentiality, pirating forms, and removing items considered proprietary to the practice is prohibited.

Acknowledgment Form for the P&P Manual

Acknowledgment Form
I have reviewed a current copy of Audiology Associates Policy & Procedure Manual. By acceptance of the manual, I acknowledge notice of all policies contained therein. I have reviewed the Privacy Policies and agree to maintain patient information in a secure fashion such that each patient's health information is protected and secured, in accord with HIPAA regulations effective April 16, 2003. I understand that changes may be made from time to time and that Audiology Associates has authority

to make any representations contrary to the statements set forth in the manual. I also acknowledge that no one employed by, or acting on behalf of Audiology Associates, is authorized to make oral statements which change the at-will employment relationship between the company and its employees. I further understand that the company or I may terminate my employment at any time for any reason.

_____
Signature

_____
Date

Employee General Compliance Document

General Compliance Document
Audiology Associates
In accord with my resignation or discharge as an at-will employee, I submit and agree to and with the following statements in compliance with office policies and HIPAA regulations:

■ *Patient records, notes, and/or other information pertaining to the patients of Audiology Associates will remain confidential and will not be removed physically or electronically.*
■ *Financial information about individual patients and/or any fiscal information pertaining to Audiology Associates will remain confidential and may not be removed physically or electronically.*
■ *Proprietary information, including, but not limited to, personnel information, supplier information and any/all statistics pertaining to the operations of Audiology and Speech Associates will remain confidential*

and will not be removed physically or electronically.

■ *Information about the current status, future plans, and other information deemed important to current and future operations of Audiology Associates will remain confidential and will not be removed physically or electronically.*

■ *Forms, computer programs, equipment manuals, patient protocols, or other documents regarding operational and patient-related matters pertaining to Audiology Associates shall remain at the office in physical and electronic forms and information contained therein will remain confidential.*

■ *Books, journals, and related materials not purchased by personal funds will remain the property of Audiology Associates*

■ *All forms developed for use at Audiology Associates are copyrighted and remain the intellectual property of Audiology Associates. As such, none may be removed nor used in whole or in part for any reason except when permission has been granted in writing.*

■ *All physical and electronic files used in the execution of duties as an employee of Audiology Associates remain the property of Audiology Associates and may not be removed in any form.*

■ *In the interests of the patients served and the continuity of their care, all charts will be completed by noon of the day immediately prior to the last day of employment.*

_____

Signature

_____

Date

Policies

Policies represent the rules of the practice. The following alphabetic list of policies with examples will not represent a comprehensive list for each and every practice. Each will provide a starting point to develop an appropriately written document for your particular practice venue. Policy language is in italics with comments in regular font.

Administrative Staff Priorities

Administrative Staff Priorities
1. *Booking patients into the office— we cannot help if they are not here.*
2. *Take care of the referral sources— referral sources and their staff are our partners in caring for their patients: Courtesy and facilitation are keys to excellent service— if you take care of them; they assume their patients will be well-cared for in our practice.*
3. *Facilitate every visit: Take the appointment from referral staff hands to your hands—let them get back to work while we book the appointment.*
4. *Take great care of each telephone call. Consider the caller your boss, as we all work for the patients in our practice. Always make decisions in favor of the patients and the referral sources. If it's a tie, they win.*
5. *Call backs and annual visits to be completed by the 15th of each month, without fail. Must try twice before leaving a voice message; if no response to voice message, send card.*

6. *Send handwritten thank you notes to those patients who have referred patients to our practice—they have entrusted their friend or relative to our care and they deserve our thanks and appreciation.*

7. *Call newly fitted patients or those with recently repaired instruments within 3 to 5 days of the (re)fitting to check their status before their return visit—if they are struggling, get them in prior to their scheduled follow-up visit.*

8. *When a patient presents a hearing instrument for repair, obtain their description of the problem, when and how often the problem occurs. If the instrument is dead, check for occlusion and battery problems. Advise need for return for repair, anticipated return time, and costs if out of warranty.*

9. *Services, instruments, and accessories are to be paid same day of service unless insurance is covering full or portion of the visit, procedure, or instrument.*

10. *All Deposits/Collections/Postings entered same day received.*

Billing and Collection Policy

Billing and Collection Policy
Every patient in our practice has signed an agreement (see below) stipulating that they are responsible for paying any and all bills incurred during their care in our practice. The billing cycle for Audiology Associates is 90 days. Accounts with unpaid balances will be sent to collection if in that time period, payment in full or partial payment with an approved schedule of payments has not been received or arranged.

There must be a written agreement on the method and dates of payment if balances are to be carried beyond the 90-day billing cycle.

Each patient must receive notification by phone or letter 15 days prior to our sending their account to collection. Once the account has been placed with the collection agent, all payments must be made to that agency. No attempt should be made to discuss accounts in collection as the account is no longer with our practice. They must be referred to the collection agency if they have questions or concerns.

Audiology Associates
Financial Agreement
Payment is expected at the time of service unless other arrangements have been made. We accept cash, checks, Master-Card, Visa, and Discover Card.

■ *We will submit charges directly to your insurance carrier as a courtesy. Submitting the charges is no guarantee that they will be paid.*

■ *Insurance policies may or may not pay for the services you receive in our office. Coverage varies with each insurance carrier; a few plans cover all charges, some cover 80%, and others cover less than 50%. The amount your insurance company pays for the services you receive is between you and your insurance carrier.*

■ *YOU ARE RESPONSIBLE FOR PAYING ALL CHARGES INCLUDING DEDUCTIBLES, CO-INSURANCE AND SERVICES, DEVICES, AND RELATED ITEMS NOT COVERED BY INSURANCE. ACCOUNTS NOT PAID WITHIN*

*45 DAYS MAY GO TO A COLLEC-
TION AGENT.*

■ *HEARING INSTRUMENTS
ORDERED AND NOT PICKED
UP WILL BE SUBJECT TO
RESTOCKING AND HANDLING
FEES WHEN RETURNED TO THE
MANUFACTURER.*

■ *EARMOLDS AND/OR IMPRESSION
COSTS ARE NONREFUNDABLE
AND MUST BE PAID IN FULL.*

*I have read and understand the
above and agree to pay all charges.
I authorize my insurance company to
make direct payment for all services
rendered. Release is hereby granted to
send records by any means appropriate
to health care providers or others deemed
by Audiology Associates to be in need of
these records.*

Signature

Date

Witness

Date

Certification and License to Practice

License to Practice
*Audiology Associates will reimburse each
member of the practice for fees associated with obtaining and maintaining
their license to practice in this state.
Board certification by the American
Board of Audiology is required as part
of the qualification for employment. It is
considered the responsibility of the holder
of the certificate to pay for securing
and maintaining their certification.*

Confidentiality

Confidentiality
*All Information pertaining to the
patients we serve must be considered
confidential. Appropriate conversations
about patients entrusted to our care
must be completed to ensure that those
in the waiting room or elsewhere in the
office will not overhear the conversation. Patient charts and other information including the appointment book
should be secured from view. At no time
should a patient be discussed outside
of the office with anyone including
another staff member.*

*As all patient information obtained
by Audiology Associates is confidential,
it may not be released to an insurance
company or any other party, without
the patient's written permission on file.*

*Breach of confidentiality of patient
information will result in immediate
termination of employment.*

Conflicts of Commitment and Conflicts of Interest

*Conflicts of Commitment and
Conflicts of Interest*
*A conflict of commitment exists when
an employee assumes obligations external to the practice which interferes with
the employee's properly discharging his
or her obligations and commitment to
Audiology Associates. Full-time employees must make full-time commitments
to Audiology Associates. Part-time employees with obligations external to the
practice must ensure they are fully committed to Audiology Associates when
discharging their duties on behalf of
our practice. Full disclosure of any obli-*

gation external to Audiology Associates is expected regardless of the numbers of hours of employment.

Obligations external to Audiology Associates that represent direct competition for similar patients, referral sources, or care contracts constitute a conflict of interest. A conflict of interest must be disclosed by the employee and a determination made as to the course of action which will resolve the issue. Expeditious disclosure and resolution of such conflicts is in the interests of all involved. Failure to resolve the conflict may result in termination of employment.

Consent Forms for Specific Procedures

Consent forms will not prevent legal action. They exist as an acknowledgment that the procedure has been explained, risks have been discussed, and the patient acknowledges having been advised of the risks by his or her signature.

Consent to Perform Cerumen Removal and/or Earmold Impression
Cerumen removal and/or earmold impression procedures involves the introduction of instruments and/or material into your ear canal(s). The audiologist will use accepted procedures to avoid adverse results. Cerumen removal and earmold impression involves the risks of discomfort, bleeding from the ear canal, puncture of or damage to the ear-drum and ear infection.

I, the undersigned patient, hereby acknowledge that I have read and understand the important notice printed above. I understand that no guarantee has been made to me as to the results. I recognize the risks of receiving the

procedure(s) described. I hereby request and consent to the procedure(s).

_____

Patient Name

_____

Signature

_____

Audiologist Name

_____

Signature

Patient Satisfaction and Complaint Resolution

Every practice must ensure that the patient has a voice in his or her care. If the patient feels as though he or she has been treated inappropriately, unfairly or has been otherwise ill treated, the patient should have a means to address the issues with the owner of the practice or the Practice Manager. The simpler the policy, the more expedient the result; complaint resolution is as much about the speed with which you reply as it is with the resolution of the complaint. The policy can be as simple as having all patients with unresolved complaints referred directly to the Practice Manager for resolution within 24 to 48 hours. He or she can deal with the situation directly after having discussed the situation with those members of the administrative and professional staffs directly involved in the patient's complaint. As the Mission Statement says, the goal is to resolve conflict in favor of the patient at every opportunity. That does not mean, however, that the Practice Manager needs to roll over every time a patient lodges a complaint. If the patient's complaint exceeds reasonable limits set forth in policies or guidelines and is beyond appropriate reasonability, resolution completely in favor of the patient might jeopardize the validity of the policies and procedures of the practice. Flexibility in favor of the patient is expected. Not responding favorably to a patient's unreasonable demand should not be construed as inflexibility. Every business has to draw the line somewhere and that includes businesses operating in the arena of health care.

Disciplinary Actions

Disciplinary Actions
Audiology Associates is proud of the reputation of its employee's high standards of patient. Employees are expected to conduct themselves in a courteous and professional manner toward patients, referral sources, and their fellow employees at all times. Policies and guidelines are to be followed to maintain the integrity of the practice and the standards of care we have established in the communities we serve. When difficulties affecting your performance or the performance of others dictate disciplinary considerations, the following disciplinary guideline represents the progressive steps that will be taken:

1. *A verbal warning*
2. *A written warning*
3. *Final warning*
4. *Termination*

Management takes into account all the facts surrounding an employee's misconduct in determining appropriate discipline. Generally, however, a verbal warning may be given for initial, minor violations of practice policies or procedures. The written warning is given for repeated violations or initial violations

of a more serious nature. A final warning, which is always in writing, is given for the most serious offenses other than those calling for immediate discharge or for continued repetition of the type of violations for which one or more written warning have been given.

Management reserves the right to bypass any of the progressive steps of discipline depending on the circumstances involved. Depending on the facts and severity of the offense, management may give an employee a written or final warning as the first warning. Management can also terminate an employee without prior warning.

When misconduct is of a very serious nature, an employee may expect immediate discharge. The following acts are examples of serious misconduct, which may result in immediate discharge, and is not intended to be an all-inclusive list:

1. *Conviction of a felony.*
2. *Theft, misappropriation of funds.*
3. *Possession, use, or sale of an alcoholic beverage, nonprescribed drugs, or illicit drugs while on Audiology Associates premises or while on duty at another practice site.*
4. *Reporting for work while under the influence of intoxicants, including alcohol, nonprescribed drugs, or illicit drugs.*
5. *Unauthorized possession of a weapon while on practice premises or while on duty at another practice site.*
6. *Fighting or attempting to injure another person while on practice premises or while on duty at another practice site.*

7. *Engaging in horseplay or using abusive, threatening, or provocative language toward another person while on practice premises or while on duty at another practice site.*

8. *Engaging in sexual harassment.*

9. *Insubordination (e.g., refusal to promptly obey a work instruction or job assignment from a supervisor or the Practice Manager);*

10. *Dishonesty, including falsification of Company records (e.g., payroll, insurance, and personnel records).*

11. *Failure to report unexcused absences.*

12. *Immoral conduct or indecency while at work.*

13. *Gambling on practice premises or while on duty at another site.*

14. *Willful destruction of Company property.*

Each employee is responsible for knowing the rules of expected conduct, as well as the procedures outlined in this manual. Should you have any questions about the application of any rule or any discipline you have received, discuss it with the Practice Manager. Nothing contained in this Disciplinary Policy shall alter an employee's at-will status.

Drug and Alcohol Policy

Drug and Alcohol Policy
Audiology Associates maintains a safe and healthy environment for its employees and the patients and referring health care providers whom we serve. The use or trafficking of illicit drugs, on or off the job has an adverse impact on our practice and will not be tolerated.

Possession of prescription drugs while on practice premises or representing Audiology Associates at a related site is permissible only if:

■ *The drug is kept in the original container with both the employee's name and prescribing doctor's name on it;*

■ *The drug was dispensed within 12 months;*

■ *Written permission is submitted from the prescribing doctor which permits the employee to work while taking the indicated dosage.*

Even if the above conditions are met, Audiology Associates reserves the right to have a second physician determine whether the drug might adversely affect performance.
Employees are prohibited from:

■ *Using, possessing, or being under the influence of any alcoholic beverage, illegal drug, or illegal substance while on practice premises or in the performance of their duties at another site.*

■ *Possessing paraphernalia used in connection with any drug or controlled substance;*

■ *Selling, purchasing, or transmitting illegal drugs or controlled substances on practice premises or in the performance of their duties at another site.*

If an employee appears to be impaired or there is reason to believe that he or she may be in possession of alcohol or drugs, the employee may be ordered to undergo a drug and alcohol screen at the expense of Audiology Associates. Employees who are directed to undergo a drug or alcohol test will be suspended pending laboratory analysis of the sample. If the test is positive, the employee will be disciplined, up to and including termination of employment. If the test is negative, the employee will be paid for any lost work time. Employees are permitted to have the same sample retested at their own expense. If you are having a problem with drugs or alcohol, you can seek help. Our health insurance benefits provide for some treatment and counseling services. Please see the Practice Manager for any questions regarding the above.

An employee who violates this policy is subject to disciplinary action up to and including termination of employment on the first offense.

Educational Allowances

Educational Allowances Audiology Associates provides a minimum of three days for CEU-eligible educational training at an approved meeting such as the Annual Meeting of the American Academy of Audiology. Registration, economy class airfare, accommodations, and reasonable expenses will be paid upon submission and approval of receipts. Additional funding for other CEU eligible educational meetings may be approved as needed.

Equal Employment Opportunity (EEO) Policy

Equal Employment Opportunity (EEO) Policy In accordance with applicable local, state, and federal law, the Company is committed to a policy of nondiscrimi-nation and equal employment opportunity. All employment decisions will be made without regard to sex, race, color, religious creed, national origin, ancestry, age, non-job-related handicap, AIDS or AIDS related conditions, or status as a disabled veteran or a veteran of the Vietnam era.

Emergency Medical Assistance Protocol

Every practice must have a plan to respond to emergency situations. In the event that an individual in the practice becomes ill and requires emergency medical care, every member of the administrative and professional staffs must follow a set of steps to secure the situation and engage emergency personnel as soon as possible. The protocol should be practiced at least twice a year. Every telephone in the practice should have the office address and cross-streets to be read into the phone—a handy reminder in the fast-paced confusion of an emergency. The steps in the protocol will vary from setting-to-setting. At the minimum, a basic plan should include the following steps:

Emergency Medical Assistance Protocol

1. *Upon determining a patient or guest is in distress, call out to other practice personnel for help.*
2. *Dial 911 and notify the operator of the situation and give the address of the practice.*
3. *Do not leave the individual; however, you must make sure that emergency personnel can access your location.*
4. *If an extra member of the staff is available, have him or her go*

outside to direct emergency personnel.

5. *The Practice Manager should follow the individual to the hospital and make sure the family is contacted.*

6. *If the individual requiring removal from your practice has been referred by their physician, contact the referring physician immediately and apprise him or her of the situation.*

7. *Follow up with the patient or the family the next day.*

Employee Access to Business Data

Access to Operational Information of the Practice
Information or data pertaining to the business operations of Audiology Associates are considered confidential. Information about the daily business and professional operations such as, but not limited to, patient care visits, numbers of instruments dispensed, billing and coding information, fiscal information, patient and referral source databases, contracts to provide services, and any similar information is considered confidential and proprietary and access to these and other operational data is restricted to the Practice Manager and his or her designees. Failure to comply with this policy will result in disciplinary action and possibly termination.

Employee Performance Review

Performance Review
The first performance review for all personnel will be completed by the Practice Manager within the first 90 days of employment and annually thereafter.

The purpose of a review is to provide each employee with an opportunity to voice his or her concerns and to express thoughts about how their particular participation in the practice enhances patient care. He or she should take the opportunity to discuss items of interest or concern with the Practice Manager.

The Practice Manager will review the employee's performance and provide suggestions to improve specific areas. If significant resolution of deficiencies is considered necessary, additional training and reassessment of performance may be established in a defined time period. The performance evaluation will be summarized by the Practice Manager in writing for the employee's personnel file and a copy will be provided the employee.

Employee Professional Appearance Dress Code

Professional Appearance and Dress Code
A professional image is important to our patients and helps solidify their positive attitudes about our professionalism and the quality of the services we provide. Good grooming and a professional appearance are expected of all employees. Employees are required to wear white lab coats with their names embroidered or a name tag. The practice will supply appropriate lab coats to all personnel. Dress shirts and ties with dress slacks or khakis and appropriate shoes and socks are expected for men. Skirts and slacks with appropriate blouses or sweaters and appropriate shoes and hosiery are expected

for women. Athletic shoes, jeans, sweat-shirts, tank tops, and blouses displaying the midriff are prohibited. Professional attire is expected to be worn when attending professional meetings.

Hearing Instrument Lost Under Warranty

Replacement of Lost Hearing Instrument Under Warranty
If a hearing instrument is lost while under warranty, a replacement instrument will be secured for the patient under the manufacturer's terms of replacement. There will be no charge for the replacement instrument. There will be an inclusive $250.00 fee for earmold impression, programming, and refitting of the instrument including adjustment(s) necessary during three follow-up visits available for 6 months following refitting.

Hearing Instrument Repairs

Hearing Instrument Repairs
Hearing instrument repairs completed after the warranty period must be paid in full on the day the instrument is refitted. The cost of the repair may include additional charges for reprogramming should the instrument be returned from the repair facility without original programming.

Hearing Instrument Return

Return of Hearing Instrument Within Four Weeks Postfitting
In the event a patient returns a hearing instrument within the 4-week period

following the initial fitting, the patient will not be required to pay a restocking charge and the charges for the hearing instrument will be refunded. If a hearing instrument is returned beyond the 4-week period, applicable restocking and earmold impression charges may apply on a case-by-case basis. Charges for hearing examination and/or hearing instrument evaluation are paid as professional services rendered and are not subject to refund in the event of hearing instrument return.

(Note: This policy may not be applicable in certain states).

Internet Usage

Internet Usage
All electronic mail (E-mail) messages, voice mail messages, and all other information contained in Audiology Associate's computer and information systems (all of which shall be referred to as "information systems") are the property of the Audiology Associates.

E-mail Procedures
1. *All E-mail correspondence is the property of Audiology Associates and is for business purposes only.*
2. *Employee E-mail communications are not considered private despite any such designation either by the sender or the recipient.*
3. *Messages sent to recipients outside of Audiology Associates, if sent over the Internet and not encrypted, are not secure. Encryption requires prior approval by Audiology Associates.*
4. *Audiology Associates will monitor its E-mail system—including an employee's mailbox—at its discre-*

tion in the ordinary course of business. Please note that in certain situations, Audiology Associates may access and disclose messages sent over its E-mail system.

5. *The existence of passwords and "message delete" functions do not restrict or eliminate Audiology Associate's ability or right to access electronic communications. The delete function does not eliminate the message from the system.*

6. *Employees shall not share an E-mail password, provide E-mail access to an unauthorized user, or access another user's E-mail box without authorization.*

7. *Offensive, demeaning, or disruptive messages are prohibited. This includes, but is not limited to, messages that are inconsistent with Audiology Associate's policies concerning "Equal Employment Opportunity" and "Sexual Harassment."*

Internet Procedures

1. *Audiology Associate's network, including its connection to the Internet, is to be used for business-related purposes only and not for personal use. Any unauthorized use of the Internet is strictly prohibited. Unauthorized use includes, but is not limited to, connecting, posting, or downloading pornographic materials, engaging in computer "hacking," and other related activities attempting to disable or compromise the security of information contained on Audiology Associate's computers (or otherwise using*

Audiology Associate's computers for personal use).

2. *Because postings placed on the Internet may display Audiology Associate's address, make certain before posting information on the Internet that the information reflects the standard policies of our practice. Under no circumstances shall information of a confidential, sensitive, or otherwise proprietary nature be placed on the Internet.*

3. *Subscriptions to news groups and mailing lists are permitted when the subscription is for a work-related purpose. Any other subscriptions are prohibited.*

4. *Unless the prior approval of management has been obtained, users may not establish Internet or other external network connections that could allow unauthorized persons to gain access to Audiology Associate's systems and information. These connections include the establishment of hosts with public modem dial-ins, World Wide Web home pages, and File Transfer Protocol (FTP).*

5. *All files downloaded from the Internet must be checked for possible computer viruses.*

6. *Any data on any computer hard drives or electronic media (disks, etc.) which pertain to Audiology Associates, its patients, or staff are considered the property of Audiology Associates and must be kept in confidence following the guidelines set forth in the Confidentiality Statement.*

7. *On termination of employment, all data must be returned to Audiology Associates intact and any copies*

must be deleted from hard drives and/or electronic media.

8. *No software or peripheral is to be installed on Audiology Associate's system without prior authorization.*

9. *Any Employee who violates this policy shall be subject to disciplinary actions including termination of employment.*

Paid Time-Off (PTO)

Paid Time-Off (PTO)
Employees are asked to schedule their vacation at least one or two months in advance of the time they desire to be away.

In the event that two employees ask for the same PTO dates and a conflict is deemed important and unavoidable, the individual who submitted his or her Request for Leave form first will be granted the PTO requested.

"Request for Leave" forms can be obtained from the Practice Manager.

All Request for Leave forms must be competed and submitted to the Practice Manager. Emergency PTO will be considered accordingly; however, we expect a telephone call regarding the situation and an estimate of time away from your responsibilities.

Paid Time-Off Schedule
Full-Time: (5 days a week; 32–40 hours and up; 50 consecutive weeks)

1st year	*7 days*
2nd & 3rd years	*15 days*
4th, 5th, & 6th years	*22 days*
7th, 8th, & 9th years	*25 days*
10th year and above	*30 days*

Part-Time: (3 days per week; 21–32 hours and up; 50 consecutive weeks)

1st year	*5 days*
2nd & 3rd years	*7 days*
4th, 5th, & 6th years	*9 days*
7th, 8th, & 9th years	*13 days*
10th year and above	*17 days*

■ *Above PTO must be used in 1-hour increments.*

■ *PTO earned but not taken during the calendar year is not cumulative from year to year and will be forfeited if not taken by December 31st (use or lose policy).*

■ *In the unfortunate event of a long-term illness, the employee will meet with the Practice Manager to discuss his or her PTO status.*

Patients with Prior Collection Actions

Patients with Prior Collection Actions
Individuals returning to our practice for reassessment, hearing instrument repairs, or follow-up visits with a history of having been placed in collections, must pay for all services on a cash or credit card basis only. Exceptions to this policy may be considered on a case-by-case basis.

Position Descriptions

Every position of employment within a practice requires a written description of general and specific duties, management responsibilities if appropriate, oversight and reporting responsibilities as well as specific areas of data handling and access. Qualifications for each position should be made clear including specific training requirements or degree requirements. Patient care responsibilities should be delineated relative to the expected clinical proficiencies necessary to provide specific services. An example of a position description for a receptionist follows:

Position Description for Receptionist

Reports To: Practice Manager

Managerial Responsibilities: None or as directed by the Practice Manager

Qualifications: Associate's or Bachelor's Degree in business or related field preferred. Past work experience should include health care or related field as front office receptionist or position that included patient or practitioner interactions.

Hours: 40 plus hours per week (flexible as needed)

Responsibilities:
1. *Opening and closing the office.*
2. *Confirming all appointments (Audiology and Speech patients) for the next business day and pulling charts.*
3. *Ordering supplies for the audiology department.*
4. *Coordinates audiologists schedules.*
5. *Schedules patient and vendor appointments.*
6. *Greets patients and gathers billing information.*
7. *Answers telephone, screens and directs calls, takes messages.*
8. *Enters selected charges and payments in the computer.*
9. *Prepares daily bank deposit.*
10. *Organizes and files patients charts.*
11. *Obtains medical concurrences.*
12. *Performs receptionist duties at satellite offices.*
13. *Researches and enters new patient data into the computer.*
14. *Assists in the orientation and training of new employees as needed.*
15. *Has joint responsibility for office maintenance.*
16. *Faxing or mailing report results to primary care physicians and others.*
17. *Other responsibilities as directed by the Practice Manager.*

Referring Patients to Other Practitioners

Referring Patients to Other Practitioners
Patients may be referred to other health care providers when needed, if he or she has come to our practice on a self-referred basis, independent of a physician or other health care provider's referral. If the patient has been referred to our practice by a primary care provider or other health care practitioner and there is a definitive need for referral to another specialist or health care entity for additional evaluation or treatment, the patient must be returned to the original referring source for disposition and management with suggestions.

Tuition Assistance

Tuition Assistance
Tuition assistance may be provided for completion of an Au.D. or Ph.D. in Audiology on a case-by-case basis. According to the Federal Tax Codes, up to $5,250.00 of payments received by an employee for tuition, fees, books, supplies, and so forth, under an employer's educational assistance program may be excluded from gross income (Code Sec. 127; Reg. 1.127-1).

Weather

Inclement Weather
When forecasts indicate inclement weather that may result in school closings due to impassible road conditions, the Practice Manager (or designee) will take a copy of the schedule home (patient phone numbers should be listed) the night before threatening weather. The Practice Owner and/or Practice Manager will decide on the following course(s) of action:

■ *If conditions are obvious, scheduled patients may be canceled and rescheduled the afternoon or evening prior to the anticipated weather situation.*
■ *If severe, inclement conditions arise in the early morning, the patients may be cancelled and rescheduled before 8:30 AM.*
■ *The Practice Owner and/or Manager will contact each member of the staff to determine their ability to arrive at the office(s) or service sites. Depending on the response, patients may be canceled and the workday may be considered canceled.*

Clinical Procedures

Each clinical procedure offered in the practice should be delineated. Every CPT code employed in the practice constitutes a procedure; each should be well described with approximate times to complete the procedure with cooperative patients.

Summary

A P&P Manual is an essential part of communication within the practice. It stands as the rulebook, the reference book, and as a reminder of why patients and referral sources are the focus of the practice. Regardless of the number of people employed by the practice, a P&P Manual should be prepared and re-evaluated on an annual basis. There are no hard and fast rules about what should or should not be available to the readers of the manual. An outline of a P&P Manual for an Audiology practice is presented in Sidebar 9–2 for your consideration. It can be easily adjusted to include speech-language pathologists, psychologists, physical therapists, or other health care providers and counselors with appropriate position descriptions and minor changes in language specific to each discipline included in the practice. Regardless of the numbers of employees and their relative contributions to the practice, the wise Practice Manager or owner will solicit as much input from every member of the practice team in the preparatory stages of the manual. After all, the P&P Manual is, at its basis, about the services and the contributions provided as members of the team that is the practice.

Sidebar 9–2
OUTLINE OF A POLICY AND PROCEDURES MANUAL

Policy and Procedure Manual
  Introduction to the Practice
  Manual as Ultimate Resource
      Document; What It is and Is
      Not (disclaimers)
  The Mission of the Practice
  Practice Philosophy
  Management Rights
  Acknowledgment Form(s)
    Acknowledges having read
        and willingness to abide by
        policies within P&P
    Compliance document
        regarding confidential and
        proprietary information
Policies
  Administrative Staff Priorities
  Billing-Collection Policy
  Certification Versus Licenses
  Collection Policy
  Confidentiality
  Conflicts of Commitment:
      Conflicts of Interest
  Consent to Perform Earmold
      Impression and Cerumen
      Removal
  Convention and Workshop Policy
  Customer Satisfaction and
      Complaint Resolution
  Disaster Policy
  Disciplinary Policy
  Discrimination and Harassment
      in the Workplace
  Drug and Alcohol Policy
  Equal Employment Opportunity
  Emergency Medical Assistance
      Protocol
  Employee Access to Business Data

Employee Evaluation/
    Performance Review
Employee Standards of Conduct
  Dress
  Demeanor
  Collegiality
  Substance Abuse
  Smoking
  Harrassment of Staff,
      Colleagues, Patients
  Review P&P Manual
      Annually
Equipment Calibration and
    Replacement
Hearing Instrument Lost
Hearing Instrument Repair
Hearing Instrument Return
Incident Report
Infection Control
Internet Usage
Leave
Liability Insurance: Malpractice
    Insurance
Outside Employment
Patients with Prior Collection
    Action
Referring Patients to Other
    Practitioners
Release of Patient Information
Tuition Assistance
Weather
Clinical Procedures
Personnel: Position
    Descriptions
Documentation
Reimbursement Capture by
    Coding Optimization

References

Burrows, D. L. (2006). Human resource issues: Managing, hiring, firing, and evaluating employees. In R. M. Traynor (Ed.), *Seminars in Hearing, 27*(1), 5–17.

Miller, R. L., & Jentz, G. A. (2006). *Business law today.* Mason, OH: Thomson Higher Education.

10

Compensation Strategies

ROBERT M. TRAYNOR, Ed.D., M.B.A.

Introduction

In the beginning, Audiology was a "helping profession" focusing on patients and how to best conduct their diagnostic or rehabilitative treatment, but not necessarily making a living as part of the process. Although audiologists have a professional responsibility to think of their patients first, this does not imply the necessity to compromise income, and subsequently lifestyle, to offer high-quality hearing care. If an audiology practice is in business to simply "help people" the practitioner is donating time and, unless independently wealthy, will soon be a destitute "helping professional" (Traynor, 2007). As doctoral level professionals, audiologists toil for 8 years in a university program acquiring their clinical credentials and, at the end of their study; should feel compensated for the time, energy, and effort spent in school and gaining experience to serve their patients.

Compensation packages for any size business have two both intangible and tangible components and, according to Elsdon (2003), the key to obtaining and keeping good employees, particularly professionals, is to create an environment in which they want to stay and grow with the practice. Although compensation packages in a small audiology practice are generally less than large firms, providing expertise and contributions to a small company has definite advantages for the employees. Shwlff (2007) indicates that these advantages include:

■ An opportunity to be more "hands on"
■ The need to wear multiple hats that result in a wider range of experiences and enhanced skills
■ Greater chance for recognition for contributions
■ The "big frog-small pond" factor that result in speedier promotions and greater personal benefits.
■ A stronger sense of ownership of work completed
■ A culture more geared to fulfilling employee needs
■ Job that better utilizes employee's aptitudes and interests
■ Flex-time and telecommuting
■ A chance to buy stock options and benefit financially from person contributions to the practice.

Generally, there are three levels of compensation packages within an audiology practice; the owner, employee audiologists, and the clerical staff. audiology practice owners are entrepreneurs, investing in a business to offer private clinical services to the public. For the practice owner, the monthly salary is sustenance. The perquisites (perks) of ownership can provide special benefits; the hope to sell the practice for a retirement income, independence, and the satisfaction of watching their small business grow into a thriving practice. Audiologist employees within a practice should be compensated to allow a good living commensurate with their credentials and experience and, possibly, an opportunity to buy into the practice over time. Clerical employees should receive salary, benefits, and other compensation based on their experience, longevity, and contributions to the practice.

Strategies for compensation are not straightforward; they are compounded by annual reviews, raise procedures, profit participation, incentives, rewards, and other specifics that can be included in these packages. This chapter aims to present perspectives into various intangible and tangible components of compensation packages for an audiology practice with special emphasis on payment arrangements for practice owners, their professional audiologist employees, and clerical staff.

The Nature of Employment

Mathis and Jackson (2004) present three general elements of employment compensation packages; the psychological contract, job satisfaction, and loyalty and commitment. A portion of the package offered by the employee and paid for by the employer includes these factors which may be an exceptional value or a substantial problem, depending on the practice situation and the employee.

The Psychological Contract

Lavelle (2003) defines a psychological contract as an unwritten expectation between employees and employers regarding the nature of their work relationship that is, to some degree, based on past experiences of both parties. This psychological contract is a direct result of the downsizing of companies over the past few years and the resulting "free agent" nature of employees. In the past, employees may have given their loyalty and commitment to a company and been disappointed as the company had minimal commitment to them, cutting their pay, or involuntarily modifying their work relationship. When a company (or a practice) has a minimal commitment to their employees, they often become free agents offering their services to the highest bidder with no particular commitments beyond the contract dates.

Although recently employees have questioned if a company (or a practice) is worth their loyalty and commitment, Lee (2001) offers that when individuals feel they have some control and perceived rights in the organization, they are more likely to be committed to the organization. Thompson and Bunderson (2003) also indicated that psychological contracts are strengthened and enhanced when an organization, such as an audiology practice, is involved in a cause employees value highly. Audiology practices, working toward a better quality of life for their patients, are very likely to obtain a psychological commitment from both the employer and the employee as they both firmly believe in the cause. Clerical employees also feel a sense of belonging to the process and usually become psychologically involved, working toward the common goal of better hearing for the patients.

Job Satisfaction

Mathis and Jackson (2004) broadly define job satisfaction as a positive emotional state resulting from evaluating one's job experience. Conversely, job dissatisfaction occurs when expectations are not met for either the employee or the employer. Figure 10–1 offers factors that affect job satisfaction. For an audiology practice the satisfaction of the employees with their positions is very important to success as often it is the employees that represent the practitioner to the patients.

Performance should never be of concern if the employee is a fully educated, licensed audiologist or an experienced clerical employee. Although an employee may have the training and the experience, sometimes motivation to provide the evaluations, products, or support services may be lacking. Motivational difficulties may include not feeling well on a particular day, a fight with a spouse that morning, a bad day, low or reduced respect for the boss, disagreement with the policies and procedures of the practice, general

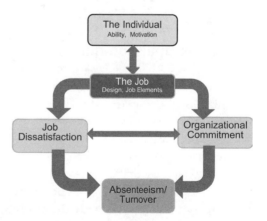

Figure 10–1. Factors affecting job satisfaction and organizational commitment. (From *Human Resource Management*, by R. Mathis and J. Jackson, 2004, Mason, OH: Thomson Learning. Copyright 2004 by Thomson Learning. Reprinted with permission.)

laziness, or myriad other factors. Whatever the motivational difficulty, it is essential that the problem be rectified as soon as possible to avoid spillover into the daily routines of the practice.

Part of creating satisfaction is the explanation of the position so the employee knows, up front, the practice owner's expectations. Job satisfaction is enhanced by openness in the job interview and is assisted by the use of position descriptions presenting the specifics of each position in the practice along with expected extra duties. This "up front" presentation of expectations leads to high overall job satisfaction which results in commitment of the employee to the organization. Motivated, committed employees have less absenteeism and are less likely to be looking elsewhere for employment. In tight labor markets or where audiologists are not readily available, job satisfaction and loyalty to the organization is a clear factor in turnover (BNA.com, 2003).

Organizational Commitment

According to Mathis and Jackson (2004), organizational commitment is the degree to which the employees believe in and accept the organizational goals and desire to remain with the organization. Their data suggest that employees with a minimal commitment to the organization are not as satisfied with their jobs and are more likely to withdraw from the organization. Wasti (2003) offers that the relationship between job satisfaction and commitment with absenteeism and turnover has been affirmed across cultures, full- and part-time workers, gender, and occupations. Findings suggest that

absenteeism and turnover are related as both involve withdrawal from the organization; absenteeism is temporary withdrawal from the organization, whereas turnover is permanent.

Types and Philosophies of Compensation

A review of the human resource literature shows that philosophical differences exist in terminology for various types of reward systems but, in general, compensation may be intrinsic or extrinsic (Mathis & Jackson, 2004; Hay Group, 2002).

Intrinsic or Intangible Compensation

Intrinsic rewards are intangible and may include praise or expressions of appreciation for a job well done or meeting performance objectives. Other psychological and social forms of compensation, such as time-off, social status, travel opportunities, and retirement plans are also intrinsic forms of employee rewards.

For many employees, the most valuable part of a compensation package is the intangible benefits offered by the position. Obringer (2007) indicates that balancing lives is becoming more important than ever, and flexible schedules, relaxed atmospheres, child-care, as well as other lifestyle benefits are becoming almost as important as salaries. Levey and Levey (2000) present a Gallup poll of 10,300 employees in the United States, Europe, Russia, and Japan that identified the five qualities most desired by employees:

1. The ability to balance work and personal life.
2. Work that is truly enjoyable.
3. Security for the future.
4. Good pay or salary.
5. Enjoyable coworkers.

Tangible compensation was fourth on their list of reasons for quitting their positions, suggesting the importance of intangible benefits and more than two-thirds indicated that they would be willing to leave their company for such opportunities. Obringer (2007) also presents another Gallup poll that indicates 90% of 1,000 workers felt that work/life balance was as important as health insurance and more than one-fourth of those surveyed felt that balancing work and family is more important than a competitive salary, job security, or support for an advanced degree.

In a study supporting the importance of indirect or intangible benefits of employment, Anderson and Zhu (2002) found that 30% of all employees planned to quit their jobs in the next 2 years. Their survey indicated that it was not necessarily due to their cash compensation package. Respondents expressed the following reasons for their dissatisfaction in order of importance:

1. Dissatisfaction with the manager
2. Lack of career opportunities
3. Job not "stretching" enough
4. Personal reasons (spouse, partner moving on, maternity, etc.)
5. Cash compensation.

Cash compensation, at least in this study, was the last reason people were quitting their jobs suggesting that intangibles are substantially more important that actual cash. Research, supports that it is not necessarily dissatisfacton with salary, but the intangibles that cause employees to explore alternative job prospects (Anderson & Zhu, 2002).

Extrinsic or Tangible Compensation

Extrinsic rewards are tangible and may be both monetary and nonmonetary. Tangible rewards are of two types:

- Direct compensation
- Indirect compensation

Direct compensation is the money that changes hands in the form of base pay and variable pay, offered by the employer to the employee in exchange for the work performed. Indirect compensation usually refers to the employee benefits, such as health insurance offered to all employees as part of employment in the organization. Figure 10–2 clarifies direct and indirect compensation for employees and represents the system by which most practice employees are compensated.

Compensation Philosophies

Professional employees can be compensated in a variety of arrangements. Shwiff (2007) offers some business models for paying professional employees that are not unlike those offered to employee physicians, dentists, chiropractors, and other health care professionals.

Entitlement-Based Programs

Entitlement programs are those that assume all employees that have worked another year are entitled to pay increases

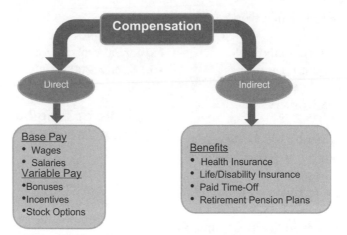

Figure 10–2. Components of a compensation system. (From *Human Resource* Management, by R. Mathis and J. Jackson, 2004, Mason, OH: Thomson Learning. Copyright 2004 by Thomson Learning. Reprinted with permission.)

with little or no regard for performance. Organizations that use an entitlement philosophy will commonly refer to these yearly increases as "cost of living" increases and they may or may not be tied to actual economic indicators. The net result of using an entitlement philosophy is that the employer will pay more for their employees each year, no matter what the performance of the business, as raises and bonuses become income to which employees feel entitled. Characteristics of entitlement compensation programs are as follows:

■ Seniority bases
■ Across the board raises
■ Pay scales raised annually
■ "Santa Claus" bonuses.

Performance-Based Programs

Lawler (2003) indicates that there is a trend to offer pay for performance among Fortune 1000 companies. In a performance-based compensation philosophy pay changes reflect the true differences among employees. Employees that perform satisfactorily or better advance in their positions and those that are poor or marginal performers fall behind in the pay scale. These performance-based systems award bonuses and incentives according to the performance of an individual, the team, or the organization. Characteristics of performance based compensation systems typically are:

■ No raises for length of service
■ No raises for longer service poor performers
■ Job market-adjusted pay structures
■ Broader compensation comparisons across the industry
■ Bonuses tied to performance results.

Realistically, compensation programs fall somewhere between these two concepts. Audiology practices need to decide what type of compensation system they want to offer. The particulars of the system offered are based on the philosophy of the practice owner, the job market, economic conditions, and the competitive compensation packages available within the region.

Straight Salary

According to Shwiff (2007), although employees often prefer the straight approach, but more companies and professional practices are moving toward the alternative methods of compensation to get more out of their employees and spread their employee costs across good and bad business seasons.

Straight salary compensation systems are the traditional method of payment where the professional audiologist works in the clinic for a period of so many hours per week for a salary. In this model the employee obtains the same amount of salary each month for the work provided if the clinic is active or slow. The individual will actually be contracted for all the work they can possibly do within the confines of the practice schedule. With no rewards for extra effort, hard work, cross-training, and/or overtime, there is usually none exerted. Whereas experience suggests that straight salaries work relatively well for clerical personnel and part-time employees, a straight salary for full-time audiologist employees usually fails to provide sufficient financial motivation. Straight salary compensation does not consider:

- The practice cash flow situations
- Incentives for the employee
- Rewards for extra work or creativity.

Practices are susceptible to seasonal highs and lows. Many patients return to spend the summer in climates they have left due to the cold in winter months.

In extremely slow periods, it would not be beneficial for the employer to pay a salary when the opportunity to produce revenue is at low ebb. Conversely, when these "snow birds" return, the audiologist employee will be working extremely hard.

Variable Compensation Model

The variable compensation model, sometimes referred to as "pay at risk," places a portion of the compensation contingent on performance. This model provides incentives for employees by allowing them to share the profit that is generated by their increased contributions to the productivity of the practice. Meek (2007) indicates that most compensation systems are boring, do not pay for performance, nor encourage commitment to the organization. In many fields, surveys point out that employees are not motivated by their current compensation system and, in fact, do not even believe their performance has any influence on compensation. She suggests that, among others, a variable compensation program should include the following components:

- *Profit Sharing*. Profit-sharing programs are employee incentives wherein a portion of the practice's profits will be set aside at year end and distributed to the employees.
- *Group Incentive*. Group incentives are given for participation in a group project or an overall goal of the practice.
- *Recognition, individual incentive, or key contributor awards*. These awards are for the individual achievement by a particular employee, such as the completion of an Au.D.,

obtaining skills that will be useful to the practice, high sales, or other individual contribution that results in benefit to the practice. These awards may take the form of a lump sum bonus, awards of stock or equity in the practice, or simply a restaurant coupon or a plaque, but are to recognize individual contribution to the overall effort that was beneficial to the practice.

■ *Project/Team Incentive*. Group awards involve a team of individuals who work together to further the goals of the practice. These awards are for group efforts that contribute to the success of the practice, such as a busy month, learning a new office management system, or other group effort that makes the practice more efficient.

■ *Participative Peer Award*. These are nominations of an employee by another employee for a job well done that may not be obvious to the practice owner. These are also individual awards that may take most any form, but are usually reserved for small rewards such as lunch or dinner, plaques, or some other simple recognition.

Designing a variable compensation program is no small task. An incentive program that rewards employee for diligent, hard work, and providing excellent, patient-centric care will go a long way to employee motivation. McNamara (2007) indicates that special care should be taken by the practitioner to design a variable pay program that offers the following:

■ A program that links variable pay to the practice business philosophy, preferably patient-centric practices.

■ A program based on long-term objectives possibly geared to partnership or practice ownership, not just short-term results.

■ Deferred compensation opportunities, such as sharing the profit of the practice to attract and retain good professional employees.

■ Well-understood details by every employee through education and regular scheduled face-to-face meetings about practice success or challenges.

■ Sets realistic goals within the reach and control of the professional employees.

■ Rewards team accomplishments, such as the clerical and professional teams, as well as individual goals.

Skill-Based Compensation

Specifically, Murphy (2004) defines a skill-based compensation program as a nontraditional pay system that ties base wages of the employee to knowledge and skills obtained rather than simply the job to which they are assigned. Shwiff (2007) indicates that these skill-based programs reward individuals for acquiring certain work-related skills or for being able to perform additional or more technical tasks. For example, if the practice conducts intraoperative monitoring, and an employee audiologist acquires the knowledge and skill sets necessary to provide monitoring services, that audiologist should be appropriately compensated. Compensation should be issued as a raise in base pay or in the form of a pay differential when providing services in the operating room. Skill-based compensation could be applied to audiologists who seek and attain specialty certification or advanced training that would enable the practice to expand or add new diagnostic or treatment protocols. Furthermore, practices often hire new audiologists directly out of school and these individuals are not initially able to conduct all evaluations on all populations in a timely manner or working with their own patients immediately. Skill-based compensation works well for these new clinicians as they will get used to the equipment, and specifics of the practice's procedures in a short time. Thus, the base starting pay for a new clinician may need to be lower and increase as the skills and the capability to work independently increases. Lawson (2006) presents that skill-based compensation programs are developed to:

- Encourage skill development
- Reward learning
- Increase individual productivity
- Encourage more flexible staffing.

Table 10-1 summarizes advantages and disadvantages of various compensation philosophies discussed above.

Computing a Tangible Base Salary and Salary Range for Employees

An important step in compensation for a practice is setting the base pay and salary ranges for all employees. This should be part of every position job description. Obringer (2007) describes the procedure for establishing a standard base pay program. She offers fixed salary ranges for employees performing the standard duties of their jobs. In her system, an audiologist who has only done diagnostics for 5 years or a new audiologist directly out of school might be on the lower end of the scale, whereas a veteran clinician able to see a full range of patients for services would be a the top of the compensation range. Setting a base pay structure can be confusing. The following points should be considered:

- Determine where your practice falls relative to competitive compensation packages within the region.

Table 10–1. Compensation Philosophies

	Straight Salary	Variable Pay	Skill-Based
Advantages	1. Easy 2. Dependable for Employees	1. Incentives 2. Rewards 3. Motivating 4. Variable cost	1. Incentive to learn new skills 2. Training for the Employee 3. Higher trained staff
Disadvantages	1. No incentive 2. No rewards 3. Fixed cost	1. Ethical concern 2. Pay varies	1. Base pay begins lower 2. Must build skills to advance base pay 3. Training costs

■ Set up your base pay levels to be competitive with other practices in the area or else you risk losing good employees.

■ Use the Internet to review salaries, nationally, and regionally. A good starting place for these salary reviews is The American Academy of Audiology (http://www.audiology.org) or Audiology Online (http://www.audiologyonline.com).

Market Banding

Mathis and Jackson (2004) offer a method called "market banding" used by human resource professionals to establish base pay and salary ranges. Market banding is used for smaller groups and classifications of employees and is ideal for use by audiology practice owners to compute base salary and salary ranges. The easy steps to tangible salary and salary ranges using the market banding approach are outlined below:

Step 1—Job Families

The first step in this process is to set job families. In most audiology practices three distinct job families will surface, the practice owner, audiologist employees, and the clerical assistants.

Step 2—Salary Review Surveys

The second step is to launch a regional survey that reviews salaries for the various job families, noting median salaries and the range in percentage from the highest and lowest salaries from the median in percentage. For example, if the median base salary for an employee audiologist with 10 years' experience is

$55,000 and a 13% adjustment up and down is noted between the highest and lowest salaries survey, then the raw survey result would be $55,000 ± 13%.

Step 3—Adjustment for Practice Personnel Expenditure

Once obtained, the median salary ($55,000) must be adjusted according to the practice budget for overall personnel expenditure. This adjustment amount is found as a result of calculations on the personnel budget by the practice owner and the accountant. The median salary amount may be either adjusted up or down depending on the practice owner's philosophy, the accountant's input, and/or the revenue of the practice relative to the overall expenditure for personnel. From the $55,000 figure (obtained from survey information) a negative personnel expenditure adjustment of $4,500 (suggested by the practice accountant) is made to adjust the median base salary to $50,500.

Step 4—Figuring the Salary Range

In the example presented here, $50,500 would be the median salary adjusted for practice personnel budget limitations. The survey also indicated that there was a 13% salary range from the adjusted medial salary. Thus, the base salary range for an audiologist employee in this practice would be ± $6,565 or a salary range of $43,935 to $57,065. Audiologists looking at this position would be able to plan as to how their experience and expertise fits into the organization and the practice owner then has the latitude to adjust the salary slightly up or down according to the quality of the application.

Step 5—Figuring the Hourly Rates for Clerical Employees

The same "market banding" procedure can be applied to hourly employees by the use of a survey to determine median hourly rates for clerical employees. For example, if the survey indicated that medial salary for a qualified receptionist with 5 years' experience and computer skills was $12.00 per hour and a negative adjustment according to practice owner's philosophy and the accountant's personnel budget recommendations of $1.00 per hour would bring the hourly employee to $11.00. If the survey indicated an hourly wage variation of ± 10% for employees with these qualifications then the hourly wage for the practice clerical staff would be $9.90 to $12.10 per hour.

Another method to compute salaries and salary ranges is to use a Web site such as SalarySource.com (http://www .salarysource.com). At this site, for a fee, average salaries for audiology employees and clerical assistants are readily available. Although often not as regionally accurate as the market banding, these sites can be valuable in the determination of salaries and salary ranges when it is difficult to obtain information from surveys and local sources.

Benefits for Employees

Audiologist employees and clerical staff may be offered a number of other tangible benefits that all add up to a package. The practice owner may decide to include all of those listed here or work out another list with their accountant and/or human resource consultant. This list of benefits for employees is modified from that offered by the Hay Group (2002) in Figure 10–3:

- *Bonus or spot rewards.* These bonuses are offered for an individual's job well done, teamwork on a specific project, or simply meeting the goals of the practice. Specifically, these rewards could be for meeting a sales goal for a particular number of hearing instruments for a particular month and might take the form of a restaurant certificate, lunch, expenses to a meeting, or just plain cash, but usually a small amount that simply serves to acknowledge the extra effort and encourage it in other employees.

- *Performance shares in the company.* As an incentive or reward, the practice owner may choose to offer shares in the company for a job well done. As the extra effort to meet a goal demonstrates interest in the success of the practice, shares in the company can be a method to reward loyalty and/or the beginning of a transition process.

- *Annual employee incentive or bonus program.* These programs reward the employee for meeting sales and/or marketing goals over the year. They are usually based on targets for the year and if the practice meets these targets then the bonus is offered. Annual bonuses can be given during the holidays, the anniversary of employment, or at other times chosen by the practice owner. Khera (2004) indicates that annual incentives and bonuses should be rewards for a job "well done" and not given all the time and

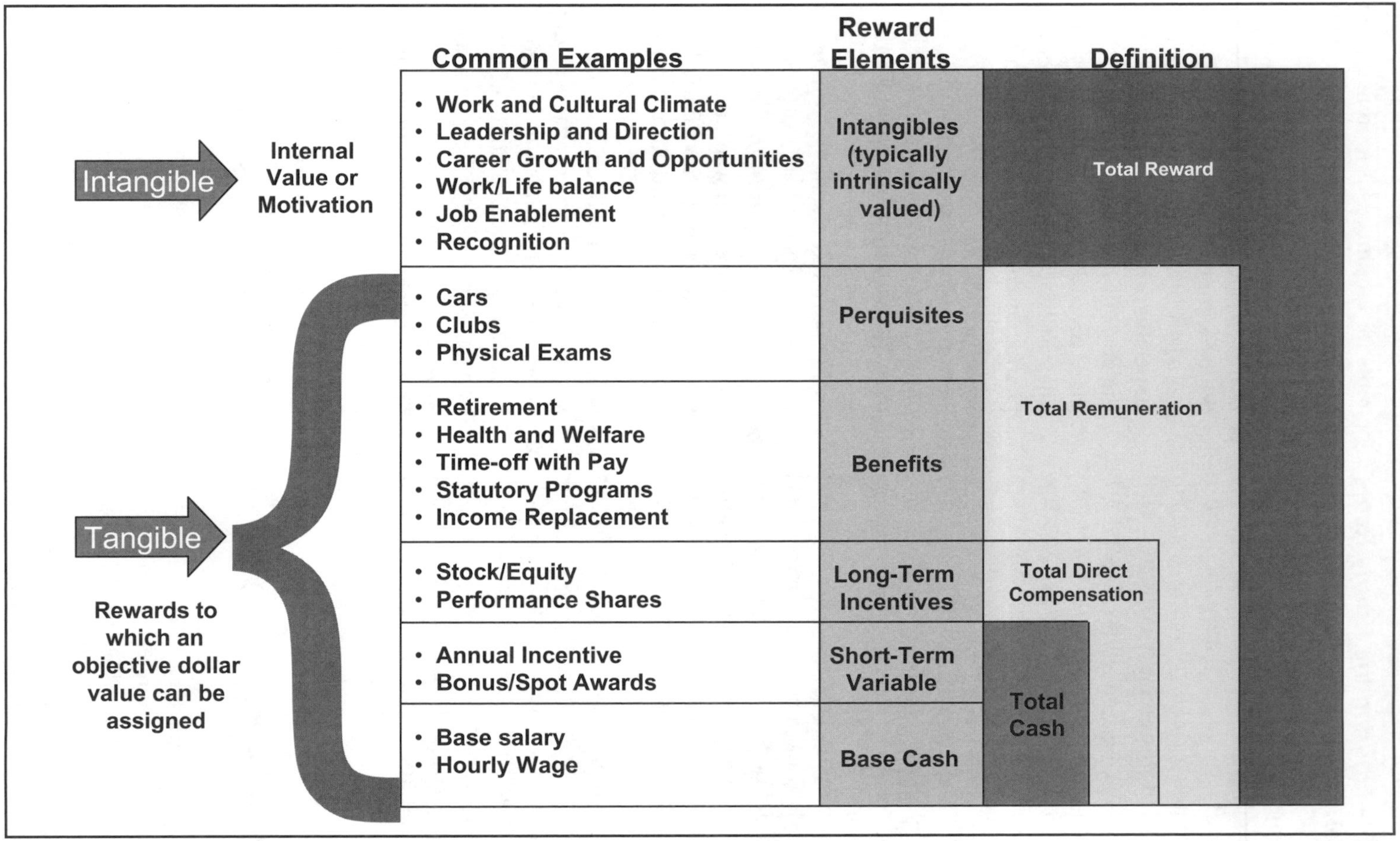

Figure 10–3. Model of employee reward program. (From *Ensuring Culture Change at Arbella: A Case Study in the Effective-ness of Rewards*, by the Hay Group, 2002, presentation at the World at Work Conference, May 13, 2002.)

in the same amounts. If given incorrectly, these incentives will be perceived by the employees not as a bonus but as part of their usual and customary compensation, defeating the purpose of the bonus program.

- *Income replacement (disability Insurance).* Short-term disabilities, such as broken ankles or hospital stays, can be outlined as part of the overall employment package or simply handled internally by the practice owner according to the policies and procedures manual. Income replacement or long-term disability insurance is not a common benefit of employment but may be offered by some practices to employees for long-term disabilities as part of the overall insurance package. Long-term disabilities are considered serious injuries that cause major life changes, such as confinement to a wheelchair, brain injuries, or other physical modifications that affect the employee's capability to be productive. Long-term disability insurance is a must for the audiology practice owner, but usually not part of the employee's package. When offered as a benefit to the employees these benefits are usually presented as an optional insurance that may be purchased by the employees through their private funds.

- *Statutory programs (workers' compensation).* In all states, it is required for employers to purchase workers' compensation insurance. Employees are never required to pay any part of the premium for this coverage as it is the employer that is covered by these policies. The purpose of these policies is to protect the practice and the practice owner from damages that could be awarded in lawsuits that conceivably could put them out of business. For example, a faulty infection control program could be grounds for a workers' compensation claim.

- *Time-off with pay.* Specific types of time-off are usually presented in the policies and procedures manual, but special time-off with pay can be awarded to employees as an incentive or reward for extra work on a specific project or reaching a goal.

- *Health and welfare insurance.* Health insurance benefits are essential to obtaining and maintaining quality employees. These benefits provide security for the employee and their family and ensure that health difficulties can be taken care of expeditiously at reasonable cost. Health insurance, discussed in detail later, is usually available through insurance brokers, specialists in the insurance business offering a variety of policies to the practice and its employees.

- *Retirement program.* Programs for retirement are necessary for employees and are usually available after a certain amount of time with the practice. These programs can take on many different forms such as stock option programs, 401(k) plans, simple savings plans, and other retirement packages. As the practice owner providing benefits to the employees, it is best to discuss these programs with financial advisors, the practice account, and the practice attorney as regulations for these programs can be quite complicated and vary from state to state.

- *Physical exams.* Some practices offer wellness exams in their clinic or at an outside office. These wellness exams are considered a nice benefit, but are usually outside the usual benefit package offered by audiology practices.

■ *Automobiles.* Transportation benefits are not part of the usual tangible package for an employee audiologist or clerical personnel. Their may be, however, special situations where travel is required that makes this benefit necessary for employees. Rather than supplying a vehicle for employees, it makes more sense to provide transportation or pay mileage and expenses according to procedures outlined in the policies and procedures manual if the employees are required to travel distances on behalf of the practice.

■ *Education benefits for employees.* Fenton (2004) indicates that most practice owners consider their employees an important investment both to accomplish the practice's current goals and to have the right people in place for the future. Practices want to hire the best and the brightest and then give them the experience and education they need to advance to the doctoral level. Continuing education benefits are now a big issue for young Master's degree audiologists who are eager to obtain an Au.D. As part of their benefit package the employer may choose to offer an education benefit to enhance the package. According to IRS 15B (2007), up to $5,250 of payments received by an employee for tuition, fees, books, supplies, and so forth under an employer's educational assistance program may be excluded from gross income. The tax code further specifies that the employer cannot cover tools or supplies that the employee retains after the completion of the course or the cost of meals, lodging, or transportation. Thus, the practice owner can offer an education package for an Au.D program and deduct up to $5,250 per year for an employee Au.D program as long as the costs covered by the employer do not cover meals, lodging, or transportation. Some practice owners will have the employee sign an agreement to work for them for a period of time after completion of the degree program. These commitments vary from 1 year to 3 years depending on the length of time required to complete the program. As with other employee benefits a discussion with the practice accountant as to how to structure the employee education benefit before it is offered is appropriate.

After the base salary, the tangible benefits of the position are incentives to provide a comfortable situation for employees so that they will be able to concentrate on their work each day as well as feel well rewarded for their labor and expertise.

Insurance Benefits

Insurance benefits are essential to any business operation and the audiology practice is no exception. To attract and retain high-quality employees the practice must offer competitive insurance benefit programs. The specific programs offered are determined by the regional employment market, the needs of the employees, and the companies that offer policies in the area.

Health Insurance

Health insurance is an important benefit for every employee, including the practice owner. There are several questions a practice owner must ask when considering health-care insurance for the practice employees:

- What coverage plans are available in the area?
- Does my insurance broker carry health insurance?
- Should I use an HMO or a PPO to save costs?
- Should I pay all of the policy for the employee or only a portion of the premium?
- What other ancillary services, such as vision and dental care, should I offer in addition to standard health insurance?

According to Palosky and Peacock (2004), the cost of employer-based coverage has increased by 59% since 2000. With such increasing costs and reduced benefits, it makes good sense to seek professional advice about these programs. The above questions and others are answered by health insurance brokers that have studied all of the various policies and providers in the area. Insurance is their business and they are eager to present a proposal to the practice considering a number of companies with the costs versus benefits presented. The broker typically has analyzed these programs and makes recommendations depending on needs of the practice. It is recommended to invite the health insurance broker to the practice to discuss insurance options at least once a year with the entire staff. All employees should participate in the discussion of this important benefit as it facilitates an understanding the advantages and disadvantages of the various health insurance options and the rationale for the choice of a particular program.

Disability and Life Insurance

The offering of disability insurances and life insurances to the employees may be a simple matter of another program offered by the insurance broker that either the practice owner can subsidize or simply have available for those employees who need these policies. This coverage is not normally part of a regular compensation package for employees of a small audiology practice but are, as presented earlier, essential for the practice owner.

Depending on the size of the practice, group life insurance can be offered to employees for as little as 5 cents per $1,000 worth of coverage. The practice employees and prospective employees appreciate this benefit as they do not usually need a physical before they are covered by the policy, and they can often convert the plan to an individual life insurance plan should they leave the practice. The actual amount of this policy should be discussed and decided by the practice owner and their accountant. Additionally, if the practice pays for the benefit, it is considered taxable income whereas if the employee pays for the benefit, it is considered insurance and is nontaxable.

Vacations, Holidays, and Personal Time-Off

Generally practitioners will spend about 10% of their payroll on paid time-off for their employees, but it is a highly rated employee benefit as people attempt to balance work, family time, and life experiences. An established policy for paid time-off (PTO) should be written and included in the policies and procedures manual. It should include the number of days granted relative to years of service, specifying lunch and break times as well as holidays paid and unpaid.

Practices usually provide paid holidays for their employees, although the specific holidays offered to the employees vary according to the individual practice owner according to philosophy, religion, region, and state. Typical holidays offered include:

- New Years Day
- President's Day
- Memorial Day
- Independence Day
- Labor Day
- Thanksgiving Day and the day after
- Christmas Eve and Christmas Day.

In addition to standard holidays, the practice may also choose to provide one to two floating holidays or personal days. These days can be used whenever the employee would like to use them and often make up for religious holidays that are not part of the practice's standard paid holiday schedule.

Obringer (2007) indicates that the average number of vacation days provided by businesses for new employees are 10 per year, with increases to 15 after 5 years and 20 after 10 to 15 years. Vacation time is usually accrued on a monthly or quarterly basis, and most practices use a calendar year to make their record keeping easier. She indicates that the business standard for a practice is to provide 6 to 9 sick days per year. Unlike vacation time, the number of sick days offered typically does not increase with increas-

ing years of service nor do unused sick leave carry over to the following year. Another necessary decision for the practice owner is if employees will be allowed to use their paid sick days to take care of the illnesses of family members. Most audiology practices have fewer than 75 people and do not fall under the Family Medical Leave requirement; thus, the practice owner is not required to provide for the employees' families (Burrows, 2006; Ellison, 1999).

Stock Options

Sometimes used as a tool to retain employees, a stock options benefit has some appeal in today's job market. Stock options represent an attractive incentive in the hiring and retention of quality professional and administrative personnel. These programs are under the control of the U.S. Securities and Exchange Commission. Consultation with the practice's accountant and a licensed securities broker is imperative before stock options are offered. The plan must also be viewed by the attorney of record for the practice.

Retirement Programs

Retirement seems like a long way off, but it is an important item to consider in attracting and retaining employees. There are several types of plans to choose from so the questions and specific needs of your practice should be considered by the practice's accountant, financial advisor, and attorney for specific advantages and disadvantages of each type.

General Profit Sharing, Cash, and Deferred Profit-Sharing Plans

Although not always a retirement program, some companies offer profit-sharing programs. Profit-sharing programs require establishing a formula for distribution of the company profits. These plans are usually based on a distribution percentage of the employee's salary, but require the employee to be in their position for a specified period of time before the profit-sharing programs are available to them. This vesting period makes profit-sharing programs primarily an incentive to retain employees.

Cash and Deferred Profit-Sharing Plans

Cash profit-sharing plans pay benefits directly to the employees in cash, check, or stock as soon as profits are determined. Profit sharing allows the practice owner to decide if a contribution will be affordable and, if affordable, how much the company will contribute to the plan. AllBusiness.com (2007) indicates that a designated profit level should be established as a goal to achieve allowing the program automatically to go into effect when profits of a certain amount are achieved for the year. The percentage of profits or the arbitrary level at which the program initiates is usually with shared the employees and is normally established and articulated in advance. For example, the practice owner may say that 10% of all profits over $50,000 will be set aside for the profit-sharing program.

In corporations, profit-sharing contributions are usually made by a fixed formula or an amount decided by the Board of Directors (BOD) (often the BOD is simply the practice owner). In high-profit years, contributions are made, during less profitable years contributions can be deferred. Profit-sharing plans also allow the practice owner to control how the money is invested and is not as expensive to administer as other plans that require expensive administrative professionals for management. The major drawback to a cash profit-sharing programs is these programs do not qualify as a retirement plan as it is difficult to predict contribution schedules and they are at the discretion of the practice owner (Armstrong, 2007).

Deferred profit-sharing plans are profit-sharing plans designed to provide benefits on retirement. The benefits at retirement are based on the total of the contributions and the results of the investments made over time. The difference between cash and deferred plans is that a deferred plan must provide a definite predetermined formula. The benefits at retirement are based strictly on the sum total of the contributions made according to the formula and the quality of the resulting investments.

401(k) Programs

PSCA.org (2007) defines a 401(k) program as a contribution plan that enables employees to choose between receiving current compensation and making pretax contributions to an account through a salary-reduction agreement. Employers may, but are not required, to make contributions to employees' accounts. These plans defer federal income taxes and, in most cases, state income taxes as 401(k) contributions are made before payroll tax deductions. This is conducted to effectively reduce an employee's income before taxes are calculated thereby allowing them to invest with pretax dollars and defer taxes on the income until later when their incomes are lower during retirement. As part of the process, the employee receives an investment return on their money, often with the practice matching their contributions. This use of "pretax dollars" to defer taxes allows the employee to simplify their investment decision and contribute through a payroll deduction. The U.S. Department of Labor (2007) states that when the practice owner establishes a 401(k) plan there are certain basic preparations that must be conducted:

- Find an administrator or service provider for the plan;
- Decide if the practice will make a contribution to the plan;
- Inform the employees that there is a 401(k) plan;
- Arrange for a trust fund or other account to receive the proceeds of the 401(k) program;
- Submit a written plan to the IRS that describes the type of 401(k) plan, and how it operates. Most of the administrators, such as banks, or mutual funds can assist with this requirement;
- Learn about the fiduciary responsibility, reporting, and disclosure requirements that come with a managing a 401(k) plan.

The 401(k) plan is a major commitment to employees. Although there may be years when there are no contributions, the employees still have their own contributions and are making money with pretax dollars that allow them to benefit greatly from the program. For the practice owner, there is a significant amount of paperwork and administrative monitoring that goes along with these programs but, once organized, the day-to-day operation of the plan will be handled by the administrator who works out the payroll deductions and makes the appropriate deposits of practice profits to the appropriate accounts.

Base Salary, Benefits, and Perquisites for the Practice Owner

There must be tangible and generous monetary rewards for the practice owner to offset the risk assumed in the initial and continuous investment in the practice. Market banding works very well to figure base salaries and salary ranges for employees, but not for practice owners. Most practice owners do not readily offer their salary and benefits to others in a survey and, therefore, these market banding ranges are difficult to obtain for practice owners. A good "rule of thumb" here is for the practice owner to set their salary about the same or slightly above the employee audiologists and then use the perks and management skills to offset the difference.

In close consultation with the practice accountant the perks of practice ownership can be used to glean other forms of direct and indirect compensation that generally goes along with business ownership or executive level employment. Increased perks will sometimes work to the practice's advantage as they are often partially or fully deductible.

Virtually all of the tangible and intangible rewards presented in Figure 10–3 from the Hay Group (2002) and, possibly others not listed, may be available as compensation to the practice owner. Compensating the owner of the practice who is often the Chairperson of the Board of Directors (BOD) for the practice's corporation, may require a formal discussion and a resolution at a corporate board meeting to allow the practice owner certain perks. The BOD of these small corporations usually consist of the owner's accountant, attorney, and relatives so they will likely vote for a liberal salary and benefits. Most states allow the practice owner who is Chairperson of the BOD to have compensation for their service on the board which may consist of extra perks, or actual tangible salary. Although the practitioner may choose a salary that is virtually unlimited; as presented above their base salary should follow some logical compensation sequence similar to the other audiologist employees of the practice.

Benefits and rewards of being in business or perks belong to the practice owner. Bank prizes for depositing money, benefits from suppliers (if the ethical choice is to accept them), and other incentives normally available to business owners are a tangible benefit of entrepreneurship. Other tangible rewards include other short- and long-term monetary compensation that make practice ownership worth the investment and more comfortable as the practice develops over time. For example, it is quite common for audiology practices to pay many of their supplier accounts payables on credit cards. The benefits of the credit cards, such as airline miles, cash rebates, points for merchandise, and other benefits are usually a tangible reward for the owner of the practice.

When business is good, the practice owner can present themselves a handsome bonus, a reward, an incentive, extra retirement contributions, time-off, or other benefit, provided that all legal, corporate, and tax regulations are observed. Benefits such as travel to meetings, books, continuing education, and country club memberships for themselves and their families also may be written off as legitimate business expenses.

Disability and Life Insurance

Insure.com (2005) indicates that nearly one-third of all Americans will suffer a serious disability between the ages of 35 and 65. Practice owners need to consider these statistics and consider disability and life insurance as an essential part of their compensation package. Disability and life insurance policies on the practice owner allow an income cushion to continue practice operations in the event of the disability or death of the owner. These benefits are not necessarily just for the practice owner, but also for the good of the employees, the owner's family, and the patients.

Short- and Long-Term Disability Insurance

Short-term disability, in the United States, is not provided by many employers, and certainly not by most private practices, even for owners. Short-term disability insurance, however, is designed to replace an employee's income on a short-term basis as a result of a disability. Short-term disability (STD) would pay a percentage of the practice owner's salary if they are temporarily disabled. Temporarily disabled is defined by Insure.com (2005) as not able to work for a short period of time due to sickness or injury (excluding on-the-job injuries, which are covered by workers' compensation insurance). Short-term disability policies typically provide a weekly portion of the practice owner's salary, usually 50, 60, or 66⅔% for 13 to 26 weeks, depending on the program selected. If the practice owner has enough in savings to meet personal and practice needs for a 3-month period without working, then short-term disability insurance is not necessary. However, if there is not much in savings or the practice is a solo operation, a short-term disability policy is essential.

Long-term disability is not required by law, but it should be considered as an essential benefit for the practice owner. Long-term disability insurance helps recover about 60% of the insured income for an extended period of time, usually ending after 5 years or when the disabled person turns 65, when Social Security benefits usually pick up the disability benefit. There is usually a period of time before the long-term disability policy will pay benefits, usually 30 to 180 days or when the short-term disability policies end. As the practice owner, audiologists in self-supporting private practice must consider long-term disability insurance. The economic security of the practice and, therefore, the practitioner, all the employees, and their families are at risk when illness or injury strikes the practice owner. Although some degree of protection is secured automatically from Social Security Disability through FICA deductions, Social Security only guards against catastrophic loss of all work capability. When dealing with the government, there are specific rules and regulations that must be adhered to by these agencies. Qualification for Social Security disability requires that a claimant must be unable to perform any gainful work at all; there is no partial or percentage disability under the Social Security Act (DeBofsky, 2006). Private insurers, however, offer income protection in the event of a disability over a wide range of disability types and levels, including temporary disruption of capability (short-term disability) to perform in your profession, permanent or long-term disability, and partial disability coverage. Qualifying for private disability benefits is not as demanding, and in some cases not as demeaning, as meeting the requirements of Social Security. Less demanding qualification does not mean that an assessment of your ability to perform your duties will not be evaluated. Private insurers will assess the capabilities of the insured and cover needs relative to that assessment.

In any event, disability income insurance is an important benefit that should be paid with after-tax dollars, especially for the practice owner. As there are many variables in the selection of these policies, it makes sense to use an insurance broker to assist in their selection. These policies are often handled by the same broker as the practice's health insurance and their job is to present an insurance package that includes the state minimums as well as some optional program that meet the needs of the practice. Some of the variables of these policies include everything from the exclusion period, which can be based on different time periods for an injury or illness, to pre-existing condition limitations, self-reported claim limitations, own-occupation protection, and rate guarantee. The specifics of the amount of income replacement and the benefits to the practice should be discussed in detail with the practice accountant to ensure cash flow to the practice as well as cash flow to the practice owner will replace their income.

As with disability insurance, life insurance for the practice owner is essential. Proceeds of the policy insure the survival of the practice in the event of the death of the owner. Although the proceeds of the policy will pay necessary practice expenses until arrangements for its disposition are finalized, the actual amount of life insurance should be discussed with the practice accountant.

Automobiles

The practice may lease or purchase a vehicle for use by the practice owner. This vehicle is technically to make deliveries, and provide transportation to peripheral clinics during the day and other places required for business. Any other use of the vehicle is considered personal use and is usually taxable to the practice owner. Thus, most practices provide the practice owner with a company vehicle (either leased or purchased)

and declare a percentage (85–95%) to be used for business purposes and another percentage (5–15%) to be used for personal purposes. Of course, the practice owner gets to choose the car, drive it most of the time, and deduct all of the acquisition costs and maintenance expenses.

Summary: The Road to Self-Actualization

In summary of compensation for a practice, an analogy that is offered by Jensen, McMullen, and Stark (2007) draws a parallel between employment compensation and the Hierarchy of Needs theory (Maslow, 1943). According to Maslow's theory, once a person has satisfied their basic physiologic and safety needs, atten-

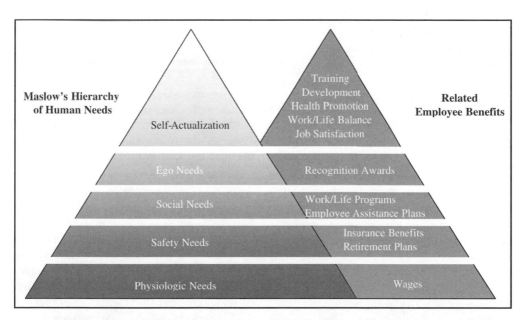

Figure 10–4. Comparison of employee compensation to Maslow's hierarchy of human needs. (From *The Manager's Guide to Rewards*, by D. Jensen, T. McMullen, and M. Stark, 2007, New York: American Management Association. Copyright 2007 by American Management Association. Reprinted with permission.)

tion is then focused on social and ego needs with self-actualization being the pinnacle of achievement. Figure 10–4 offers correlation between components of compensation packages and Maslow's theory suggesting that Self-Actualization or job satisfaction will only exist if there is a fair salary that meets physiologic needs; health benefits, ensuring safety needs; work/life programs, for the social needs; recognition to feed the ego; as well as training and employee development. The road to Self-Actualization, or job satisfaction, seems to follow a clear progression from tangible compensation components to the intangible and, once the tangible needs are met, it appears that intangibles become extremely important to job satisfaction and ultimately retention of good employees.

As practice owners, consideration of the Self-Actualization theory as to how and why we compensate employees and ourselves offers perspective to an otherwise complex issue. This concept simplifies the compensation issue into certain specifics that can be considered in light of the practice, its revenue, and the owner's philosophy.

References

AllBusiness.com. (2007). *Profit sharing programs*. Retrieved July 21, 2007, from http://www.allbusiness.com/human-resources/compensation-profit-sharing/491-1.html

Anderson, K., & Zhu, G, (2002). *Organizational climate technical manual*. Chicago: Hay Group.

Armstrong, F. (2007). *Profit sharing and 401k plans*. Retrieved July 21, 2007, from http://www.investorsolutions.com/v2content/Profit%20Sharing%20and%20401K%20Plans.pdf

BNA.com, (2003). Study says 30% of workers are loyal. *Bulletin to Management*. Retrieved June 28, 2007, from http://www.bna.com/products/hr/btmn.htm

Burrows, D, (2006). Human resource issues: Managing, hiring, firing, and evaluating employees, In R. M. Traynor (Ed.), *Seminars in Hearing, 27*(1), 5–17.

DeBofsky, M. (2006). What every physician needs to know about disability insurance. *Journal of Medical Practice Management, 22*(2), 113–118.

Ellison, K. (1999). *Managing employees*. Lectures for CAS 7803, Business and professional issues, University of Florida Working Professional Doctor of Audiology Program, University of Florida, Gainesville, FL.

Elsdon, R. (2003). *Affiliation in the workplace: Value creation in the new organization*. Westport, CT: Praeger.

Fenton, E. (2004). Employer provided education benefits. *Journal of Accounting* (On-line issues). Retrieved July 18, 2007, from http://www.aicpa.org/PUBS/JOFA/sep2004/fenton.htm

Hay Group. (2002). *Ensuring culture change at Arbella: A case study in the effectiveness of rewards*. Presentation at the World at Work Conference, May 13, 2002.

Insure.com. (2005). *The basics of short-term disability insurance*. Retrieved July 20, 2007, from http://info.insure.com/disability/shorttermdisability.html

IRS publication 15B. (2007). *Employers guide to employee benefits*. Retrieved July 18, 2007, from http://www.saonm.org/pdf/additional-employers-tax-guide.pdf

Jensen, D., McMullen, T., & Stark, M. (2007). *The manager's guide to rewards*. New York: American Management Association.

Khera, D. (2004). Establishing an incentive compensation program. *The profit advisors*. Retrieved May 13, 2007, from http://www.morebusiness.com/running_your_business/profitability/tip16.brc

Lawler III, E. (2003). Pay practices in Fortune 1000 companies. *World at Work Journal, 4*, 45–54.

Lawson, F. (2006). *Skill-based pay: Results of a national survey*. Fox Lawson and Associates. Retrieved May 13, 2007, from http://www.foxlawson.com/newsletter/newsletters/v3n1.cfm

Lavelle, L. (2003, Sept. 29). Coming next: A war for talent. *Business Week, 1*.

Lee, G. (2001). Towards a contingent model of key staff retention: The new psychological contract reconsidered. *South African Journal of Business Management, 32,* 1-9.

Levey, J., & Levey, M. (2000). Reflections for leaders. *Journal of the EAPA Exchange.* Employee Assistance Professionals Association, Florida State University, Tallahassee, FL.

Maslow, A. (1943). A theory of human motivation. *Psychological Review, 50,* 370-396.

Mathis, R., & Jackson, J. (2004). *Human resource management* (11th ed.). Mason, OH: Thompson Learning.

McNamara, C. (2007). The basics of employee motivation (the steps you can take). *Free Management Library*. Retrieved July 19, 2007, from http://www.managementhelp.org/guiding/motivate/basics.htm

Meek, C. (2007). *Variable pay*. Meek and Associates, Retrieved May 12, 2007, from http://www.meekassoc.com/opinion/variable_pay.htm

Murphy, S. (2004). *Design and implementation of a skill-based compensation program in a physician group practice*. University of Kentucky Capstone Project. Retrieved May 13, 2007, from: http://www-martin.uky.edu/~web/programs/mha/2004mha_capstones/murphy.pdf

Obringer, L. (2007). How employee compensation works. *How Stuff Works*. Retrieved May 14, 2007, from http://money.howstuffworks.com/benefits1.htm

Palosky, C., & Peacock, C. (2004). *Premiums increased at five times the rate of growth in workers' earnings and inflation*. Kaiser Family Foundation. Retrieved July 21, 2007, from http://www.kff.org/insurance/chcm090904nr.cfm

PSCA.org. (2007). *Profit sharing 401(k) Council of America*. Retrieved May 18, 2007, from http://www.psca.org/starting.html#types

Salarysource.com. (2007). Salary source Web site. Retrieved July 10, 2007, from: http://www.salarysource.com/articles.cfm

Shwiff, K. (2007). *Best practices: Hiring people*. Irvington, NY: Hylas.

Thompson, J., & Bunderson, J. (2003). Violations of principle: Ideological currency in the psychological contract. *Academy of Management Review, 28,* 571-586.

Traynor, R. (2007). Business essentials in audiology private practice. In R.S. Ackley, N. Decker, & C. Limb (Eds.), *An essential guide to hearing and balance disorders.* Mahwah, NJ: Lawrence Erlbaum and Associates.

U.S. Department of Labor. (2007). *401(k) business plans for small business,* Employee Benefits and Security Administration. Retrieved May 17, 2007, from: http://www.dol.gov/ebsa/publications/401kplans.html

Wasti, S. (2003). Organizational commitment, turnover, intentions, and the influence of cultural values. *Journal of Occupational and Organizational Psychology, 76,* 303-321.

11

Hearing Instrument Manufacturers and Suppliers

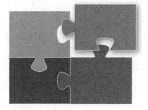

ROBERT G. GLASER, Ph.D.

Introduction

All hearing instruments are not the same. Likewise, all hearing instrument manufacturers are not the same. Both instruments and those who develop and manufacture them differ in many and varied ways. It is just as important to know when to move on to another manufacturer as it is to select a manufacturing group and their line of hearing instruments. How to select and when to leave manufacturers are two very different decisions. Each impacts the quality of services provided by your practice as well as the financial health of the practice. This chapter will help you create a foundation on which to make these important decisions. Consider the following scenario:

Patients and their family members are, generally speaking, a forgiving lot. However, that is true only up to a critical point of intolerance that is consistent in today's health care consumer. How many times has this happened in your practice?

A patient returns to pick up his repaired hearing instrument, wife waiting patiently in the room with him. You enter the room with appropriate greetings, perhaps a comment on the weather and full confidence that the hearing instrument about to be replaced in the patient's ear is in full working order with the same programming, the same shell, all ready to go when you notice that the serial number does not match the patient's records or the instrument fails to ignite despite a new battery. Or you have a left instrument in your hand when you sent a right one in for repair; or the patient says the hearing aid sounds terrible in his ear and objective measures confirm there is a gross mismatch between need and output.

As beads of sweat develop on your forehead, the patient and his wife look at you like this is some sort of cruel joke as you are responsible for all things that make up the total picture of hearing care including the repair, the replacement, and successful rededication of patient and instrument.

It matters not to the patient that the audiologist-case manager could not open the instrument and replace a chip or a microphone assembly if life depended on it: It is the audiologist's responsibility, not the repair team at the manufacturing facility. Because the audiologist will bear the brunt of patient and family dissatisfaction, it is up to you as the care provider to step up to the plate and swing away as the patient's advocate. That duty is unequivocal and clearly defined no matter the venue of your practice.

"I Am Only as Good as You Will Permit Me to Be"

The line above should be reserved for every repair manager and inside sales representative until such time that each

finally begins to see the big picture of having patients in your office appropriately disgusted by the fact that their hearing instrument needs to be sent to the manufacturing facility for its third repair in as many months. They sit at their desk on the phone while you are facing down an angry patient who is convinced the hearing instrument you placed in their ear will never work despite extensive diagnostic testing, counseling, and emotional preparation to the contrary.

Repair managers do not have to figure out a reasonable apology scheme for disgruntled patients and family members. However, it is true, as the audiologist, you are only as good as the repair team (or manufacturer in the case of new instruments received dead-on-arrival) will permit you to be. As clinicians, each of us has experienced this type of disappointment such that we begin to dream up clever ways to jam our hands through the telephone and around the neck of the repair manager or inside sales representative each of whom promised the world and delivered more problems.

Hearing Instrument Manufacturer and Audiologist: A Symbiotic Relationship

Audiologists and hearing instrument manufacturers alike both have contributions to make and responsibilities to assume in a patient's journey from diagnostic assessment to wearing hearing instruments with a high degree of satisfaction. It is the responsibility of the audiologist to blend the needs of the patient with the manufacturer offering the most appropriate technology. It is their primary contribution of assessment, instrument selection, and application/adjustment that is the continuum of successful aural rehabilitation.

The hearing instrument manufacturer has the responsibility to provide sophisticated instruments and support systems such that audiologists can readily apply these technologies within the continuum of aural rehabilitation. A symbiotic relationship exists when reliance becomes mutually beneficial so that the patient is the direct recipient of the interdependent function of each group.

The instrument manufacturer has tremendous responsibilities in the relationship. It is the responsibility of the manufacturer to provide audiologists with innovative solutions to hearing loss—improved chip technology and transducers, better clarity in noise, improved reliability of operation, user-friendly fitting software, ease of modifiability, and excellent in-house service. The instrument manufacturer logically and for obviously intrinsic reasons, accepts the burden of educating audiologists about all of the options and instrument-specific advantages available to maximize the benefits obtainable in their product lines. Whether the training is delivered in the audiologist's office by a manufacturer's field representative, provided at their facility, or in a Continuing Education Unit (CEU) event, the manufacturer must have a readily available, systematic training program to ensure that audiologists are optimizing the potential of their technology. If the instruments and their particular technological advantages are not applied effectively in the patient's ear, the expense of extensive research and development is essentially lost.

It is also the responsibility of instrument manufacturers to produce solid evidence that all claims made about their products are valid, unequivocal, and, most importantly, readily noticed by the patients wearing the instruments. The ultimate metric of success of the symbiotic relationship between manufacturer and clinician is the level of patient satisfaction and the observations of those around the patient wearing the hearing instruments.

Patient Satisfaction and Digital Technology

Patient satisfaction with their hearing instruments has been steadily improving over the last 7 years and it appears to be directly related to increasing numbers of fittings of hearing instruments with digital signal processing (DSP). Kirkwood (2001) surveyed audiologists and commercial hearing aid dealers regarding their patient's satisfaction and DSP hearing instruments. They rated overall patient satisfaction to be 78% better with DSP instruments, 89% better in sound quality, 82% in listening comfort, 77% better in speech recognition in noisy areas, and 70% better in feedback reduction or suppression.

From 2000 to 2005, DSP hearing instruments as a percent of fittings grew from 5 to 90%. The use of digital hearing instruments is associated with significantly higher ratings of overall user satisfaction and benefit, improved sound quality, reduction in feedback, improved performance in noisy situations, and greater utility in a number of important listening situations (Kochkin, 2005).

In the final analysis, a practice is often viewed by patients to be only as good as the hearing instrument. Therefore, choosing a hearing instrument manufacturer is critically important to both the immediate and long-term success of your practice. Audiologists should choose a hearing instrument manufacturer based on much more than "the best technology choice for my patient, and how can I keep my costs as low as possible" (Smriga, 2004). Technologic and connectivity considerations, instrument costs, warranties, financial operations, repair resolution, and educational opportunities are but a few important items to consider when choosing a hearing instrument manufacturer for your particular practice venue.

Technology

"In the United States, roughly 90% of all hearing aids dispensed in 2006 were digital, offering improved fitting flexibility, feedback reduction, and multichannel compression strategies to ensure audibility for soft, moderate, and loud sounds. Open-fitting platforms have regained in popularity due to improved fitting flexibility in combination with feedback phase inversion systems that may be used to dynamically cancel feedback" (Fabry et al., 2007).

There is little question that advances over the last 10 years in hearing instrument technology and the ear-instrument interface can appropriately be viewed on a logarithmic scale in comparison to the advances noted since the first vacuum tube hearing aid was invented by Hanson in 1920. The Vactuphone was made to order for the Globe Ear-Phone Company by the Western Electric company and was commercially distributed in 1921 (Berger, 1984).

When evaluating a manufacturer's lineup of available hearing instruments, a number of characteristics should be considered. The most logical starting point in the evaluation should be the needs of the patients seen in your practice. What are the general characteristics and range of hearing levels commonly seen in your practice? For example, if your practice is in a highly industrialized area, there will be a higher percentage of noise-induced hearing loss with attendant high-frequency "noise notch" configurations. The manufacturer's lineup therefore, should include high-frequency emphasis offerings with open-fit platforms. If you are practicing in a pediatric hospital seeing youngsters with moderate-to-severe losses, your fitting needs will differ and the manufacturer should have a well-developed series of pediatric-focused instruments with adequate power and processing capabilities linkable to FM systems. A manufacturer should have sufficient breadth of offerings to cover at least 85% of the hearing loss parameters seen in your particular practice venue.

If you are an independent practitioner seeing children and adults in a community with a broad base of employment opportunities and noise exposure possibilities, the same 85% criteria should hold comfortably true. Most major manufacturers offer realistic technological opportunities from open-fit platforms for steeply sloping sensorineural hearing loss to powerful behind-the-ear instruments with appropriate compression and feedback management systems for moderate-to-severe sensorineural hearing loss. Of course, there is no rule that you have to maintain allegiance to only one or two manufacturers. However, the ease of knowing one line of instruments thoroughly and maximizing the utility in one programming system are only two reasons to seek a single manufacturer as the primary source of your hearing instrument needs. If a single lineup of instruments covers only 85% of your patients needs, there will always be room to seek solutions elsewhere for the remaining 15% of your clinical population.

Assistive Technologies and Compatibility

There are a host of adjuvant devices to improve hearing and listening in specific conditions that are coupled to hearing instruments via direct audio input, infrared and Bluetooth integration, and by electromagnetic inductance. Both assistive listening systems (ALS) and assistive listening devices (ALDs) require specific interfacing technologies from tele-loop compatibility to inductor coils specifically designed to enhance cell phone use. Compatibility with an ever expanding group of devices developed to improve the signal-to-noise ratio and enhance speech recognition in difficult listening situations must be considered an important part of every aural rehabilitation effort. A manufacturer should have a well-developed grouping of ALS or ALDs or have easy access or modification routines so that their hearing instruments can interface readily with systems available elsewhere in the market. Whether it be something as simple as enjoying a sermon at church or hearing well at a meeting in a hard-walled, highly reverberant conference room, these new technologies are critically important to the patient and to their families as well. They lend a level of communication integration in difficult listening situations and reduce the number of environments or communication situations which may have been avoided altogether.

Connectivity: Ease of Connecting to the Instrument

With the advent of programmable hearing instruments a dilemma developed for both instrument development engineers and for audiologists fitting the hearing instruments: How best to connect the instrument with the programming system? This dilemma seemingly went from bad to worse in a brief period. Initially most of the connectivity was completed with cumbersome yet easy to connect plugs to fit into capped receptacles on the instrument. Once connected, they remained connected and data transfer was relatively easily completed. Pull the connector, replace the cap to the programming port, and the commands or data were transferred and the session was done. The ports were large and the economy of space issue inherent in the miniaturization process of hearing instruments began to win out as programming ribbons and other smaller connection systems were developed.

These attempts at size reduction created, in some instances, an entirely new set of problems for the end-user. The manufacturing community could have come together and agreed on consistent usage of size and shape of connectors but that would have been too easy. As it stands, every audiologist must have an ugly array of connecting gear and ribbons and "whatnot" to access the hearing instrument for programming or adjustment of the instrument.

There are problems within a single manufacturer's lines where ribbons must be changed for this or that reason or another cable must be used here or there. And none of the software appears to be sensitive to this dilemma, save one which gives a description and number of the cable and ribbon to be used for the instrument specified in the fitting software. It is truly a puzzle as to why hearing instrument manufacturers seemingly have to compete right down to the connectivity of their instruments to a universal linking system. It does, however, give the audiologist a reason to evaluate a manufacturer on the basis of ease and speed of connectivity. If a hearing instrument cannot be connected with data on screen within 2 minutes, serious consideration must be given to looking for another manufacturer with better connectivity throughout their product line. Time is money no matter the venue of your practice and connectivity problems are not a good sign to a patient awaiting his new instruments or the replacement of a repaired instrument that has to be reprogrammed. Connectivity should not be an issue; connecting hearing instruments to a programming system should be essentially instantaneous.

User-Friendly Software

There are great differences in the usability, efficacy, and simplicity of hearing instrument manufacturers' programming software systems. Some require wading through two or three screens before approaching the initial programming screen. Other programming software has little or no navigation indicators to let the user know exactly where he or she is in the programming sequence. This can create a sense of being lost within the program and often results in having to restart the programming sequence. Time and confidence in the programming system are lost as the patient perceives palpable frustration. No matter the intent of the software developers, programming

protocols that require disproportionate amounts of time and effort will subject the manufacturer to the financial risk of losing valuable dispensers.

Evaluating the usability of programming software systems does not require the skills or knowledge of a software developer. The audiologist working with patients every day quickly develops a sense of usability and the inherent time constraints a poorly designed program brings to the patient's visit. There are several, basic aspects of software programs that can be used to evaluate hearing instrument programming software. Although not a set of absolute rules, these recommended actions, programming transformations, screen prompts, and messages adapted from Hedge (2007), provide guidelines to be used in comparing software program offerings of hearing instrument manufacturers:

1. A time-focused hearing instrument software system should permit initial programming within four keystrokes after auditory data describing the patient's hearing loss is entered in the program.
2. The software should provide an instant reading of the instruments being programmed and display the serial number and specific model details on initial connection to the software.
3. Software users (hereinafter, audiologists will be considered the "users") must be able to accomplish their task in a naturally occurring order of events—the programming task must be in an order that makes sense to the user so that he or she does not have to change screens or otherwise search for solutions in other levels of the software.

4. Wording in on screen messages and instructions should be easily understood, concise, and unambiguous.

5. All recent actions or commands completed by the user should be easily reversible by "undo" commands which would allow escape routines from specific operations in motion.

6. The programming software should be solution driven with "go to" symptom and solution selection lists to logically help the patient with their various performance complaints. The more automatic the resolution of definable problems, the faster the instruments are programmed or reprogrammed and the quicker the patient can begin to adjust to their new instruments.

7. The software must permit access to all definable parameters of the hearing instrument. Compression ratios, output by channels or frequency bands, processing speed, and integration of attack and release times and similar modifiable functions should be accessible to the audiologist programming the instrument for the patient.

8. The software must provide pull-down lists and reminders to foster recall by the clinician. With so many opportunities for optimizing the instrument fitting, it is difficult to commit to memory various routines and subroutines that may be important for the unique needs of individual patients.

9. The software must be configured to provide a printout or easily retrievable electronic record of actions by dates for each instrument programmed or adjusted after the initial programming. This record is important as it is not uncommon to have to undo programming that failed to improve a patient's particular situation. If a record is retained, the original programming configuration can be reinstated in the hearing instruments. This is an important feature as many patients unsure of the adjustments made following the initial fitting will want to return to the initial settings to compare their performance in varied environments.

10. Photos of the hearing instruments in situ and patient-friendly lists of features along with audiologic findings superimposed on the effective fitting range of the instruments should be readily available to the audiologist and patients in the initial phases of counseling and preparation for the fitting. Additional information, readily visible on screen or in a printout for the patient, should include the battery size, estimates of battery life, and information about compatibility with assistive technologies including cell phones and land-line telephones.

Costs and Financial Operations

One of the most important determinants in selecting a hearing instrument manufacturer is instrument acquisition cost. More than just the cost of the instrument should be included in the assessment. Some of these issues may not seem to be related to costs. Their impact will, nonetheless, impact your practice and how it is viewed as a professional health care provider. A good example of an important yet nonmonetary cost factor involves the time span from placing an order to the arrival of the new or repaired hearing instrument. If Manufacturer *A* takes 10 days to 2 weeks to deliver a new or repaired instrument and Manufacturer *B* delivers in 7 days, these different schedules can be critical to patient satisfaction and, therefore, the long-term success of your practice. A few days to a week from order to arrival is often a critical time frame for a patient and family waiting for a new or repaired hearing instrument. There are other determinants involving costs and financial operations to consider in choosing a hearing instrument manufacturer.

Wide Range of Instrument Costs Across the Product Lineup

Most major instrument manufacturers develop a wide-ranging lineup of circuitry and instrument types within their product line. Manufacturers strive to provide a comprehensive array of offerings so that an audiologist will be able to select an instrument appropriate to a broad base of patient needs. In essence, each line should be able to cover 85% of the fitting needs represented by most clinical presentations. That is important to instrument manufacturers for a variety of reasons not the least of which is developing brand loyalty in the ranks of audiologists using their products.

Paying the Bills

Instrument manufacturers generally function on a 30- to 45-day payment policy. You are expected to pay the bill for the instrument completely (net) within the specified payment period. The longer the payment cycle, the greater the time the manufacturer has granted to pay the bill in full. In effect, the manufacturer is providing you with a loan for the period of the defined payment cycle. There might be penalties or interest charges if the bill is not paid within a specific time period. Depending on your status as a customer, you might be able to get an extended payment time period. The terms of payment should be taken into consideration when choosing a manufacturer. The longer the payment cycle, even by as little as 15 days, the longer you keep your operating fund intact. Penalties for overextending the payment deadlines should be clearly stated and if not, contact the accounting department and have someone clarify the situation, preferably in writing. An additional measure of a good manufacturer is a readily available accounting department focused on account resolution and most are quite happy to review your statement and assist you in resolving any confusions or correcting wrongs.

The statement of your account should be easy to read and it should balance relative to known orders, payments and credits for returns. The accounting department must produce a readable and logical account statement. If your office personnel or your accountant has trouble making sense of the format of the account, ask to have the format changed. Should the accounting department fail to consistently provide an accurate statement, a true accounting of the orders, payments, and credits, do not stop at the head of the accounting department to resolve the problem. Statements should be carefully confirmed on receipt and errors resolved swiftly. If they cannot figure whether you have appropriately scheduled payments to your account or if the accounting department is calling to request payments when your records indicate payments have been made in full and on time, consider another manufacturer. Resolving errors on your statement is time consuming and frustrating for you and your office personnel and your part of the bargain in the business transaction is paying their bills on time. Their part is to provide an accurate accounting of transactions in your statement and that is not an inordinate expectation.

Repair Resolution and Warranties

Hearing instrument repairs are perplexing to the wearer and to the audiologist managing the patient's aural rehabilitation. Despite the improvement in patient satisfaction with digital hearing instruments, there remains the ever present issue with hearing instrument repairs. Clinically, it matters little to the patient and their family whether the repair was necessitated by their actions. They are, generally, more interested in how long the repair will take and why their instrument cannot be repaired in the office. In an odd sense, their concern is less an unrealistic expectation as it is a tribute to the effectiveness of the instrument in need of repair. Their response is coincidental to the observations reported by Kochkin (2005) wherein 93% of digital hearing instrument wearers noted a significant improvement in the quality of life.

Rates of Repairs

It is difficult to determine the rates at which hearing instruments require out-of-office repairs. Although statistics on hearing instrument repairs are kept by manufacturers, neither the consuming public nor the audiology community is commonly privy to these data. Conventional wisdom (largely based on the experiences of clinicians) suggests rates of repairs on most instruments in the first year postfitting ranging from 10% to as much as 18% of instruments dispensed. The second and third year rates of repairs flatten to approximately 20 to 25%. By the fifth year postfitting, 30 to 40% of instruments will likely undergo an out-of-office repair.

With greater market penetration of digital products in the last 3 to 5 years, repairs on instruments in their first year post fitting appear to have decreased. Glaser (2007) has monitored the incidence of repairs and postfitting rates of occurrence in his practice for over 25 years across several manufacturers, instrument styles and various levels of circuitry. The data indicate there have been 12% fewer returns to manufacturers for repairs within the first postfitting year from 2003 to 2006. Additionally, the rate of rerepairs (defined as a repaired instrument returned to the manufacturer within 45 days of the original repair date) has declined at a similar rate within the same period. The reasons for the improvements most likely include improvements in the stability of transducers and chip technology to better preventive measures to reduce repairs related to cerumen. Wax screens and coils alone may be responsible for a significant decline in the rate at which instruments are returned to the manufacturer for in-warranty repair.

Establishing a Benchmark for Instrument Repairs in Your Practice

It is difficult to establish a benchmark for an "expected" number of hearing instrument repairs. From the patient's viewpoint there should be zero toler-ance for repairs. Audiologists agree there should be zero tolerance for repairs. The reality of the situation, however, dictates reasonable acceptance of some repairs as electronic equipment in general and hearing instruments specifically are inherently prone to failure from time to time. It is unreasonable to assume that hearing instruments can be developed that are not subject to the need for out-of-office repairs. It is also difficult to develop a benchmark on repairs without an accurate accounting of numbers of repairs occurring as a function of the date of the instrument being fitted. Knowing the pattern of repairs as a func-tion of the fitting date provides an opportunity to develop a prospective guide of what to expect of a specific model within an instrument line.

Based on well-kept anecdotal records of a single practice (Glaser, 2007) de-scribed above, the following represents an example of an anticipated repair rate which has been generated on the basis of previous data for an approximated volume of 250 instruments per year:

- Fewer than 10% of instruments fit within the first year require out-of-office repair (250 instruments fit; up to 25 returned for repair);
- Fewer than 15% of instruments in the second and third years postfit-ting required out-of-office repairs (250 instruments fit; up to 37 returned for repair);
- Fewer than 20% of instruments in the fourth and fifth years postfitting required out-of-office repairs. (250 instruments fit; up to 50 returned for repair).

Considering the numbers of repairs that will require returning an instrument to a manufacturer for repair, it becomes readily apparent that out-of-office repairs cost a great deal of time and money as well as increased levels of patient dissat-isfaction and discord. However, by reduc-ing the repairs encountered in the first year from 10 to 5%, from 15 to 10% in the second and third years of service, and from 20 to 10% in the fourth and fifth years of service, not only will the prac-tice have more time to schedule new patients, but there would be a concur-rent increase in patient satisfaction. No matter how fast you return the repaired instrument nor how many warranty extensions the manufacturer is willing to issue, repairs are unacceptable to patients and family members who have come to appreciate the benefits of appropriately fitted, functional hearing instruments.

Counseling Patients About Hearing Instrument Repairs

Beyond counseling and advising the rates of repairs known to your practice, there are few methods to assist patients in developing realistic expectations about hearing instrument repairs. As with counseling the patient and family about the importance of developing realistic expectations of what they should expect from hearing instruments, counseling about the incidence of hearing instru-ment repairs should be equally realistic. Zero percent repairs is an unrealistic expectation despite remarkable advances in contemporary hearing instrument technology. Warranty periods are made available to the patient for a reason. They stand as indicators of likelihood that instrument repairs will be needed within a 2 or 3 year period after the fitting— why else would a manufacturer build the cost of anticipated repairs into the single unit price of their hearing instruments with additional years of coverage available at an additional cost? The simple fact remains that hearing instruments are subject to a variety of external and internal forces that work against developing a performance history without at least one repair.

Patients and family must be given appropriate training on maintenance and about the importance of consistent instrument care and cleaning. They must be given every opportunity to develop good maintenance habits. At the fitting and during the immediate follow-up visits, care and maintenance routines should be assessed, restated, and all involved must demonstrate competencies in care and cleaning, proper insertion and removal of the battery, and use of dehumidifying equipment. Routines should be suggested, including removing the instrument only when the patient can reasonably expect to place it in the safety case. The more the family is involved in the care and maintenance of the patient's hearing instrument, the less likely it will be misplaced or require an out-of-office repair.

Return of Repaired Instruments by the Manufacturer/Repair Facility

Repairs should be returned to the practice by the manufacturer/repair facility within 7 working days. Most repairs require a 2 or 3-day in-house period. Shipping to and from manufacturers and repair facilities is commonly facilitated by retail shippers (FedEx, UPS). Pickup and delivery at the practice door reduces critical out-of-ear time and reduces the risk of loss and damage in transit. With improvements in shipping, the onus to improve the in-house time to complete and return

the repair rests with the repair manager and the productivity and accuracy of his repair technicians. And then there is the extra cost of an expedited repair. Does it really warrant the extra cost? Does the repair turn-around in-house faster with the extra fee? The answer, of course, depends on the manufacturer or repair facility but there is usually a savings of 1 or 2 days at the most—perhaps worth it to the executive who has an important board meeting or to a mother who must hear her children in the middle of the night. If repair facilities can improve turnaround time to your practice for an additional charge, it seems reasonable to expect that same repair department to improve their turnaround time without an additional charge levied for expected work.

Repair turnaround time should be monitored consistently and reviewed regularly. If the data indicate turnaround time is increasing, it must be considered a critical measure in deciding whether to seek another manufacturer or repair facility. Repairs are always a rough spot for our patients. The longer it takes to return the instrument to the patient's ear, the greater the probability of reduced patient satisfaction and a loss of confidence in both the hearing instrument and the practitioner.

Rerepairs

If the patient experiences greater than three repairs in an 18- to 24-month period postfitting, manufacturers commonly replace or replate (replace all major components within the shell) the instrument at no charge to the patient. If they do not consider this an option, they should be urged to do so on behalf of your patient and your practice. This replacement scheme covers the patient's needs; however, it does not account for diminishing profits in the practice when greater time is spent in repeated visits, reprogramming efforts, refitting, and recounseling the patient and family to regain at least a bit of confidence lost in the instrument and the practice. Too many unplanned "re-'s" result in lost revenue and respect that will not be replaced by an instrument manufacturer or repair facility.

Beyond Improving Rates of Repair: What Manufacturers Can Do

As manufacturers generally do not reimburse practitioners for lost time and revenue due to multiple repairs, there are a few items or issues manufacturers could incorporate to lessen the burden of audiologists responsible for fitting their products:

Return Repairs with Programming Intact

Repaired instruments returned without the original programming is irritating, time consuming, and, in many repair situations, an unnecessary addition to the mayhem. Granted, it may take only 15 minutes or so to resurrect and inject the data back into the hearing instrument, but it is not simply about the time and effort it takes to technically restore the instrument to prerepair status. It also includes the fact that a significant number of patients perceive differences in performance with the repaired instrument. No matter the programs nor manufacturer nor whether or not we have informed them of the need for the reprogramming. Even if the chip must be

replaced it is best for all concerned for the repair technician to spend the time transferring the programming information rather than having to repeat the programming in the office with patients and family members overseeing every move the audiologist makes. Retrieving and reprogramming the instrument at the repair facility must become an institutional priority and duty of repair technicians and every instrument manufacturer or repair facility.

Software Upgrades for Chips in Use

When chip technology and accessibility become readily available to clinicians, upgrades can be provided to the practice patient base. Upgrades could be purchased from or provided by the instrument manufacturer. Patients with accessible chip technology could be called in for an upgrade at no cost or at a nominal fee relative to what the manufacturer charges to download the upgrade. Upgrade availability would go far in reducing the concerns of purchasing a sophisticated hearing instrument that is subject to technologic obsolescence. Unlike a safety recall common to the automobile industry, upgrades will be viewed as a positive opportunity for a practice to offer additional opportunities for improved hearing with their instruments. It affords the audiologist another, positive opportunity to preserve the patient's confidence in both instrument and practitioner alike.

Liberal Warranty Extensions on Rerepairs

Rerepairs are poison to a patient and to a practice as well. Rerepairs provide the greatest source of broken confidence in both the hearing instrument and the practice—*"What is it with you people? You can't even get a broken instrument repaired correctly at the manufacturing plant? That damn thing hasn't worked right from day one and here I am a year and a half later and it still doesn't work right and you can't get it right even with two tries."*

Little will satisfy a frustrated patient after having had his instrument repaired only to have it fail a second time within a month or two. Rerepairs should be discussed at the initial fitting but few practitioners dwell on the topic for obvious reasons. A realistic expectation about a repair is one thing; there is no reality to the patient when it comes to multiple repairs in a brief time period. Rerepairs should not happen in this digital era with the levels of quality control used by most manufacturers and repair facilities. Unfortunately, rerepairs do happen and the manufacturer should provide a liberal warranty extension after the fact. Issuing an additional 6 to 12 months of warranty on a 4- year old-instrument may represent a formula for loss for a manufacturer but it should be the minimum consideration given the patient for no other reason than to stand as an indication of confidence by the manufacturer that another rerepair will not be an issue.

Manufacturer's In-House Staff Dedicated to Rapid Resolution of Problem

The members of a call staff in a manufacturer's repair section are the first responders in the calamity that is a hearing instrument repair. They must be well trained in complaint resolution, knowledgeable about the product line in general and specific idiosyncrasies of each

particular circuit, and they must know the internal tracks to resolution. They must be as efficient and accommodating as your front office associates and just as available for consultation and inquiry. They represent the human touch of a system that can quickly become impersonal and inattentive. And if they cannot solve the problem over the phone or by quickly consulting with the repair section, they should request the instrument be sent to their desk for personalized attention. Each member of this important team must be dedicated to complaint resolution and acknowledging the caller's problem as unique to his or her practice deserving an equally unique response and resolution.

Effective in-house teams work closely with manufacturer's field representatives. These are the unsung heroes of the hearing instrument manufacturing community and constitute a critical element in solving quirks in fitting software, connectivity issues, and a variety of missteps on the part of the practitioners dispensing their products. Field representatives can make or break a manufacturer's effectiveness in a market place. From putting out fires to counseling the dispenser on optimal uses of specific features of new products, the manufacturer's field representative should be considered an important member of the practice staff (Sidebar 11–1).

Monitoring Performance: Products and Providers

Part of maintaining a practice as a center of excellence requires evaluating the performance of others as they integrate their products or services into your practice.

Sidebar 11–1
ON THE IMPORTANCE OF MANUFACTURER'S FIELD REPRESENTATIVES

Manufacturer field representatives provide a great service to practitioners and patients alike. They offer fast-track, pragmatic information not readily available in printed bulletins or product descriptions issued by the manufacturer. Some of the services they provide include:

- Training regarding products, software, and specific technical information
- Establishing which patients are best suited for specific instruments
- Offers circuit-by-circuit comparisons of products offered by others
- Training to maximize fitting utility of fitting software and instruments
- Sharing tricks, gimmicks, insights gleaned from other users of the product
- Solving specific patient difficulties
- Assisting in developing realistic pricing for the practice's demographic
- Assistance in resolving billing errors
- Stands as the practice's in-house liaison to the manufacturer
- Assist in marketing strategies and co-operative marketing opportunities.

The practice, after all, is only as good as the sum of its parts. Each part must be consistently monitored with expectations defined in the parameters of participation that affects the overall performance of the practice. Just as administrative and professional staff members should undergo performance evaluations on a regular schedule, so too should hearing instrument manufacturers and other suppliers to the practice undergo consistent performance assessment.

Evidence-Based Decision Making

Evidenced-based practice in health care requires explicit and judicious use of information (data-as-evidence) in making decisions about matters that directly influence the quality of care provided to patients. In health care, it covers the gamut from counting numbers of visits to a patient's bedside by nursing personnel during hospitalization to counting the numbers of repairs sustained within a specific hearing instrument model or, more generally, by a specific manufacturer.

Incidence of Repairs

The incidence of hearing instrument repairs by manufacturer must be monitored on a weekly basis (Figure 11–1). When repaired instruments are sent or received, a few minutes spent logging information about the repair provides

Patient Name	Instrument Make/Model	Acquisition Cost	Running Total Manufacturer	Dates Ordered/Received

Figure 11–1. Example of data sheet to record repair data.

compelling information about the manufacturer, instrument model, and repair history of the instrument. It takes little effort to gain additional important information beyond counting the number of repairs. By documenting repairs by circuit class or model, the practice will get a failure rate for each class of instrument dispensed. Should a spike in the incidence data occur, an analysis will be at hand and a call to the manufacturer to discuss the dilemma must be made. If the particular circuit class or model of interest continues to fail, it would be appropriate to stop fitting that particular instrument class or model. It would also be appropriate to reassess the past records of repairs and determine whether it is time to consider finding another source for hearing instruments.

How much data should be required to contact the manufacturer? That depends on several factors. Certainly volume should be a factor: If the practice is dispensing a significant number of a specific model, the data will dictate the need quite readily if there is an inherent problem within the circuit class or model. If the data signals a developing panel of evidence that one in five instruments requires a return for repair, the manufacturer should be contacted immediately. Advise the manufacturer of the findings and ask if they have noted similar difficulties with that particular model. They may have a fitting or modification suggestion that will resolve the repair issue completely. If the repair manager replies they have not seen a pattern in that particular instrument model, advise them that in your hands, the instrument is failing. After you have stated your case with the data, make it clear that if these failures continue, there will be no more orders forthcoming from the practice for this particular instrument model.

Confirm the telephone conversation with the repair manager via E-mail and include copies to the inside sales staff member assigned to your account and to the President of the company. Presidents of hearing instrument manufacturing companies are sometimes the last to know there is a flaw in a specific model or circuit class. They understand that you stand as your patient's advocate in these matters. They also understand that you will cease to dispense their products if situations such as repeated failures continue. Consistent problems in your practice should become known to every level within the product side of the instrument manufacturer's hierarchy.

Changing Manufacturers: When It's Time to Go

Patient satisfaction is tied to a variety of factors. When managing patients, audiologists must recognize and accept the fact that patient satisfaction is tied directly to the hearing instrument and to the services provided by the audiologist directing the patient's hearing care in about the same measure.

Factors to Consider in the Decision

Hearing instrument manufacturers must share in the responsibility for declining patient satisfaction when directly relatable to the hearing instrument. Lack of or lethargic responses to inquiries in the face of well-documented evidence that a segment of their product line is consis-

tently failing, should be a strong factor in the decision to seek another source for hearing instruments. In some cases, it may be the most important or singular reason to move to another instrument manufacturer. If the incidence of repairs exceeds established practice benchmarks; if turnaround time on repairs is excessive; if the incidence of rerepairs is increasing, the need to move to another instrument manufacturer becomes undeniably evident—a "no-brainer." The bottom line of the practice requires optimum product reliability and fast and reliable resolution to patient-centered problems by each hearing instrument manufacturer involved in the practice.

Establishing Perspective: Continuous Monitoring of Acquisition Costs

Practice owners and managers tend to overlook the amount of money spent in the purchase of hearing instruments. To monitor continuous acquisition costs, add a column for a running tabulation of instrument and shipping costs for each manufacturer supplying instruments on the Record of instruments ordered and received (Figure 11-2). It takes little time to read the invoice and do the addition and it clarifies the amount of money the practice sends to each manufacturer. It will put each manufacturer into a financial perspective and appropriately embolden the practice owner or manager to become more assertive in their advocacy efforts for their patients. The previous year's total amount spent should be in the heading of the column to further recognize the level of participation with each manufacturer. A running tabulation of acquisition costs is a simple statistic

	Jan	Feb	Mar	Apr	May	Jun	Jul	Aug	Sep	Oct	Nov	Dec
Model No.												
1–2 yrs												
2–3 yrs												
3–5 yrs												
Rerepair												
Cost												
Turnaround												

Figure 11–2. Record of instruments ordered and received.

to maintain relative to the perspective it provides.

Factors to Consider Other Than Product Lines and Repair Parameters

An interesting revolution in the profession of audiology began in the late 1990s, when major hearing instrument manufacturers decided to solidify distribution outlets for their products. In essence, manufacturers determined the need to secure and manage clinical outlets that would dedicate dispensing efforts specifically within their respective product lines. These efforts paralleled ongoing activity in "managed care," where health care services are delivered to member-patients of a Health Maintenance Organizations (HMO) or networks at specified locations by a panel of participating providers or employee-providers of the HMO or network. In managed care organizations, medical care, therapies, and hospitalization are controlled by corporate entities.

Managers assign patients to participating providers or employee-practitioners for general or specific health care. Medication regimen, surgical intervention, selection of specialists, specific testing protocols, and other utilization activities are carefully controlled with strict guidelines and utilization reviews. Participating providers may suggest particular therapies or medications; however, these suggestions are subject to review and approval by corporate managers. Similar efforts have been ongoing within the hearing care industry in the form of corporate and practice consolidation.

Consolidation Efforts on Two Fronts: Corporate Buyouts and Practice Buyouts

Over the last decade there have been considerable efforts within the hearing instrument industry at consolidating manufacturing concerns as well as consolidating providers into networks of participating providers serving as a network or distribution system dedicated solely to their respective product line.

Manufacturer Consolidation

Powerful, well-financed hearing instrument manufacturers have been actively acquiring the interests of other instrument manufacturers over the last 5 to 7 years. The result has been a consolidation of six or seven "major manufacturers" controlling the primary marketplace world wide. Soaring operating costs including research and development, production, facilities, personnel, and a host of other costs have contributed to this trend. So too has the opportunity for greater control and profitability within the marketplace in the United States and throughout the world. On the positive side, concentrated resources will likely foster improved technologies and, therefore, greater opportunities for patient success and satisfaction. With those successes will come greater acceptance of advanced technologies and an increased likelihood that the vastly untapped group of potential patients will begin to seek appropriate, professional hearing care.

Those hearing instrument manufacturers without well-developed distribution networks will, in the long term, likely lose whatever position within the hierarchy of their peers that "numbers of instruments produced" brings to the roster of the major manufacturers seated at the Hearing Industries Association (HIA) table (Sidebar 11–2).

Distribution System Consolidation

Smriga (2004) suggests three strategic ways hearing instrument manufacturers have pursued consolidation of the hearing instrument distribution in the United States. These include company-owned outlets, manufacturer branded distribution (MBD), and affiliated providers:

- Company-owned outlets are retail outlets purchased and owned by the consolidating instrument manufacturer. Both administrative and clinical staff members are employees of the manufacturer and overhead considerations such as rent, utilities, office outfitting, and leasehold improvements are the responsibility of the manufacturer.
- Manufacturer branded distribution (MRD) facilities are recognizable members of a chain of retail outlets exclusively dispensing the retail brand of the instrument manufacturer. The manufacturer covers expenses for advertising and promotion and supplies leads to the chain's participating providers. Overhead costs remain the responsibility of the owner of the distribution outlet.
- Affiliated providers are independent practices with a contract to purchase instruments and related products from a distributor-consolidator. The practice agrees to buy instruments form the same corporation that owns retail outlets and MBD chain locations. The corporation sets the prices the practice pays for the instruments. Overhead costs including administrative and professional staff are the responsibility of the practice owner.

Smriga (2004) collapsed available data on distribution segments in the United States and determined that "54% of current U.S. distributions outlets (as described

---

Sidebar 11–2
HEARING INDUSTRIES ASSOCIATION (HIA)

In the mid-1950s the leading manufacturers of hearing aids joined together in a membership organization they called the Hearing Aid Industry Council (HAIC). At the time of its creation, HAIC represented companies that both manufactured and dispensed hearing aids in "authorized factory dealerships," and worked on manufacturing and retail issues. They created the Hearing Industries Association (HIA) Quarterly Statistical Report, which remains the sole source of U.S. hearing aid sales data today. Like its dispensing association counterparts, HIA is organized as a 501 C (6) nonprofit trade association. It is governed by a nine-person Board of Directors elected by the members, and its work is funded by annual dues paid by member companies.

In the 1970s, most of the companies divested themselves of their dispensing operations, and the HAIC focus switched to legislative and regulatory issues as the U.S. Food and Drug Administration (FDA) classified hearing aids as "restricted" Class II medical devices and developed a special regulation for the labeling and conditions for sale of hearing aids. The new challenges of communicating about hearing aids to people with hearing loss was met by the manufacturers with the creation of the Better Hearing Institute (BHI) and its public information programs.

The contemporary HIA took shape—and its current name—at the start of the 1980s as in-the-ear hearing aid technology, evaluation, and testing advances, the emergence of dispensing audiology, and an array of other trends restructured the hearing aid industry. HIA continued its legislative and regulatory programs, enhanced its statistical reporting initiatives, and launched a program of market development that drove sales into double-digit annual growth, topped by the watershed event of having then-President of the United States Ronald Reagan appear in public with hearing aids. Today, HIA members manufacture well over 90% of the hearing aids sold annually in the United States and the programs that their dues support help to ensure that the HIA vision—"everyone with a hearing loss should have the opportunity to benefit from the use of hearing aids"—someday becomes a reality.

(Special Thanks to Carol Rogin, Executive Director, Hearing Industries Association.)

---

above) are funded either in whole or in part by corporate consolidators." He continued: "The remaining 46% of U.S. distribution outlets are independent, autonomous and unaffiliated practices." Considering the stated and anticipated growth plans of several of the major manufactures at the time, Smriga (2004) projected consolidation plans for the U.S. market for the next 3 to 5 years (2007 to 2009). His projections suggest that 78% of U.S. distribution outlets will be funded, in whole or in part, by corporate consolidators with only 22% of the U.S. distribution outlets remaining under independent or unaffiliated practices.

After the Fall: How to Optimize Relations After the Departure

The practice owner or manager must recognize the need to maintain a good relationship with the sidelined instrument manufacturer. It is best to keep the door open as there are hearing instruments which remain under warranty and some repairs or adjustments may be required on an out-of-warranty basis.

The decision to move to another manufacturer was a well-documented, well-considered business decision: It was not personal nor did it require complete severance of all ties to the manufacturer. Doors always swing both ways in business. Should the manufacturer contact the practice with a proposal to re-establish a business relationship, the practice is in a favorable situation to negotiate better terms of operations. Practice owners should never say "No," but always put a price on "Yes." If relations are re-established, the practice must once again begin recording the parameters that lead to the decision to leave in the first place. At the slightest development of similar statistics, the decision-making process to go or stay begins all over again. This time around, the decision will be made with greater speed and less tolerance for slow response or poor resolution by the instrument manufacturer.

The Final Note: Patient Advocacy

Patient advocacy is a time-honored tradition of all health care practitioners: Whatever it takes to guarantee the quality of patient care, dedicated health care practitioners work diligently on behalf of their patients. Whether it is establishing or improving licensing and regulatory issues for audiologists or whether it is the concerted efforts of an entire profession actively advancing providers to doctoral level training and expectations, patient welfare and quality of care are at the core of professional health care providers.

Audiologists are advocates in the relationship between hearing instrument manufacturers and the end-users of their products. It is the audiologist's job to work diligently on behalf of the patient to ensure appropriate instrumentation is placed and applied relative the patient's need. No matter the situation or circumstance, the audiologist-as-health-care-provider, must ultimately put the interests of his or her patients before those of the practice and the hearing instrument manufacturer. The audiologist must function as the patient's intercessor in matters of conflict that may arise from time to time with hearing instrument manufacturers and suppliers. The practice must insist that instrument manufacturers, suppliers, and related vendors participate as actively as any member of the front office or professional staff in placing the patient's interest first in all deliberations and resolution of conflict. In contemporary hearing health care, adhering to the concept of patient centric care is as much the responsibility of the audiologist managing the patient's aural rehabilitation as it is the responsibility of instrument manufacturers and suppliers.

References

Berger, K. W. (1984). *The hearing aid: Its operation and development.* (3rd ed., p. 87). Livonia MI: National Hearing Aid Society.

Fabry, D. A., Launer, S., & Derleth, P. (2007). Hearing aid technology vs. steeply sloping sensorineural hearing loss. *Hearing Review, 14*(1), 18–24.

Glaser, R. G. (2007). Unpublished data on rates of hearing aid repairs.

Hedge, A. (2007). Ergonomic guidelines for user-interface design. *CU Ergo*. Retrieved January 28, 2007, from http://ergo.human.cornell.edu/ahtutorials/intrface.html

Kirkwood, D. H. (2001). Most dispensers in Journal's survey report greater patient satisfaction with digitals. *Hearing Journal, 54*(3), 21–32.

Kochkin, S. (2005). Marketrak VII: Satisfaction with hearing instruments in the digital age. *Hearing Journal, 58*(9), 30–37.

Smriga, D. J. (2004). Are we asleep at the wheel? The delicate future of audiology private practice in America. *ADA Feedback, 15*(4), 7–15.

12

Marketing the Practice

ROBERT M. TRAYNOR, Ed.D., M.B.A.

Introduction

No matter what the venue, it is absolutely necessary to market an audiology practice. The days of complacency in presenting the clinic to the market are gone forever. In the past, audiologists could often simply establish a few referral sources and make a rather good living by offering good reports and customer service to their patients. There are many reasons for these changes in practice patterns that have made marketing essential to success but the big one is the same as other fields, *competition*. As greater numbers of colleagues have chosen to offer their services privately, competition presents a challenge for all practices to make their clinic stand out from the crowd. This does not mean that patient care is compromised or that audiologists need to become high-pressure salespeople, it means that without proper marketing the patients will go somewhere else. Practitioners should keep in mind that to offer the best possible patient care, they must first be brought into the practice by some type of marketing program.

Marketing is conducted to increase traffic and subsequently increase the units of service provided and numbers of hearing instruments dispensed. Marketing is not simply ads in the paper, a senior guide, or other local publication. It is more than an isolated presentation at the Kiwanis Club or a marketing trip to a physician's office, it involves an organized, targeted effort to present or brand the practice to the marketplace. Commonly, marketing in audiology practices peaks when office traffic slows down and is frequently a disjointed process incorporating little evidence-based information on what works best. When practitioners respond to a lull of activity in their practice by pulling together a marketing-after-fact plan, they will find their reflexive marketing response to be inefficient and costly relative to the meager outcome of their actions.

To properly brand a practice in a community it is necessary to do market research and link the information about the market to a simple or comprehensive marketing plan. The purpose of this chapter is not only to present basic marketing principles but to discuss the critical elements of market research that are essential to a marketing plan that brands the practice in the marketplace.

Professional Marketing Defined

Marketing, as defined by Kotler (2001), is a process of identifying and meeting human wants and needs profitably. Although it may have a social or managerial purpose, marketing is the creation of demand for a particular product or service by establishing public awareness. Obringer (2006) presents marketing as the process of planning and executing the conception, pricing, promotion, and distribution of ideas, goods, and services to create exchanges that satisfy individual and organizational goals. What does that mean to you? It means marketing encompasses everything you have to do in coming up with a needed product or service, making potential customers aware of it, making them want it, and then selling it to them. Put simply, marketing is basic communication between a collection of sellers (such as audiologists) and a collection of buyers of services or products (such as hearing-impaired consumers), as presented in Figure 12–1. This collection of sellers offers goods and services to the market consisting of

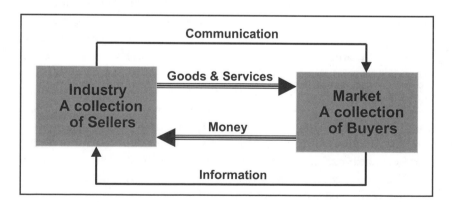

Figure 12–1. Simple marketing system. (From *Marketing Management,* by P. Kotler [p. 6], 2001, Upper Saddle River, NJ: Prentice-Hall. Copyright 2001. Adapted with permission.)

a collection of buyers who pay money for those goods and services. Although this concept is how the system works, in marketing the goal is to get this collection of buyers to choose one seller over another. One of first decisions that must be made in presenting the practice to this collection of buyers is how it will be branded. As branding is the key to the image that will be marketed to the consumers, it must be considered as the first component of any marketing exercise.

Branding Your Practice

Hansen (2006) presents that each day brand promises are made to your patients and prospects. These promises are made through literature, signage, advertising, and other means of communication. Although promises are certainly easy to make, the key to winning new patients and keeping existing clientele loyal to the practice is the delivery of those promises. Delivery is exhibited through the practice, in the attitude of your team as well as the products and services that are offered. This connection between promises and their ultimate delivery is what leads the consumer to choose a particular practice over the competition.

The purpose of a marketing program is to distinguish a particular audiology practice from the other practices that appear similar to the consumer. The goal should be to make a particular practice or "brand of audiology" stand out from all other possible options that could meet the consumer's wants and needs for hearing care. This involves "branding the practice" with a marketing campaign that establishes in the consumer's minds that this particular practice is the place for them to receive hearing care above all the other possible options.

Branding, according to D'Alessandro (2001), is an old business practice that can be described as whatever the consumer thinks of when they see or hear a company's name. For example, what comes to mind when thinking of BMW, Apple, or Harley-Davidson? Some of the best products world wide have built strong brands so that in consumer's minds, the thought is of quality, image, reliability, and customer service. Audiology practitioners build their brand every time they see a patient, present a market offering, participate in a public relations activity, or simply interact with the community. Hansen (2006) further indicates that it is not just what is done with the patients that build a brand; it is the office environment, location, and atmosphere. As purchase rates and satisfaction ratings are connected, negative in-office experiences can lead to a loss of 10 to 30% of a clinic's business and create negative branding in the community. If, for example, Audiology Associates is to be branded successfully as *the place* for hearing care; market offerings to the com-munity must be ethically directed toward generating in the minds of perspective patients and others, that the Audiology Associates "brand of audiology" makes it the *best place* in the market area to receive hearing care. Additionally, from arrival to completion of the hearing care experience, Audiology Associates, must deliver on the promise that was presented their marketing communications.

Prior to the age of digital hearing aids, most of the amplification products were essentially the same and the real difference among them was simply the *place* they were obtained or the hearing aid *brand name*. In today's high technology world, there are substantial differences among products and consumers are bombarded constantly with market offerings via print media, radio, direct mail, television, and even via the Internet. This constant interaction of the market with consumers makes it even more difficult to brand a particular practice as the special place to receive hearing care.

Compounding the problem of branding is the Doctor of Audiology (Au.D.) degree which has forever changed the landscape of audiology private practice. As a universal brand for the profession, the Au.D. generates images of high-quality hearing care in the minds of consumers. Consumers can generally feel more comfortable in the knowledge that a professional branded with the Au.D. is an audiologist educated to certain standards and offers the typical skills that are commensurate with a doctoral level profession. Although the Au.D. has significantly branded the audiology profession to consumers, the unique designator for audiologists makes it increasingly more difficult to distinguish one practitioner's practice from another. When all Au.D professionals are branded the same, how does one practice stand out among the others? Consider that audiologists generally conduct similar evaluations and sell (more or less) similar products from a closed set of manufacturers. Thus, in a world where all practitioners have the same credential, the Au.D. how are these practices different? Under conditions where all clinicians look the same, it may be the personality of the practitioner, the convenience or physical environment of the practice, and/or the atmosphere created by the staff that can make the difference. In a world of intense competition among audiologists and other hearing health care providers, there are a number of competitors simultaneously attempting to brand themselves through market offerings to the same population. All of these competitors may be formidable and it is essential that a specific practice present the difference between their "brand of audiology" and other "brands of audiology" or hearing care offered elsewhere. To better understand the nature of competitive branding, four distinct categories of branding competition have been offered by D'Alessandro (2001):

- Brand competition. All competitors that *are like me*. This category, for example, represents all Au.D. audiologists that offer hearing care in the same market area. These competitors look exactly alike to the consumer, as they have the same "brand" for their credentials. In the consumer's mind, without proper market offerings, they would presume that products and services for their needs could be obtained from any Au.D. professional. Thus, it is not enough to brand the credential; branding of the particular clinic is necessary to ensure success.

- Industry competition. All competitors that *look like me* offering hearing care. Pertaining to the field of audiology, this would include doctoral level audiologists (Ph.D., Ed.D., Sc.D.) other than the Au.D. or otolaryngologists. Similar to "brand competition," many professionals appear to be the same in the capability to provide products and services to the hearing impaired to the consumer and many of these people already have an established relationship with a professional for their hearing care. Again, it is the intensity and the direction of the market offerings that can ensure the branding of the practice by separating a particular clinic as the facility of choice.

■ Form competition. All those *in the same business.* This category would include audiologists of all brands, otolaryngologists, hearing aid dealers, drug stores, wholesale warehouse corporations, Internet offerings, or other establishments that offer hearing care or sell similar products. Form competitors are those where considerable diversity may exist in the capability to serve consumers. Branding a practice by a tasteful and ethical market offering that presents the type of hearing care offered, can often provide the differentiation of hearing care providers desperately needed by consumers. Indeed, it may be an ethical responsibility to present market offerings that direct consumers to the most qualified professional.

■ Generic competition. All products *that cost the same as hearing care.* In this instance, patients weigh the costs of hearing care against other (possibly more desirable) recreational activities, required services, or products; such as, cars, foreign vacations, cruises, appliances, or, on the service side, office visits, physical therapy, eye exams, and so forth. This is simply an application of a basic principle of economics; the principle of "opportunity cost." This principle suggests that there is only a finite amount of funds and if the funds are utilized to purchase an item, then those funds are not available to use for another purpose. It is a simple fact that the products sold in audiology practices, especially

hearing instruments, are expensive to most consumers, and compete for attention with other products of similar value. Furthermore, it is also well known that consumers want these other competitive products or services more than those offered in audiology clinics. It is more fun and, sometimes of more mental health benefit, to take a cruise, a foreign vacation, or purchase a car rather than obtain amplification. Thus, there are many products in competition for the same funds. It is the marketing campaign, and sometimes, the specific market offerings, that will convince the patient to make the more prudent decision.

Although marketing is what builds a particular brand of audiology in the consumer's minds, D'Alessandro (2001) indicates that it is not easy to build a great brand. He states that it takes an artistic sense of proportion and timing as well as a ruthless willingness to distinguish yourself from the competing brands and, one hopes, "bury them" in the process.

Marketing Research

Marketing research is conducted for many different purposes. It can be used for planning, problem-solving, or control purposes to provide insight and serve as the basis for a simple or comprehensive marketing plan. Churchill and Brown (2004) indicate that when market research is used for planning, it deals largely with determining which market opportunities are viable for the practice. When a viable opportunity is uncovered, marketing research provides an estimate of the size and scope of the opportunity so that it can be better managed. The use of market research for problem-solving focuses on making short- and long-term decisions relative to the mixture of market communications that will be used in presenting and branding the practice to the community. For example, one of the major problems of audiology practice can be the rise and fall of demand for products and services. The example presented in Figure 12–2 summarizes the problem that a practice may have with the seasonal demands for our products and services. In this example, the demand for hearing aids is less early in the year with a demand spike in May followed by a downturn in the summer. It also presents that the greatest demand for hearing instruments is in the last part of the year. As the product demand changes throughout the year, it must be stimulated at certain times of the year by an organized marketing plan based on sound market research. This pattern of demand, or, *demand analysis*, would suggest that the marketing plan would need more funds when the demand was low (early in the year and summer) and less funding

when demand was high (September–December). A demand analysis can be conducted for all products and services offered in the clinic, including hearing aids, routine audiometric evaluations, OAEs, ABRs, VNGs, operative monitoring, and ALDs as well as small accessories. Additionally, these product and service analyses can be as detailed as necessary even describing the specific brands of products or components of audiometric evaluations that were purchased. As marketing is an expensive process, successful practices spend their valuable funds presenting their brand of audiology to the community based on their demand predictions and market research.

Marketing Plans

A good marketer will communicate their brand to the market and receive feedback that can be used to stimulate demand for products and services. Planning a successful marketing program involves conducting marketing research

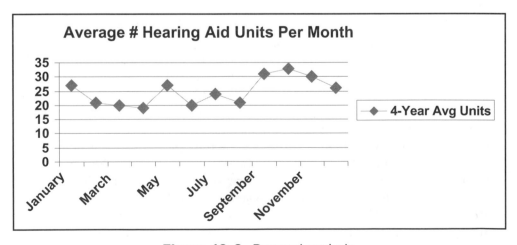

Figure 12–2. Demand analysis.

to know how, when, and where to wisely expend that hard-earned marketing budget.

Berry and Wilson (2004) offer that marketing should be a set of planned activities designed to positively influence the perceptions and purchase choices of individuals and organizations. KnowThis.com (2006) states that a marketing plan is a highly detailed, heavily researched, and well-written report that many inside and some outside the organization will evaluate. Although there is no one format for the marketing plan, it is an exercise that essentially forces the practitioner to look internally into the practice. This is done to fully understand the results of past marketing decisions, the market in which the practice operates, and set goals while providing direction for future. As with business plans, marketing plans can be a key component in obtaining funds to pursue expansions, equipment, or other operational modifications but, generally, is pursued for any of the following reasons:

■ The plan is needed as part of the yearly planning process.
■ The plan is needed for a specialized strategy to introduce something new, such as new products, entering new markets, or generating a new strategy to fix an existing problem.
■ The plan is a component within an overall business plan, such as a new business proposal to the financial community.

Marketing research can be divided into three distinct purposes, planning, problem-solving, and control. Planning is the key to successful marketing programs and marketing research must be conducted to know how to wisely direct the marketing funds. Market research that is used for problem-solving is incorporated to review issues relating to product, price, place, and promotional whereas control-oriented marketing research assists the practice manager in the isolation of trouble spots in the practice and promotes knowledge of how the clinic is performing. In Sidebar 12–1, Churchill and Brown (2004) outline these three general categories of marketing research into questions used in successful businesses. Although some of the questions are more applicable to general business; most of these market research questions can be directly or indirectly applied to an audiology practice. The application of Churchill and Brown's marketing research outline to audiology practice greatly organizes and simplifies the marketing process.

Generating the answers to the questions is a great place to start in the marketing of a practice. In the planning phase, the answers to the questions vary substantially from one service or product to another. For example, the demand may be constant for hearing evaluations, but rise and fall for hearing aids, or vestibular evaluations. There may be one overall marketing plan for the practice, another for specific products, and still another for specific services.

The answers to these planning questions also develop an understanding of the market in which the practice operates. In the business world, the answers to these questions are called target *market segmentation*. Traynor (2006) describes the target market segmentation as the identification and profiling of consumers into categories or different components of the market. The target market segmentation answers the questions generated by Churchill and Brown's

---

Sidebar 12–1
OUTLINE OF MARKETING RESEARCH
(Churchill and Brown, 2004)

I. Planning
   A. What kinds of people buy our products? Where do they live? How much do they earn? How many of them are there?
   B. Are the markets for our products increasing or decreasing? Are there promising markets that we have not reached yet?
   C. Are channels of distribution for our products changing? Are new types of marketing institutions likely to evolve?
II. Problem-solving
   A. Product
      1. Which of various product designs is likely to be the most successful?
      2. What kinds of packaging should we use?
   B. Price
      1. What price should we charge for our products?
      2. As production costs decline, should we lower process or try to develop higher quality products?
   C. Place
      1. Where, and by whom, should or products be sold?
      2. What kinds of incentives should we offer to push our products?
   D. Promotion
      1. How much should we spend on promotion? How should it be allocated and to geographic areas?
      2. What combination of media, radio, television magazines, the Internet should we use?
III. Control
   A. What is our market share overall? In each geographic area? By each customer type?
   B. Are customers satisfied with our products? How is our record for service? Are there many returns?
   C. How does the public perceive our company? What is our reputation with the trade?

---

outline, but can be very simple or quite complex. To conduct the target market segmentation, market segments are divided into major areas such as:

- Geographic
- Demographic
- Psychographic
- Behavioral.

These general categories of the market can then be further delineated to identify a specific population or segment of individuals that are the most likely candidates for the market offering or the product. The geographic category can be reduced from a large area such as a state to a region, a city, a neighborhood, or even segmented for seasonal offerings to offset the rise and fall of demand.

Demographics are a large category often utilized to target the product or service offering into categories of individuals that may be interested. These categories identify specific groups or segments of the market by age, income, race, family size, occupation, generation, family life cycle, education, nationality, religion, gender, social class, and others. For example, the demographic target market for an audiology practice that offers hearing aids is usually individuals above age 55, mid to upper incomes, any race, one or two in the family, retired or employed person, any occupation, without children at home, of any education level, nationality, religion, or gender from any social class.

Psychographic segmentation is usually by lifestyle or personality. For example, all of those individuals at an assisted living center or that have a particular personal style might be singled out for a specific marketing campaign.

Behaviorally, segments can be made from occasions or events, such as birthdays or anniversaries; from a status, such as warranty expiration; or battery use. One very useful segment in audiology practices can be the readiness stage, such as when the patient reaches a certain hearing loss level that begins to affect their interactions with family members, or when their attitude toward

the product changes. Although accessing a consumer in this stage can be difficult, patients that have been seen a year or so before can be targeted for access when they may be more psychologically ready for treatment.

The real benefit of target marketing is when these general segments are further delineated and utilized together as multi-attribute segmentation in the presentation of the marketing material. These multiattribute segmentations create a population composed of individuals that have a need and want for your products or services. Generally, the better the segmentation, the better the response to the market offering. Although it is necessary to find a portion of the segmentation that requires audiology goods and services, Wood-Young (2000) indicates that a common mistake is to identify too broad of a market. Thus, you must be accurate in your target market segmentation; too broad will minimize the efficiency of the marketing program and too small of a market will reduce the number of individuals presented with the market offering.

The problem-solving portion of the outline in Sidebar 12-1 focuses on the short and long-term decisions that must be made with respect to the marketing mix. The marketing mix, according to Day (1994) and Borden (1994), is the specific combination of how the basic marketing elements are used to present the practice. Often called the *Four Ps* of marketing, product, price, place, and promotion are put together to make up the overall marketing plan for the practice. The marketing mix concept is presented in Figure 12-3. Churchill and Peter (2002) state that the purpose of marketing is the creation of value for customers where customer value is the difference between

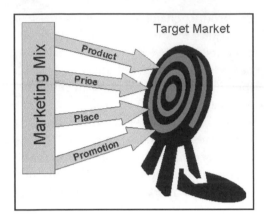

Figure 12–3. Marketing mix.

customer perceptions of the benefits they receive from using the products and services, and their perceptions of the costs they incur to exchange for them. Customers are willing and able to make exchanges and will do so when (1) the benefits of the exchanges exceed the costs of exchanges and (2) the products and services offer superior value compared with the alternatives.

Churchill and Brown (2004) indicate that marketing managers, in their attempts to create customer value, generally focus their efforts on the Four Ps, namely the product or service, its price, its placement or channel in which it is distributed, and its promotion. These Four Ps are closely related to the four customer or patient-related variables that Lauterhorn (1990) calls the *Four Cs*. The Four Cs look at the marketing mix from the patient benefit point of view and suggests that products are the *customer solution*, price is the *customer cost*, place or channel is the *customer convenience*, and promotion is the *customer communication*. Thus, the Four Ps should be considered in light of the Four Cs to provide perspective to the marketing process. The questions in the second por-

tion of the Churchill and Brown outline deal with how to market the practice, given the specific mixture of product, price, place, and promotion.

Product

Product Tangibility

Murphy and Ennis (1986) describe three characteristics of products that must be understood for effective marketing. These include durability, tangibility, and consumer use. Durability and tangibility include both nondurable and durable goods.

In an audiology practice, batteries are an example of a nondurable in that they are purchased and used for a period of time, then another one is required to power the hearing aid again. The marketing strategy for nondurable goods is to have them available in many locations and charge only a small markup, with some advertising and/or demonstrations to build brand loyalty and preference. An example of a durable good is the hearing instrument itself as it is, one hopes, used each day for several years. Durable goods are tangible products that require more personal selling and service. As there is greater involvement in time and attention, durable goods require a higher margin to offset the dispenser education, research and development, and the necessary guarantees. Services, however, are intangible, inseparable, variable, and perishable products and as such require more quality control, supplier credibility, and adaptability. Thus, audiologic services are highly influenced by the provider, their credentials, and how well they can adapt to the variables of the evaluation and offer other necessary services.

Product Mix

Most audiology practices have basically the same mix of products. They offer hearing instruments, nondurable goods in support of the hearing instruments, and rehabilitative efforts as well as a mix of services including diagnostic hearing and balance assessment. Some practices offer additional items in the mix such as cerumen management, intraoperative monitoring, and various levels of hearing conservation programming. When the patient looks to find a solution to a problem, it is the product mix, both goods and services, tangible and intangible, offered by the practice that meets their want or need.

In a business sense, Berry and Wilson (2004) describe a product offering as something that offers benefits or satisfaction to the target group. Although part of the product mix is the practice's image, Kotler (2001) offers that there are specific factors about products that cause them to be chosen as part of the product mix. The following are some characteristics that can be a part of choosing the products that make up the product mix:

- Product variety
- Quality
- Design
- Features
- Brand name
- Packaging
- Sizes
- Services
- Warranties
- Return policy.

A hearing instrument manufacturer must have the correct technology mix in their product line to make them appealing to an audiology practice. Certain brand names have a reputation for quality and functionality. Above and beyond a manufacturer's respective technologic offerings, peripheral factors such as packaging, utility of the fitting software, warranty parameters, access to inside support personnel, low repair rates, quick repair turnaround time, and well-informed field representatives are a few important components that add to (or detract from) their attractiveness to practitioners.

Product manufacturers, especially hearing instrument companies, are very willing to give audiology practitioners marketing assistance in both advertising and public relations. Many hearing instrument manufacturers offer funds to assist in marketing costs incurred for a campaign that features their products. Although these campaigns are effective and usually available for simply the use of the manufacturer's product during the marketing effort, these product marketing efforts should be accompanied by offers that present the practice's brand of audiologic expertise. Many audiologists use the same brands of hearing instruments so it is best to market your brand of audiology rather than the manufacturer's brand of product that the patient can obtain from many different sources.

From the patient point of view, the want or need for hearing can be met by the simple acquisition of the product, and not necessarily from your practice. If they perceive that they do not need the audiology expertise, then they will simply attempt to acquire the hearing instrument at the lowest possible price. Hearing instruments and some related products are in the process of becoming commodity products. Commodity products are those products that are perceived as the same by consumers no matter where they are purchased. As they are the same, then consumers tend to purchase them at the lowest available price, no matter the location. Until recently, hearing instruments have only been available though audiologists and commercial hearing aid dealers. Many patients, especially those seeking these products for the first time, do not understand the differences among instruments or the services that are required to dispense them properly. This lack of understanding the complexity of hearing instruments, fitting techniques, and rehabilitative intervention, causes consumers to consider the Internet and discount stores as realistic options.

Currently, Killion (2006) indicates that about 7% of hearing instrument sales are completed on the Internet and Smriga (2004) adds that about 6% of hearing instruments are dispensed through discount stores. Patients not only look at these delivery systems, but seriously consider that they might save a lot of money by going to the discount store, or an Internet purchase. The products look the same, sound the same, but usually do not have services included with them or the that included services are inferior to those offered by a private practice audiologist. In markets where discount stores or the Internet are major concerns the services and follow-up should be a marketing focus. Patients do not appreciate that they are the beneficiary of the unique rehabilitative efforts of the audiologist that make the difference in the outcome in this patient-professional interface. Practitioners are uniquely qualified by their academic and practical training to provide both the necessary diagnostic studies as well as developing a rehabilitative treatment plan relative to the practical findings.

"It is the position of the American Academy of Audiology that every person seeking treatment of hearing disorders through the use of amplification devices receive a comprehensive audiological evaluation prior to purchasing a hearing instrument. . . . The comprehensive audiological evaluation must be performed by an audiologist who is licensed or registered in the state wherein the evaluation is completed. The diagnostic evaluation is not conducted for the purposes of selecting or fitting a hearing aid, but rather to assess the functional status of the auditory system, and to assure that amplification or other assistive listening devices are an appropriate treatment strategy" (American Academy of Audiology [AAA], 2000).

The focus on a specific product for a marketing campaign is not a good idea as patients will review their alternatives to acquire the same product a lower price. It is far better to focus on the branding of the practice so that consumers come to expect a specific brand of hearing care service than to spend the marketing money branding the manufacturer's product. As it is the benefits of the product that the consumer purchases, the marketing program should focus not only on product features, but also the expertise required to fit and maintain the device to achieve full benefit.

Price

Wood-Young (2000) indicates that setting correct pricing for products and services is a great challenge. It could be that pricing is one of the biggest keys to success as it has such an effect on profit. If the price is high, sales are usually lower but with higher profit, whereas if the price is low, sales are high with minimal profit. Traynor (2006) presents that from a business standpoint; the goal is to price the product mix where the most products are sold for the highest price possible without discouraging the consumer as to its cost. Although this seems a simple process, it is difficult in that correct or incorrect pricing has a direct effect on the bottom line or the actual profitability of the practice.

Once the product has been chosen then it is simply a question of how much the patient is willing to give up for the product. Nagle and Holden (2004) suggest that pricing is a game because success depends not only on a practice's own pricing decisions but also on how patients and competition react to them. They further present that pricing decisions should always be made as part of a longer term marketing strategy to generate and capture more profit contribution. Otherwise, it is possible to win many individual battles for market share and still end up losing the war for profitability.

For a comprehensive review of pricing fundamentals and procedures as they directly apply to the audiology practice the reader should review Chapter 3.

Once the manager has calculated the product prices, the components of the "pricing mix" can then be established. These would include:

- List price—Full retail price as determined by a particular method.
- Discounts—A discount from the full retail price.
- Allowances—Cash allowances on the trade-in of valuable products.
- Payment period—Period of time allowed for the consumer to pay for the product taking into account the amount put down at the time of order and how much deposit is lost if the product is returned.

- Credit terms—Terms for financing of goods and services by internal and external financing programs.

Place

Place is where the services are offered, the atmosphere, and the image in which the product mix is provided. In any business, a product is anything that can be offered to a market to satisfy a want or a need. Products not only include physical goods but also services, experiences, events, places, properties, organizations, information, and ideas.

Indeed, part of the product that is presented to the market is the practice's image. From the first phone call until referral or dismissal of the patient the whole experience is part of the product branding of the practice. The more centrally located the clinic is in the community, the more comfortable for patients to find and facilitates a relaxed situation to them as they arrive. Parking should be easy with a number of handicap spaces provided, as well as wheelchair and walker accessibility; if possible, even a handicap door allowing easy, convenient accessibility for those with disabilities. Although it is helpful to have a number of convenient locations, the viability of multiple locations must be weighed with the expansion costs incurred from a business standpoint.

The practice should offer a clinical, but not stuffy, atmosphere so as to allow for relaxation and comfort, reinforcing that they have come to the right place for hearing care.

Generally, the clinic should have a neat, uncluttered waiting room with a tasteful decor. The front office staff begins setting the brand image presented on the telephone scheduling the appointment, greetings on arrival, as well as being courteous, interactive, and sympathetic if they have difficulty communicating. The audiologist should dress to see patients and wear a lab coat to present the professional doctoral level image. Simply dressing for image is a good start toward branding the product image offered by the practice. In the past, even many doctoral level audiologists did not use lab coats. These were the days before the profession was a doctoral level profession and this attire was considered unnecessary by some professionals. The profession has totally changed in that more audiologists are in private practice, working for themselves, branding their practice at the doctoral level. Thus, the use of a lab coat promotes the image of a doctor offering services in a professional operation and an individual with credentials to ethically recommend further testing or rehabilitative products that will be of benefit to them.

Image is so important to success in practice that McCall and Dunlop (2004) suggest that it is a good idea to check the brand that is being presented to the community. They feel that is essential to conduct these checks occasionally by calling the office using the main number and to try to make an appointment, checking on the elements of the experience:

■ How were they greeted?
■ Was it easy to make an appointment?
■ How long did they have to wait for an appointment?
■ Were they put on hold?
■ Were they advised of what to bring for the first appointment?
■ Were they made to feel important?

They also suggest that every so often the professional should park where the patients park.

■ Is the signage easy to read?
■ Is the entrance to the practice clearly designated?
■ Is the parking lot clean?

Professionals should also walk into the practice through the front door and see the practices' first impression from the patient's eyes.

■ Is the entrance easily marked?
■ Is the entrance inviting?
■ Is the waiting room pleasant and comfortable?

McCall and Dunlop (2004) also suggest that it is a good idea to check the brand presented to consumers by asking the patients a few good questions. First, they will appreciate being asked and it will convey to them that these details are of concern and that their satisfaction is important.

■ How were they treated when they called in for an appointment?
■ Did they visit the Web site? Was it helpful? If not what can be done to make it better?

Product brands are built by "doing the homework" necessary to make a particular brand of audiology stand out from the other brands already offered in the community. Once your brand is known as the most competent, professional, relaxed, and convenient clinic most of the marketing is already done and the goods and services almost sell themselves.

Promotion

Audiologists must communicate with the market to take advantage of the ever changing market conditions that may be beneficial to the presentation of products or services. There are three specific types of consumers that require promotional intervention:

- Referrals from medical colleagues
- Existing patients in database
- Patients recruited from the general public.

The first consumers that need attention are those that are referred by medical colleagues. The best source of patient referral for general diagnostic and rehabilitative audiology services is from family practice, internal medicine, and occupational medicine. Although General Surgeons are a good source of referral for operative monitoring, otolaryngologists usually have their own service providers and often dispense hearing instruments. As marketing to referral sources requires these colleagues to entrust their patients to you this is a special relationship requiring a different interactive marketing approach and presented in detail in Chapter 6. Once the referral is made, however, it is the responsibility of the audiology clinic to support the referral source and deliver the expected brand of audiology services or products presented to them. Subsequently, however, the relationship is then between the patient and the audiology practice with interaction back to the referral source.

The second group are existing patients included in the clinic database. An established practice will benefit from the consumers knowledge of their brand of audiology and often minimal marketing to existing patients nets a rather large return. This is done by generating special promotions through a newsletter, Web site, or other communication.

The third and most expensive source of patients is from the general public. Market communications to this group are called a *market offering* that can be in the form of advertising in newspapers, radio, television, direct mail ads, newsletters, or other communication media. As these media require the purchase of space, time, and other expensive commodities it can require use large amounts of marketing funds to get these individuals into the practice. Any of these specific advertising mediums may be used in isolation, but the best result is usually achieved by an organized marketing effort that incorporates a number of these modalities simultaneously. These coordinated market offerings allow multiple exposures that gain maximum interaction with the audience by stimulating a number of senses. In addition to advertising to the general population, a marketing program should also include a coordinated public relations or awareness campaign, conducting presentations to service groups, as well as interaction with physician's offices. The demonstration of products, services, and professional expertise to these groups can be a great source of new patients either from the audiences or their family and friends.

General Considerations in Promotional Activities

Promotions can be easily over- or underused in marketing the practice. A practice with no promotions will have a difficult time competitive markets. No matter what specific promotional method is incorporated it is better to begin the discussion with some evidence-based themes woven into promotions that ensure for success. Staab (1992) offers some general experiential tips that ensure success with promotional programs:

■ Try to add value, rather than discounting products.
■ Put your imprint on your promotions; make them exclusive and identifiable to your office.
■ Focus on the future; look for repeat business, not just new business.
■ Give your promotions a theme to help reinforce your other promotional efforts.
■ Target your promotions as specifically as you can to make the results measurable.
■ Try to find ways to reward your best patients, the life blood of your business.
■ If the promotion does well, look for cross-promotional opportunities.
■ Find ways to make your patient feel good about you and your office.
■ Promotions should be presented in a quality manner within an affordability range.
■ If you have sales staff involved, the promotion should be exciting and rewarding for them to participate, or it will not perform as well.
■ Make promotions fun and easy to execute.
■ Keep testing different promotions, even if specific promotions are working well.
■ Design the promotion asking the question, "What do hearing-impaired patients want us to do for them" or rephrased, the patient should be able to ask, "What's in it for me?"

Many general areas can be included in direct marketing efforts for practice differentiation. These marketing efforts can achieve results by diversifying the message or offering into a number of specific areas such as goods, services, experiences, events, persons, places, organizations, information, ideas, or technology, . and so forth. Kotler (2001) leads practitioners to believe that all of these areas can be considered and varied in their marketing programs:

■ *Marketing through the goods—* These are products such as hearing aids, batteries, accessories, and other physical products for sale in the clinic. The selling of goods can use manufacturer-produced or practice-generated ads and discuss technology, product changes, and/or product features and benefits.
■ *Marketing through the services—* Depending on the audience for the marketing campaign, evaluations and other services offered in the clinic can be presented as an alternative to the traditional. Highlighting other services besides audiometric evaluations such as ABRs, OAEs, balance testing, programming of hearing aids, aural rehabilitation classes, and cerumen removal, presents the practice as a facility that can help the whole patient. Consumers often view the offering of these other services as an indication of a "patient-oriented" facility and may not only seek services at this clinic, but may also be inclined to refer others.
■ *Marketing through the experiences—* Although audiologists are aware of how new products can change the quality of life of hearing-impaired

individuals, the patient is most likely unaware of the broad range of benefits that they will receive from items, such as new technology amplification, a special telephone, or from just reprogramming their current hearing aids. Offering services "beyond the basics" in the form of focus groups and aural rehabilitation classes can set a practice apart from the competition. These unique offerings are, in fact, a form of informal marketing as it encourages the sharing of experiences among patients with similar problems. Good first-hand experiences are probably the best form of advertising and testimonials are a good source of advertising not only for new hearing aid fittings, but also for refits, reprogramming, and services

■ *Marketing through events*— Sponsoring or offering screening services at special events, such as health fairs, will foster awareness of hearing loss and treatment and thus draw people into the practice. Additionally, offering community lectures on hearing impairment to service groups, such as the Lions Club or Sertoma, is a good marketing tool for visibility. Other events, such as "open houses" must be conducted at strategic times and coordinated with multimodality advertising to ensure success.

■ *Marketing through people*—This can be the marketing of a special individual, the practice owner/ audiologist, or other expert, such as a manufacturer's representative as a spokesperson for the practice. Events that market a specific individual are usually more successful when combined with a special market offering with a timed response.

■ *Marketing the place of service*—The promotion of a specific location, such as rural, conveniently located, accessible by public transportation, plenty of available parking, or other relevant aspects pertaining to the locale of the practice can be a special marketing edge.

■ *Marketing through organizations*— It is possible to gain recognition by building a strong, favorable image relative to organizations such as senior centers, church groups or other local groups for the elderly, or the hearing impaired.

■ *Marketing with information*— Information, such as explanations about hearing loss, hearing instruments, assistive devices, middle ear disease, and so forth, can be disseminated in brochures made available in displays in the office or through direct mailings.

■ *Marketing the benefits*—This is the selling of the key features and benefits of your product. Benefits that are often utilized liberally relative to hearing instruments include: help with speech understanding, reduction of background noise, elimination of feedback, and comfort. Although these "catch phrases" are substantially overused, it is necessary to present the same ads occasionally so that the practice is seen as offering the same benefits as others in the surrounding area.

Although there are marketing firms that advertise in professional journals to develop specialized mailing lists for practices, these marketers may know less about the appropriate market segment than the practitioner. There are many Internet sites offering assistance in designing multiattribute market segmentations that allow the practitioner to design a direct mail list targeted for their specific market at about one-third the cost of a list generated by professional marketing services. Although care must be exercised to communicate realistic expectations, various ads and marketing efforts can be made relative to specific characteristics of a product.

McCall and Dunlop (2004) present a 1-year marketing map in Sidebar 12–2 that can be used for a small practice in conjunction with the Churchill and Brown (2004) outline. These are simply suggestions and may vary from one practice and community to another.

Detailed Marketing Research and Marketing Plans

Berry and Wilson (2006) present information about the development of detailed marketing plans. They indicate that a marketing plan must fit a need and a particular situation, yet recognize there are common elements to most marketing situations. Although the rudimentary marketing plan offered by Churchill and Brown (2004), presented in Sidebar 12–1, may likely suffice in the first early years of practice, a more detailed marketing

---

Sidebar 12–2
1-YEAR MARKETING MAP

Month 1. Develop a two-page marketing to-do list for the year.

Month 2. Improve practice signage (inside and out).

Month 3. Enhance the Web site; add patient education links and directions to the practice.

Month 4. Hold customer service training for staff on how to be a brand ambassador.

Month 5. Hold a patient education event.

Month 6. Contact local reporters; offer the audiologist as a source for hearing health care stories.

Month 7. Send out direct mail piece to potential patients in market area.

Month 8. Improve waiting room decor, install a computer for patient use.

Month 9. Participate in local health fair or other "show."

Month 10. Contact local civic organizations or speaking opportunities.

Month 11. Sponsor a community event, preferably health-related event.

Month 12. Place an ad in a newcomer publication.

plan will be necessary as the practice grows or if expansion of the practice is planned. It will be needed to supplement the business plan when seeking loan funding from your banking partner for that new office, the new equipment, or the hiring of that new person.

Detailed marketing plans should be conducted with computer software, such as Market Pro Plus (2006). As these programs are readily available and relatively inexpensive, usually about $100, they are an inexpensive method of organizing and presenting your detailed plans for marketing the practice. These software programs actually "walk" the first time marketing planner or the seasoned veteran through the step by step process. Figure 12–4 presents the specifics of software in these marketing software packages which assist the practitioner in analysis of the market, developing a marketing strategy, setting the financials, and organizing the controls of the marketing program (Palo Alto Software, 2006, http://www.bizplan.com). For minimal costs the audiology practitioner with virtually no marketing experience can have years of "user friendly" marketing expertise assisting the generation of a detailed, professional market program.

Organization of the Plan

Most marketers agree with Obringer (2006) that there are four major components to developing a marketing plan:

- Researching and analyzing your business and the market;
- Planning and writing the plan;
- Implementing the plan;
- Evaluating the results.

Researching and Analyzing the Business and the Market

Research and analysis are critical because they lead you to the identification of your product's target audience. Researching and analyzing the market is a detailed analysis of the situation in which the marketing will take place. The situation analysis consists of a market summary or review of demographics, the target market segmentation; and a review of the needs, trends, and possible growth of the market for the products and services offered by the practice. Although similar to that presented above in the Churchill and Brown (2004) outline, data for detailed marketing plans are substantially more specific and often reviewed over a 5-year period to understand the historical trends of each analyzed component. Specific charts and graphs should be presented for each of the trends reported within the plan so as to explain and depict the target market segmentation, needs, trends, and market growth.

A review of the market situation is enhanced by a self-analysis (Berry & Wilson, 2001; Obringer, 2006; Porn, 2004). In an audiology practice, a serious look at the strengths (S), weaknesses (W), opportunities (O), and threats (T) (SWOT) leads to the identification of the practice's target audience and usually involves both a qualitative and quantitative review (Porn, 2004). The qualitative component is simply the audiologist's own opinion of the situation, whereas the quantitative is an actual review of data. The effectiveness of the SWOT analysis will depend on the amount and accuracy of the data on which it is based. In the SWOT analysis, strengths and weaknesses are considered internal to the organization whereas opportunities and threats are external.

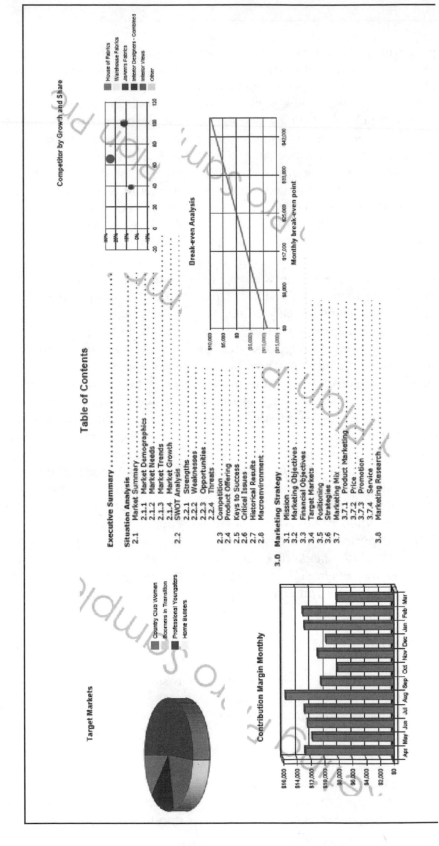

Competitor by Growth and Share

- House of Fabrics
- Warehouse Fabrics
- Jewels Fabrics
- Interior Designers - Combined
- Interior Views
- Other

Break-even Analysis

Monthly break-even point

Target Markets

- Country Club Women
- Boomers in Transition
- Professional Youngsters
- Home Busters

Contribution Margin Monthly

Table of Contents

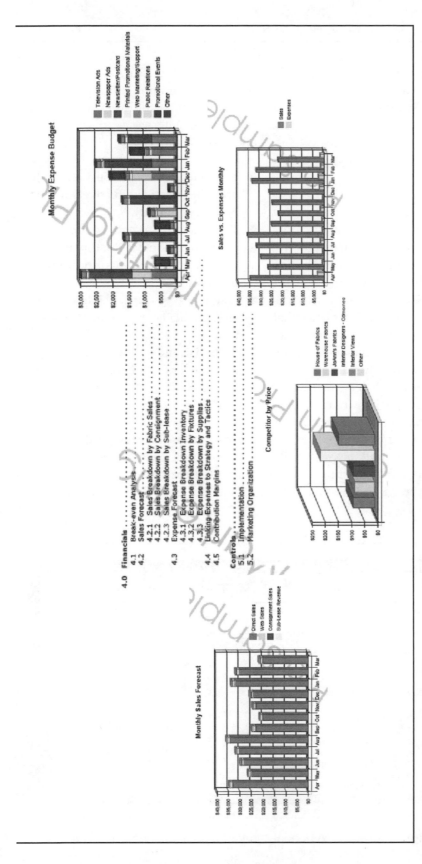

Figure 12–4. Marketing plan sample software program. (Palo Alto Software, 2006, Marketing Plan Pro 6.0. Palo Alto, California. Retrieved May 26, 2006, from http://www.paloalto.com/ps/mp/?CFID=1181365&CFTOKEN=1572385 3dba44657-7605AB31-A3B0-0DE1-D66FDA589 B4866FC)

Marketers suggest reviewing the opportunities and threats first, and then moving on to the strengths and weaknesses (Figure 12–5).

SWOT: Strengths and Weaknesses Assessment

Strengths and weaknesses are Internal factors and important to determine how (or if) the practice can manage the opportunities and threats. Strengths can be anything that will increase market share or financial performance whereas weaknesses are internal problems that can reduce the market share or the financials. Strengths and weaknesses are more of an internal qualitative analysis, but consist of issues which the practitioner is more familiar. Especially in marketing, closeness to the issues sometimes clouds judgment. Often the practitioner is too close to the issues and has difficulty seeing some of the marketing issues. Caution must be exercised that this closeness to the issues does impact on the analysis and presents a clear picture of the strengths and weaknesses. Analysis of these internal factors is essential and should center on:

■ The practice's operational leadership, how the practice effectively operates in the community.
■ The financial strength of the practice to combat the threats and take advantage of the opportunities observed.
■ Practices physical capabilities, large enough facility, equipment, and so forth.
■ Responsiveness of workforce in the practice, enough people, motivation, and so forth.

SWOT planning is conducted to gain knowledge of the competitive environment and to facilitate a plan of attack for going after the competition's business as well as the new business that might go

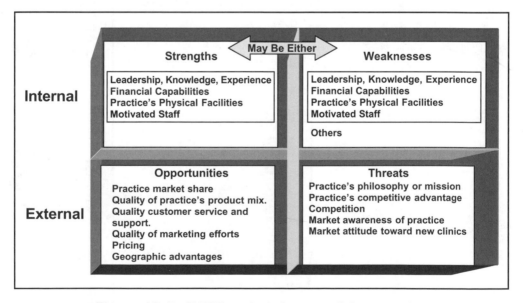

Figure 12–5. SWOT analysis for an audiology practice.

either way. How is the competition different from the practice to be marketed? What is offered by the practice that is not available in the competitive clinic? What does the competition do better or worse than your practice?

SWOT: Opportunities Assessment

The analysis of opportunities includes a review of problem-solving, product use cycles, creative methods of providing services, or ideal scenarios. As opportunities are external to the practice analysis review of the opportunities should center on market oriented factors such as:

- Practice market share
- Practice's ability to meet the needs and trends of the market.
- Value the practice brings to the target market.
- Quality of the practice's product.
- Quality of the practice's customer service and support.
- Quality/effectiveness of past promotions and other marketing efforts
- Pricing in the practice compared to others for the value obtained.
- The practice's geographic or other service advantages.

Both the threats and opportunities should utilize as much data as possible as they are external factors to the practice. These are concerns that may or may not arise, but they can be a major problem if not considered as part of the analysis.

SWOT: Threat Assessment

While conducting the SWOT analysis, Obringer (2006) suggests some general areas of investigation that can direct the assessment of threats facing the practice.

When reviewing the threats at least the following should be considered:

- Practice's philosophy or mission?
- The practice product (both goods and services) features, benefits, or quality?
- The competitive advantage of the practice? (Is there a competitive advantage?)
- How the services are conducted, patient and referral source satisfaction.
- Practice pricing structures? Are the goods and services of this practice priced much higher or lower than the competition?
- Target market's awareness of your practice and its services?
- Target market's attitudes toward the audiology, hearing aids, and new referral sources?
- Target market's brand loyalty to your practice?
- Competition's activities? (New product launches, price changes, new companies, etc.)
- These areas of investigation offer the audiologist a good start in the review of the practice and its place in the market and the possible threats to be encountered.

The Competitive Analysis

When reviewing the practice and its ability to stand up against the competition, Harrison and St. John (2004) indicate that there are four distinct areas that can lead to competitive advantage (Figure 12–6).

1. *Financial Resources*—include excellent cash flow, a strong balance sheet, and superior past performance.

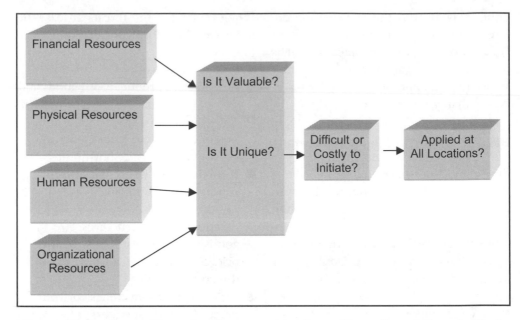

Figure 12–6. Competitive advantage considerations. (From *Foundations in Strategic Management* [p. 47], by J. Harrison and C. St. John, 2004, Dayton, OH: Thomson Learning. Copyright Thomson Learning. Adapted with permission.)

2. *Physical Resources*—include the physical premises of the practice, the atmosphere, location, parking, equipment, and other physical parameters of the practice.

3. *Human Resources*—include management capability, well-trained and motivated staff, and doctoral level professionals with certification to ensure the best possible experience for patients.

4. *Organizational Resources*—the organization that has been around for a time will have a reputation or a well-known "brand" that has been presented to the community in the past. The clinic might be known for its competence, products, excellent customer service, flexibility, and other specifics of operation that cause them to stand out.

Other components of the situation analysis involve developing some specific keys to success while reviewing critical issues that must be considered, analyzed, and surmounted. Additionally, situation analysis involves the specific media channels in which these issues will be addressed as well as macroenvironment or economic conditions of the area in which the practice resides.

Developing a Marketing Strategy

Berry and Wilson (2004) indicate that strategy is focus. In audiology practice, there is usually too much to do with too little resources, it is essential to focus on specific targets within the market. These targets can be patients of a certain age, hearing loss, or demographic situation. Patients often say, "I get so much mail from hearing aid places, how do they know that I have a hearing loss?" Obviously, this is the competition sending their marketing material to a specific age group (a targeted market segmentation) with a high chance that a member of the household has a hearing loss.

Marketing is most successful when priorities are established and focus is sharpened. If there are too many priorities, the marketing objectives and the branding of the practice will never be accomplished. The limited resources of audiology practice make it necessary to maximize the profit generated by the marketing effort. An example of this focus defining a demographic of interest then identifying a specific audiometric configuration, degree, or type of loss for a specific hearing instrument with new technology is focusing the marketing effort for maximum attention. No matter what the media, when a message goes to those that are most ready to hear it, the results are much greater.

In the development of a focused marketing strategy, it is essential that audiologists understand the difference between features and benefits. Kotler (2001) and Krarup (2001) have indicated that consumers purchase benefits, not merely product features. For example, a hearing evaluation is not simply an assessment of hearing; the patient is purchasing information about their hearing difficulties. Patients do not buy directional microphones they seek the benefit of better hearing capabilities in noisy environments due to the benefits of direction microphones or microphone arrays.

Generally, Obringer (2006) summarizes the critical components of a marketing plan as:

■ Research and analysis are critical because they lead to identifying the target audience, as well as its strengths, weaknesses, threats, and, most importantly, opportunities.

■ Knowing the threats and opportunities the practice faces helps to realistically set sales goals and objectives.

■ Knowing your opportunities, target audience, and sales goals will present the information required to set marketing goals to take advantage of the opportunities and meet the sales goals.

■ Knowing the marketing objectives will net the information necessary to set positioning, pricing, distribution, and other marketing strategies.

■ Having marketing strategies set will deliver a road map to set up the tactical elements of your marketing plan, such as advertising, promotions, branding, packaging, and so forth, items that must be tailored to specific markets.

■ Once tactical elements are determined, creative elements, budgets, and calendars can be organized.

Probably the most important component of any marketing effort is to track its effectiveness. This is an evidence-based section that requires assessment of the marketing program by defining the important items to be tracked and evaluated. For example, numbers of instruments dispensed in the first 90-day period after implementation of a particular section of the marketing plan can be tabulated and compared to a similar period prior to instituting the new marketing plan. Another evidence-based example would be to ask each patient at the reception desk if they had heard about the practice before their friend or physician referred them for hearing care. Patients are willing to relate their experiences. If they had read an ad or heard about the practice from another source prior to their referral, they will be forthcoming in their response to your inquiry.

Advertising Options for Audiology Practitioners

Audiologists can choose from a number of methods of advertising that are appropriate to the specific makeup of a particular practice. Here are some methods of advertising that have been used in audiology practices:

Advertising Specialty Item

These specialty items are often great awareness reminders for your patients and others. They can be issued after the hearing examination or included in promotional mailings. Specialty items include items such as refrigerator magnets, rolodex cards, coffee cups, pens, or pencils with logos and practice information.

Articles and Columns

Articles in the newspaper and local magazines are important for image, and brand awareness of the practice, and they provide a forum for your specialized expertise as an audiologist. The practice manager should take every opportunity to place the name of the practice in front of the public at all times. A method of obtaining this type of advertising is to offer routine press releases to the local press or by talking with your newspaper advertising representative and have him or her seek insertion of your article into the main body of the newspaper or in a special advertising section. Audiology practitioners have leverage with the paper if a regular advertiser. As May is Better Hearing and Speech Month, newspapers are looking for articles about communication disorders and hearing loss in the months of April, May, and June. Other months or weeks are devoted to specific yet related topics. Hearing and cognition are closely intertwined; National Alzheimer's Week would be a good opportunity for an article on the effects of hearing loss in dementia. Christmas time brings noisy toys and an article about noise-induced hearing loss and prevention would be appropriate (Sidebar 12–3).

Billboards

Not for everyone and extremely local, billboards represent an innovative type advertising opportunity for the practice. Billboards are most frequently used in isolation for the awareness of a particular practice. Personalizing the billboard with staff pictured in white coats near equipment will lend to the branding of the practice as a professional and technologically advanced site for hearing and balance care.

Sidebar 12–3
TO EAR-BUD OR NOT TO EAR-BUD: HOW TO AVOID PERMANENT HEARING LOSS

There have been a number of articles appearing in newspaper and magazines and on several Internet sites recently about the effects of high sound levels delivered through ear-level receivers. Each item discusses noise-induced hearing loss and offers recommendations about how to protect your hearing and how to use earphones and "ear-buds" (ear canal insert speakers) without causing permanent hearing loss. The good news—the new ear-bud speakers provide a wonderfully clear and clean signal: This is high fidelity at a technologic sophistication never heard before. The bad news—the sound pressure levels, the decibels that can be reached with personal music systems and ear-bud style speakers, rival damaging sound levels from jackhammers, chain saws, and loud rock concerts at or near 115 to 120 decibels.

It is not just younger people who are at risk for hearing loss. Runners, readers, restaurant workers, bikers, truck drivers, and others are using insert earphones to listen to music, talk shows, or Spanish lessons at levels that can cause permanent hearing loss. It doesn't matter whether it's Beethoven or Black Sabbath, high sound levels delivered through high fidelity earphones or ear-buds will cause hearing loss if precautions (and common sense) are not used consistently.

Your hearing is very important. Helen Keller said " . . . blindness separates you from things, hearing loss separates you from people." Here are four simple ways to protect your hearing while enjoying your personal music system:

Turn It Down

If a person next to you can hear your music, the volume is too high: If you cannot hear a person within five feet, the volume is too high. It is unsafe to drive when using any form of earphones and may be illegal in some states: Should you choose to wear earphones while driving, the volume is too high if you are unable to hear your turn signals. Just as joggers using earphones cannot hear bicycles coming from behind, loud volume settings can mask sirens and other signals that could help avoid an accident. Best suggestion: Do not turn the volume control beyond 50% of the available volume control rotation—at any time.

Give Your Ears a Break

The louder the volume, the less time it will take to permanently damage hearing. Best suggestion: Take a break while wearing your personal music system; for every two hours, take at least a half hour silence break. Be careful, silence might become addictive! Audiologists are not yet able to predict who will be more likely to develop hearing loss from exposure to loud sounds. As such, everyone is considered equally susceptible to noise-induced hearing loss and everyone should take a break from his or her earphones.

Use Hearing Protection

If you are in noise that requires you to raise your voice above the noise, you are in a situation that could damage your hearing. Using earplugs and/or muffs consistently when in loud noise will reduce the likelihood of permanent hearing loss. This is true at work or home, at NASCAR events or loud concerts. Recognize that personal music system "ear buds" are not designed to reduce noise levels. They cannot be used for hearing protection. Never use your personal music system in the presence of other loud noise. For example, if you are riding a lawnmower and using your personal system, you will likely turn the music levels well above the potentially damaging noise levels from the lawn mower. Best suggestion: Use hearing protection in noise at all times to limit your total exposure time to loud sounds.

See an Audiologist for an Evaluation

If you suspect hearing loss or are experiencing "dull hearing" or ringing in your ears (tinnitus) after exposure to loud sounds, make an appointment to see an audiologist for a comprehensive hearing examination. The audiologist will discuss the findings and recommend appropriate measures to improve or conserve your hearing. He or she will provide your family doctor with a complete report of findings and recommendations.

May Is Better Hearing and Speech Month

The national organization for speech-language pathologists (SLPs) has fostered May as Better Hearing and Speech Month to focus on issues such as noise-induced hearing loss. May is only one month. As harmful noise levels are in our communities and available via a multitude of opportunities for both children and adults, the job of hearing conservation and education about the effects of noise exposures must be considered a 12-month job for parents, SLPs, educators, and industry and recreation professionals. Peace and quiet: Emphasize the latter and enjoy the former!

For more information, including items appropriate for classroom use, explore the following links:

http://www.hearingconservation.org (best resource for noise and protection)

http://www.hearingconservation.org/rs_forKids.html (great classroom resource)

http://www.audiology.org (professional home of audiologists)

http://www.audiology.org/professional (go to; hearing conservation)

http://www.audiology.org/news/20060330.pdf

http://www.cdc.gov/niosh/topics/noise (great resource and definitions)

Brochures and Circulars

Practice brochures should form the advertising and public relations cornerstone of your practice. Brochures must be well done and printed on high-quality, glossy paper. A professional designer should be consulted to maximize the message and imagery to be included in your practice brochure and weave these messages into the marketing mix offered by the practice. Practice brochures should be issued to every new patient coming into your office. They will serve as calling cards and sources of information for potential patients, potential referral sources, and when a reporter calls inquiring about a story. They should be "high end" and should be displayed in as many offices as possible throughout your particular demographic. Many primary care providers will simply hand your brochure to their patients and instruct them to call the office for an appointment. Practice brochures are powerful tools. Health care professionals and other referral sources will judge your practice on what is most immediately available making the practice brochure extremely important to the marketing mix (Berry & Wilson, 2004). Your practice will be judged on the message and images created in your practice brochure.

Web Sites

Web sites are an essential component of contemporary audiology practice. As the "Baby Boomer" generation reaches maturity, visibility on the Internet will become more important as more patients, potential patients and referral sources visit Internet sites before considering professional services, purchasing hearing instruments, or considering other health care-related products such as eyewear or glucometers for immediate blood sugar levels. Your practice Web site opens your doors to the community-at-large. Virtual marketing should help to create the image of the practice and clarify the services and products available through your practice and the professional staff. Staff information should include information such as degrees and experience, particular areas of expertise, as well as items that will "personalize" the particular staff member's participation in the practice.

The Web site should set forth the menu of clinical services provided and information about hearing instruments and the hearing aid fitting process from initial hearing examination to instrument fitting and subsequent follow-up visits. Additionally, the messages on the site should be woven into the marketing program with the same messages and visuals that are offered elsewhere, that is, the practice brochure, print media ads, and so forth. The practice Web site should also offer educational information about the ear, hearing loss, and assessment and treatment of balance disorders. If the practice has a referral base from physicians, it might even be beneficial to have a physician page where information of interest to referral sources is relayed efficiently.

The Web site should be easy to remember and relate to your practice as best as possible as it is the practice's distinct location in cyberspace. As Web site registration has increased at a phenomenal pace, creative Web site addresses using terms "hearing," "care," "aids," "associates," "professional," and the like are less available. New doors are opening with the issuance of newer suffix locations such as ".net" or ".biz."

The practice Web site should be custom designed by designers that can capture the "feel" of the practice and make it stand out from the competition. There are Web site hosting groups that provide server hosting and a formulaic design strategy. Although most of these often look very much alike, the information is different practice-to-practice. Although these sites are less costly and provide an organized place for patients to find audiologists, it is important to stand out in the arena that is cyberspace.

Those coming to the Web site address for the first time (unique hits) must be quickly motivated to deepen their search for the information they are seeking. Web site designers are knowledgeable in arranging the topography of the Web site to maximize unique hits. They will design the site relative to the practice goals and objectives. The site can be informational, educational, or geared to getting new patients in the doors for hearing evaluation. The site developers may visit the practice, review practice brochures, and provide recommendations for integration of the messages offered to the market for better use of the eCommerce format. They may even suggest that you put a virtual tour or video on the site to offer some personalization to the experience. After a few iterations and modifications, the site will become a space that is unique to your practice.

Classified Advertising

Although classified advertising sections are not usually the place that consumers go for audiologic services. They can be used for retrieving a few hearing-impaired consumers for the trial of a specific product, or if the clinic is conducting a research project. These are an inexpensive source of patients for these procedures.

Coupons

Staab (1992) suggests that coupons be used cautiously when they are attached to reducing the price of hearing instruments or services. Patients may suspect that the original pricing was set too high for purposes of using promotional coupons. Coupons can be effective depending on their use. For example, if a goal is to have members of the practice's existing hearing instrument patient database return for a visit, coupons offering a pack of batteries, hearing instrument cleaning, and hearing screening (to assess changes in sensitivity that might need re-evaluation) for a nominal fee will likely produce surprising numbers of returnees. To be optimally effective, coupons should be tied to a reasonable marketing goal. Possible outcomes from this particular coupon-based promotion to the existing database would be hearing examination, hearing instrument repair, or the need to consider new hearing instruments depending on the age and operational status of the instruments in use.

In the promotion section, coupons must be utilized cautiously so as not to give the impression that the regular price was too high. When used effectively coupons can get consumers through the door generating new business and new customers. Once the customers are there, then the practice needs to give them a reason to return.

Product Demonstrations

Demonstrations work best in a place where perspective patients are already gathered such as trade shows or health fairs. This offers a chance for the patient to see what the device can do for them in a relaxed, social environment. Demonstrations within the practice, as in a trial period of amplification use for a specified time period, are not uncommon and enable the patient and those around him to evaluate the efficacy and communication improvements to be expected with advanced hearing instrument technology.

Direct Mail

Direct mail marketing has a response rate of 0.5 to 1% of the number mailed directly to a specifically tailored list of recipients. The key to direct mail solicitation is in defining the demographic of the intended group. With the rise of the Internet, direct mail sales of over-the-counter hearing instruments have resulted in greater numbers of mail order instrument sales. It is more common today than in any other period to have a patient schedule an appointment for an earmold impression to be sent with their check to a mail order house. Direct mail hearing aids are illegal in the United States in all states except Illinois. It is no accident that the largest direct mail hearing instrument sales group sends their products throughout the United States and the world from Illinois.

Direct-Response Radio and Television

Unless the audiologist is an invited guest, these shows are effective but expensive. A Saturday morning talk show about hearing health care every other week for 5 to 6 months can cost upward of $20,000.00 depending on the broadcast market. Often the practice can be invited to these talk shows and asked to make a presentation, thereby making these invitations a substantial bargain and well worth the time.

Exhibits and Fairs

This is a good source of prospective patients. Selecting the right health fair is critical and should always consider the demographic of the attendees. These fairs are an opportunity to present the practice to the public face-to-face and eye-to-eye. Be prepared to offer some sort of demonstration, presentation, or give-away to get attention and draw participants to your booth space.

Magazine Advertisements

Local magazines are a good place to present a high-end message. It is a good idea to try to get an article in the magazine and place the ad in close proximity to the article. This reinforces the fact that you wrote the article and refers to your brand of audiology to the consumers.

Newsletters

Newsletters are effective tools to communicate with your patients and prospective patients and referral sources. They should contain updates on hearing instrument technology, highlight important regulatory changes or changes in insurance coverage, and should provide information about the front office and professional staff. In Audiology practice marketing to existing patients is a major source of revenue and the newsletter is one of the most efficient

methods of communicating with the existing customer base. It not only breeds good communication but also substantial word of mouth advertising.

Newspaper Advertisements

Long a staple in practice advertising, the focus of the newspaper ad has centered around two distinct topics; price and time-sensitive deadlines to action; however, not all newspaper ads have those goals. Getting the practice recognized in the community as a center of excellence, a location where professional services prevail, and where primary care providers send their patients will also have an impact on newspaper readers. Of course, the price shoppers will respond to "special pricing offers" and if those are patients you would like to target for your particular practice then newspaper ads pushing price is the way to go. If, however, you would like to have patients coming to your office to participate in a continuum of professional, rehabilitative care, your advertising presence in the newspaper will look vastly different from price-based ads. At east initially, it is good to have a marketing consultant assist in the generation of a few good ads that can be placed strategically, no matter your marketing strategy.

Personal Letters

Personal letters are appropriate to referral sources, prospective patients, and those previously evaluated but who have decided not to act on your recommendations to consider the use of amplification. The initial mailing should be accompanied by your practice brochure or specific brochure about hearing instruments or hearing rehabilitation. The letters must be brief, no longer than three short paragraphs.

Radio Advertisements

Radio is an expensive yet strong and vital medium that can brand your practice in a very short time. Using clever, humorous, and testimonial spots, the listener can develop an image of your practice and what to expect from a visit. As consumers spend a lot of time in their cars and offices, the expense is often worth the exposure. In radio, the station will usually help the practice manager organize a radio marketing program, preparing spots and suggesting communication formats that have worked in the past for other businesses. Testimonials work particularly well in radio advertising where a locally prominent person discusses their experiences in the practice. These testimonials further brand the practice as the place to go for hearing care.

Educational Seminars

No obligation seminars are another form of advertising that can be used effectively. The concern with this type of advertising is that it must be conducted in an environment conducive to presenting the material in a nonobligatory way in a classroom-style arena.

Signage

It sounds simple, but signs are a true form of advertising. Each time the consumer passes the practice, or looks for the practice good signage is necessary. The sign outside the practice is basic communication with a wide expanse of potential consumers. It presents what you do at that location and should be professional in the truest sense of the word to reinforce the professional "brand" of service delivery available at that particular location.

Telemarketing

Although used in the hearing industry, it is only typically utilized by the high-pressure sales operations. Telemarketing is the offering of information by paid individuals using a script about products or services via the telephone to special targeted lists of consumers. Berry and Wilson (2004) indicate that more and more people view this as an invasion of their privacy. With increasing public resistance and the advent of "no-call" lists, telemarketing is not a technique to be considered as a viable marketing alternative.

Television

Much less expensive than in the immediate past, television, especially local cable channels, offer an opportunity to visually engage potential patients.

Internet Advertising

Although coming up first in an Internet search for hearing care services may not seem important to your practice in your local market, you must recognize that those in your local area seek out information pathways via Google and other search engines in greater numbers than those reading papers, listening to the radio, or watching television. Mothers interested in having their child's hearing evaluated or seniors wondering what is available for the communication difficulties they are experiencing will be pleased to see your practice come up on their Google (or other) search.

Yellow Pages

Yellow Pages used to be the primary advertising location for hearing care. If you were not listed, no one would know that you existed. Although not nearly as necessary as in the past, smaller advertising with less display is now the trend as fewer people consult the Yellow Pages with the advent of cell phone, and Internet access. One trend that helps the Yellow Pages ads is the tying of the Yellow Pages to the Internet with Web pages, phone numbers, and other specifics only offered by the various phone companies to keep their Yellow Page-customers.

Experiential Marketing

This is a new marketing concept that allows the consumer to experience the product before they take it home. For example in the audiology practice, this would include a room that has a capability to project large images of manufacturer's audio/video presentations that attempt to have the patient involved in the listening experience. These programs are readily available and can be utilized in conjunction with the mounted speakers and amplifiers to create a place where the patient can see if they can hear well, before they ever leave the practice.

Kotler's 8 Steps to Designing and Managing Marketing Communications

To summarize marketing and marketing plans Kotler (2001) suggests that an efficient design and management of marketing communications requires remembering the following eight steps:

- Identify the target audience.
- Determine the communication objective.
- Design the message.
- Select the communication channel.
- Establish a marketing communications budget.
- Develop and manage the marketing communications mix.
- Measure the results of the marketing effort.
- Manage the integration of the market communications process.

Kyle (2006) reminds practitioners that a marketing plan is more than something you "have to do" each year. It is the framework on which your company's marketing success depends and a guide to follow until it is time to replan. As you begin the planning process, it is necessary to keep the following practice elements in mind:

- Be strategic.

There are many good marketing programs that will be offered to your practice. The job of the practice manager is, through a planning process, to determine which of those marketing programs makes strategic sense. The marketing plan can then help you stay focused throughout the year and will result in achieving your business goals. It is a good idea to start with the big-picture objectives then define general strategies that support those goals. The right actions and programs for a particular clinic can vary dramatically, depending on the goals and strategies. Consequently, strong strategic analysis behind your marketing plan can make a dramatic difference in the success of your marketing efforts.

■ Understand that feeling uncertain is normal.

Feeling overwhelmed or incredibly confused at the beginning of the planning process is expected. The purpose of planning is to find your way to the best actions for the business. As you progress toward the end of the analysis, the best programs to include in *your* marketing plan to grow *your* particular business will become clearer. Consider seeking the advice of a practice management specialist or marketing consultant who will help focus your efforts relative to the goals you have established for your practice.

■ Be realistic.

Optimism is a plus in marketing the practice, but understands the clinic's limitations. A small or one-person practice can implement only a fraction of the marketing programs larger operations. So, choose programs carefully and concentrate on seeing them through as the year progresses.

■ Stay focused.

The marketing plan is only as good as your implementation. Keeping your "eye on the ball" rather than spreading too thin and implementing poorly can make the difference between profit and loss.

■ Watch the budgets.

For each marketing program included in your plan, spend some extra time and collect real-world costs to use in the budget. At implementation, stick to the budget and the plan to avoid the temptation to throw more money into the mix should a lull in traffic occur in the middle of the plan schedule.

■ Put measurements in place.

Evidence-based practice management requires that assessment dictates the direction of many clinical and business actions in a practice. Certainly evaluating marketing programs is a prime example of evidence-based management. If your plan is not performing well based on your measurements, the plan should be recalled, reconsidered, and re-appropriated.

■ Don't forget the four marketing Ps.

Promotion gets a lot of attention but pricing, place, and product are equally important to the bottom line. Consider adding new or improved products/services to the mix, evaluating pricing strategies, and improving distribution, along with advertising and promotional campaigns.

References

American Academy of Audiology. (2000). *Position statement for hearing impaired seeking treatment.* Reston, VA.

Berry T., & Wilson, D. (2004). *On target: The book on marketing plans.* Eugene, OR: Palo Alto Publishing.

Berry, T., & Wilson, D. (2006). *Market Pro Plus (6.0).* Palo Alto, CA: Palo Alto Software. http://www.biz.plan.com

Borden, N. (1994). The concept of the marketing mix. *Journal of Advertising Research, 4*(6), 2–7.

Churchill, G., & Brown, T. (2004). *Basic marketing research*. Mason, OH: South-Western.

Churchill, G., & Peter, J. (2002). *Marketing: Creating Value for Customers* (2nd ed., p. 15). Burr Ridge IL: Irwin/McGraw-Hill.

D'Alessandro, D. (2001). *Brand warfare: 10 rules for building the killer brand* (p. xvi). New York: McGraw-Hill.

Day, G. (1994). Capabilities of a market-driven organizations. *Journal of Marketing, 58*(4), 37–52.

Glaser, R. (2006, May 13). To ear-bud or not to ear-bud: How to avoid permanent hearing loss. *Dayton Daily News*.

Hansen, K. (2006). Successful practice branding. *Advance for Audiologists, 8*(1), 53–554.

Harrison, J., & St. John, C. (2004). *Foundations in Strategic Management*. Dayton, OH: Thompson Learning.

Killion, M. (2006, March). *Over-the-counter hearing aid debate*. Presentation to the American Academy of Audiology, Minneapolis, MN.

KnowThis.com (2006). *How to write marketing plans*. Retrieved April 30, 2006, from http://www.knowthis.com/tutorials/marketing/marketingplan1/0.htm

Kotler, P. (2001). *Marketing management*. Upper Saddle River, NJ: Prentice-Hall.

Krarup, N. (2001). Personal communication. September 11, 2001, Bern, Switzerland.

Kyle, B. (2006). *Tips to calm marketing panic*. Retrieved May 7, 2006, from http://www.websitemarketingplan.com

Lauterhorn, R. (1990, February). Marketing litany: 4Ps passé; C-words take over. *Advertising Age*, p. 26.

McCall, K., & Dunlop, D. (2004) Marketing a practice. In B. Kaegy & M. Thomas (Eds.), *Essentials of physician practice management* (pp. 394–409). San Francisco: John Wiley & Sons.

Murphy, P., & Ennis, B. (1986). Classifying products strategically. *Journal of Marketing, 7*, 24–42.

Nagle, T., & Holden, R. (2004). *The strategy and tactics of pricing* (3rd ed.). Upper Saddle River, NJ: Prentice-Hall.

Obringer, L. (2006). What is marketing. *How stuff works*. Retrieved May, 1, 2006, from http://money.howstuffworks.com/marketing-plan1.htm

Porn, L. (2004). Developing a business plan. In B. Keagy & M. Thomas (Eds.), *Essentials of physician practice management* (pp. 357–358). San Francisco: John Wiley & Sons.

Smriga, D. (2004). Are we asleep at the wheel? The future of audiology private practice in America. *ADA Feedback, 15*(4), 7–15.

Staab, W. (1992). Sales promotion for office traffic control. In W. Staab (Ed.), *Applied hearing instrument marketing* (pp. 201–254). Livonia, MA: National Institute for Hearing Instrument Studies.

Traynor, R. (2006). *The basics of marketing for audiologists*. In R. Traynor. (Ed.), *Seminars in Hearing, 27*(1), 38–47.

Wood-Young, T. (2000). *Intuitive selling*. Colorado Springs CO: WY Publishing.

13

Practice Management Considerations in a University Audiology Center

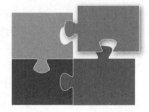

GAIL M. WHITELAW, Ph.D.

Introduction

It may seem unusual to find a chapter on the management of a university-based audiology clinic in a text on strategic practice management targeting profit-based practice models. Historically, university clinics have been based on a model in which they are viewed as a "teaching laboratory." In this lab model, services were provided at no charge or at a significantly reduced fee and often only during periods that coincided with the university calendar. The focus in this model was ensuring that students in audiology programs had subjects on whom to "practice" their clinical skills.

However, the changing landscapes of both the profession of audiology and of higher education herald the need for a transition from this "lab model" to a model that recognizes the University clinic as a business. The demands of Doctor of Audiology (Au.D.) programs require that university audiology clinics provide breadth and depth of clinical experiences delivered in an environment that prepares the Au.D. student to enter the profession of audiology. A not-for-profit mantra of "no margin, no mission" must be the guiding principle for university audiology clinics, both to provide a clinical education model appropriate for the Au.D. student and to survive in the changing university environment. This principle supports a strong clinical education model with the clinic being a critical entry point to prepare students for the demands of the profession of audiology both now and into the future. As suggested by Novak (2004), it is imperative that there is consistency of clinical preparation for students entering the profession, so that the transition from university audiology clinic to clinical sites that partner with the university support the development of the knowledge and skills required entering the profession. This statement makes the assumption that the university clinic will be the first clinical placement for the Au.D. student, an assumption that is certainly accurate for the vast majority of current Au.D. programs. Therefore, the university audiology clinic must be an environment that sets the standard to nurture the entry of young audiologists into their profession.

Funding and Support

The landscape for funding of higher education has also changed significantly, as universities face rising costs and declining support (Lundy, 2006). Universities are viewed as businesses and administrators are charged to be fiscally responsible and there has been a trend toward "responsibility based budgeting" within the university structure. This type of budgeting system requires cost shifting so that costs incurred by an individual unit (e.g., Department or Clinic) are assigned to that unit. In the past, the cost of "education" was typically borne by the university, usually in a centralized model. The university, as an entity, received tuition revenues from students, but in turn, covered the full cost of the education of the student. In the current model, the differential cost of education, such as additional costs incurred in a clinical education program, is assigned to the individual "unit" providing the education, such as the Department or the Clinic. In this decentralized model, the audiology clinic is responsible for covering costs associated with its operation and, presumably, the revenue generated by the audiology clinic is "earned" by the clinic and can be assigned to the costs of running the business. Any revenue that exceeds cost, or the audiology clinic profit per se, should be available for the clinic to expand programs and services, provide care for the indigent, or purchase equipment. However, it may be difficult to generate a profit in this environment due to the demands and expectations of the university. Costs allocated to the clinic may be similar to those of practices in the private sector; leasehold and other space-related costs, insurance costs, specific facility charges, and other overhead costs. In addition, audiology clinics housed within universities are often viewed as "earnings units," with the expectation that the clinic has both the ability and responsibility to generate revenue to the point of being self-sustaining. In many university settings, this business model for the audiology clinic is a paradigm shift from the past. It is, however, clearly a trend that will continue into the foreseeable future (Lundy, 2006). This shift coincides with changes in professional preparation in audiology to result in the need for the university clinic to be based on a business model.

The Changing Landscape for Service Provision in the University Setting

The strategic management tenets identified in this text certainly apply to the management of a university audiology clinic. Effective management is a critical topic; however, a review of the literature suggests a dearth of information specific to this practice setting. A chapter on administration of speech-language-hearing programs within the university setting by Hardick and Oyer (1987) highlighted some of the same issues that are identified in this chapter. This chapter serves to emphasize the significant changes impacting the delivery of audiology services that have occurred since the time that chapter was written. The challenges of implementing a clinic technology platform, the ever changing human resource environment, and enhanced government regulation, as mandated in the privacy and security components of the Health Insurance Portability and Accountability Act (HIPAA), were not anticipated 20 years ago. This suggests the importance of developing a clinic model that emulates other practice settings, as the changes facing the university clinic are more similar to those in other practice settings than in the past, with this trend likely to continue.

The Council of Academic Programs in Communication Sciences and Disorders (CAPCSD) is an organization with a mission to support undergraduate and graduate programs in communication sciences and disorders. CAPCSD has as one of its goals to support the clinical education process; thus, the organization has an interest in both the university-based audiology clinic and the "town-gown" partnership between the University program and the community preceptors. A review of the proceedings of the annual meeting of Council of Academic Programs in Communication Sciences and Disorders (CAPCSD) for the past 10 years reveals articles on the topic of university clinics; however, the vast majority focus on the broader perspective of clinical education. These topics include changes in certification requirements, approaches to clinical supervision, or the focus of preparing future personnel to meet general requirements in the workplace (ASHA, 2000; CAPCSD, 2007). In addition, only four articles that deal exclusively with issues related to university clinic administration have been published among the nearly 200 articles that have appeared in the newsletter of ASHA's Special Interest Division Eleven: Administration and Supervision since its inception (ASHA, 2006).

This chapter focuses on the unique challenges and opportunities of running a practice within the university environment: including physical facilities, personnel, pricing of goods and services, and marketing.

Physical Facilities and the Practice of Audiology

The university setting provides a unique environment in which to develop and maintain an audiology practice In addition to the number of audiologists employed, number of patients served, and other services, such as speech-language pathology, available in the practice, a number of issues are distinctive in the university environment. The type of university, whether state funded or privately funded, can have a significant impact on the federal and/or state rules that govern the function of the clinic and types of funding support that may be available to support the clinic's mission. The college or "unit" in which the clinic is housed can have a significant impact on the practice. University clinics are located in a wide variety of units, including Colleges of Allied Medicine, Education, Social and Behavioral Sciences, Arts and Sciences, Optometry, and Medicine. In many cases, the audiology clinic may be the only clinical education program within the college, a lone "earnings unit" and/or facility providing patient care within the college. Deans of Colleges with backgrounds not related to audiology will often comment on the expense of clinical education, often without recognizing the benefits of the clinic to the department, college, or community.

University audiology clinics receive significant benefits from being housed within the university. These benefits may commonly include access to legal services, assistance with purchasing, fiscal management services, and marketing consultation. The clinic may benefit from the economy of scale available based on the size of the university and also the specialized knowledge and skills of those employed by the university. Specific benefits may include access to services that facilitate contract negotiation with knowledge specific to this setting, understanding of target marketing within the university community, and access to dis-

counts on office equipment and supplies based on the purchasing power of the university.

Challenges of Operating in the University Environment

The university environment can provide unique challenges to effectively operating an audiology practice. Choices that are available in other practice settings, such as location, signage, or decor of the office may not exist in the university setting. University clinics may be required to pay physical facilities assessment, similar to rent; however, they may have little ability to make decisions about the space and literally no ability to negotiate the amount charged for the space assigned. This also applies to the overhead rate charged by the university. Assuming the university audiology clinic operates on a business model, the clinic should expect to pay for the resources utilized. However, there must be a vehicle to negotiate. Information is power and the clinic director must know the cost per square foot for the "rent" charged and how these decisions are made by the university. The clinic director should carefully analyze the space needs for the clinic and ensure that the clinic is not paying for more space than is actually needed. In addition, space needs should be analyzed in terms of purpose of the space. If the space is used primarily for research or shared with department administration, only the actual space utilized for clinical activities should be counted in this process. This also requires that the Department Chair and/or College Dean understand the use of space and acts as an advocate in the space allocation process. In addition, the clinic may receive benefits from developing a coalition with other clinical education programs providing services on campus. This type of coalition may be either formal or informal and may include clinics such as those housed in optometry, psychology, and/or education. Such a partnership can provide leverage in discussions with the university related to rates or overhead and opportunities to educate university administrators about the breadth of clinical education.

As mentioned above, the university clinic location may be fixed. Most clinics are housed within their department, which limits choices of location on campus. Decisions are not likely to be based on patient need, but rather on where space is available, the location of the college in which the department is located, and other factors which do not address the needs of clinical service provision nor the population being served. In an era of privatization in higher education, some university clinics may be able to take advantage of opportunities to rent space off campus or generally think outside of the proverbial clinic location "box." An example of this would be the model at the University of Pittsburgh, which does not have an "in house" university audiology clinic, but utilizes partnerships throughout the Pittsburgh community. Au.D. students are placed in these sites and supervised by university employed preceptors, who fulfill the role of clinical supervisors for the university and in clinical service provision for the sites.

In addition, a program may raise funds through university development to build their own clinical facility or share with similar programs within a college. An example of this is the Bill Wilkerson Center for Otolaryngology and Commu-

nication Sciences at Vanderbilt University, designed to encourage interdisciplinary collaboration and research in all the speech, language, and hearing sciences, and otolaryngology specialties. The amount of funds required to build a facility along with space being at a premium in most universities are factors that would limit the feasibility of this model in most universities. In addition, most audiology programs in universities cannot easily move locations due to these types of constraints.

Patient Care Considerations in the University Audiology Clinic

Assuming that the clinic location is generally non-negotiable, a number of factors that impact patient care must be considered. On most campuses, parking is a valuable commodity. Parking generally reflects a delicate balance of supply and demand and the supply of available parking is often a significant distance from the location of the clinic. Universities have historically been designed to meet the needs of young adults for whom parking a distance from academic or recreational facilities may be less of a physical challenge than for clinic patients and their families. However, with changes in the demographics of higher education, demands for accessibility on campus, and an increased focus on consumerism on campuses, improvements in parking services are likely to occur. In addition, increases in on-line education and virtual classrooms even on traditional campuses suggest changes in demand for parking in the future. The current situation is generally the same on most college campuses: although physical access to the clinical facility may be appropriate, the distance from the parking area may be significant, parking options may be limited, or the parking area may present challenges in terms of related factors, including grading of walkway that take into account the clinical population served or signage that clearly marks the clinic. Parking may require that creative solutions, such as valet or dedicated parking options available only to audiology clinic patients, be implemented. These types of solutions can facilitate access to a clinic, but often come at a cost higher than would be negotiable in a private practice setting. In addition, if the clinic building is "landlocked" within a university campus, limited options may be available. In this case, the growth of the clinic may be constrained by how many patients may park to access the building at any given time. Obviously, it is critical to educate those in both administration and customer service at the university's Department of Transportation or Parking regarding the missions and functions of the clinic and the special needs of those seeking hearing and balance services at the clinic. Utilizing specially designated clinic spaces or spaces designated for those with disabilities can provide options that increase both access to the clinic and number of patients that can be accommodated. Patients may be able to access special parking permits or tokens to park in restricted areas or be able to access parking meters located close to the clinic. Patients, however, may be sensitive to the additional cost of parking, a factor which may be viewed as a negative in utilizing services at the university audiology clinic. Paying a parking meter to access services is consistently cited as the most frequent complaint on patient satisfaction surveys over the past 10 years in the author's clinic setting.

Other types of overhead assigned from the university may include building services, such as housekeeping/cleaning. As discussed earlier in this chapter, communication regarding the mission of the clinic, the patient population served, and consumer expectations are critical to successful management of a patient-centric practice within the structure of the university. University services, such as cleaning, are often hired as subcontractors based on a bidding process. The bidding criteria should include specifications for the specialized needs of the audiology clinic population, such as vacuuming after hours to minimize noise interference during audiometric testing or additional cleaning needs when serving young children. The audiology clinic director should participate in developing the bid criteria or communicate specific needs in working with janitorial subcontractors. In addition, the clinic director should participate in the evaluation of services provided as a criterion of the contract between the service provider and the university. This participation allows for clear communication regarding expectations of cleaning, providing a vehicle to document these expectations, and the ability to develop corrective actions if the criteria are not met. These corrective actions may include the ability to modify the contract or to hire a cleaning service independent of that provided by the university.

Personnel in the University Audiology Clinic

There are a number of personnel challenges that are unique to the university setting. First, the person that oversees the clinic may be a skilled clinical supervisor, researcher, or teacher, but may have little preparation for administrative and management demands of an audiology practice. This person may be selected based on seniority or as part of their "service load" within the department and have little knowledge, skill, or interest in running a business. A clinic director dedicated to managing a business helps to ensure both the fiscal success of the clinic and its strength in the clinical education process. It is important that both the personnel in the department and college understand the demands of running a practice and the unique skills and knowledge required to effectively administer this practice.

Administration of the Clinic

The university clinic director must have many of the same skills as an audiologist in private practice in functional areas such as marketing, finance, and human resource management. However, the clinic director may be constrained from making independent decisions available to those in private practice due to restrictions inherent in the university setting. Based on the university model, the clinic director may be required to utilize the skills and knowledge of others within the department, such as a fiscal officer, or employees within another unit, such as purchasing or business and finance. These employees may have little knowledge or interest in issues related to practice management, and the tasks required for clinical management may differ significantly from the skills required in a traditional university department. Bartlett, McNamara, and Peaper (2006) describe the balancing act of clinical education

demands with clinic operations demands in an era of shrinking resources in higher education. Their survey of clinic directors in university settings described personnel challenges including an inadequate number of clinical supervisors and inadequate or nonexistent clerical staff that are critical for managing a successful clinical practice.

In addition to the clinic director, audiologists are employed in university-based clinical settings. These audiologists may either have a role as a clinical supervisor or preceptor, as a direct service provider, or a hybrid of the two. Historically, services were only provided in the university audiology clinic when students were available and audiologists employed in this type of setting did not provide direct service. This trend has changed with consumer demand and the fact that hearing instruments do not stop functioning only on the university schedule. This requires that audiologists employed in university settings are not only knowledgeable in the process of clinical supervisor and clinical education, but also in the current practice of the profession. In many university medical center settings, a marketing slogan is related to the concept of "we practice what we teach," which characterizes the current trend for university-based audiology clinics. Another issue is how to address continuity in patient care, so that patients both understand that services are provided in a clinical education environment yet have their needs effectively and efficiently met. The scheduling of appointments must be as realistic as possible to strike a balance of providing the opportunity for clinical education yet to ensure that the patient's time is valued. These are challenges in the clinical education process and the audiology preceptor has to balance the importance of patient care with the demands of clinical education. Patients should be given the opportunity to request that clinical services be provided by a specific audiologist or Au.D. student, often in the case of a referral to the clinic, and every effort should be made to ensure that the patient will be followed by that individual. Although it is generally the audiology supervisor with whom the relationship will be established, it is also not unusual for patients to request a particular Au.D. student to provide continuity of care. The limitations of this type of schedule may discourage some patients from seeking services in the university clinic; however, others will see the benefits of participating in a clinical education model as of significant benefit. Just as with any practice setting, it is impossible to be all things to all patients and audiologists employed in this setting must capitalize on the strengths of the setting.

Guidelines for clinical supervision are evolving with changes in accreditation and certification guidelines. These changes require new approaches to supervision and new methods of assessing student performance, often developed by the audiologists employed as supervisors. Audiologists employed in the university may also be responsible for developing and nurturing partnerships with audiologists in the community who provide clinical supervision. In addition to their clinical responsibilities, university-based audiologists are often engaged planning the fourth-year preceptorship for Au.D. students, thus strengthening the "town-gown" partnership that is critical in preparing students for independent practice of the profession of audiology. The critical nature of this relationship cannot be underestimated and the importance of developing and maintaining strong relationships with community practioners to participate in the clinical education process is key to the future of the profession. As clinical education in audiology has moved from the Master's degree profession with a separate Clinical Fellowship Year or Professional Experience Year model to an intended four-year program the university has a significant role in developing this educational program. The clinical education program must follow a plan in which the university and preceptor enter into a relationship that is mutually beneficial and contributes positively to the student's educational program. To that end, university-based audiologists must make the professional contacts with preceptors and not rely on students to contact preceptors independently. In addition, preceptors must understand the mission and vision of the clinical education program and that they will participate in an educational partnership with student. Several programs have been developed that address these partnerships by integrating academic and clinical education across settings and providing training in being a mentor. These programs include Mentoring Au.D.'s (MAuDs), a program sponsored by the Illinois Academy of Audiology, and the preceptor education model developed by the Northern Ohio Audiology Coalition (NOAC), the joint partnership between the University of Akron, Kent State University, and the Cleveland Clinic.

Clinical Faculty Rank

Many universities have a clinical faculty rank that provides an appropriate framework for hiring, retaining, and promoting those employed in clinical education. This classification differentiates from the traditional faculty ranks, for which the requirements may have little flexibility to recognize the clinical education component of these positions and recognize teaching and research as the primary criteria for evaluation. Other universities have administrative and professional classifications for those employed in the clinic. Although this model may provide a mechanism that reflects the types of skills required for service provision, it can fail to recognize the critical role that these professionals have in the student's education. An important consideration in this discussion is whether the audiologist is on a traditional university 9-month contract or employed year round. Obviously, the need for 12-month employment of audiologists in a university setting is critical, as most practices cannot be successful if they cannot meet the ongoing needs of patients, which are full time and year round. Most Au.D. programs operate year round with required courses offered during summer quarter/semester.

In addition to audiologists/clinical supervisors, appropriate support personnel are as critical in the university setting as they are in the private practice setting. These may include a clinic business/financial manager, billing personnel, clinic secretary, and/or office manager. In some settings, these roles may be filled by one person, and in some cases, a person who has other job responsibilities within the department and the clinic responsibilities are "add-ons." Every effort should be made to ensure that the clinic has dedicated personnel with knowledge and skill sets appropriate to advance the mission of the clinic. Just as in the private practice setting, training of front office personnel is critical. The number of sup-

port personnel, and therefore the need for a generalist and/or specialists, is driven by a number of factors, including the number of patients served, the amount of revenue generated, and the size of the program. All personnel should have appropriate training in both their functional areas, such as accounts payable or receivables, and in university procedures related to these areas. A cost-effective approach for expanding support personnel may be hiring graduate assistants from among students enrolled in the Au.D. program. These graduate student assignments may include checking in hearing instrument deliveries, scheduling appointments, or assisting with processing insurance claims. The employees, because of their status as students, may bring skills and ideas to the work setting, such as technology savvy, that others in the clinic do not possess. In addition, they have knowledge of audiology. The benefit to the clinic is obvious; however, the student also obtains a more intimate understanding of business-related functions of audiology and an appreciation of attention to detail required in these functions. Hiring graduate assistants may be a cost allocated to the clinic budget or may be an option for the department to provide as a benefit to the clinic in partnering in the clinical education function.

Salary and benefits in most university settings are structured and lack flexibility. Some university employees, depending on their classification, may be members of unions so that benefits and working conditions are prescribed with minimal options. The clinic director may need to actively develop mechanisms that recognize audiologists and support staff for their productivity and service, which may include paying for continuing education opportunities, licensure and certification, and liability insurance. The challenge in the university audiology clinic is to elicit "buy in" from audiologists and support staff when the opportunities for "reward" are limited by the constraints of university policies that emphasize a didactic education model. As professional education in audiology evolves, it is important for the audiology clinic director and the administration of the department and college to advocate models that recognize the contributions of the clinical staff for productivity in the university clinic environment (e.g., patient satisfaction, revenue generation, and student outcomes are some possible measures that may reflect the staff contribution).

The option of housing a clinic that is established like a private practice or a faculty practice model is available in some university settings while prohibited in others (Windmill, Cunningham, & Preminger, 2004). A faculty practice is arguably a more effective clinical education model that emphasizes a business, due to increased autonomy afforded to the partners in the practice. Regardless of the relationship between the university and the practice, all university employees are required to sign Conflict of Interest statements. These statements should be reviewed carefully so that audiologists affiliated with the university understand the opportunities and limitations of their specific employment setting.

Issues Related to Clinical Education Activities in the University Clinic

A critical component of clinical education and personnel development in the university audiology clinic is the Au.D. student. For too long, the "corporate culture" of the university audiology clinic reflected that of a "teaching lab" referred to earlier in this chapter. Students may have had a relaxed approach to clinical service provision, assuming that they were "students who were learning in this process" and someone else, usually the audiology clinical supervisor, was the one responsible for assuring that the patient (often referred to as "client" in university clinics, particularly in the past) was well served, that the paperwork was filed appropriately, and that the clinical areas were clean and organized. As noted by McCarthy (2006), the Doctor of Audiology degree was developed in response to external factors including evolutions in health care, advances in information and technology, and the changing demographics of those requiring hearing and balance services. The Master of Arts degree was inadequate at preparing students academically or clinically to meet the escalating demands of the workplace; thus, the knowledge and skill sets were expanded to meet the needs of professional preparation (McCarthy, 2006).

It is imperative that university clinics challenge Au.D. students by defining clinical service broadly and by setting the expectation of professional behavior that is also modeled by the clinical staff. Generally not paid employees of the clinic in their clinical rotation (although a fourth-year placement may be in the university clinic based on a different model), every effort should be made for students to understand that they are to view their placement in the university clinic as that of an employee. Students must understand that placement in the university audiology clinic is a critically important segment of their professional preparation. This may require a number of paradigm shifts including those related to dress and behavior. The dress code must be clearly communicated and enforced for clinic employees and student clinicians alike. Students may be required to wear a lab coat and must wear a name tag clearly identifying their affiliation with the university audiology program and their role in the clinic as an Au.D. student. Au.D. students should have firm understanding of how to greet patients in an appropriate, professional manner. Students should have the opportunity to observe, develop, and execute skills related to conflict resolution with patients, counseling patients regarding the need for and acceptance of hearing instruments, and providing timely, effective, and efficient clinical services. Flexibility is certainly a cornerstone in the profession of audiology and should be an expectation that is nurtured in the university clinic.

As noted earlier in the chapter, continuity of patient care should be a focus for the audiology student placed in the university audiology clinic. In some university audiology clinics, student assignments are based on one's level in the program or clinical experience in a specific area, such as diagnostics or hearing instruments. In these cases, the student is assigned to a "diagnostic only" clinic during a semester or quarter. Although this may have good face validity as a clinical teaching model, there is no empirical evidence to support that this is the most effective model. From a patient-centric approach, a model which provides a broader training experience will yield better continuity of care. This provides a more realistic clinical education model and requires that the audiology supervisor/preceptor and student clinician work together as a team to meet the patient's needs.

The university clinic setting should allow students to develop the knowledge, skills, and values that will transfer to other clinical placements and to the practice of audiology. Au.D. students should understand their role on the "team" in the clinic by showing respect to the clinic staff and their colleagues. Students must see the clinic as their own and should treat the equipment, facility, patients, and staff with the same respect as if it were their own business. They should have a clear understanding of the policies and procedures of the clinic, as outlined in clinic manual or handbook. This handbook should be viewed as similar to an employee policy and procedures manual in a private practice setting and should outline expectations, policies, and protocols that apply to the Au.D.student. This handbook or manual should be reviewed by the university attorney to ensure it is consistent with university policies. A mechanism for documentation of clinic requirements outlined in the handbook, such as criminal background check, immunizations, training in HIPAA and/or universal precautions procedures, and annual liability insurance update, is necessary, along with a protocol to update this information on a regular basis. This documentation should be provided by the student and kept in a secured area.

The university clinic provides an excellent opportunity for students to learn about issues related to human resource management, even if discussed through hypothetical scenarios. At this point, most university clinics do not employ audiology assistants; however, it is likely that during their careers, audiologists currently being educated will be responsible for hiring, supervising, promoting, and terminating employees, including assistants. Peer supervision may provide an excellent mentoring opportunity and enhance patient care, as is implemented in clinical education in other fields (Williams, 1996). These areas of personnel management and supervision are appropriate topics for clinical seminars, courses within the program, or as part of a specialization that a student may choose to take as part of their degree. In addition to providing supervised clinical services within the university clinic environment, students may be given other assignments or projects related to their clinical education. Such projects may include development and publishing brochures and patient newsletters, participating in community education events, and maintaining a hearing instrument loaner stock and hearing-related informational materials. These types of projects may result in materials that can be utilized immediately by the student, provide templates for future reference, and represent a set of transferable skills that will be desirable to employers.

Just as students have a responsibility to the clinic, they have a right to expect certain types of support within the university clinic. Students must have access to equipment that provides the opportunity both to serve the patient population of the clinic and to learn new procedures and techniques. The number of individuals and relative inexperience of these individuals using clinical equipment should be considerations when purchasing equipment and budgeting for repair. The replacement cycle for equipment may differ from that in other practice settings due to these factors. The clinic and department should work together to allocate equipment costs associated with patient care and those costs associated with clinical education so that an equitable plan

for equipment calibration, repair, and replacement is developed. This also applies to associated materials and disposable accessories, such as electrodes.

If the expectation of the student is to view their position as an employee of the clinic, resources must be provided to support this approach. In the past, audiology students performed clinical responsibilities only related to direct patient care. Currently, the expectation is that student's should perform all aspects of professional care, including ordering hearing instruments and providing patient follow-up with appropriate supervision and direction. Due to confidentiality issues, the student should have telephone access in a private office area adjacent to relevant patient charts. Private areas should also be available to complete chart notes, write reports, contact manufacturers, and return patient phone calls, as requested by their clinical supervisor. Computer data base access with appropriate software programs including access via personal digital assistant technology must also be available.

Cost of Services and Reimbursement Issues

A confusion held by many involved in clinical education in universities and by potential patients of university clinics is that services should be provided at no charge. These attitudes are based on a number of misconceptions including that patients are somehow "guinea pigs" in the education process or that taxpayer dollars cover the operation of the clinic. The mission and vision of the clinic should certainly drive decision-making regarding patient care and service provision. Establishing fees for the services rendered should also be in line with the mission of the audiology clinic as well as the university's policy on fee-for-service charges for faculty-supervised service provision. In addition, a patient-centric approach to clinical education is critical. Students must be supervised appropriately so that patients receive professional care and do not feel as if they are participating in an "audiology experiment." Participation in research studies associated with the clinic may be an added opportunity and benefit to the patient; however, such participation must be clearly differentiated from the clinical services provided. In this era of strict regulation and protection of human subjects participating in research, the rules established for subject participation established and enforced by the Institutional Review Board (IRB) differ greatly in need and scope in comparison to patients receiving clinical services.

As noted earlier in the chapter, most university clinics are viewed as earnings units which are expected to cover some or all of the cost of operation. University audiology clinics face the same issues as the public universities in which they may be housed: decreased state and federal support, increased regulation, and economic uncertainties. The university clinic cannot count on long-term support from the university to survive or thrive. States continue to reduce taxpayer support for public, higher education, offsetting those reductions with higher tuition (Fish, 2003). A model may exist in which the audiology clinic can access some portion of the tuition paid for the clinical education courses to support the clinic operation. In addition, many professional education programs in universities assess students a lab or clinic fee that is designed to acknowledge the added cost of clinical education. The university clinic may be able to access a portion of this fee, if it currently exists, or to advocate for the development of such a fee if it does not.

A brief discussion on the nonprofit status of the clinic is included to address some possible misconceptions about the implications of this classification. Nonprofit organizations are incorporated, exist for education and/or charitable purposes, and from which trustees or shareholders cannot benefit financially. One of the cornerstones of nonprofit organizations has been to build capacity (e.g., financial resources, facilities, personnel) in which to meet their mission. These capacity-building activities are generally based on money, and may be based on private contributions, grants, or other sources, viewed as "indirect customers" that are able to support the mission of the organization (Foster & Bradach, 2005). Receiving revenue from goods and services provided to "direct customers" is another method for nonprofit organizations to build this capacity. There is a national trend toward nonprofit organizations engaging in earned-income ventures as they become "more businesslike" and attempt to reduce their reliance on other sources of funds, such as grants or development gifts, which may be less stable sources of income in the current economic and higher education environments (Foster & Bradach, 2005). However, it is noted that these organizations are often poorly prepared to meet the demands of running a successful business. Foster and Bradach (2005) point out that those running nonprofit organizations must have knowledge of issues related to pricing and generating revenue to be successful and meet their missions. This principle should guide decisions made related to pricing products and services in the university environment.

Determining pricing of services and products is covered in other chapters in this book and is not reviewed here. However, the clinic director must have a strong knowledge of the cost of providing services within the university environment. Concerns regarding the university "undercutting" cost of products, such as hearing instruments, are often noted by audiologists in the community who may also participate as critical partners in the clinical education of students. The university clinic must price products and services in the same manner as every other business: pricing should be based on the actual cost to provide the services or products with an appropriate profit margin. Each audiology practice sets its prices based on its cost of doing business, and the university clinic should be no different. Prices of goods and services in the clinic should reflect a business model that incorporates the cost of doing business in this environment. This model should be carefully reviewed by the university administration to ensure that pricing of services is also consistent with university policy.

The mission of the university clinic may provide some options in services and products not readily available or feasible in other practice settings. University programs may find benefit, for example, in providing education opportunities in adult group aural rehabilitation or educational audiology. The clinic may develop a contractual relationship with a nursing home or school district for provision of services to meet the educational mission but is also mutually beneficial to the facility receiving the services and the clinic. These contractual relationships should be billed on a fee-for-service basis as sug-

gested above. The benefit to the clinic is that these types of contractual relationships follow a fee-for-service model and are not subject to the types of "discounting" experienced in working with third party payors wherein a specific discounting structure is commonplace. These contracts provide an important platform to teach the economics of engaging in fee-for-service health care delivery. They also provide an opportunity for the student to develop awareness that the services he or she provides has economic value. Their services are meaningful both clinically and fiscally.

In the current environment, it is likely that university clinics will have relationships with third party payors, including private health insurance companies, Medicaid, and Medicare. It is critical that students understand the requirements of dealing with third party payors in terms of coding, supervision, and accurate attention to detail related to paperwork. If the clinic accepts third party payment, an employee who is knowledgeable in this area must be on the clinic staff or hired as a consultant. As with any practice setting, third party billing is complex and constantly changing and requires the attention of dedicated personnel. Many universities are self-insured and this fact may drive decision-making regarding provider status with third party payors. It may be most efficient and effective to focus efforts in the university insurance plan, as there is consistency in the plan, presumably ease of access to those developing and administering the plan, and a built-in marketing benefit, due to the ability for the clinic to participate in university health fairs and plan sponsored wellness events.

Regardless of the source of reimbursement, the university audiology clinic must have an effective billing system in place to track payables and receivables and a mechanism for ensuring that bills are paid in a timely manner and that receivables are collected effectively. Students should be exposed to this aspect of practice management by becoming directly involved in these critically important efforts. The audiology clinic should integrate effective software that tracks patient visits, services provided, and procedural and diagnostic codes and charges, among other information. Software programs should be carefully evaluated and matched to the needs of each clinical venue. Those designed for a small private practice or for use within the framework of a hospital setting may be inappropriate for the university audiology clinic. Clinic directors should consult with others in university audiology and or speech/language/hearing clinics to determine options and to obtain feedback about the benefits and glitches of particular clinic management software currently available. As with any business, a certain percentage of patients will not pay for services or products they receive. A plan that addresses collections to recover as much of these funds as possible must be in place, along with clearly established write-off criteria. The university setting may limit the types of collections options available to the clinic, and may include a collections department within the university or the state Attorney General's office. The clinic director and/or business manager must clearly understand the university policies for collection.

The university will have specific rules related to purchasing and accounts payable that are likely to limit some decisions available to the clinic. Vendors may be required to participate in a "competitive bid" procedure, the clinic may have to select from "University-approved vendors," or there may be categories in which minority vendors must be considered. Based on the nature of the hearing instrument industry, the clinic staff will need to educate those in procurement regarding options for selecting hearing instrument manufacturers. The audiologists involved in hearing instrument dispensing should be able to put their specifications and criteria in writing. Universities have protocols that provide multiple cross-checks related to purchasing, based on concerns related to ethics, conflict of interest, and prudent use of taxpayer funds. The challenge for the university audiology clinic is to implement these protocols without collapsing under the weight of the bureaucracy. This requires communication with those in purchasing regarding the mission and function of the audiology clinic along with the desire to operate as a business within the constraints of these policies. A relationship with accounts payable is of particular importance due to the fact that hearing aids will not be received by the clinic if payables do not take into account the patient service mission of the clinic and the need to pay invoices in a timely manner. There may also be more than one clinic on a campus that provides hearing and balance care services and procedures must be in place to ensure that charges and refunds are assigned to the appropriate clinic.

Other Considerations

As in all practice settings, the university clinic should have a marketing plan, even if it is basic. The clinic may have a plan designed by the staff, or may consider other options. Participating in a buying group, like Sonus or American Hearing Aid Associates (AHAA), could provide marketing support to the clinic, along with other benefits. The clinic director may be able to take advantage of marketing or communications resources within the university that will capitalize on a consistent marketing message or program that promotes the clinic utilizing the university's slogans and materials. In addition, the clinic may benefit as a volunteer as a "case study" with a marketing or business class which can provide a market analysis and recommendations at no charge, with the side benefit of educating future marketing professionals about the profession of audiology. The cost of marketing must be included in the clinic budget and should include current needs and methods to address the future, such as the clinic's presence on the Internet.

Referrals to the university clinic may come from a variety of sources, including university faculty and staff, physicians and health care providers within the community, and self-referrals. The marketing adage of "perception is reality" may apply to the University clinic more than to any other practice setting in audiology. On the one hand, there may be a perception that services and products provided in the university setting are the most up-to-date and cutting edge due to the educational mission of the clinic. On the other hand, there may be a perception that services are provided by students with little experience making decisions independently. Marketing programs should target referral sources and the community and address these perceptions. Certainly, the name of the university provides a competitive advantage in certain markets. However,

marketing should also highlight the clinical education mission of the clinic and the implications of this mission.

Clinic staff and students should be involved in all marketing activities, including activities that recognize and thank referral sources, promote services in wellness events, and provide community presentations. Understanding patient expectations, perceptions, and responses is enhanced by participation in these types of activities and is critical in the clinical education process. These experiences also reinforce clinical education activities and expectations, such as the importance of delivering services in a timely and efficient manner, a frequent criticism of university audiology clinics. Conversely, everyone involved in marketing of the clinic must understand the mission and vision of the clinic and communicate the message that the model utilized in the university audiology clinic may not be one that meets the needs of a specific patient. If all services are provided by students supervised by a licensed audiologist, the patient should understand that the supervising audiologist may not be providing direct or exclusive services to the patient. As stated previously in this chapter, this falls in the category that the university audiology clinic cannot or should not try to be "all things to all people" and understanding the target market helps to utilize time and resources most effectively.

As noted earlier in this chapter, it may be a paradigm shift for a university to have a patient-centric service focus, as historically they have been established primarily to address the educational needs of students. This trend is certainly changing in universities and it is the responsibility of all associated with the clinic to promote the "patient-centric" focus described in this text both within the clinic and in the larger environment of the university. This focus is the right thing to do if optimal patient care is to be provided. It builds a clinical education model that will guide students effectively, and may have unintended benefits to the university community. A satisfied patient may be a significant factor in the marketing plan, as word of mouth is often a strong marketing component in the university setting. This may generalize to other clinical settings within the university, making this patient a "loyal customer" of other service providers available within the university. In addition, patients who are satisfied with the services they receive at the clinic often donate to a clinic development fund, which can support the missions of the clinic such as new equipment or a loaner hearing aid bank, which enhance both patient care and clinical education.

In the current era of higher education financing, it is clear that there is increased pressure for clinical programs and University-based clinics to be self-sufficient; however, these clinics may be constrained by regulations and policies that impact autonomy in options and decision-making. Despite all of these considerations, the transition to the Au.D. has provided both an opportunity and imperative to transform the university audiology clinic to an efficient and effective nonprofit business. The tenets set forth in this book should help guide this plan, along with specifics addressed in this chapter. The university audiology clinic has a critical role in meeting patient needs, providing clinical education, and facilitating clinically relevant research. This role will increase with demands for services, changes in Au.D. education, and with greater emphasis on evidence-based prac-

tice. This is framed by continued issues in funding of higher education and reimbursement for hearing and balance services. To be successful, the university clinic will need to transition to a nonprofit business for the new millennium. The clinic may benefit from the development of an advisory board made up of community partners, patients, families of patients, and other health care providers that may provide insight into issues facing the clinic, such as marketing and development fundraising. New collaborations will be developed with community partners to meet patient needs while expanding the clinical education component (Doran, Solomon, & Brasseur, 1997; McCready, 2000; Solomon-Rice, 2004). Most importantly, the concepts that drive successful practices in the "real world" must be those that guide the university clinic: provision of cost-effective, time-efficient patient-centric services.

References

American Speech-Language-Hearing Association. (2000, March). *Responding to the changing needs of speech-language pathology and audiology students in the 21st century* (A briefing paper for academicians, practitioners, employers, and students). Website: http://www.asha.org/students/changing.htm

Bartlett, S., McNamara, K., & Peaper, R. (2006, November). *Factors influencing the activities of clinic directors in university settings*. Presentation at the Annual Convention of the American Speech-Language-Hearing Association, Miami Beach, FL.

Council of Academic Programs in Communication Sciences and Disorders. (2007). Web site: http://www.capcsd.org/proceedings.html

Doran, M. C., Solomon, B. S. W., & Brasseur, J. A. (1997). Partners in professional preparation: Collaboration between universities and off-site settings, *Administration and Supervision Newsletter, 5,* 17-21.

Fish, S. (2003, Oct. 31). Give us liberty or give us revenue. *Chronicle of Higher Education*, p. 4.

Foster, W., & Bradach, J. (2005). Should nonprofits seek profit? *Harvard Business Review, 83*(2), 92-100.

Hardick, E. J., & Oyer, H. J. (1987). Administration of speech-language-hearing programs within the university setting. In H. J. Oyer (Ed.), *Administration of programs in speech-language pathology and audiology*. Englewood Cliffs, NJ: Prentice-Hall.

Lundy, E. (2006). University facilities respond to the changing landscape of higher education. *APPA Thought Leaders Series 2006.* Alexandria, VA: APPA.

McCarthy, P. (2006). Clinical education in audiology: The challenge of change. *Seminars in Hearing, 27*(2), 79-85.

McCready, V. (2000). The changing face of the university clinic: Reaching out to the community. *Council of Academic Programs in Communication Sciences and Disorders conference,* San Diego, CA.

Novak, R. (2004). Thoughts on the development of our audiology profession. *Audiology Today, 16*(4), 18-19.

Solomon-Rice, P. (2004). Enhancing university clinical programs through collaborations with non-profit organizations. *American Speech-Language-Hearing Association convention*, Philadelphia.

Williams, A. L. (1996). Modified teaching clinic peer group supervision in clinical training and professional development. *American Journal of Speech-Language Pathology, 4*(3), 29-38.

Windmill, I. M., Cunningham, D. R., & Preminger, J. E. (2004). The University of Louisville: The Au.D in a medical and business environment. *American Journal of Audiology, 13*(2), 110-117.

14

Establishing the Value of Your Practice

ROBERT G. GLASER, Ph.D.

Introduction

Reality is often a rare commodity when it comes to buying or selling a practice. The value of a business to the owner is usually much greater than the value of the same business to a potential purchaser (Peltz, 2006). Sellers inherently tend to over value their practice. After all the blood, sweat, and tears of getting the practice started or having gone through the rigors of buying others out, sellers become emotionally as well as economically attached to the practice. Buyers,

being less emotionally attached, tend to move toward under pricing the opportunity regardless of the value. Somewhere in between the positions of the two parties lie the actual value and an acceptable purchase price.

Value is an economic term based on a specific set of financial data generated by the practice over a specified time period. It is customary to assume that value is not only tied to price but tied to the best price to be paid. Conventional wisdom suggests that if a high price is paid, there is ipso facto high value. If a low price is paid, the perception of value may not seem to decline if the purchaser perceives a bargain—a valuable item purchased at a low price. The realities of both value and price become clear when the item of interest is clarified by accurate fiscal data. In the case of an audiology practice, when an appropriate valuation has been completed by a qualified assessor, a dollar figure is set and a starting point for negotiations is established.

Value Versus Price

Value is derived: Price is negotiated. Price is the result of negotiations between two parties or their representatives wherein both sides are interested in transferring ownership of the practice. The greatest accomplishment, and often the most difficult, is to develop a realistic appraisal of the worth of the practice. The term "realistic" implies that the value established reflects what the practice is worth to *both* the seller and the buyer.

The seller must develop a reasonable price point based on an accurate assessment of the practice. If the price is unrealistic relative to the actual value of the practice, the practice will languish as an opportunity available to a fool with too much money and little or no professional guidance. Additionally, the price for the practice must be within a range that potential buyers can qualify for as well as service their indebtedness while earning a living in the practice. No one should buy a practice that over extends their financial capabilities. Most banks will not permit such fiscal disability to occur no matter how appealing the inertia of the active patient and referral base of the practice under consideration.

Reasons for Valuations

Although buying or selling a practice is the most likely reason an owner would seek a comprehensive valuation of their practice, there are a number of other reasons to secure a formal valuation: Merger negotiations; developing loan guarantee information; buy-in by a potential partner; partners seeking a buy-out; divorce proceedings involving a principal shareholder in the practice; disability or death of a principal shareholder within the practice; or estate and retirement planning (Sidebar 14–1).

The reason to secure a valuation will often dictate the method of appraisal. The scope of this chapter does not permit extensive consideration of valuation methods nor the reasons which would differentially trigger one form of valuation over another. We do, however, consider a common valuation strategy frequently used in evaluating audiology practices. As hospital-based and nonprofit community center practices are rarely involved in buy-sell arrangements (beyond corporate mergers occurring well above the departmental level) the primary focus is on audiology practices operating in the private, for-profit sector.

Valuation Methods

There are a variety of opinions about which is the best method to appraise a closely held, health care practice. Choosing the most appropriate valuation method is critically important as each method produces relatively different numbers depending on the relative value of assets, cash available in the practice,

---

Sidebar 14–1
BUY-SELL AGREEMENTS

Any shareholder in a corporation or partner in a venture with several other owners must agree to and sign a buy-sell agreement. It is an important document that stipulates the terms under which a shareholder or partner is to be bought out of his or her holdings within the practice. If there is a buy-sell agreement and a partner dies or decides to retire, the process is triggered under specific circumstances, a valuation is completed and the derived figure serves as the basis for the agreed on payout. The buy-sell agreement will establish the method of valuation and may even list the individual or group to do the valuation of the practice. Without such an agreement in place, legal fees will likely deplete a significant portion of the payout and could possibly lead to the financial ruin of the practice.

---

services delivered, and products dispensed. Drullinger (2006) suggests that service-related practices such as audiology practices pose a challenge to value as the "worth" of these businesses is often tied to the services performed by the owner of the practice. He suggests that the largest asset in an audiology practice is goodwill and adds that valuation specialists have adopted two specific methods to accurately define the value of an audiology practice; book value and valuation based on historical precedent.

Bartolacci (2002), by comparison, provides a different viewpoint on valuation methodology: Asset-based valuation should not be the foundation for valuing medical/health care practices, which are labor intensive and heavily dependent on human resources. Although medical or other health care practices will most likely have tangible assets, it is not the primary basis for increasing the wealth of the owner of the practice. The fiscal intention of health care practices is to increase owner wealth through practitioners who generate cash flow. Therefore, he suggests that the most appropriate valuation method (for medical/health care practices) should be based on practitioner-generated cash flow.

Linton (2005) takes issue with using book value assessment: The book value of a company is the net worth shown on the company's balance sheet, that is, the historical net assets minus the net liabilities. She levies another criticism about using book value assessment based on the fact that the assessor will be using historical cost numbers which rarely have any relationship to fair market value. She adds that assessment methods that include a forecast of earnings or projected earnings data be included in the assessment along with another method that considers the trends in performance found in the historical data of past balance sheets.

Finding a Qualified Practice Valuation Professional

There are a variety of opinions as to who should complete a valuation of a practice—from both the seller's side as well as that of the potential buyer. Buyers are securing their version of the future in buying an ongoing practice. Sellers are relying on past performance data to stand as evidence that the practice has done well and will likely continue to do well. As each method of valuation varies in scope and application and the data generated will sometimes favor the seller and sometimes the buyer, it is best to rely on the suggestions of a qualified valuation analyst to select the most appropriate method(s) to be used in the assessment of the practice.

Not only is the value of a practice viewed differently by a buyer and seller, there are differing points of view on what method of valuation should be used. Whether you are considering selling your practice or buying an ongoing concern, a comprehensive assessment by a qualified valuation analyst is critically important. Consult with other trusted advisors to the practice who have had occasion to work with qualified practice valuation analysts. Additional information about valuation analysts can be found by contacting one of the nationalprofessional organizations for those involved in business or practice valuations to find members in your area who can be contacted for information or interview:

■ American Society of Appraisers (http://www.appraisers.org)
■ Institute of Business Appraisers (http://www.instbusapp.org)
■ National Association of Certified Valuation Analysts (http://www.nacva.com)

The Most Common Valuation Method for Audiology Practices

It is not the intent of this chapter to provide a short course on practice valuation methods. It is, however, valuable to explore a common method of valuation so that an idea of the depth of analysis and the effects of some of the variables to be considered in the valuation process can affect the derived price point for the practice.

A Basic Valuation Method: Book Value

Determining the book value of a practice is one of several commonly applied methods of valuation to assess health care practices. The book value of a practice is the difference between total assets and liabilities of the practice; the net worth of a practice. The balance sheet contains the necessary numbers but it may not contain the whole story of how the practice owner minimized net income while making a good salary with excellent benefits including a car allowance, unlimited cell phone usage, travel allowance, and personal accounting and legal fees. These expenses should be considered in the valuation.

Recasting is the process of removing unnecessary expenses from historical financial statements so that they more accurately reflect a realistic financial assessment of performance. Drullinger (2006) indicates that once the practice income has been reviewed and normalized, the final step to determining a value for the practice is assigning a multiple that will be factored with the adjusted net worth to arrive at a figure to be used to begin the negotiations. He states that multipliers used in the hearing industry range from 2.0 to 6.0 with an average of 3.5. Therefore, if the adjusted net worth of a practice is $200,000.00, and the average multiplier of 3.5 is applied, the value of that practice is set at $700,000.00. Drullinger lists several factors that, if present, would indicate the need to use a higher multiplier: He includes several factors that would signal the need for lowering the multiplier (Sidebar 14–2). Based on his list, there are no hard and fast rules to establish an appropriate multiplier.

Drullinger (2006) states that goodwill is "the largest asset in an audiology practice" and that he considers goodwill to be unequivocally tied to the principal clinician/owner of the practice. It is interesting to note, however, that several of the items included in the list to either raise or lower the multiplier are clearly items that can be considered elements of "goodwill" of the practice itself as much as the practitioner.

Goodwill: An Important, Multifaceted Commodity

Goodwill: considered ephemeral by some, nonexistent by others. It is the reputation of the practice and should be considered one of the most important assets in any audiology practice. Goodwill is embedded deeply within a practice. It is the heart of a practice; it is the character of a practice. Without specific character, there is little to differentiate one practice from another. Goodwill is

---

Sidebar 14–2
FACTORS AFFECTING THE SELECTION OF A MULTIPLIER FOR BOOK VALUE ASSESSMENT

Factors that increase a multiplier:

- Strong referral base in place
- Validated, active charts
- Length of time in the marketplace
- Less than 50% of the revenue is generated by the owner
- Higher percentage of private pay versus third-party pay patients
- Revenue growth year after year of the periods examined

Factors that decrease a multiplier:

- 100% of the revenue generated by a retiring owner
- High third-party pay patients
- High accounts receivable
- Revenue decline year after year in the periods examined
- Low number of active patient files

Source: Adapted from Drullinger (2006)

the reason the practice flourishes. It is why referral sources send patients and why patients return to the referring health care provider to report on their positive experiences. It is also the reason patients return to a practice to ensure the continuity of their care.

Goodwill can be measured by patient retention, which exemplifies patient loyalty to the practice. It is that remarkable commodity that need not vanish nor diminish if the ownership changes. Goodwill is not solely bound to an individual in the practice or the owner. Practice goodwill relates to the practice's ability to maintain and build the business separate from an individual professional (Linton, 2005). It is interwoven in the fabric of the practice. It has inertia that can be captured by a buyer if the buyer recognizes the components that have come together to establish the goodwill of the practice. The buyer will wisely capitalize on the fluidity of the practice's goodwill and bolster those characteristics of the practice that must continue to flourish and grow.

The initial stages of the practice's stability and growth immediately following purchase will rise or fall on the extent to which the new owner embraces and advances the rhythm of goodwill within the practice. As a new owner in a purchased practice, it would be wise to initially move with the rhythm of the practice before jumping headlong into the fray and changing direction or otherwise altering the flow of the practice. Give it some time, get a feel for the practice as an entity, not just what appears in the balance sheet or the projections provided by the practice broker.

After a realistic period of assessment, consider changes that will impact patient, front office and professional staff, and cash flow the very least and begin implementation. Those who interact with patients will be most immediately affected by changes in policies or procedures set forth by the new owner. Implementation will go much smoother if the professional and front office staff "buy in" to the changes and become stakeholders. Their input to the proposed changes must be considered and included whenever possible. As the transition continues, new ideas may develop or a better vantage point may come about simply by observing the reaction of the entire system to change. Call it a measure of the practice's "fluidity" but know that it provides a clear snapshot of how the system will react to changes of greater magnitude.

Above all, do not forget to ask the patients what their opinions are about the practice. Given an opportunity to provide input, most patients will be more than happy to render an opinion: After all, if they feel a part of the practice, as they indeed should, they will be proud to have been asked and to have participated in securing the future of "their" practice. If they have not been given an opportunity to provide input under the previous ownership, they will note the interest of the new owner and will feel that much more involved—and more likely to stay within a practice that cares enough to ask their opinion. Patient loyalty is the highest metric of success and security a valuation can uncover. Referral source retention is a photo finish second to patient loyalty.

A Cautionary Note on Rule-of-Thumb "Guestimates"

Linton (2005) insists that rules-of-thumb valuation techniques are arbitrary formulas based on unsubstantiated data applied to undifferentiated company financial information: Rules-of-thumb assume that you are valuing an "average" company in the industry, which is similar to analyzing the "average" American family with 2.3 children. She continues: "Just as you won't find any average American family with 2.3 children, you won't find an average American company that you can accurately value with a shorthand value."

Despite the caution, rule-of-thumb formulas are used by accountants and owners, buyers and sellers, and others to get a snapshot view of the financial status of a practice. A rule-of-thumb formula can be used to test the reasonability of a formal valuation based on one or multiple methods of valuation. Common rules-of-thumb valuation formulas include:

- 1.0 to 1.5 times net practice income
- 1.25 times net revenues after expense adjustment
- 1.0 to 1.5 times annual revenues
- 50 to 70% annual collections plus furniture, fixtures, and equipment (Sidebar 14-3)

A Tale of Two Practices

Consider two practices with the same net revenues of $500.000.00. If the formula of 1.25 times net revenues is applied, the valuation figure of the practice will be $625.000.00.

Practice No.1 is located on a high volume thoroughfare in an upscale section of town. Equipment is on a scheduled replacement plan, leasehold improvements have been made within the last 2 years; staff turnover is low; 2:1 marketing strategy in place—markets to referral base twice as much as to the general public.

Practice No. 2 is located near a neighborhood with declining property values and increasing rentals over the last several years; high staff turnover; no schedule of equipment replacement; marketing strategy depends on cash flow.

Which practice is more appealing as a potential purchase? It is not all to be found in the numbers regardless of the valuation method or multiplier used.

Sidebar 14–3
DEADLY SINS IN SELLING A PRACTICE

- Not getting it in writing
  Verbal agreements do not count, are not enforceable in court, and disable the thinking process concerning the multiple issues involved in selling a practice.

- Not using professional legal, tax and other counsel
  Consulting a qualified practice valuation analyst, the attorney, and accountant of record for the practice to review purchase documents and assess price points from their perspectives on the practice is important. The more input from trusted advisors, the better.

■ Not knowing the practice value
Sellers must never base an asking price on emotions over the market value of the practice nor on "guestimates" of the worth of the practice derived by rule-of-thumb analysis. Buyers must be mindful of the valuation techniques and never purchase a practice that can hinder making a living while servicing the debt incurred to purchase the practice. Buyers must be satisfied with the price paid and the potential seen in the practice.

■ Waiting too long to sell
The best time to sell a practice is when you do not have to sell it. Do not wait until you have to sell the practice under duress, which commonly results in a lower sales price. Recognize that it may take 2 or more years to get the practice into salable form—and it might take a year or so beyond that to complete the sale.

■ Keep the practice current
Make sure the equipment is current and up-to-date and that services provided within the practice matches or exceeds the competition within the demographic.

■ Not making cosmetic upgrades
First impressions are lasting. Upgrade the carpeting, wall coverings, landscaping, or whatever it takes to make the surroundings (whether owned or not) have a current and up-to-date feel.

■ Small stuff requires attention and action
Practice transactions take time and require attention to details that you as the seller might think are meager points of contention. If the buyer thinks an issue is imperative, consider it so and correct the situation and move on.

■ Avoid seller's remorse
Every seller will, at some point toward the end of negotiations or at the signing of the sale documents, develop seller's remorse. They think they can hold out for more or that the potential buyer has no appreciation for all the years of blood, sweat, and tears it took to build the practice. Get over it. If you are satisfied with the offer and if it meets your fiscal needs, take it and go on to the next phase in your life. And do not look back except to say that I got what I could and remain satisfied with the deal—if you do not think you can say that at the end of the sale, perhaps you are not ready to sell the practice. It is your choice.

Assets

An audiology practice has a variety of assets. Some prefer to consider tangible and intangible assets, the latter referring primarily to the goodwill of the practice. All assets are tangible—whether "touchable" or woven into the fabric of the practice and considered the goodwill of a practice.

Besides cash and accounts receivable, the most important asset of an audiology practice are the active patient charts. There are other touchable assets including the office building or condominium (if owned), audiometric and related instrument dispensing equipment and inventory, vestibular testing equipment, clinical computers, and a host of patient-interface items such as video-otoscopes.

Assets have value. How much value depends on the merit of the asset. Certainly the building or office condominium has well-defined value as it is real estate and can be readily and accurately appraised. Audiometric equipment has value; however, once the equipment is purchased it becomes used equipment with markedly lowered cash value—far worse than the depreciation suffered when you drive a new auto off the showroom floor. There is not much of a market for used audiometric and vestibular testing equipment—a great argument for considering leasing arrangements. Assets are considered "current assets" if they can be sold and turned into cash within one year.

Active Patient Charts

Active patient charts can be defined a variety of ways. They are commonly defined by the frequency of patient visits and the time frame from the last visit to the valuation date. Depending on the practice philosophy, a patient must be seen in the office within a specific time period to be considered an "active" patient. Some practices consider all charts of those patients fitted with hearing instruments within a 5-year period to be "active" charts. Those charts within 3 to 5 years of a visit for hearing examination might be considered "active" diagnostic charts or "tested, not fitted" charts. They may be retained as active charts so that follow-up visits can be readily scheduled or, if categorized as "needing amplification but not fitted," the patient will be contacted from time to time to determine their readiness to consider hearing instruments.

Active "contact" charts can be defined as any patient chart that has a related contact with a member of the front office staff without having interaction with professional staff members. An example of an active "contact" chart would be the patient who occasionally calls or stops by to purchase batteries.

When assessing the value of a practice, time spent scrutinizing active patient charts will be both revealing and rewarding. Depending on the practice and the practitioner, the charts will tell the tale of the true potential for future hearing instrument dispensing and the need for repeat hearing evaluations. If a representative numbers of charts are pulled from active patient files (including "contact" charts), a clear picture of the potential of the practice can be generated. The examiner will get an immediate feel for the completeness of the system; how patients are evaluated; an indication of follow-up care; the report style and interactions with referral sources; how the services provided can be improved, and what levels of amplification have been used over the service years of active charts. By carefully examining the numbers and styles of instruments placed, the sophistication of the circuitry used, the numbers of post fitting visits until patient satisfaction is reached, and the numbers of returns, a remarkably complete picture of the needs of the active patients in the practice will develop.

For example, if 40 or 50% of the instruments placed in a specific period consist of digitally programmable or entry-level digital instruments, there is a firm likelihood that the charts will produce a list of patients classified as being in need of upgraded circuits or to be recalled for assessment and reprogramming. The chart review will enable the new owner(s) an opportunity to develop recall protocols that can be worked by the front office staff over a specified period after the office is up and running smoothly under the new management (Sidebar 14-4)

Sidebar 14–4
DEADLY SINS IN BUYING A PRACTICE

- Not getting it in writing
  Verbal agreements do not count, are not enforceable in court, and disable the thinking process concerning the multiple issues involved in buying a practice.

- Make sure the practice is available
  Have the parties involved sign a statement that the intention of the negotiations is to complete a sale of the practice. Sometimes practices go on the block just to go through the valuation process so that the owner(s) can assess the appropriateness of the timing to sell.

- Not using professional legal, tax, and other counsel
  First and foremost as the buyer, make sure someone is representing your interests from the legal aspect, whether the attorney-of-record for your practice or your personal attorney. Beyond that, the same goes for the buyer as the seller: Consulting a qualified practice valuation analyst, the attorney, and accountant of record for the practice to review purchase documents and assess price points from their perspectives on the practice is important. The more input from trusted advisors, the better.

- Not having good financial records
  Review the last 3 years' financial and tax records for the practice with great attention to detail and trends. It is best to have your accountant

review the figures with you. Determine the need for questions about discrepancies, normalization of principal's expenses, and whether the financial records match the tax returns.

■ Paying too much for the practice
When the seller finances the sale, you lose the important, objective perspective the bank provides as the lender. Consider other options including leasing the practice with an option to buy at the end of a specified period which will permit savings to accrue while you work the practice

■ Taking too long to complete the deal
The more time it takes to get to the signing table, the greater the likelihood the seller can change his or her mind or find additional costs features to put on the table. Time is of the essence when you have committed to the venture.

■ Waiting for the "perfect" practice opportunity
Perfect today may not be so perfect in 3 to 5 years. Find an opportunity that meets your salary and location needs and has at least two other motivating reasons to buy. If you wait for the perfect practice opportunity to come along, it will be time to retire.

■ Small stuff requires attention and action
Practice transactions take time and attention to details that you as the buyer might think are important points of contention. If the seller thinks your concern is less an issue than it appears to you, consider that the seller may be right and put the situation in perspective. If it is important to be a deal killer, perhaps the deal is not right for either the seller or the buyer.

■ Avoid buyer's remorse
Every buyer will, at some point after the purchase develop buyer's remorse. They will rethink their negotiation strategy, the purchase price, the location, the status of the active charts, and in so doing, simply drime themselves crazy with unwarranted regret. Get over it. If you are satisfied with what you determined was important in the practice before you signed the contract to purchase, all of those characteristics and financial indicators still exist. Do not look back except to say that I did the best evaluation and consulted with trusted advisors and remain satisfied with the deal. Now get back to making your dream come true!

Capitalizing on the First Visit "Under New Management"

The first visit will represent an opportunity for the patients to come in and meet the new staff. It will provide the new management to present their philosophy in the office and to review the patient's chart so that a fresh start can be established. The review might find some disgruntled patients willing to start over or patients who refuse to come in for whatever reasons. That patient could be reclassified as inactive or he or she could be asked if they want to continue to receive a newsletter or reconsider their position about the practice at a later date. Patient retention is the critical lever that will provide the long-term lift a practice needs over time to maintain financial viability and success. Patient retention is part goodwill, part patient loyalty, and all about the practice—defined by the patient refit, retest, and return records. Never give up on a patient who feels as though the practice has given up on them!

Referral Base Analysis

Just as patient charts should be carefully analyzed as part of the valuation process, referral sources and their respective referral patterns need to be equally evaluated. As part of the patient chart evaluation, the original referral source for the patient should be noted. As the list of referral sources grows, each can be considered an "active referral source" based on the rate of their referrals to the practice. The practice owner should have a well-defined referral source roster which should contain each referral's relative frequency of referrals.

If there is a defined list of referral sources, it is a good idea to evaluate each care provider listed. Depending on their years in practice or graduation date from medical school, they may be near retirement. Loss of a referral source is mitigated to some extent if the referring physician has partners in his or her practice and if they too refer to the practice. Information may be available through local medical societies. They may have rosters with members' graduation dates and other information that can be considered in evaluating the longevity of anticipated referrals from current listings of health care practitioners who consistently refer to the practice. The current owner/seller of the practice should issue a review and history of each referring health care provider with projections of continued referrals to the practice. Contacting each referral source personally should be a first-order goal of the new practice owner.

Assessment of Effective Marketing

The owner/seller of the practice should have examples of marketing plans that have been effective in getting patients to the practice. Examples of marketing brochures, print advertising, and other media that has produced specific results in the practice demographic area should be available as part of the valuation process. This information will be especially important to a prospective purchaser of the practice if he or she is not familiar with the demographics of the area. Marketing and advertising efforts that have proven successful should be evaluated, modified, and continued to match the character of the practice under new ownership. If patient flow is determined to be intimately related to a particular blend of promotion, there may be little need to change the schedule and format of the effort. If a combination of visits to referral sources, periodic presence in print media, and lectures in health care facilities or social organizations has been successful, keep the inertia moving in a positive direction until the need for change presents itself clearly.

Summary

Valuation of a practice is critically important for both the seller of the practice as well as the potential buyer. Regardless of the method of valuation used, a figure will be generated and price negotiations will begin around the price point or range of price points established by the valuation analyst. To be on the safe side, it is recommended that more than one valuation method be used, that a qualified analyst be secured and that reasonability prevail on both sides of the price figure so that the deal can be consummated. The goal of the process remains buyer and seller satisfaction. The buyer needs to be satisfied that the price he or she has paid represents the value of the practice now and in the future. The seller must come away from the table satisfied in knowing the practice was appreciated in the final price and that the patients will be well cared for in years to come. The practice evaluation checklist presented in Sidebar 14–5 should focus the reader's attention on key elements to be considered by potential buyers and sellers of an audiology practice.

Sidebar 14–5
PRACTICE EVALUATION CHECKLIST FOR POTENTIAL BUYERS AND SELLERS

When engaging in the valuation of a practice, whether it is the practice you own or one that you might be considering to purchase, this checklist can serve to focus on matters of importance that can affect the perceived value of the practice. It can also be used as a checklist for a successful practice. The more positive responses to the questions, the more successful the practice and the greater the likelihood an equitable price can be determined and agreed on.

☐ Is the office staff well trained and qualified for their specific duties?

☐ Is each office staff member cross-trained?

☐ Does the office staff communicate with one another well?

☐ Is there good communication between the office personnel and the owner or principals in the practice?

☐ Do you have a policy of regularly scheduled performance evaluations for the office staff?

☐ Are the members of the office staff held accountable for their actions and performance?

☐ Are specific goals and expectations set forth in job descriptions?

☐ Do you promote office staff development and discourage turnover?

☐ Do you allow employees to speak their mind and feel comfortable in recommending improvements to the practice?

☐ Is there a policy on employee benefits and compensation?

☐ Is your practice competitive in compensating office staff?

☐ Is the owner(s) or principals in the practice considerate of the office staff?

☐ Is there a strong belief that within the practice that serving the patient with quality and professionalism is the number one priority of the practice?

☐ Is the administrator of the office sensitive to the needs of the employees yet able to complete the necessary tasks required to run the practice efficiently?

☐ Are formulas for the buy-in and buy-out processes in place and agreed on in buy-sell agreements?

☐ Do your financial records give a clear picture of your practice's status?

☐ Are your financial reports prepared according to Generally Accepted Accounting Standards (GAAS)?

☐ Do the accounting data provide for variance analysis?

☐ Is there a mechanism to review expenses to reduce costs and control increases on a regular basis?

☐ Do your financial statements enable comparisons to prior year data?

☐ Do you consider the financial statements for fiscal trends over a 1 to 2 year period?

☐ Is your staff aware of the balances that are outstanding and require collection action?

☐ Are collections appropriate within the practice?

☐ Is there an aggressive collection policy in effect in your practice?

☐ Is your billing system appropriate for your collection rate?

☐ Are charges billed within 24 hours of service delivery?

☐ Are bad debts a significant problem within your practice?

☐ Do you use an outside collection agency to collect unpaid balances?

- ☐ Is the fee schedule reviewed to make sure it is competitive and accurate for the level and extent of services provided?
- ☐ Are there internal controls in place to reduce embezzlement of practice funds?
- ☐ Do you evaluate the reason for and amount of patient refunds prior to sending issuing the refund?
- ☐ Is the billing aspect of your practice efficient with timely processing of claims and follow-up with patients with outstanding balances?
- ☐ Is there proper cash management within the practice?
- ☐ Is a disaster recovery plan documented and in place?
- ☐ Are there opportunities to improve on the rental space by negotiating a better lease or reduced rent?
- ☐ Do you use the space and facilities to their maximum potentials?
- ☐ Is there a need to consider a move or to begin looking elsewhere for space?
- ☐ Have you done a recent demographic study of the practice to determine where the patients are coming from?
- ☐ Is the equipment in the practice able to provide appropriate clinical information as well as billable items for the time spent with the patient?
- ☐ Have you developed an equipment replacement schedule for the practice?
- ☐ Is there an equipment replacement fund in place and actively receiving monies on a regular basis?
- ☐ Is your appointment scheduling method current?
- ☐ Does your practice comply with state guidelines for the services provided?
- ☐ Is the practice in compliance with all aspects of HIPAA?
- ☐ Do you have a well-organized and comprehensive Policy and Procedures Manual?
- ☐ Is there an organized policy on employee compensation?
- ☐ Is there a protocol for complaint resolution for patients?
- ☐ Is there a protocol for complaint resolution for employees?
- ☐ Do your patients understand office policies regarding billing and insurance processing?
- ☐ Do your patients understand the collection policy of the office?
- ☐ Have the patients signed an indication of understanding that they are liable for all charges incurred?

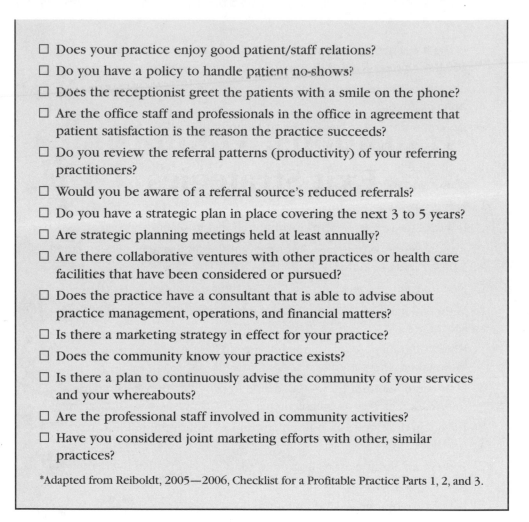

☐ Does your practice enjoy good patient/staff relations?

☐ Do you have a policy to handle patient no-shows?

☐ Does the receptionist greet the patients with a smile on the phone?

☐ Are the office staff and professionals in the office in agreement that patient satisfaction is the reason the practice succeeds?

☐ Do you review the referral patterns (productivity) of your referring practitioners?

☐ Would you be aware of a referral source's reduced referrals?

☐ Do you have a strategic plan in place covering the next 3 to 5 years?

☐ Are strategic planning meetings held at least annually?

☐ Are there collaborative ventures with other practices or health care facilities that have been considered or pursued?

☐ Does the practice have a consultant that is able to advise about practice management, operations, and financial matters?

☐ Is there a marketing strategy in effect for your practice?

☐ Does the community know your practice exists?

☐ Is there a plan to continuously advise the community of your services and your whereabouts?

☐ Are the professional staff involved in community activities?

☐ Have you considered joint marketing efforts with other, similar practices?

*Adapted from Reiboldt, 2005—2006, Checklist for a Profitable Practice Parts 1, 2, and 3.

References

Bartolacci, R. (2002). Fundamentals of finance in a practice. In J. S. Sanfilippo, T. E. Nolan, & B. H. Whiteside (Eds.), *MBA handbook for healthcare professionals* (pp. 215–230). New York: Parthenon.

Drullinger, R. (2006). Practice valuation: The buying and selling of an audiology practice. *Seminars in Hearing, 27*(1), 57–67.

Linton, H. S. (2005). *Business valuation*. Avon, MA: Adams Media.

Peltz, S. (2006, Sept.–Oct.). How to Value a buy-in/buy-out. *Journal of Practice Management*, pp. 71–74.

Reiboldt, M. (2005a). Checklist for a profitable practice. *CokerConnection, 5*(11), 8.

Reiboldt, M. (2005b). Checklist for a profitable practice: Part 2. *CokerConnection, 5*(12), 7.

Reiboldt, M. (2006). Checklist for a profitable practice: Part 3. *CokerConnection, 6*(1), 6.

15

Transitions: Optimizing Exit Strategies

GAIL M. WHITELAW, Ph.D.

Introduction

Audiology is a profession that continues to evolve. The Au.D. now represents the entry level degree for the profession, with an estimated 70% of audiologists having an Au.D. by 2010 (Smriga, 2006). This evolution heralds a focus on new types of transitions that may occur at each new stage of an audiologist's career. New Au.D. graduates focus on establishing themselves as professionals while developing career goals. Experienced audiologists face career decisions related

to a desire for greater autonomy which may lead them to pursue private practice options. Mature audiologists may be focused on winding down their clinical practices and preparing for the next stage in their life. The issue of buying or selling an audiology practice may apply in each of these stages and requires different considerations in each stage. This chapter aims to address the critical transition presented when an audiologist chooses to sell an established private practice. The transition process is not simply initiated one day and executed the next; it takes much planning time and energy to prepare for the purchase or sale of a practice.

The sale of a practice requires a succession plan to facilitate the transition. Developing a succession plan focuses on preparing for the financial, professional, and emotional aspects of the sale. This plan will likely take a year or more to develop; however, 3 to 5 years has been suggested as a more realistic time frame to reach the goal of selling the practice in the manner which the seller desires: selling the practice for a fair price and addressing a goal, whether retirement or change to a different role within the practice (Franks, 2006; Nemes, 2006; Patsula, 2001). This lead time ensures that the audiologist owner will have the ability to address a number of issues, including the valuation of the practice as discussed in Chapter 14, updating the business plan, making necessary improvements in the physical structure, planning for legal and fiscal responsibilities related to employees, and the critical transition of patients. The seller will need to use the same type of care and due diligence in developing the succession plan as a buyer would in making a purchase decision. The process outlined in this chapter is designed to develop a smooth transition in the sales process.

When Is the Best Time to Sell a Practice?

The simple answer to the question of when is the best time to sell a practice is *when the seller does not have to sell!* Timing of the sale of a practice is critical in terms of strategic positioning of the practice, both now and in the future (Mayer, 1998). Barlow, as cited in Nemes (2006), advises that audiology practices should be operated as if they will be sold in the near term, even if the owner has no intention of selling the practice, with all business decisions directed by the goal to develop a sustainable structure and measurable profits, in part to be attractive to a potential buyer. This philosophy also helps to establish a process for successful transition in the case of unexpected illness or death of a practice owner.

Once the seller has made the commitment to develop a succession plan, there are several practical considerations that will maximize the value of the practice in preparation for sale. To summarize the information presented in Chapter 14, the value of the practice is ultimately based on two factors: tangible assets and intangible assets, or goodwill (Franks, 2006). Both types of assets will contribute to a favorable appraisal and make the practice attractive to potential buyers. The practice owner should take an objective look at the physical appearance of the practice to ensure it is inviting and attractive. An unbiased party will be able to more effectively evaluate the condition of the physical space, particularly in a long-standing practice with a stable staff. In addition, the seller should be committed to increasing the productivity and profitability of the practice, as this reflects an upward trend in the practice and assurance that the buyer will purchase a vigorous practice (Franks, 2006).

Planning for the Ultimate Change: Exit Strategies

The sale of an audiology practice is clearly more difficult than selling a home. Unlike the sale of a home, where valuation is often simply based on the floor and yard plan, the valuation of the practice encompasses both the physical space and other tangible and intangible assets that are potentially part of the purchase, including referral sources, equipment, employees, and patients. However, just as with home sales, the selling price can reflected diligent preparation and careful market research, as outlined in this chapter (Sullivan, 2006).

Although there is no standard for practice valuation from the perspective of the seller, a professionally conducted appraisal is most likely to ensure that the seller receives the maximum value for the practice and the buyer has sufficient information about the practice and its key features to understand why it is an attractive opportunity. Specific aspects of practice valuation are outlined in Chapter 14. The seller should be aware of models of valuation that may be considered in appraisal of the practice. Professional appraisers often use several methods for calculating the value of assets (McDonald, 2005). A market approach compares the practice for sale to other similar practices that have recently been sold in the market. This method is difficult to apply in audiology due to the relatively small number of practices for sale in a given market at any period of time. A cost approach estimates the amount of money that would be required to duplicate the asset. This approach relies heavily on assumptions and is generally used as a secondary method in practice valuation. A book value approach, which is the sum total of cash, supplies, furniture, equipment, leasehold improvements, real estate, liabilities, and accounts receivable, is based on both fair market and depreciated costs. Although this method typically is not used for practice sales of an ongoing practice, it may be appropriate in situations where the practice must be closed, such as with illness or death. A modification of the book value approach takes into account the book value of the practice plus the value of "goodwill."

One model widely accepted in the health care industry is the composite valuation method, which compares common elements found in a practice—gross receipts, profitability, location, growth potential, collections, new patients, lease, equipment, staff, recall system in place, competition, patient base, transferability, practice production components (e.g., specialty services in the practice), and patient types—with an ideal practice to develop a percentile rating (Mattler, 2000). The model is heavily weighted toward practice income and patient base and the resulting percentile rating is then multiplied by factors addressing profitability and other market issues based on the appraiser's subjective judgment.

The seller should develop a sales package, discussed later in this chapter, which presents a "turnkey" operation to the buyer. This "turnkey" operation will ensure that the practice is ready to generate income from the first day of ownership, provide a salary to the owner and practice staff, and secure the capability to pay back the funding source. Even when a practice is a "turnkey" operation, there will be challenges for the new owner that go along with management of the practice. Some issues for the buyer may include:

- Inherited employees and office staff
- A patient database and referral base created and maintained in a method that may not reflect that of the buyer
- The "goodwill" (or "bad will") generated by audiologist owner or their staff
- The physical location of the practice: semipermanent and often difficult to change

- The decorating, furnishing, paint, and fixtures
- Clinical equipment inherited by the buyer.

In general, the above can either be benefits or liabilities to a turnkey operation. It is the responsibility of the seller to disclose information that provides insight into components of the practice purchase. Whereas a seller's responsibility is to provide the information and leave the clinic salable, it is the buyers responsibility to recognize that there are issues that need to be discussed and, where necessary, rectified.

The process of selling a practice requires a due diligence similar to that necessary on the part of the potential buyer. The audiologist selling the practice must prepare for the sale by working through myriad considerations to address potential problems and to ensure that the practice is in a salable condition, discussed in detail later in this chapter. Although the sale of a practice can be a long process, a relatively fast transition can occur if both parties are motivated and build a relationship of mutual trust Building trust between buyer and seller of a practice begins with the condition of the office and the financials. Buyers of practices do not want to purchase a clinic that is struggling, shabby, and requires substantial investment to make it profitable. At the first sign of recalcitrance, the buyer may wonder if the seller has something to hide. Reluctance on the part of the seller to provide information critical to the sale can erode the trust that has been built between the parties and result in a less than smooth transition to a new owner. Additionally, it may cause the buyer and their practice appraiser, accountant, attorney, and the

financial institution funding the purchase to be suspicious of hidden negative information. Failure to produce items of interest to the potential buyer and/or their representatives may result in delays due to the need to seek information for disclosure related to the sale. If a sale is to occur in good faith, it is necessary to ensure in advance that there will be full cooperation with the buyer and their representatives or there is no reason to progress to this stage of the sale. An audiologist purchasing a practice independently should be viewed as a colleague who will expect to make a living from conducting business in the practice and, after paying the purchase price of the practice, should have no surprises. Conversely, the seller should be assured that the potential buyer is negotiating in good faith, is serious regarding their inquiry into the practice, and will be able to secure funding to purchase the practice.

Preparing the Practice for Acquisition

General Considerations

Although there are situations and conditions where a sale can be obtained for a practice in "as is" condition, improvements made by the practice owner to prepare for a sale will make it more attractive. Drullinger (2006) indicates that there are specific items that the practice appraiser is looking for during the assessment process. Whereas some of these items lend themselves to preparation over a 3 to 5-year period, others are simply due diligence performance issues that must be presented when the sale is in progress. McAllister (2005) suggests that the first step in the assessment of the readiness of a practice for sale is for the seller to take an objective look at the practice. Although emotional clouding makes viewing the practice as others see it difficult, objectivity is absolutely necessary for the seller to obtain the best price. In preparation for the sale of the practice, many hard questions must be answered:

- What would an outsider think of this practice?
- How does it compare to other practices in the area?
- Has the neighborhood changed over the years?
- Is there a need to update the cosmetics?
- Are the financials such that they will look attractive to a potential buyer?
- How is the practice management system?
- How are the equipment and computers in the practice?
- Are the employees ready for a sale?
- Will the practice accountant be available to assist in the sale?

These questions must have answers as they are what the buyer and their appraiser will consider basic information about the practice. The buyer may be considering the purchase of a number of practices; therefore, it is paramount for the seller to make their practice stand out among those being evaluated.

History of the Practice

As a component of the practice appraisal, the owner should prepare a history of the practice and put this information into a written document. This information should focus on the audiologist(s) in the practice, the length of time the practice has been in existence, current and previous locations, and special attributes, including specialized audiologic procedures performed (Mattler, 2000).

Leasehold and Physical Improvements

An initial consideration in the sale of the practice may revolve on an objective assessment of the community in which the practice is located. There may have been substantial changes in a neighborhood or a community over the time that the practice has been located there that may not be evident to the owner or employees due to the familiarity of the setting. In preparing for the sale of the practice, the ,audiologist should evaluate the neighborhood and become reacquainted with the advantages and disadvantages of the area as it has developed over time and with the demographics of the community (Mattler, 2000; McCall & Dunlop, 2004).

The building in which the practice is located also requires objective review. It is difficult to be objective about one's own practice, but this step is essential. Seeking consultation from someone outside of the practice who is willing to objectively assess the physical setting of the practice can help to provide a realistic assessment of the perception of the practice to help avoid surprises in the salability of the practice. It is critical to demonstrate to a potential buyer that the practice has been progressive and has changed over time, which may require updates of interior design, carpeting, and furniture The potential buyer may have funds tied up in the purchase of the practice and, therefore, lack the financial resources for remodeling or relocation of the practice. The need for major cosmetic modification may result in a potential buyer rejecting the purchase for a practice that requires less updating. One of the reasons to begin the sales process well in advance is to complete these cosmetic overhauls and present the practice at its best; although a practice facelift may be expensive, it can help to attract interested buyers and/or enhance the practice price.

McCall and Dunlop (2004) suggest a number of considerations that should be attended to in evaluating the physical cosmetics of the practice:

- Exterior of the building in need of paint or modification in order to look more contemporary
- Sidewalks and approaches adequately lighted and in good repair
- Parking lot with an appropriate number of well-marked parking spaces designated for the practice
- Carpet and tile, cleanliness, up-to-date style and color
- Paint and woodwork: up-to-date color, cleanliness, and touch-up is recent
- Photographs and artwork current, not dated
- Attractive front desk area
- Display fixtures clean and up-to-date
- Adequate coat rack
- Adequate and attractive seating for patients in the waiting room.
- Up-to-date magazines and product literature available to patients
- Clean restroom area, with appropriate decorations and up-to-date features.
- If there is an elevator in use in the building, it should be safe, clean, and operable.

- Patient files and filing system clean and up-to-date
- General atmosphere of the sound room and counseling/fitting rooms
- Adequacy of the laboratory
- Signage: positioning, style, and visibility
- Windows washed, lettering is readable and not deteriorated.
- All ALDs and accessories in a position that does not appear cluttered.
- All light bulbs replaced and operating.
- If available, storage should be clean and free of old equipment, cords, tables, and materials, as these items may be perceived as clutter to the buyer

Attention to basic aspects of the facility are likely to yield significant benefit to the seller. Franks (2006) suggests that the seller should clean their office and desk prior to visits by potential buyers. McCall and Dunlop (2004) stress that it is critical that the overall atmosphere of the waiting room is pristine. A dated waiting room presents a shabby image that may justify a lower purchase price. An update of the waiting room may pay off in image presented to the patients, be consistent with the branding of the practice, and offer a contemporary image to a potential buyer.

Furthermore, both the seller and the buyer should know the current lease terms and monthly rent. The specifics of the lease should be critically reviewed by the attorneys for the seller and the buyer, with specific options related to escalation and renewal capabilities for 5 years postpurchase/sale discussed. If the facility is owned by the audiologist selling the practice, the terms for lease to the buyer should be carefully presented, with options for purchase of the real estate clearly addressed (Mattler, 2000).

Audiometric and Office Equipment

As discussed earlier in this chapter, the potential buyer of the practice is generally seeking a turnkey operation. An important component of a turnkey practice is audiometric and office equipment. A practice that utilizes an appropriate equipment depreciation schedule and funds equipment replacement as part of the business plan will have a clear advantage at the time of sale compared to the practice that has not addressed this critical aspect. This ongoing investment in equipment enhances the value of the practice both in capital and in "good will" as patients will perceive the practice as "state of the art," enhancing the practice reputation in the community. Audiologists using older equipment (e.g., equipment for electronystagmography rather than videonystagmography) may receiver a lower offer for their practice as a potential buyer will need to add equipment purchase or lease payments to the fixed expenses presented in the due diligence process. As the addition of the new fixed expenses will add to the overhead of the practice, these expenses may reflect a change in the multiple selected for the practice by the buyer's appraiser and result in a price reduction to the seller.

Office equipment, such as computers, printers, office management software, and accounting programs must be replaced and/or updated in a systematic and organized way based on an infrastructure replacement cycle outlined in the business plan. This replacement cycle should be based on the usable life of the equipment and the schedule of depreciation. This cycle is less likely to be based on a fixed financial schedule but closely linked to business practices of the individual office (Ohm, 1999) Evidence of addressing software upgrades is critical in providing state of the art clinical care and assuring potential buyers that the office is well managed and up-to-date.

Filing and file management needs to be an organized systematic method that allows for easy access to the records for each individual patient. Two options may be available, either a hard copy or an electronic medical record (EMR). Some audiology offices have moved toward a "paperless" system, storing most or all information electronically. These systems require less physical space for storage, may be less costly, and provide for efficient access and retrieval of patient information. Although increasing in popularity, paperless systems are not yet the standard in audiology practices; thus, not required to sell a practice. Having a paperless system is likely to garner the attention of potential buyers that are looking for a state-of-the-art practice. McAllister (2005) describes this as a critical time to ensure that the practice management system (PMS) is running effectively and efficiently and to objectively assess the potential need for a new PMS.

Staff Considerations

It is paramount that employees know that the practice is being sold. Employees that are satisfied and well-trained can be a significant asset to the practice; conversely, issues with disgruntled or poorly performing employees can present a sticky situation during the transition/sale (Franks, 2006; McDonald, 2005). Knowledge of a potential sale allows employees to plan for their future, whether seeking another position or ensuring their role in the transition with a new practice owner. If a potential buyer is interested in a turnkey business, the audiologists, the receptionist/office manager, and billing personnel may be of particular interest to them. To facilitate this turnkey approach in relation to personnel, it is recommended that the audiologist selling the practice inform the employees of the impending sale, review the ethical/legal responsibilities to the employees, review retirement and health care plans and responsibilities to cover unused benefits (e.g., vacation or sick leave), and provide incentives for employees to stay during the transition period, if this is the desire of the new owner (American Medical Association, 1997).

The revenue generated by the business and productivity of each audiologist who contributes to that bottom line are important considerations in the purchase of a practice. Part of the practice valuation will be based on the productivity of the staff and which employees generate the revenue. If the majority of the revenue is generated by the audiologist who owns the practice, the owner is essential to the financial success of the practice. If the owner is leaving the practice, there is a risk of significant decrease in business if patients choose not to stay with the practice under the new ownership. Typically if the audiologist selling the practice is the primary income producer, the valuation will be lower. However, if, 50% or more of the revenue production has been transferred to a professional employee, the valuation is likely to be higher, particularly if the audiolo-

gist employee plans to stay with the practice after its sale. When a smaller percentage of revenue is generated by the audiologist owner, the chances of keeping existing patients within the practice on the owner's departure are likely to be greater. If the owner of the practice is using the sale as an exit strategy for retirement or as a career change, the seller should plan the transition by slowly transferring patients to other audiologists in the practice (Bauer, 2004). This is typically done slowly so that the patients and staff in the practice gradually become accustomed to the original owner no longer being available to address issues or concerns. To a professional appraiser valuing a practice, this may be viewed as a solid indication that when the owner leaves the practice, business will be much the same and patients will remain loyal.

Normalizing Income and Expenses

As described in Chapter 14, normalizing income and expenses is a critical step for the audiologist owner who may run legitimate personal expenditures through the practice. In this case, the seller adds back as income the amount of the expenses that are accrued by the practice owner, such as car lease expenses, travel expenses, and club membership and dues. Separating these major expenses accurately reflects the profitability of the practice and provides the buyer's financing source the actual income available to service the purchaser's salary and the debt created by the purchase (Lowes, 2006). These expenses should be separated prior to the appraisal so that their impact is obvious prior to the practice valuation.

Creating the Sales Package

Patsula (2001) indicates that once the practice components are in place, a sales package should be constructed. This gives the perspective buyer a concise orientation to the practice and organizes the discussion between the two parties as to the positives of the practice and the concerns of the buyer. This package provides essential information about the practice and serves as a checklist of discussion topics. The following items should be included in the practice sales package:

- History of the practice
- Description of how the practice operates
- Description of the physical facilities
- Discussion of the suppliers
- A review of marketing practices
- Description of the competition
- Review of personnel, including an organizational chart, job descriptions, rates of pay, and willingness of key employees to stay and work for the new owner.
- Identification of all the owners
- Explanation of Insurance coverage
- Discussion of any pending legal matters or contingent liabilities
- A compendium of 3 to 5 years of financial statements
- A valuation report that states how the practice arrived at its asking price.

Basically, the sales package mirrors the practice's business plan, with the addition of real historical financial data offered by the seller. The practice owner must realize that they are selling their practice based on historic performance whereas the buyer is purchasing the practice on unknown future performance.

The better the sales package tells the story of historic performance, the more likely the practice is to present a case for positive future performance.

Another portion of the sales package preparation is the anticipation of various discussion questions from the buyer, as thorough due diligence is essential for any buyer that plans to acquire a health care entity (Doty & Campbell, 2000). Issues that concern the future viability of the practice may include:

- The age of the audiometric equipment and computers
- The anticipated transferability of patients to the new owner
- Patient relations, patient loyalty
- Practice reputation and image
- Competition threats, weaknesses
- Leasing costs for premises and equipment
- Location conditions
- Maintenance costs, heating, air conditioning, and other utility bills
- Parking availability
- Staff turnover.

The seller should be prepared to answer these and other specific questions key to any serious consideration of the practice purchase. The buyer may also request information about compliance plans and the billing audit to ensure no undisclosed issues with billing or fraud and abuse problems exist (Doty & Campbell, 2000).

Generating Interest in the Practice: Marketing to Independent Practitioners

There are many reasons why a buyer will find one practice more attractive than others. It could be a significant financial opportunity, the location, the opportunity to learn and conduct specific procedures, the specifics in the sales package, or myriad other reasons. Interest can be generated by a practice broker, discussed in a separate section of this chapter, or it may be generated by the audiologist owner marketing the practice on their own. For audiology practice sales, interest is often created by three major sources:

- Print advertising
- Trade journals
- Word of mouth/networking.

Audiology is a relatively small profession; therefore, facilitating communication regarding the potential sale of a practice is fairly uncomplicated but does require a targeted approach in order to be effective. The size of the profession certainly facilities the ability to communicate about the sale; however, it should be noted that marketing of practice will eliminate any possibility of confidentiality regarding the sale. Print ads advertising the practice for sale may be placed in both trade journals, such as *The Hearing Journal* or *Hearing Review*, and communications from professional organizations, such as *Audiology Today*. A number of web sites also provide information to those interested in buying or selling a practice, including *Audiologynline.com* and *AuDNet.com* . State audiology academies may provide a strong network to advertise the sale of a practice and to attract local buyers who may be particularly familiar with the reputation of the seller, thus understanding the goodwill aspects of the practice. Advertising on the state academy web site and/or in newsletters is an effective approach for marketing the practice.

The marketing of the sale of a practice through word of mouth approaches requires taking advantage of networking opportunities in the profession of audiology. Manufacturer representatives and equipment distributors interface with a significant number of audiologists in an area and may be able to reach a large number of audiologists in a short period of time. Continuing education events and state, regional, and national conventions provide an opportunity to interact with audiologists and to market the practice. Networking with Au.D. programs may identify new audiologists who are seeking a practice.

Independent Versus Corporate Practice: Selling to a Corporate Entity

The corporate purchase of private practices is a trend that has affected medicine and other health care fields over the past several decades. This trend has recently become a consideration in private practice in audiology. In recent years, corporate entities in hearing care have been seeking to acquire independent audiology practices to expand their regional or national practice networks (Nemes, 2006). Affiliating with a corporate buyer may provide access to capital, expertise in billing and coding, specialized management services, and economies of scale not possible in an independent practice (Carlson, 1998). These potential advantages must be weighed against the practice mission, vision, and values.

Just as due diligence is required in the seller's development of a succession plan and the buyers research into practice options, the practice owner must consider the same diligent approach to the decisions related to whether to remain independent and sell to an independent audiologist or to join or sell the practice to a corporate entity. Some corporate contacts are unsolicited and may be viewed as an opportunity to learn more about the market and as an opportunity to obtain additional viewpoints on the value of the practice, even if the seller has not considered a sale or affiliation with a corporate buyer. However, caution must be exercised to avoid potential pitfalls which may include providing detailed financial information regarding the practice or accepting claims that other practices in the market have committed to an affiliation (Carlson, 1998). Corporate buyers may seek several approaches to obtaining independent private practices. They may seek a practice with reduced profitability in order to expand their network at minimal cost. Conversely, corporate buyers may seek independent practices that are well run in a desirable location, with diverse referral sources, and with a growing patient base (Nemes, 2006).

A number of publicly held corporations are players in this corporate market and have been expanding market share in specific regions for much of the past decade. This makes them a significant force in the audiology market, thus viewed by some as competition to independent private practices. These corporate practices are often associated with a hearing instrument manufacturer which provides a significant distribution network for their products. Sonus, a national hearing care chain, is a division of Amplifon USA, in which Siemens Hearing Instruments has a substantial interest. Oticon owns the Avada corporate chain and has a significant investment in Amer-

ican Hearing Aid Associates (AHAA). GN ReSound now owns the long established Beltone chain of franchises. According to American Hearing Aid Associate (2005), growth in corporate purchase of audiology practices has increased the number of retail outlets by 16% in recent years and it is estimated that by 2010 manufactured sponsored outlets for hearing instruments will approach 25%.

Discount stores, such as Costco and Wal-Mart, are now actively offering hearing instruments as a product line in their stores. Although not actively purchasing independent practices, these stores have the potential to be formidable competition for hearing instrument sales in a given region, and thus may impact the value of a practice in view of their proximity to the practice.

When contemplating sale to a corporate entity, it is critical that the owner perform due diligence related to this sale. Selling a practice to a corporate entity may result in a substantial economic windfall. However, it is critical to determine if the corporate group is truly interested in obtaining the independent practice or is merely investigating the practice to determine the competitive aspects of the independent practice to open an outlet close to the practice, without intent to purchase the practice. Conversely, talking with a representative of a corporate audiology entity may be a great opportunity to learn more about the marketplace and to help determine the value of a practice, information which may be useful in the long run. According to Carlson (1998), to avoid some potential pitfalls, it is important to consider the following:

■ Avoid signing a "letter of intent" that restricts discussion with other corporate entities prior to the sale;

■ Do not provide detailed financial data regarding the practice until the negotiations have advanced to the point where this is necessary, when the potential seller has determined that such an affiliation would be the right move for the practice;

■ Do not take claims at face value that other practices in the market have committed to an affiliation with the corporate entity.

Another method of assessing the willingness of the corporation to enter as a partner in negotiation is to obtain a nonrefundable earnest commitment, suggested to be in the range of at least $2,000 to $5,000. This "earnest investment" would offset the time and effort involved in the due diligence and, of course, apply to the purchase price if the practice is actually purchased but would be forfeited if the practice is not purchased by the corporation.

The decision to affiliate with a retail/corporate practice or to remain in an independent practice setting is certainly influenced by financial considerations, but other factors should also be considered. Corporate affiliation has impacted optometry over the past few decades and there are certainly potential parallels with the profession of audiology. In optometry, the number of retail chains resulted in direct competition with those in independent private practice, with optometrists entering the profession attracted to commercial/corporate optometry to earn an income without accruing the debt load associated with starting or purchasing a private practice (Smriga, 2006). In contrast to other professions, such as optometry and medicine, the significant majority of dentists have maintained solo independent practices, which is thought to result in improved autonomy for the profession and earning ability for individual dentists (Mertz, 2002). Audiologists who sell their practice to a corporate/commercial entity must be prepared to yield control of their practice and understand that the philosophy and corporate culture of the practice may change under the new ownership (Nemes, 2006). However, the ability to focus on patient care while receiving a salary and benefits package as an employee without the responsibilities of owning a practice may motivate an owner to consider a corporate audiology sale. Carlson (1998) advises a potential seller to recognize the risks in affiliating with a corporate organization and not to sell the practice based on the financial aspects only, as the affiliation should result in a partnership that the audiologist can live with, making their life easier, and their practice more competitive.

Using a Professional to Sell a Practice: Practice Brokers

Most audiologists have little knowledge or experience in negotiating the sale of a practice. Even with a strong business team, relying on the skill and knowledge of a practice broker can help to facilitate the sale of the practice. Using a real estate analogy, a practice broker would be similar to using a realtor to sell a home. McDonald (2005) suggests that selling a practice by the owner might be equated to a "for sale by owner" home sale: the home may be overpriced and the owner "in love with their own home," optimistic, and a "bit greedy," a scenario sometimes observed in the sale of a practice. Specific knowledge in a number of key areas including practice valuation, marketing, real estate, negotiation, and advertising, may be of benefit in the sale of a practice. The buyer may have a team of professionals working on their behalf, including a practice appraiser. Adding a practice broker to the seller's team may provide considerable value and help the seller.

A practice broker can be viewed as a "matchmaker" between the buyer and seller. This independent broker may be able to address a number of complex tasks related to the sale of the practice. Reiboldt (2004) suggests that some of these activities may include:

■ Market analysis
■ Providing guidance in setting the sales price
■ Assisting with negotiations
■ Networking and advertising the practice
■ Providing direct mailing to potential buyers
■ Creating an Internet presence
■ Working with medical specialty lenders to maximize the amount of the loan to a potential buyer (which may assist the seller in obtaining a higher sales amount)
■ Screening calls and inquiries from potentially interested buyers; procuring purchasers through recruiting and reference checks
■ "Showing" the practice.

The preparation for the sale may include a consultation with a practice broker who can provide the proper presale advice to assist the audiologist in obtaining the most for their investment in the practice. Selling a practice can be a sensitive situation for the audiologist owner, as they have considerable emotional and financial investment in the practice. A potential buyer will ask questions regarding how decisions have been made, why things are done in certain ways, and offer ideas about new services that may put the seller on the defensive. Beiting (2006) notes that a third party, such as a practice broker, can be helpful in reducing the emotion associated with the sale, being able to collate information for the seller, and negotiate a buy-sell agreement. The practice broker may also coordinate activities with attorneys, accountants, and lenders.

Although practice brokers can substantially reduce the burden of the sales process, they handle their business like a real estate broker. Similar to a real estate agent for a home, a practice broker is paid a commission for their services. Generally, these fees are about 10% of the purchase price of the practice (Reiboldt, 2004). Commission and other fees should be negotiated prior to the sale and the listing agreement should be reviewed by the seller's attorney.

Sales Alternative: Employee Purchase of Practice

The audiologist interested in selling their practice may need to look no further for a potential buyer than in the staff of audiologists employed in the practice. This type of sale may include a number of options including out and out sale of the practice or selling portions of the business to employees using a number of approaches. The benefit to the audiologist owner may include infusion of cash into the business, reduced employee labor costs, or simply the ability to retire at a planned time. Grau (2007) states that an employee group is a perfect option as they already know the patient base and mesh well with the business philosophy. In this sense, the employees become informed buyers, with considerable knowledge of the practice. Christensen (2003) suggests that one of the motivations for bringing a new associate into a practice is as a logical candidate to take over a practice. He adds that selling the practice to an employee/associate/partner is "the most painless way to exit from a practice."

Applegate (2002) notes that when the owner of a small business, such as an audiologist, wants to sell the practice to employees, there are several viable options to do so. Although the audiologist owner might be willing to negotiate a deal with an employee so that they may become a partner, audiology salaries are usually not conducive to obtaining the funds for a down payment on the practice without substantial collateral. Additionally, young practitioners that have considerable debt related to their education may find that financing a practice, even with favorable terms, is a challenge. The audiologist owner may choose to fund the practice sale themselves, as it may be difficult for a young audiologist to borrow the full value of practice at a reasonable interest rate (Beitling, 2005).

Sale to employees often includes setting up options that may augment or replace some portion of salary or benefits in order to assist employees in being able to "own" the practice while providing a favorable situation for the owner. One such option is Employee Stock Ownership Plans (ESOP) that provide for the owner to sell company "shares" of the practice to employees at a fair price.

Employees that own shares in the practice may be more loyal and driven to perform, resulting in an increase in practice productivity. Selling stock in the practice may also provide a significant tax advantage in terms of capital gains, a topic addressed later in this chapter (Egerton & Egerton, 2005). A number of methods for establishing an ESOP are available, and if an owner is interested in setting up this type of plan, consultation with an attorney and accountant are critical.

Retained Involvement

Some audiologists sell their practices and stay on to work in them for a specified period of time, often as a condition of sale. This option provides continuity of patient care and/or ongoing management the practice during the transition. Retained involvement is a common practice in sales to corporate entities as the corporate owner may need a practice manager for continuity and to provide patient care This allows for an effective transition for patients and staff alike and maximizes opportunities for success under new management.

Some audiologists may take advantage of a retained involvement approach known as "transitioning" in which the audiologist planning to sell a practice will look for another audiologist to join the practice that will purchase it and succeed the current audiologist at the time of their retirement (Wilson, 2005). If a favorable agreement can be reached, the senior audiologist will mentor the buyer for a period of time, often outlined in a legal document referred to as a "phase-out" agreement (Reiboldt, 2004). This transitioning period, although it may take several years to plan and implement, can be profitable for both the buyer and the seller.

There may be pros and cons to the audiologist being retained in the practice after sale. The audiologist, as a former owner, can be relieved of the pressures of management such as billing, insurance, and human resources, and can attend to patient care. This allows the audiologist to work as a salaried employee and have a greater degree of flexibility in their schedule. However, as noted in Nemes (2006), the audiologist retained as an employee in the practice must recognize that they will lose much of the autonomy to which they are accustomed. There may be a shift in the corporate culture of the practice (e.g., the new owners may change fundamentals such as marketing tactics or human resource option) and the audiologist retained in the practice must be able to accommodate this change if they are to stay on as a successful and productive employee. The new owner may take advantage of the knowledge and skills of the retained audiologists and include their input in decision-making regarding the practice. However, the audiologist selling the practice and staying must be able to accept this potential loss of control.

The Successful Sale of the Practice: Tax Considerations

A goal in the sale of the practice is to maximize the profit to the seller. Attention to tax issues is critical in pursuit of this goal. The seller must seek appropriate counsel, including input from their attorney, financial advisor, and accountant. Burg (1995) suggests that the main tax goal in the sale of a practice should be to minimize the profit that is considered ordinary income and to assign the maximum profit possible to capital gains. Nearly everything that is owned and used for personal purposes, pleasure, or investment is a capital asset. According to the IRS (2007), when a capital asset, such as an audiology practice, is sold, the difference between the selling price and the amount paid for the asset is a capital gain (or loss). There are number specific areas that the seller should consider in addressing tax aspects of the sale that may also impact the amount of capital gains.

One area of consideration is depreciation recapture. The owner of the audiology practice has had the tax benefit of depreciation of tangible business property, such as audiometers, computers, and office furniture, over the life of the asset. The sale of these assets can qualify as capital gains only to the extent that the sale price exceeds the original cost of the asset, a rare situation (Bobryk, 1998). Generally a buyer will not pay more for an asset than the original purchase price; therefore, the revenue from sale of these types of tangible business assets is taxed as ordinary income. An alternative approach that may result in benefits to both the seller and buyer is for the seller to lease equipment to the buyer (Burg, 1995). The seller will still be able to write off some of the depreciation, which offsets the revenue received from lease payment, whereas the buyer will benefit from having less working capital tied up in equipment.

Another consideration is leasehold improvements. Leasehold improvements are depreciated over a period of 31.5 or 39 years, depending on when the practice was purchased, and a longer period than for other types of tangible assets (Burg, 1995). The advantage for the seller is that the remaining leasehold write-off may be deducted in the sale year. If a $90,000 renovation was completed 5 years prior to the sale of the practice, it is possible that only $15,000 has been depreciated at the time of the sale. This would result in a $75,000 deduction for leasehold improvements at the time of sale.

Goodwill and the patient database are capital assets so the portion of the sale related to these are taxed as capital gains. Although this may provide benefit for the seller, the buyer may prefer to negotiate more of the sale be allocated to equipment or furnishings, as intangible assets are written off over 15 years but tangible assets can be written off two to three times as quickly (Burg, 1995). However, sale of these "hard assets" are taxed as ordinary income for the seller.

The tax and financial implications of the sale of an audiology practice are complex and require professional advice. An old adage is "it's not what you earn, it's what you keep"; this suggests that the seller may benefit from accepting a slighter lower price if the sale can be structured to result in a more favorable tax structure, as the long-term capital gains are currently taxed at a rate of 28%, with ordinary income taxed at a rate of 40% (Eastern, 2006). In addition, there is currently a substantial review of tax regulations in Congress that may modify tax implications of practice sales in the future. Trusted advisors in the sale of the practice will ensure that the profit to the seller will be maximized in a legal and ethical manner.

Informing Patients That the Practice Has Been Sold

A critical task in the sale of a practice is informing patients about the impending transition. Practice management consult-

ants encourage the audiologist selling the practice to contact patients by letter at least 3 months in advance of the sale or transition (Franks, 2006). The letter should inform active patients of the sale, the plan for the practice, and the assurance of continuity of care. If a colleague is to be taking over the practice, this audiologist should be introduced in the letter. If the audiologist owner will be remaining in the practice in a different role, this should also be addressed in the letter. Assuring patients that the practice infrastructure (e.g., location, staff, etc.) will remain constant will serve to ease the transition.

Exiting the practice can be an emotional time for the audiologist, their staff, and patients that have been loyal to the practice. Attention to the detail of communicating with staff will help to ease the transition, provide the patient with information that will ensure goodwill in the practice, and provide both the owner and patient the opportunity for closure. Some consultants also recommend that the audiologist buying the practice contact patients via letter to introduce themselves and again ensure continuity of care.

Closing the Practice Without Selling

There may be situations in which an audiology practice will be closed without a sale. These situations, such as a health condition that precludes the owner from continuing to work, often occur suddenly. These again address the importance of having a succession plan in place. However, if this plan is not in place, the audiologist may have limited time to prepare the practice for closure.

If addressed appropriately, the process for closure will require similar attention to detail as in the case of the sale of the practice. Weiss (2004) suggests that walking away from a practice should be the last resort after serious attempts to sell the practice; however, in some situations, such as a rural practice with no buyers, there may be no other options. The audiologist will need to work closely with an accountant and attorney to ensure that all patient, legal, and financial responsibilities are carefully considered prior to, during, and after the closing of the practice.

Audiologists simply cannot abandon or abruptly withdraw from their patient responsibility. The continuity of audiologic care is critical and attention to the disposition of patients to another audiology practice is absolutely necessary. It is also important that the audiologist(s) receiving these patients have a patient-centric approach and assure new patients that their hearing instrument warranties and other commitments from the practice that is closing will be honored.

To ensure continuity of care for patients, the audiologist closing the practice should notify patients by letter, preferably at a minimum of 3 months prior to closure of the practice. This letter should include the following information:

- Practice closing date
- Name(s) of audiologists recommended and willing to accept new patients
- How copies of audiologic records can be obtained or transferred to the new audiologist
- An authorization form for the patient to sign for release of records
- Where audiologic records will be stored after the practice is closed (Reiboldt, 2007; Weiss, 2004).

The audiologist should also plan on placing an announcement of practice closure in local newspapers a few weeks prior to the actual closing, a step that may be required in some states (Weiss, 2004).

In the case of the closure of the practice, special care should be given to the retention of patient records. An attorney should review a retention policy, with consideration to the statute of limitations for various potential lawsuits that may be faced by the audiologist or the practice (Reiboldt, 2007). A custodian for records must be established with previous patients being able to access records as necessary (Weiss, 2004). Records that are retained must be stored in a secure place and in a confidential manner. Options for storage, such as copying onto microfilm or scanning into read-only storage media, should be explored. Records that are no longer needed should be disposed of by utilizing a reputable record-shredding business.

In addition to notifying patients, closure of a practice requires communication with other entities and individuals, including:

- Liability/malpractice insurance company
- Medicare, Medicaid, and other third party payors
- State licensing board
- Affiliated hospitals/referral sources
- Professional associations in which the audiologist holds memberships
- Insurers covering the practice, its employees, and facilities (Reiboldt, 2007; Weiss, 2004).

A location to receive practice mail and telephone calls must be established. The assets of the practice will need to be sold, which can be done through a local equipment distributor or on a forum for selling used equipment, such as that at *AudiologyOnline.com* . The final order of business is to address accounts receivable, as it may be possible to collect up to 90% of the outstanding AR (Weiss, 2004). It is recommended that a staff member be retained for a period of time to work on collections. Alternatively, a billing service may be more cost effective in the case of practice closure (Reiboldt, 2007).

Summary and Conclusions

Sale of a practice can be both exciting and challenging. It signals an important transition in the life of an audiologist, such as retirement, career change, or taking on additional clinical opportunities in exchange for administrative ones. Developing a succession plan early in the practice is an effective way to ensure that the transition will be seamless and maximize benefit to the buyer and seller. Updating business plans and attending to ongoing strategic positioning within the practice ensures that the audiologist is prepared for all eventualities, including sale of the practice or a need to close. The time to begin thinking about the sale is early in the life of the practice.

As noted by McDonald (2005), beginning with the end in mind suggests that an audiologist who opens a practice will eventually want to sell it. Significant time should be spent in designing and developing a practice that will increase operational efficiencies and goodwill. McDonald (2005) suggests that "this investment of time and energy will result not only in a higher practice valuation but also in a more enjoyable (and profitable) professional life."

References

American Hearing Aid Associates. (2005, Nov). *Corporate audiology in America*. Reno, NV: American Hearing Aid Associates.

American Medical Association. (1997). *Closing your practice: 7 steps to a successful transition*. Chicago, IL: Author.

Applegate, J. (2002). *20 great ideas for your small business*. Princeton, NJ: Bloomberg Press.

Bauer, C. (2004). Plan for emotional changes, too: Here's how to make your transition out of practice a truly positive time. *Medical Economics, 81*(10), 60.

Beiting, J. (2006). Part VI: Riding into the sunset: Many optometrists have discovered that if they can find a way to stay on the horse without having to manage the stable, "retirement" can be sweet indeed. *Review of Optometry, 143*(12), 27-31.

Bobryk, J. (1998). Tax traps in buying and selling a medical practice. *Physician's Management, 38*(1), 36-42.

Burg, B. (1995). Selling your practice? Avoid these tax traps. *Medical Economics, 2*(20), 68-73.

Carlson, R. P. (1998). When a physician practice management company comes calling. *Family Practice Management, 5*(6), 10.

Christensen, G. J. (2003). The best way to bring a dentist into your practice. *Journal of the American Dental Association 134*(3), 367-369.

Doty, L. W., & Campbell, A. T. (2000). Well-planned due diligence can protect buyers of healthcare entities. *Healthcare Financial Management, 54*(10), 56.

Drullinger, R. A. (2006). Practice valuation: The buying and selling of an audiology practice. *Seminars in Hearing 27*(1), 57-76.

Eastern, J. S. (2006). Selling a medical practice. *Skin and Allergy News, 37*(11), 72.

Egerton, J. R., & Egerton, J. M. (2005). Selling our practice: A real roller-coaster ride. *Medical Economics, 82*(21), 73-76.

Franks, D. (2006, November). Practice succession. *Southern California Physician*, pp. 1-3.

Grau, D. (2007). Linked in. *Financial Planning, 37*(5), 89-91.

IRS. (2007). Tax facts about capital gains and losses. Internal Revenue Service, Internal Revenue Service. Retrieved May 27, 2007 from http://www.irs.gov/newsroom/article/0,,id=106799,00.html

Lowes, R. (2006). How to value your practice: Whether you're selling to a hospital or getting a divorce, you need ropes. *Medical Economics, 83*(5), 66-70.

Mattler, M. G. (2000). When and why should I have my practice appraised? *Journal of the American Dental Association, 131*(11), 1622-1624.

Mayer, T. (1998). Selling your medical practice: Calculate more than cash value in the bottom line. *Postgraduate Medicine, 104*(5), 25.

McAllister, D. (2005). Taking steps to prepare your practice for sale. *Coker Connection, 5*(9), 5-6.

McCall, K., & Dunlop, D. (2004). Marketing a practice. In B. Keagy & M.Thomas (Eds.), *Essentials of physician practice management.* San Francisco: John Wiley & Sons.

McDonald, K. (2005). "Practice Builder" Understanding the factors that add to the value of a practice. *Podiatry Today, 18*(4), 20-25.

Mertz, E. (2002) *UCSF report finds dental practice patterns add to oral health disparity in the United States* (press release). San Francisco: Center for the Health Professions, University of California, San Francisco, 9/27/02.

Nemes, J. (2006). Ready to sell? Experts offer advice on doing so successfully. *Hearing Journal, 59*(8), 19-26.

Ohm, N. (1999). How IT can move finance to change depreciation periods. *Gartner Group Archive Report.*

Patsula, P. (2001). Selling your company. *The Entrepreneur's Guidebook Series.* Mansfield, OH: Patsula Media.

Reiboldt, M. (2004). *Buying, selling, and owning the medical practice* (2nd ed.). Chicago: American Medical Association.

Reiboldt, M. (2007). *Financial management of the medical practice* (2nd ed.). Chicago: American Medical Association.

Schell, J. (2007). Exit strategies: Selling your company to your employees. *All Business.* Retrieved May 30, 2007, from http: allbusiness.com/buying-exiting-businesses

Smriga, D. J. (2006). For audiology, dentistry offers a good model for preserving independent private practice. *Hearing Journal, 59*(9), 36-42.

Sullivan, J. D. (2006). Divesting strategies for medical practices. *Journal of Medical Practice Management: MPM, 22*(3), 159-161.

Weiss, G. G. (2004). How to close a practice: whether you're turning your practice over to a colleague, selling it, or simply walking away, take the time to do it right. *Medical Economics, 81*(1), 69-73.

Wilson, K. (2005). Don't retire your practice; "Transition" it. *Cosmetic Surgery Times, 8*(3), 46.

Index